Excel

ADVANCED SKILLS

MATHS

YEAR 6

AGES 11–12

ADVANCED MATHEMATICS

Get the Results You Want!

PASCAL PRESS

Allyn Jones

Written for the NSW Curriculum and the Australian Curriculum Version 9.0

Reprinted 2025 (twice)

ISBN 978 1 74125 659 8

Pascal Press
PO Box 250
Glebe NSW 2037

www.pascalpress.com.au

Publisher: Vivienne Joannou
Project editor: Rosemary Peers
Edited and proofread by Rosemary Peers
Answers checked by Peter Little
Cover and page design by Sonia Woo
Typeset by Grizzly Graphics (Leanne Richters)
Printed by Vivar Printing/Green Giant Press

Contents

Introduction

The aim of the ***Excel*** Advanced Skills: Advanced Mathematics series is to build on and extend students' skills in Mathematics. Each book in the series supports the requirements of the Australian Curriculum (Mathematics) at each year level.

The series consists of six books, one for each year level, from Year 1 to Year 6. The series is supported by other books in the ***Excel*** Mathematics range.

Structure of the book

Level of difficulty key Level ★★★★★

The level of difficulty of each page is shown by a key at the top of the page showing a number of stars, with three stars being the least challenging questions and five stars being the most difficult.

Section 1

This section consists of ten double-page units of teaching and learning activities, each focused on a specific topic from the Number, Algebra, Measurement, Space, Statistics and Probability areas of the syllabus.

- **Unit A** provides work at an advanced four-star level
- **Unit B** provides work at the most advanced five-star level.

Section 2

This section consists of 30 carefully graded double-page units of teaching and learning activities. Each page provides questions from all areas of the syllabus: Number, Algebra, Measurement, Space, Statistics and Probability.

- **Units 1 to 15 A** provide introductory work at a three-star level
- **Units 1 to 15 B** and **16 to 30 A** provide work at an advanced four-star level
- **Units 16 to 30 B** provide work at the book's most advanced five-star level.

NAPLAN–style Tests

There are two mini NAPLAN-style tests. These tests:

- provide practice for the Year 7 NAPLAN Numeracy test
- contain a non-calculator section (four questions) and a calculator-allowed section (16 questions)
- are graded so that the questions in Test 2 are more challenging than in Test 1.

Worked Solutions & Answers

Worked solutions are provided for every question to support students' learning. Answers are also provided in bold for quick reference.

How to use this book with the *Excel* Advanced Skills English series

For a complete weekly English and Mathematics program use this book in conjunction with the ***Excel* Advanced Skills English Year 6** book. This way a student will have work set for four days a week—two days for English and two days for Mathematics.

How to assess students' progress

The results of the work undertaken in each unit can be recorded on the marking grids. The marking grids on pages 7, 8 and 9 (please see the example on page 5) are easy-to-use diagnostic tools that indicate where students' strengths and weaknesses lie in relation to specific areas of Mathematics. These results can be used to gather extra information about students' progress and their further revision needs.

The *Excel* Advanced and Basic Skills Series

If students are experiencing difficulty, require additional practice or need extension in any area of the course, further books are available to support them in the ***Excel*** Basic Skills and Advanced Skills series. (Please see the comprehensive list of ***Excel*** books on page 6.)

The *Excel* step-by-step improvement plan

Step 1

Read the introduction on page 4.

Step 2

The results of the work undertaken in each unit can be recorded on the marking grids.

These are an easy-to-use diagnostic tool that indicate both where each student's strengths and weaknesses are in relation to specific areas of Mathematics as well as their ability to work at different levels of difficulty.

These results can be used to gather extra information about each student's progress and their further revision needs.

When marking answers on the grids, simply mark incorrect answers with 'X' in the appropriate box. This will result in a graphical representation of areas needing further work.

Section 1 Marking grid

See the sample Section 1 marking grid below:

Questions	1	2	3	4	5	6
Unit 1A ★★★★☆						
Unit 1B ★★★★★		X	X	X	X	
Unit 2A ★★★★☆						
Unit 2B ★★★★★						
Unit 3A ★★★★☆						
Unit 3B ★★★★★						
Unit 4A ★★★★☆						
Unit 4B ★★★★★						

This grid indicates that the student needs extra help and practice with the most advanced five-star level questions in Unit 1 (Number and Place Value)

If a student has only a few crosses marked in Unit 1A but a lot in Unit 1B then they are finding the more advanced questions in this topic challenging. This topic will therefore require more practice.

Section 2 Marking grid

See the sample Section 2 marking grid below.

If a student is consistently getting more than one in five questions wrong in any topic they need help in this area.

An example for the first five units is shown below.

		Number properties	Integers	Whole numbers	Fractions 1	Fractions 2
	Questions	1	2	3	4	5
Unit 1A	★★★☆☆					
Unit 1B	★★★★☆					X
Unit 2A	★★★☆☆					
Unit 2B	★★★★☆					X
Unit 3A	★★★☆☆					
Unit 3B	★★★★☆					X
Unit 4A	★★★☆☆					
Unit 4B	★★★★☆					X
Unit 5A	★★★☆☆					
Unit 5B	★★★★☆					X

This grid indicates that the student needs extra help and practice with advanced four-star level fraction questions.

Step 3

Refer to page 6: *Excel* books to help you *get the results you want*!

Under each topic there is a comprehensive list of books in our range to help students practise the topic they are having difficulty with.

For example, if a student wants more practice with fractions questions the books shown will help them. Each ***Excel*** book has a comprehensive contents page that will identify the appropriate pages in the book to target the specific topic area that is causing problems.

Excel books to help you *get the results you want!*

NUMBER AND ALGEBRA

Number, place value, fractions and decimals

Excel Basic Skills · *Excel* Advanced Skills · *Excel* NAPLAN-style Tests

9781741255904 · 9781864412901 · 9781741252798 · 9781741252644 · 9781741254167 · 9781741253887 · 9781741254259

Percentages and financial mathematics

Excel Basic Skills · *Excel* Advanced Skills · *Excel* NAPLAN-style Tests

9781741255904 · 9781864412901 · 9781741252798 · 9781741252644 · 9781741254167 · 9781741253887 · 9781741254259

Number patterns and order of operations

Excel Basic Skills · *Excel* Advanced Skills · *Excel* NAPLAN-style Tests · *Excel* NAPLAN-style Tests · *Excel* NAPLAN-style Tests

9781741252798 · 9781741252644 · 9781741254167 · 9781741253887 · 9781741254259

MEASUREMENT AND SPACE

Length and area

Excel Basic Skills · *Excel* Advanced Skills · *Excel* NAPLAN-style Tests · *Excel* NAPLAN-style Tests · *Excel* NAPLAN-style Tests

9781741252798 · 9781741252644 · 9781741254167 · 9781741253887 · 9781741254259

Volume, capacity, mass and time

Excel Basic Skills · *Excel* Advanced Skills · *Excel* NAPLAN-style Tests · *Excel* NAPLAN-style Tests · *Excel* NAPLAN-style Tests

9781741252798 · 9781741252644 · 9781741254167 · 9781741253887 · 9781741254259

Shape, location, transformations and geometric reasoning

Excel Basic Skills · *Excel* Advanced Skills · *Excel* NAPLAN-style Tests · *Excel* NAPLAN-style Tests · *Excel* NAPLAN-style Tests

9781741252798 · 9781741252644 · 9781741254167 · 9781741253887 · 9781741254259

STATISTICS AND PROBABILITY

Chance and data representation and interpretation

Excel Basic Skills · *Excel* Advanced Skills · *Excel* NAPLAN-style Tests · *Excel* NAPLAN-style Tests · *Excel* NAPLAN-style Tests

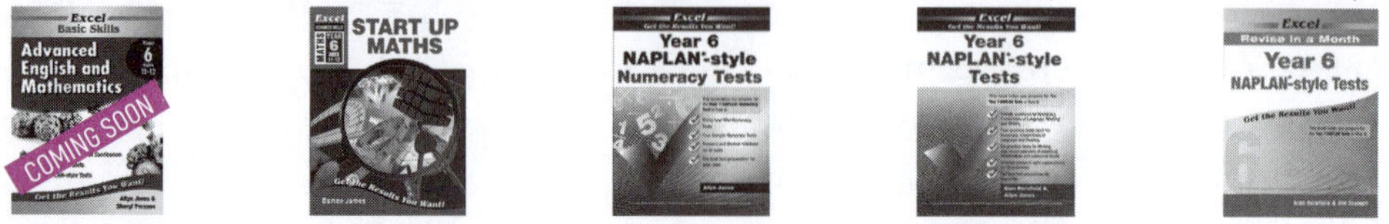

9781741252798 · 9781741252644 · 9781741254167 · 9781741253887 · 9781741254259

Section 1 Marking grid

Number and Algebra
Units 1A & 1B: Number and place value
Units 2A & 2B: Fractions
Units 3A & 3B: Decimals
Units 4A & 4B: Percentages and financial mathematics
Units 5A and 5B: Number patterns and order of operations

Measurement and Space
Units 6A & 6B: Length and area
Units 7A & 7B: Volume, capacity, mass and time
Units 8A & 8B: Shape, location, transformations and geometric reasoning

Statistics and Probability
Units 9A & 9B: Chance
Units 10A & 10B: Data representation and interpretation

Questions	1	2	3	4	5	6	7	8	9	10	11	12	13	14	15	16	17	18	19	20	21	22	23	24	25	26	27	28
Unit 1A ★★★★☆																												
Unit 1B ★★★★★																												
Unit 2A ★★★★☆																												
Unit 2B ★★★★★																												
Unit 3A ★★★★☆																												
Unit 3B ★★★★★																												
Unit 4A ★★★★☆																												
Unit 4B ★★★★★																												
Unit 5A ★★★★☆																												
Unit 5B ★★★★★																												
Unit 6A* ★★★★☆																												
Unit 6B* ★★★★★																												
Unit 7A ★★★★☆																												
Unit 7B ★★★★★																												
Unit 8A ★★★★☆																												
Unit 8B ★★★★★																												
Unit 9A ★★★★☆																												
Unit 9B ★★★★★																												
Unit 10A ★★★★☆																												
Unit 10B ★★★★★																												
Questions	1	2	3	4	5	6	7	8	9	10	11	12	13	14	15	16	17	18	19	20	21	22	23	24	25	26	27	28

* These units have more than 28 questions.

Section 2 Marking grid

		Number and Algebra										Measurement and Space						Statistics and Probability	
		Number properties	Integers	Whole numbers	Fractions 1	Fractions 2	Decimals	Converting fractions, decimals & percentages	Financial mathematics	Patterns	Order of operations	Length & area	Volume, capacity & mass	Timetables	Shapes	Location & transformations	Angles	Probability	Statistics
	Questions	1	2	3	4	5	6	7	8	9	10	11	12	13	14	15	16	17	18
Unit 1A	★★★☆☆																		
Unit 1B	★★★★☆																		
Unit 2A	★★★☆☆																		
Unit 2B	★★★★☆																		
Unit 3A	★★★☆☆																		
Unit 3B	★★★★☆																		
Unit 4A	★★★☆☆																		
Unit 4B	★★★★☆																		
Unit 5A	★★★☆☆																		
Unit 5B	★★★★☆																		
Unit 6A	★★★☆☆																		
Unit 6B	★★★★☆																		
Unit 7A	★★★☆☆																		
Unit 7B	★★★★☆																		
Unit 8A	★★★☆☆																		
Unit 8B	★★★★☆																		
Unit 9A	★★★☆☆																		
Unit 9B	★★★★☆																		
Unit 10A	★★★☆☆																		
Unit 10B	★★★★☆																		
Unit 11A	★★★☆☆																		
Unit 11B	★★★★☆																		
Unit 12A	★★★☆☆																		
Unit 12B	★★★★☆																		
Unit 13A	★★★☆☆																		
Unit 13B	★★★★☆																		
Unit 14A	★★★☆☆																		
Unit 14B	★★★★☆																		
Unit 15A	★★★☆☆																		
Unit 15B	★★★★☆																		

Section 2 Marking grid

		Number and Algebra										Measurement and Space						Statistics and Probability	
		Number properties	Integers	Whole numbers	Fractions 1	Fractions 2	Decimals	Converting fractions, decimals & percentages	Financial mathematics	Patterns	Order of operations	Length & area	Volume, capacity & mass	Timetables	Shapes	Location & transformations	Angles	Probability	Statistics
	Questions	1	2	3	4	5	6	7	8	9	10	11	12	13	14	15	16	17	18
Unit 16A	★★★★☆																		
Unit 16B	★★★★★																		
Unit 17A	★★★★☆																		
Unit 17B	★★★★★																		
Unit 18A	★★★★☆																		
Unit 18B	★★★★★																		
Unit 19A	★★★★☆																		
Unit 19B	★★★★★																		
Unit 20A	★★★★☆																		
Unit 20B	★★★★★																		
Unit 21A	★★★★☆																		
Unit 21B	★★★★★																		
Unit 22A	★★★★☆																		
Unit 22B	★★★★★																		
Unit 23A	★★★★☆																		
Unit 23B	★★★★★																		
Unit 24A	★★★★☆																		
Unit 24B	★★★★★																		
Unit 25A	★★★★☆																		
Unit 25B	★★★★★																		
Unit 26A	★★★★☆																		
Unit 26B	★★★★★																		
Unit 27A	★★★★☆																		
Unit 27B	★★★★★																		
Unit 28A	★★★★☆																		
Unit 28B	★★★★★																		
Unit 29A	★★★★☆																		
Unit 29B	★★★★★																		
Unit 30A	★★★★☆																		
Unit 30B	★★★★★																		

FOCUS ON NUMBER AND PLACE VALUE

1 Write the first 10 prime numbers.

2 Chelsea wrote this two-digit prime number: 2☐. Circle all the possible digits.

3 5 7 9

3 Write the square numbers between 0 and 100.

4 What is the difference between 11^2 and 7^2?

5 What are the first two consecutive numbers that are composite numbers?

6 How many composite numbers less than 80 are square numbers?

7 What are the prime factors of 210?

8 What is the difference between *P* and *Q*?

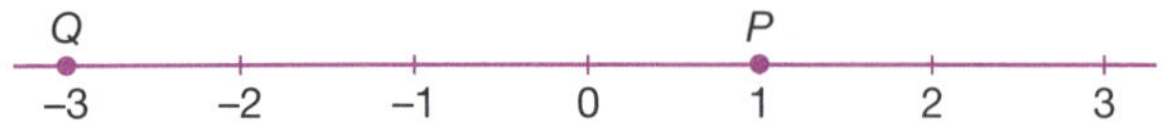

9 Rewrite this list of numbers in order from lowest to highest:

–6 3 1 –4

10 Put a cross (**X**) on the number 4 less than 3.

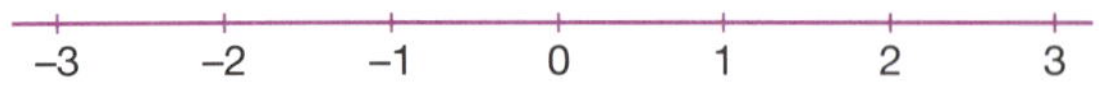

11 What is the combined effect of riding a lift down 4 floors and then up 7 floors?

12 What is the combined effect of travelling 4 km north then 6 km south?

13 The arrows on the number line are used to write a number sentence.

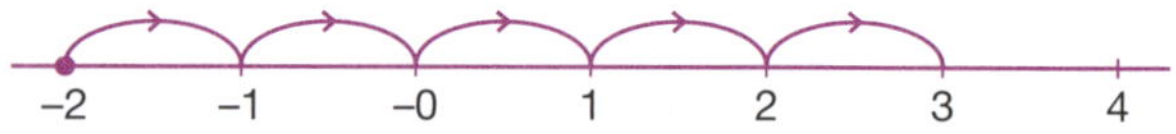

Complete the number sentence:

–2 + ☐ = ☐

14 Write the whole numbers between –6 and –2.

15 What is the difference between the temperatures –1 °C and 4 °C?

16 Here is a pattern of numbers.

–8, –5, –2, 1, ☐

What is the missing number?

17 Eddie places a counter on the number 1 on a number line. He moves the counter 5 units to the left. What is the new position of the counter?

18 There are 51 passengers on a bus. Twenty-seven are women, 18 are men and the rest are children. How many children are on the bus?

19 What is the average of 8, 11, 16 and 21?

20 345 ÷ ☐ = 5

What is the missing number?

21 Sofia travelled 644 km in 7 hours. What was her average speed in km/h?

22 Which two numbers multiply to give eighty thousand? Circle the two numbers.

40 80 200 400 800

23 Find the missing number:

☐ ÷ 45 = 9

24 What is 69 200 ÷ 400?

FOCUS ON NUMBER AND PLACE VALUE

1 How many composite numbers lie between 17 and 37?

2 Carter wrote this three-digit composite number: 12☐. Circle all the possible digits.

5 6 7 9

3 1, 3, 6, 10 … are triangular numbers. What is the tenth triangular number?

4 The product of a square number and a triangular number is 150. What are the two numbers?

5 Mr Graham gave each of his 28 students a number from 1 to 28. When he asked those students with a composite number to stand, how many remained seated?

6 What is the third prime number larger than 50?

7 Here is a list of square numbers:

576, 625, 676, 729, ☐, 841

By considering the differences between the numbers, what is the missing number?

8 What is the difference between the temperatures −11 °C and −2 °C?

9 Rewrite this list of numbers in descending order:

−7 1 −2 3 −5

10 Put a cross (**X**) on the number 4 less than −6.

11 What is the combined effect of a temperature fall of 6 °C and then a rise of 2 °C?

12 What is the combined effect of winning $30, losing $50 and then losing $10?

13 The arrows on the number line are used to write a number sentence.

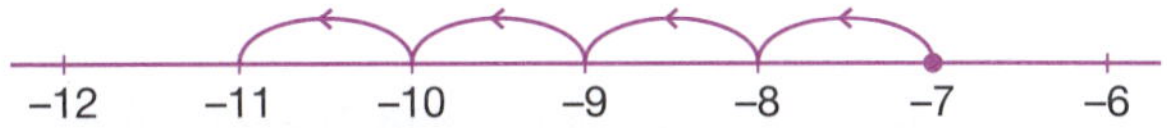

Complete the number sentence:

.... − .... = ...

14 How many whole numbers are between −3 and 5?

15 What is the difference between the temperatures −6 °C and −13 °C?

16 Here is a pattern of temperatures.

−12 °C, −16 °C, ☐, −24 °C, −28 °C

What is the missing temperature?

17 Golf scores can be positive or negative and the person with the 'highest negative number' score wins. Here are four scores: Dustin −2, Rory −6, Aaron +5 and Beau −4. Who is coming third?

18 The sum of two numbers is 237. The smaller number is 93. What is the product of the two numbers?

19 The average height of three friends in Year 6 is 146 cm. If Zoe is 141 cm tall and she is 6 cm shorter than Amelia, how tall is Claire?

20 11 760 ÷ ☐ = 60

What is the missing number?

21 Christian's plane took off at 10 am and flew west for 4340 km. If he arrived at his destination at 5 pm, what was the average speed of the plane?

22 Find the value of 250 × 48 × 23.

23 Find the missing number:

☐ ÷ 24 = 68 × 48

24 A pallet holds 12 boxes of containers of motor oil. Each box contains eight 4-litre containers of oil. If a store ordered a shipment of five pallets, how many litres of oil are in the shipment?

FOCUS ON FRACTIONS

1 Circle the fraction of the shape that is shaded.

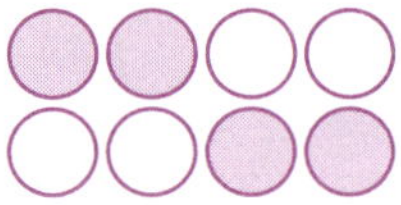

$\frac{1}{4}$ $\frac{4}{5}$ $\frac{1}{2}$

2 What is one-third of 735?

3 $\frac{1}{6}$ of 618 =

4 In a class of 24 students, 16 have borrowed a book from the library. What fraction of the class have borrowed a book?

5 In a bunch of 8 balloons, 4 are red, 2 are white and the rest are pink. What fraction of the balloons are pink?

6 There are 40 cards in a complete collection. Sebastian has 24 of the cards. What fraction of the total set does Sebastian own?

7 Complete the equivalent fraction: $\frac{15}{18} = \frac{\square}{6}$

8 Complete the equivalent fraction: $\frac{7}{\square} = \frac{56}{96}$

9 Rewrite the fractions $\frac{2}{3}$ and $\frac{1}{2}$ as sixths.

10 By changing these fractions to eighths, rewrite from smallest to largest:

$\frac{3}{4}$ $\frac{1}{2}$ $\frac{3}{8}$

11 Insert either <, = or > to make a true statement.

$\frac{2}{3} \square \frac{5}{8}$

12 On the number line, locate and label $\frac{1}{4}$ and $\frac{2}{3}$.

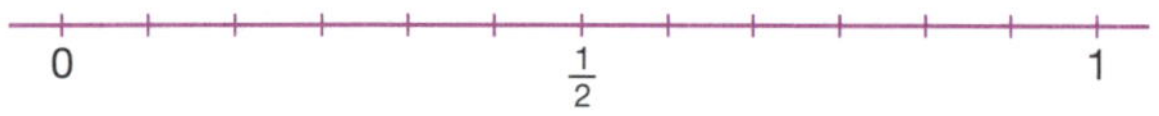

13 $\frac{2}{10} + \frac{4}{10} + \frac{3}{10} =$

14 $\frac{1}{2} - \frac{2}{5} =$

15 Find the sum of $\frac{2}{3}$ and $\frac{4}{5}$.

16 What is $1\frac{3}{4} - \frac{1}{4}$?

17 Find the missing number.

$\frac{7}{8} + \frac{6}{8} = 1\frac{\square}{8}$

18 Find the missing number.

$\frac{3}{5} + \square = 1$

19 Before lunch Michaela drank $\frac{1}{4}$ of her water bottle and then another $\frac{1}{3}$ of the bottle later in the day.

What fraction of the water bottle did she drink?

20 What is $\frac{3}{5}$ of 45?

21 Pearl is building a 24-metre-long fence. She has already completed two-thirds of the fence. What length of fence remains to be built?

22 A recipe Jacinta is following needs 2 cups of sugar. As she has only $1\frac{1}{3}$ cups, she borrows the remainder from her neighbour. How much sugar did Jacinta have to borrow?

23 Three-fifths of the teapots in Edna's collection come from Europe. If she has 100 teapots, how many come from Europe?

24 The distance from Chloe's home to work is $2\frac{1}{4}$ km.

She walks to and from work 4 days every week. What is the total distance she walks?

FOCUS ON FRACTIONS

1 Circle the fraction of the shape that is **not** shaded.

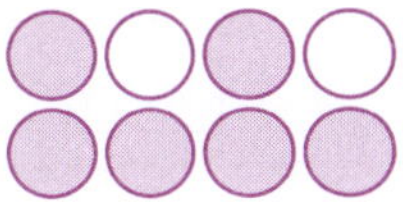

$\frac{1}{3}$ $\frac{3}{4}$ $\frac{1}{4}$

2 What is $\frac{3}{4}$ of 360?

3 A box contains 85 bananas.
If $\frac{3}{5}$ of the bananas are ripe, how many are **not** ripe?

4 This morning 184 out of 200 students arrived at school on time. What fraction of the students were late to school?

5 In a box of 20 chocolates, 12 are milk chocolate, 6 are dark chocolate and the remainder are white chocolate. What fraction of the chocolates are white?

6 What fraction of the positive numbers less than 20 are composite?

7 Complete: $1\frac{9}{12} = \frac{\square}{4}$.

8 Reduce $\frac{24}{144}$ to its simplest form.

9 Rewrite the mixed numerals $2\frac{1}{4}$ and $3\frac{2}{3}$ as improper fractions with the same smallest possible denominator.

10 Express these fractions in ascending order:

$\frac{5}{6}$ $\frac{2}{3}$ $\frac{5}{8}$ $\frac{3}{4}$

11 Insert either $<$, $=$ or $>$ to make a true statement.

$\frac{15}{4} \;\square\; \frac{11}{3}$

12 On the number line, locate and label $2\frac{1}{2}$ and $3\frac{1}{4}$.

13 $\frac{5}{6} + \frac{3}{6} + \frac{5}{6} =$

14 Indira has $\frac{7}{8}$ L of detergent. She uses $\frac{1}{3}$ L when cleaning her bathroom.
What amount remains?

15 Levi worked for $4\frac{1}{2}$ hours on Thursday and $6\frac{1}{4}$ hours on Sunday. What was the total number of hours he worked over the two days?

16 $1\frac{1}{5} - \frac{4}{5} =$

17 Find the missing number.

$\frac{7}{8} + \frac{1}{6} = 1\frac{\square}{24}$

18 Find the missing number.

$\square + \frac{7}{10} = 1\frac{1}{10}$

19 Last week Dylan started reading his novel. He read $\frac{5}{8}$ of the novel, and this week he read another $\frac{1}{4}$ of the novel. What fraction of the novel remains?

20 A group of 48 people were surveyed at a local supermarket. If $\frac{5}{8}$ of the people surveyed were women, how many men were surveyed?

21 Grayson has already cycled 135 km of a charity bike ride. If he has completed $\frac{3}{5}$ of the distance, what is the total length of the ride?

22 Lyle bought a case of oranges at a market. He gave $\frac{3}{10}$ of the oranges to each of his two sisters and kept the rest. What fraction of the oranges did he keep?

23 When half-full, Noah's tank contains 1600 L of water. How much water is in the tank when it is $\frac{4}{5}$ full?

24 After his death, Jamie's estate is allocated as follows: Sam and Kate receive $\frac{1}{5}$ each, Jack $\frac{1}{4}$ and the remainder is given to Bruce. What fraction of the estate is given to Bruce?

FOCUS ON DECIMALS

1 Find the sum of 8.07 and 12.9.

2 18 – 9.4 =

3 Round 17.786 to two decimal places.

4 What is 12.7 – 5 + 3?

5 8.03 × 5 =

6 23.872 × 100 =

7 $5\overline{)23.85}$

8 48.86 ÷ 100 =

9 Divide 34 by 5, writing your answer as a decimal.

10 Fiona needs 1.6 m of material to make a child's skirt. How much material is needed for her to make three skirts?

11 Find the answer:
0.73 × 20 × 5

12 A block has a mass of 14.06 kg. What would be the total mass of eight blocks?

13 What is the missing number?
2.3 – ☐ = 1.6

14 What is the sum of 12.78, 0.239 and 18.096, correct to two decimal places?

15 A cube has a mass of 26.7 g. What is the total mass of 30 cubes?

16 What is 14.671 × 10^2?

17 On five mornings Jason completed an average of 38.6 push-ups. What was the total number of push-ups?

18 Wyatt, Layla and Eli decided to split their total restaurant bill evenly. If each paid $65.75, what was the total cost of the meal?

19 The difference between the maximum and minimum temperatures in Hobart last Monday was 9.6 °C. If the maximum temperature was 23.5 °C, what was the minimum temperature?

20 From a 4.2-metre plank, Colin cut five equal pieces. What was the length of each piece, in metres?

21 Anastacia removed four 3.6-metre lengths from an 80-metre ball of string. What length remained?

22 Max drove at an average speed of 84.2 km/h for 5 hours. What distance did he drive?

23 Find half of 0.0465.

24 Corey won his race in a time of 24.9 s. Linus came fourth, finishing 1.26 s after Corey. What was Linus's time?

25 When planted, a shrub is 0.8 m tall. If it grows 20 cm each month, what will be its height, in metres, in 6 months time?

26 What is the largest number with two decimal places that can be rounded to 8?

27 Jake had a timber plank measuring 3.6 m in length. He cut 50 cm from one end and 20 cm from the other end. What length of timber remained?

FOCUS ON

DECIMALS

1 9.28 + 0.098 + 13.4

2 4 – 1.8 – 0.58

3 Round 43.598 to two decimal places.

4 Find the answer: 9 – 4.26 + 3.075.

5 97.4 × 36 =

6 What is the missing number?

9.481 × ☐ = 948.1

7 $4\overline{)3.156}$

8 What is the missing number?

64 ÷ ☐ = 0.64

9 What is 146.4 divided by 4, to the nearest whole?

10 Bananas are priced at $2.69/kg and mandarins at $3.49/kg. Hope bought 2 kg of bananas and 1 kg of mandarins. What is the total cost, to the nearest 10 cents?

11 250 × 0.0378 × 4 =

12 Find the value of 1.7 × 5 + 4.2 × 6.

13 Find the missing number:

1.672 × 100 = 200 –

14 Find 316.814 ÷ 100, writing your answer to the nearest hundredth.

15 What is the average of 3.9, 12.8, 6.1 and 5.2?

16 Find the value of $\frac{178.3}{10^2}$.

17 The average temperature at midday across 4 days is 23.6°. On the fifth day the temperature at midday is 26.1 °C. What is the average temperature across the 5 days?

18 What is the missing number?

☐ ÷ 2.4 = 36

19 Matthew mailed three packages. Two packages had a mass of 2.15 kg each and the other package was 0.8 kg heavier. What was the total mass of the packages?

20 In winter this year, Ulladulla received 116.7 mm of rain. In June there was 43.1 mm, and in July another 32.9 mm fell. How much rain fell in August?

21 The temperature in Jindabyne at 6:15 am was 2.9 °C. By 2:30 pm it had increased by 16.4 °C and then by 7:00 pm it had dropped by 11.8 °C. What was the temperature at 7:00 pm?

22 Jasmine is paid an hourly rate of $18.75. What will she be paid for working 36 h?

23 What is $\frac{3}{4}$ of 6.2?

24 What is the middle of 17.8 and 25.47?

25 Two numbers are represented on the number line as *A* and *B*. What is the value of *B* – *A*?

26 The average mass of three packages is 3.2 kg. The heaviest parcel has a mass of 4.6 kg. What is the average mass of the other two packages?

27 Jack finished first in a 400-metre race at the state championships. He ran a time of 58.13 s. Thomas finished second and Bryce came third with a time of 59.38 s. If Bryce finished 0.68 s after Thomas, how much time was between Jack and Thomas?

FOCUS ON PERCENTAGES AND FINANCIAL MATHEMATICS

1 Circle the fractions that are the same as 50%.

$\frac{3}{6}$ $\frac{1}{50}$ $\frac{15}{25}$ $\frac{50}{100}$

2 What percentage of the rectangle is shaded?

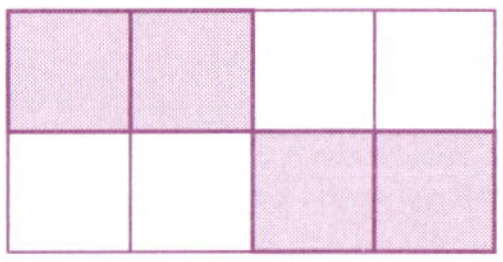

3 The rectangle contains squares. Shade 75% of the rectangle.

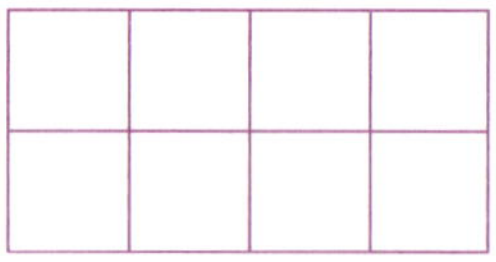

4 Circle the largest: 0.8, 60%, $\frac{65}{100}$, $\frac{3}{4}$.

5 A survey at a supermarket found 16 out of 20 shoppers were buying milk. What percentage of the shoppers were buying milk?

6 What is $\frac{2}{5}$ as a percentage?

7 What is 50% of 436?

8 When completely full, a swimming pool has a capacity of 36 000 L. If the pool is 25% full of water, how much water is in the pool?

9 A packet of toilet paper contains 24 rolls. If 6 rolls have been used, what percentage of the packet remains?

10 What is 45% written as a fraction in simplest form?

11 Charlotte has read four-fifths of her book. What percentage of the book remains?

12 80% of the girls in a group of 30 students have had their ears pierced. What number of girls do **not** have their ears pierced?

13 A pendant originally priced at $860 has been discounted by $275. What is the new price?

14 Five years ago Cooper purchased a motorbike for $23 400. Today he sold it for one-third of the original price. At what price did Cooper sell his motorbike?

15 After a discount of $65, Theo paid $378 for a lawnmower. What was the original price of the lawnmower?

16 The price of a television is discounted by 10%. If the original price was $2290, what is the discounted price?

17 A shoe store is offering a 'Buy one pair, get the next pair half price' sale. What will Zoe pay for two pairs of shoes priced at $89 each?

18 The price of a pair of jeans has been discounted from $100 to $65. What is the discount as a percentage?

19 Olivia spent half of her birthday money on a necklace and 25% of her money on a pool toy. If the necklace cost $48, what was the cost of the pool toy?

20 The price of a microwave dropped from $200 to $160. Find the discount as a percentage.

21 Loki's electricity bill is $651.90. He plans to pay the bill early to receive a discount of 10%. How much will Loki save?

22 Lexie saves $95 when she buys a clothes dryer at a store with a 20% discount sale. What is the usual price of the clothes dryer?

23 Thomas buys a painting for $28 000 and later sells it at a profit of 10%. What was the selling price of the painting?

24 The price of an apartment for sale is $800 000. The real-estate salesperson drops the price by 10%. What will be the new price?

FOCUS ON PERCENTAGES AND FINANCIAL MATHEMATICS

1 Circle any decimals and fractions that equal 25%.

$\frac{2}{5}$ 0.25 2.5 $\frac{3}{12}$

2 What percentage of the rectangle is shaded?

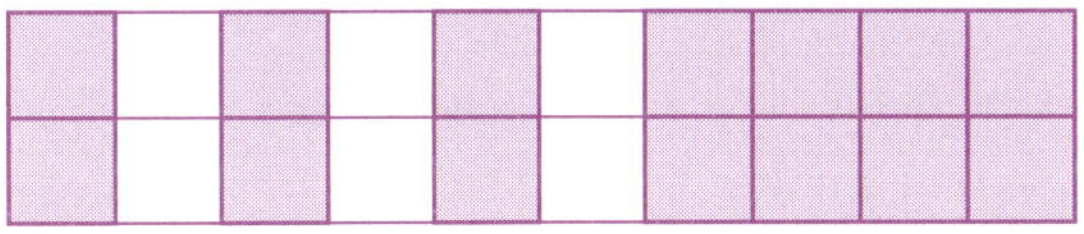

3 The rectangle contains squares. Shade 35% of the rectangle.

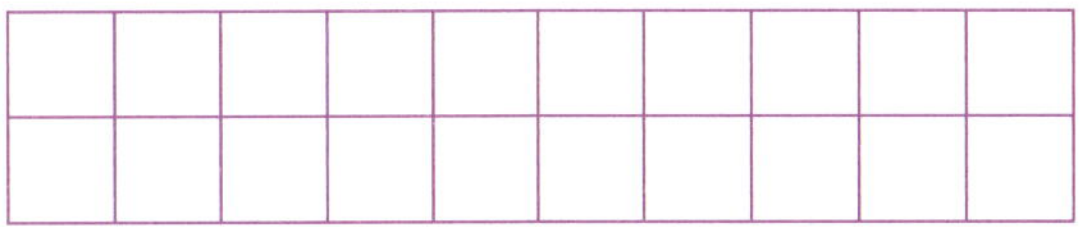

4 Rewrite these in ascending order:

$\frac{9}{20}$, 0.4, $\frac{23}{50}$, 35%

5 Write the fraction $\frac{72}{200}$ as a percentage.

6 What is $\frac{3}{8}$ as a percentage?

7 Find 20% of 640.

8 This week Colton cycled a total of 460 km. Next week he plans to increase this distance by 25%.

How far does Colton plan to ride?

9 There are 25 students in a class. 80% of the students have handed in their signed permission note. How many students have **not** handed in the note?

10 What is $7\frac{1}{2}$% as a decimal.

11 In a bag of balls, 50% are red and 10% are green. If the remainder of the balls are blue, what fraction of the balls are blue?

12 A survey of 850 audience members at an opera found that 30% of the audience were at their first opera. How many had never been to the opera before?

13 A set of headphones has been discounted by $65. If the new price is $138.99, what was the original price?

14 The price of a used car has been reduced by one-quarter. What is the new price if it was originally priced at $15 600?

15 After being damaged in a hailstorm, the price of a new caravan is discounted by one-fifth. If the new price is $48 000, what was the original price?

16 At a sale, all computers have been discounted by 25%. What will be paid for a laptop originally priced at $1780?

17 What is saved if a pizza oven originally priced at $399 is discounted by 20%?

18 Sarah works as a waitress and is paid $24 per hour. If she is to receive a 5% pay rise, what will be her new hourly rate?

19 A furniture store is having a sale. An entertainment unit originally priced at $2500 is on sale for $1200. Circle the best estimate of the discount as a percentage.

13% 20% 50% 75%

20 Which of these is closest to $\frac{1}{3}$?

20% 30% 40% 50%

21 What is 4% of $78?

22 All potting mix is discounted by 50% at a 'Spring Sale'. Will buys four bags for $24. What was the normal price of a bag?

23 As a tradesperson, Chloe receives a 5% discount on all purchases at the local hardware store. How much does she save on plumbing supplies totalling $860?

24 The price of a ladder drops by 10% and then by another 10%. If the original price was $200, what is the final price?

FOCUS ON NUMBER PATTERNS AND ORDER OF OPERATIONS

1 What is the next number in the sequence?

2.3, 3.55, 4.8, [ ]

2 What is the missing number in the sequence?

120, 12, 1.2, [ ], 0.012 ...

3 What is the next number in the sequence?

75, 15, 3, 0.6, [ ]

4 What is the next number in the pattern?

$\frac{3}{5}$, 1, $1\frac{2}{5}$, [ ]

5 Write the first four numbers in the pattern:

'Start with 2.4 and subtract 0.3 each time.'

[ ]

6 Write the first four numbers in the pattern:

'Start with $2\frac{2}{3}$ and add $\frac{1}{6}$ each time.'

[ ]

7 Samir wrote a sequence starting with 8 and subtracting 0.6 each time. Circle the number that is in the sequence.

6.4 5.8 5.6 5.1

8 Here is a pattern of three shapes made of matchsticks.

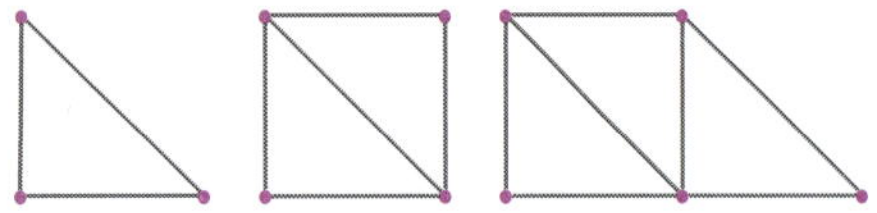

How many matchsticks would be used to make the fifth shape in the pattern? [ ]

9 Here is a pattern of three shapes made of dots.

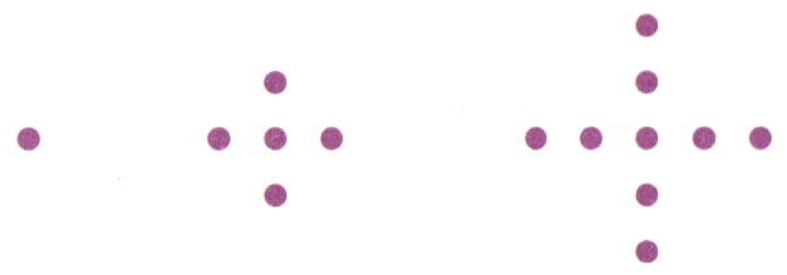

How many dots would be used to make the seventh shape in the pattern? [ ]

10 A table uses a rule to link two numbers.

First number	1	2	3	4	5
Second number	9	18	27	36	?

What is the missing number? [ ]

11 A table uses a rule to link two numbers.

First number	3	3.6	4.4	4.9	5.8
Second number	6.3	6.9	7.7	8.2	?

What is the missing number? [ ]

12 What is 12 – 5 × 2? [ ]

13 What is the value of 16 – (4 + 8)? [ ]

14 Find the value of 36 ÷ 4 + 6 – 1. [ ]

15 What is a quarter of the sum of 8 and 12? [ ]

16 What is the product of 6 and the sum of 8 and 3? [ ]

17 Find 12.1 – 2.8 × 3. [ ]

18 What is $\frac{9}{10} - (\frac{1}{10} + \frac{5}{10})$? [ ]

19 Insert grouping symbols to make the number sentence correct:
12 – 3 × 4 = 36 [ ]

20 Corey works 28 hours one week and 22 hours the following week. If he is paid $20 per hour, what is his total pay?

21 What is 60 – 4 – 4 – 4 – 4 – 4? [ ]

22 What is $\frac{24 - 16}{2}$? [ ]

23 What is the missing number in this number sentence?

30 – 5 × [ ] = 10

24 Find the value of $6^2 \div (6 + 6)$. [ ]

FOCUS ON NUMBER PATTERNS AND ORDER OF OPERATIONS

1 What is the next number in the sequence?

11.38, 13.66, 15.94, ☐

2 What is the missing number in the sequence?

0.037, ☐ , 370, 37 000, …

3 What is the first number in the sequence?

☐ , 16, 0.8, 0.04, 0.002, …

4 What is the next number in the pattern?

$5\frac{1}{2}$, $4\frac{3}{4}$, 4, ☐

5 Write the first four numbers in the pattern:

'Start with 8.4 and add 1.37 each time.'

☐

6 Write the first four numbers in the pattern:

'Start with 8 and subtract $1\frac{1}{4}$ each time.'

☐

7 Amara wrote a sequence starting with 3.5 and adding 0.45 each time. Circle the number that is in the sequence.

5.25 5.3 5.4 5.45

8 Here is a pattern of three shapes made of matchsticks.

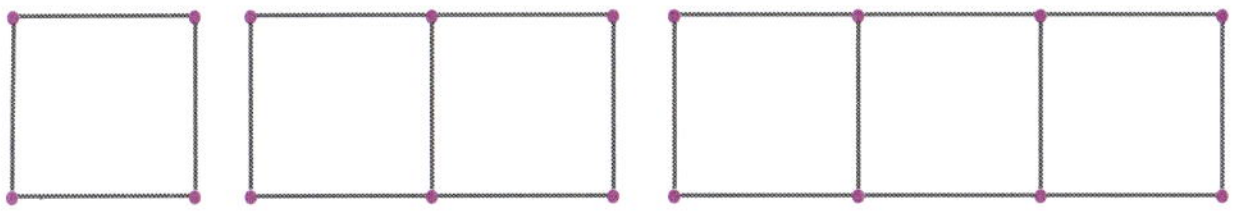

How many matchsticks would be used to make the tenth shape in the pattern? ☐

9 Here is a pattern of three shapes made of matchsticks.

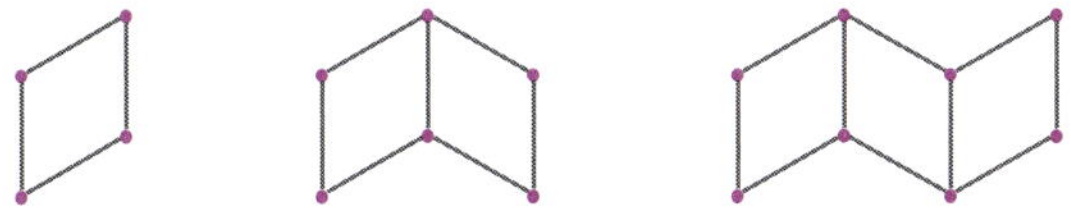

Shape 1 Shape 2 Shape 3

Which shape would be made using 25 matchsticks? ☐

10 A table uses a rule to link two numbers.

First number	4	5	6	…	?
Second number	24	30	36	…	132

What is the missing number? ☐

11 A table uses a rule to link two numbers.

First number	4.8	7.6	10	?	13
Second number	1.2	1.9	2.5	3.2	3.25

What is the missing number? ☐

12 What is 32 ÷ 8 + 8 × 3? ☐

13 What is the value of 5.8 – (4 – 2.7)? ☐

14 What is 5 × 6 ÷ 3 + 12 × 4 ÷ 2? ☐

15 Find three-quarters of the difference between 64 and 48. ☐

16 What is the difference between the product of 8 and 4, and the quotient of 63 and 9? ☐

17 Find the value of $16 - (2.3 + 0.7)^2$. ☐

18 Find the value of $\frac{5}{8} - (\frac{3}{4} - \frac{1}{2})$. ☐

19 Insert grouping symbols to make the number sentence correct:
16 ÷ 4 + 3 + 1 = 2. ☐

20 Every morning Joshua buys three juices and four coffees for his workmates.
A juice costs $6 and a coffee $5.
What is the total cost over 5 days? ☐

21 Kenny budgets $200 for his work lunches.
On 8 days he spends $9 and on another 12 days he spends $10.
How much of his budget remains? ☐

22 What is $\frac{2 + 3 \times 6}{12 - 8 \div 4}$? ☐

23 What is the missing number below?

9 + 40 ÷ (☐ + 3) = 14

FOCUS ON LENGTH AND AREA

1 Change 2.876 m to millimetres.

2 How many metres are in 8500 cm?

3 How many millimetres are in 38.62 cm?

4 Convert 60 000 m^2 to hectares.

5 Add these lengths, writing your answer in millimetres:

370 mm and 5.21 m

6 Saanvi removed 1200 mm of string from a 10-metre roll.

What length, in metres, remained on the roll?

7 Naomi is 1.72 m tall. Her sister Morgan is 16 cm shorter. What is Morgan's height, in metres?

8 Complete: $\frac{1}{2}$ metre = ... cm.

9 The four legs of a sailing course are 3.6 km, 7.1 km, 6.8 km and 5.05 km.

What is the total distance of the course?

10 Josiah is participating in his school's fundraising walkathon. He has already walked seven laps and plans to walk a total of 6 km.

If each lap is 600 m, how many more laps will he need to complete?

11 Write these lengths from smallest to largest.

5100 mm 520 cm 5.05 m

12 How many kilometres are in 19 600 000 mm?

13 Each side in a regular hexagon is 5.9 cm.

What is the perimeter of the hexagon?

14 Each side of an equilateral triangle has a length of $\frac{2}{3}$ m. What is the perimeter of the triangle?

15 The perimeter of a square is 10.8 cm. What is the length of each side?

16 A square has side length of 36 cm. What is the perimeter, in metres?

17 Find the area of the shape.

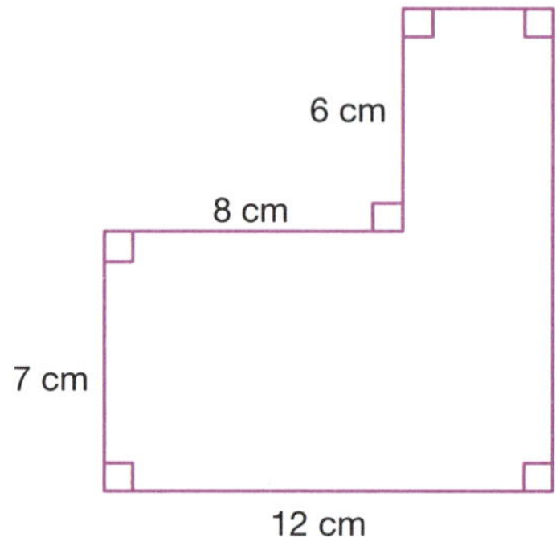

18 What is the perimeter of a rectangular paddock with side lengths of 640 m and 380 m, in kilometres?

19 Find the perimeter of the rectangle, in metres.

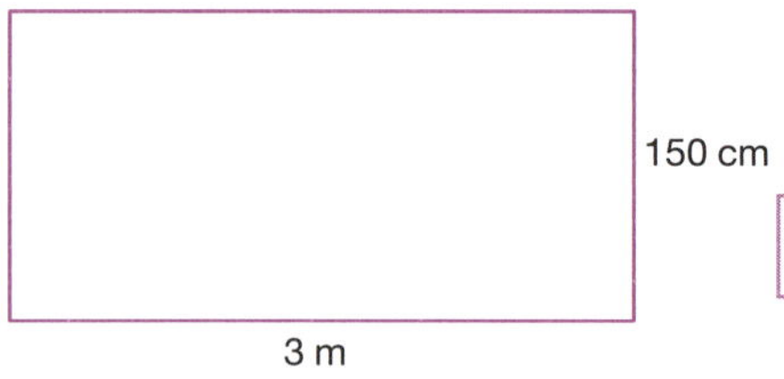

20 The perimeter of the triangle is 56 cm.

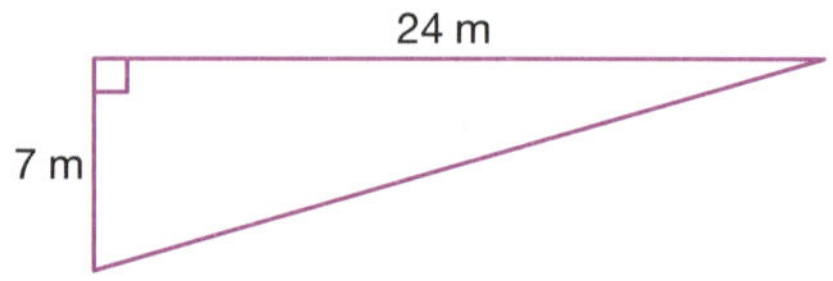

What is the length of the longest side?

21 The shape below has two equal sides. The perimeter of the shape is 54 cm.

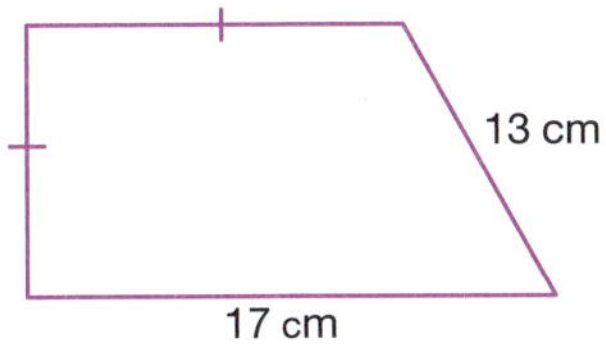

What is the length of each missing side?

22 What is the area of the rectangle, in square metres?

23 The area of the rectangle is 112 cm^2.

What is the length of the rectangle?

24 What is the perimeter of the rectangle?

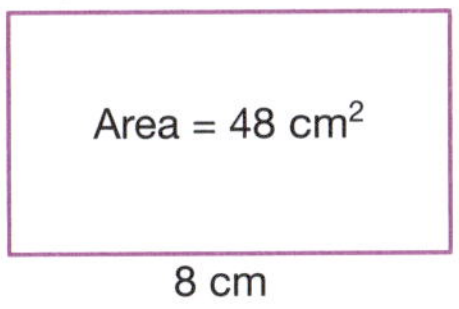

25 A rectangular patio is to be tiled. The dimensions are 6 m by 3.2 m.

What is the area of the patio?

26 Find the area of the triangle.

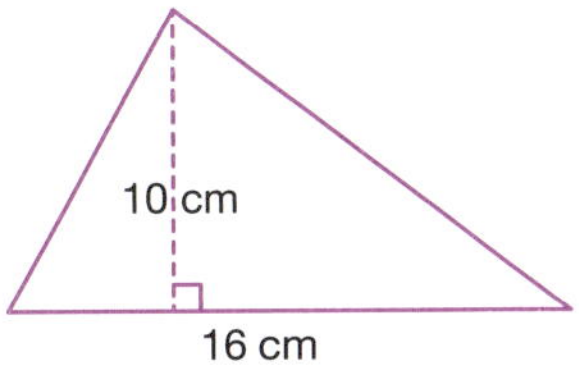

27 A piece of wire 36 cm in length is bent to form a square.

What is the area of the square?

28 One side of an isosceles triangle is 4 cm shorter than the other sides. If the perimeter is 20 cm, what is the length of the shorter side?

29 A rectangle has an area of 60 cm^2 and a width of 5 cm. If the dimensions of the rectangle are doubled, what is the area of the new rectangle?

30 A right-angled triangle is drawn inside a rectangle. Two sides of the triangle are 9 cm and 12 cm. What is the area of the rectangle?

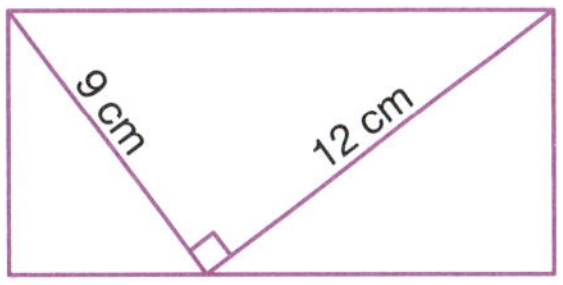

31 A length of wire can be bent to form an equilateral triangle of side 10 cm. Instead the wire is used to form an isosceles triangle where the longest side is 14 cm. What are the lengths of the other two sides?

32 The perimeter of a rhombus is 2.2 m. What is the length, in centimetres, of each side?

33 A square has an area of 16 cm^2. Two sides of the square are doubled and two sides are halved so that the shape is now a rectangle.

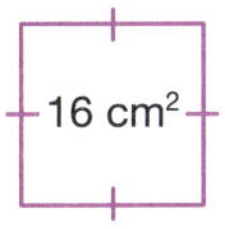

What is the area of the rectangle?

34 A wall measures 12 m by 3 m. Jannah is to paint the wall with two coats of paint. If a litre of paint covers 6 m^2, how much paint will be required?

35 The diagram shows two identical triangles.

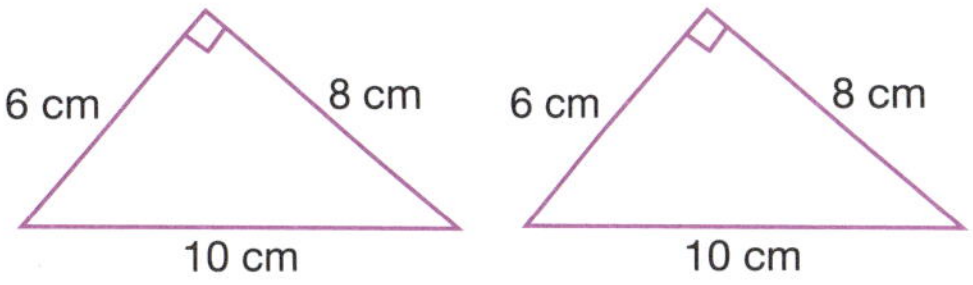

The triangles are then shifted to form a rectangle. What is the area of the rectangle?

FOCUS ON LENGTH AND AREA

1 Change 25.6 m to centimetres.

2 How many kilometres are in 6 100 000 mm?

3 Change 390 000 cm to kilometres.

4 How many square metres are in 2.43 ha?

5 What is the total length of planks that are 135 cm, 1.4 m and 750 mm in length, writing your answer in metres?

6 Arjun swam 1500 m, rode 12 km and ran 6.6 km. What was the total distance, in kilometres?

7 Dominic is $\frac{3}{4}$ the height of his father. If Dominic's dad is 1.82 m tall, what is Dominic's height, in centimetres?

8 Complete: $7\frac{1}{4}$ m = ... mm.

9 On an 18-hole golf course, the average length of each hole is 362 m.

What is the total length of the course?

10 $2 coins worth a total of $10 000 are placed next to each other to form a line of coins.

What is the length of the line, in metres, if a $2 coin has a diameter of 20.5 mm?

11 Write these lengths in ascending order.

0.409 m   403 cm   40.5 cm   406 mm

12 Convert 0.063 19 km to metres.

13 The perimeter of a regular octagon is 73.2 cm. What is the length of each side?

14 A rectangle measures $5\frac{3}{4}$ cm by $3\frac{1}{4}$ cm.

What is the perimeter of the rectangle?

15 A rectangle has a perimeter of 38 cm. If the length is 13 cm, what is the width?

16 Two identical rectangles measuring 74 cm by 37 cm are joined to form a square.

What is the perimeter of the square, in metres?

17 Find the area of the shape.

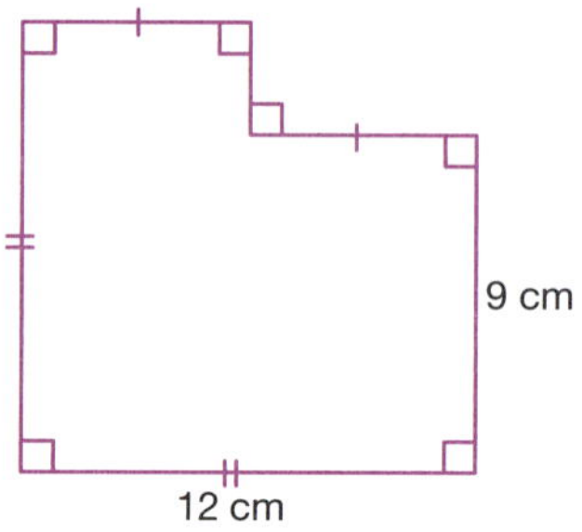

18 Find the perimeter.

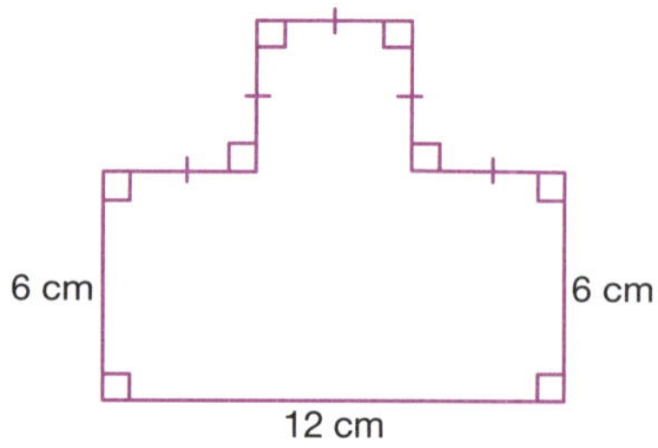

19 What is the perimeter of a rectangle with a length of 2 m and a width of 85 cm.

Give your answer in metres.

20 Three identical rectangles measuring 12 cm by 8 cm are joined to form this shape. What is the perimeter of the new shape?

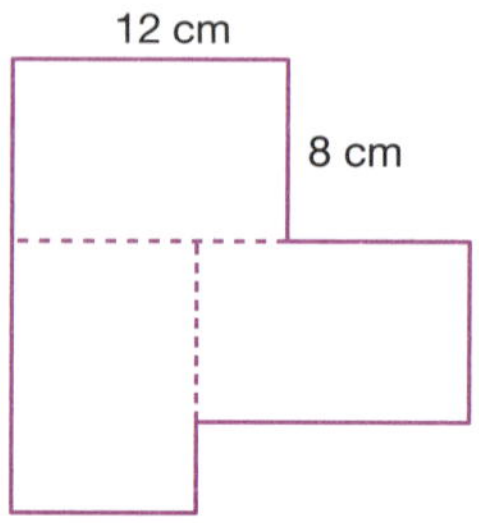

21 Three squares are placed together to form this shape.

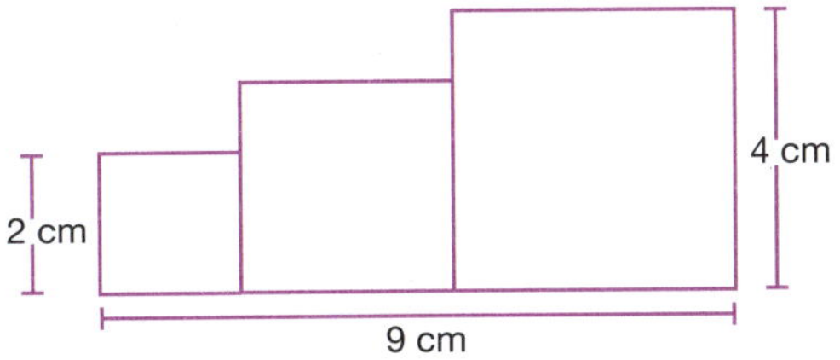

What is the total area of the shape?

22 What is the area of the rectangle?

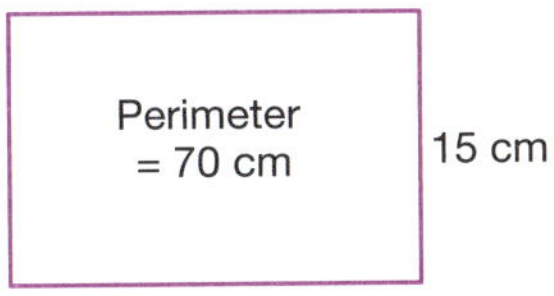

23 A rectangle has a perimeter of 72 cm. The length is twice the width. What is the area of the shaded triangle?

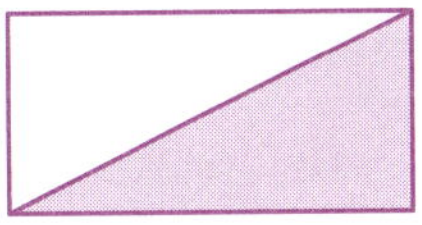

24 If the perimeter of this triangle is 24 cm, what is the area?

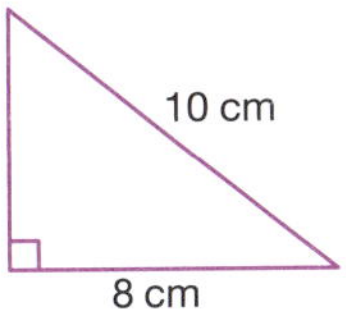

25 A piece of wire 96 cm in length is bent to form a rectangle where the length is three times the width.

Find the area of the rectangle.

26 A rectangle has an area of 40 cm^2 and a perimeter of 26 cm.

What is the length of the rectangle?

27 A square and a regular octagon have the same perimeter.

If a side of the octagon is 6 cm, find the area of the square.

28 The diagram shows two squares, one on top of the other. The area of the shaded section is 27 cm^2.

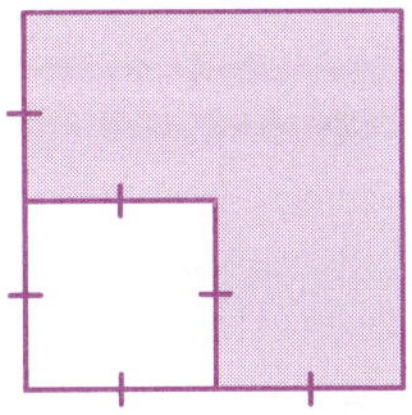

What is the length of the side of the smaller square?

29 A photo is mounted in a frame. The dimensions of the photo are 16 cm by 12 cm. A border of cardboard 4 cm wide surrounds the photo. What is the area of the cardboard?

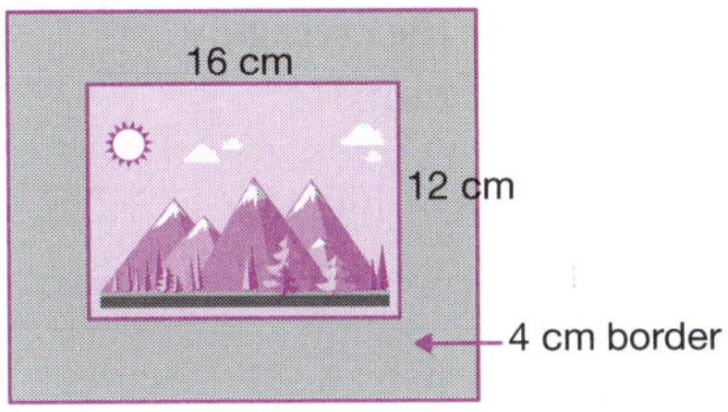

30 The diagram shows a rectangle measuring 14 cm by 8 cm. A square is removed from the rectangle, leaving a shaded part with an area of 76 cm^2. What is the perimeter of the square?

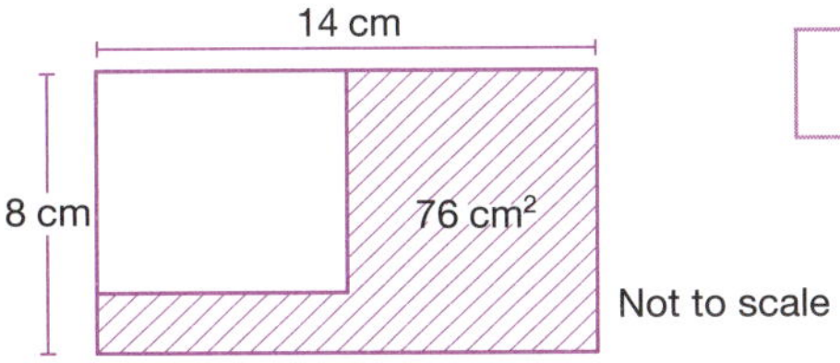

31 The diagram shows a large rectangle split into five identical smaller rectangles. The large rectangle has an area of 120 cm^2.

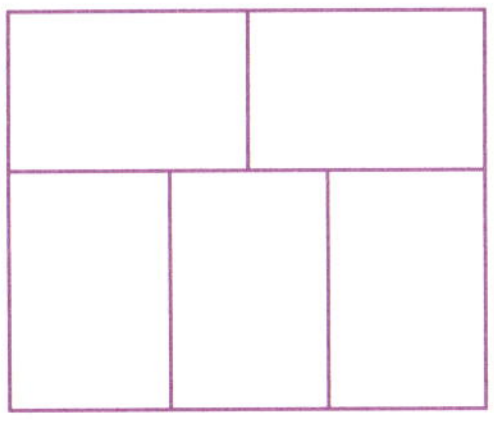

What is the perimeter of each of the small rectangles?

32 A rectangle is made up of a row of six squares and a row of eight smaller squares. Squares in each row are identical. If the area of one square on the top row is 64 cm^2, what is the perimeter of the rectangle?

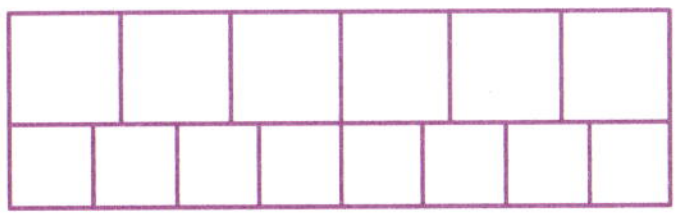

FOCUS ON VOLUME, CAPACITY, MASS AND TIME

1 How many grams are in 3.08 kg?

2 Complete: 7840 g = ... kg.

3 What fraction of a litre is 400 mL?

4 How many cubic centimetres are in 1.5 L?

5 Krystal bought three tomatoes which had a total mass of 1.05 kg. What was the average mass of each tomato, in grams?

6 A litre of honey has a mass of 1.44 kg. What is the mass of 5 L of the honey?

7 At the supermarket, Sam used a set of scales to weigh two pieces of watermelon. What is the average mass of the pieces if they weigh 4.8 kg and 3.6 kg?

8 How many kilograms are in 3 kg 590 g?

9 If a litre of water has a mass of 1 kg, what is the mass of 3 kL of water?

10 What is the volume of a rectangular prism with dimensions 14 cm, 10 cm and 6 cm?

11 How many kilolitres are in 12 650 L?

12 A cube has a side length of 20 cm. What is the capacity of the cube, expressed in litres?

13 A rectangular prism is 15 cm long, 10 cm wide and 8 cm tall. What is the capacity of the prism, in millilitres?

14 A cube with sides 6 cm is half full of water. How much water is needed to fill the cube, in millilitres?

15 A solid is made of identical cubes weighing 0.6 kg each. Find the total mass.

16 A prism has a cross-section area of 48 cm^2. If the prism is 10 cm high, what is the volume?

17 Find the volume of the prism.

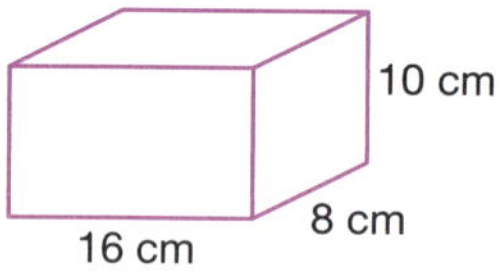

18 The diagram shows a square-based prism. What is the volume of the prism?

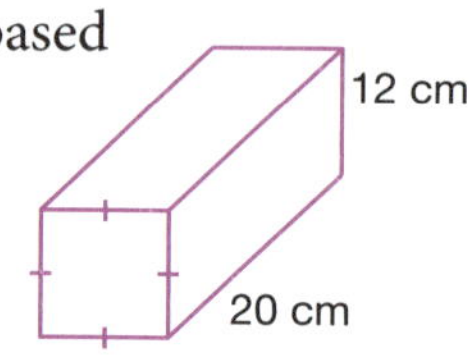

19 Record this information on the timeline: school starts (X) at 9 am and finishes (Y) at 3:30 pm.

20 A movie is shown in Cinema 5 every 2 h 30 min. If the first screening is at 1100, when does the third screening start?

21 The timetable shows two buses that travel the same route at the same speed each morning. What is the missing time?

York	0728	0830
Concord	0751	?
Richmond	0818	0920
Newmarket	0847	0949

22 The table lists movies showing at a multiplex cinema.

Film	Session times		
Extinguished	11:20	1:40	4:00
Sweetie Pie	11:45	2:20	4:55
The Gamer	11:55	2:00	4:05

Maddison arrives at the cinema at 3:30. How long does she wait until the start of *The Gamer*?

23 The table shows flights from Perth to Broome, which all have the same flight time.

	Perth to Broome schedule		
Perth	0555	1030	1110
Broome	0835	1310	1350

How long is the flight?

FOCUS ON VOLUME, CAPACITY, MASS AND TIME

1 How many kilograms are in 0.067 tonnes?

2 Complete: 0.056 kg = ______________ mg.

3 What fraction of 6 kg is 200 g?

4 Find the number of litres in 960 cm^3.

5 A box contains twenty-four 420-gram cans of lentils. What is the total mass of the cans, in kilograms?

6 A litre of saltwater from the Dead Sea has a mass of 1.25 kg. An empty 9-litre bucket has a mass of 1.5 kg. What is the total mass of the bucket when full of saltwater?

7 Here are the masses of four boys: 41.5 kg, 40 kg, 43.9 kg, 39.6 kg. What is the average mass?

8 How many litres are in 10 L 5 mL?

9 A bucket has a total capacity of 9 L. When empty, the bucket has a mass of 320 g. If 1 L of water has a mass of 1 kg, what is the total mass when the bucket is exactly half full?

10 Henry needs to fill a garden bed with soil to a depth of 30 cm. If the garden is rectangular with dimensions 12 m by 2 m, what is the volume of soil required?

11 Rewrite these from least to greatest capacities.

3080 mL   0.003 kL   3600 mL   3.27 L

12 From a 2-L bottle of soft drink, Sandun poured 330 mL into each of six glasses. What amount of soft drink remains in the bottle?

13 A box has a square base and a height of 20 cm. If the perimeter of the base is 44 cm, what is the capacity of the box, in litres?

14 A rectangular prism has a length of 12 cm, width 10 cm and height 8 cm. If the prism is one-third full of water, how much more water is required to fill the prism?

15 This solid is made using identical cubes. If the solid has a mass of 12.5 kg, what is the mass of each cube, in grams?

16 A rectangular prism has a volume of 480 cm^3. If the length is 10 cm and the width is 8 cm, what is the height?

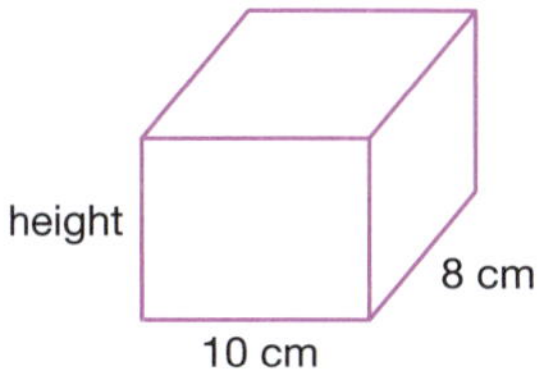

17 The diagram shows the net of a prism. What is the capacity of the prism?

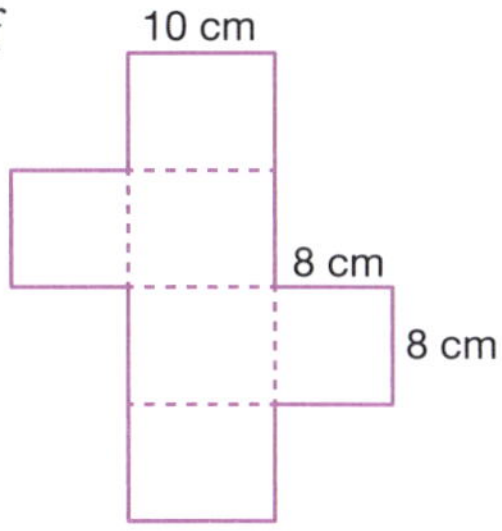

18 An empty container has a capacity of 40 L. Nicola is filling the container with water at a constant rate of 200 mL per second. How long will it take Nicola to fill the container?

19 Record this travel information on the timeline: left on cruise (A) on 15 January, arrived London (B) on 1 April and left San Francisco (C) on 20 May.

20 A movie is shown in Cinema 3 every 2 h 45 min. If the first screening is at 1130, when does the fourth screening start?

21 The timetable shows one of the many buses that travel the same route at the same speed each day. If another bus arrived in Newmarket at 1106, what time had it left Concord?

York	0728
Concord	0751
Richmond	0818
Newmarket	0847

FOCUS ON SHAPE, LOCATION, TRANSFORMATIONS AND GEOMETRIC REASONING

1 What are the coordinates of *P* and *Q*?

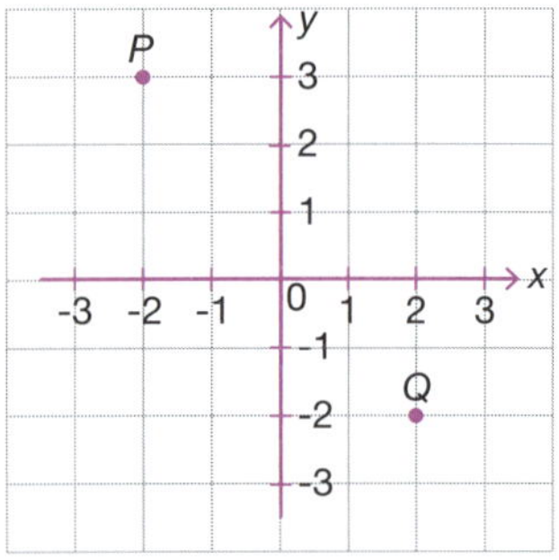

2 On the number plane, plot the points *S*(−2, 2) and *T*(3, 2). What is the length of *ST*?

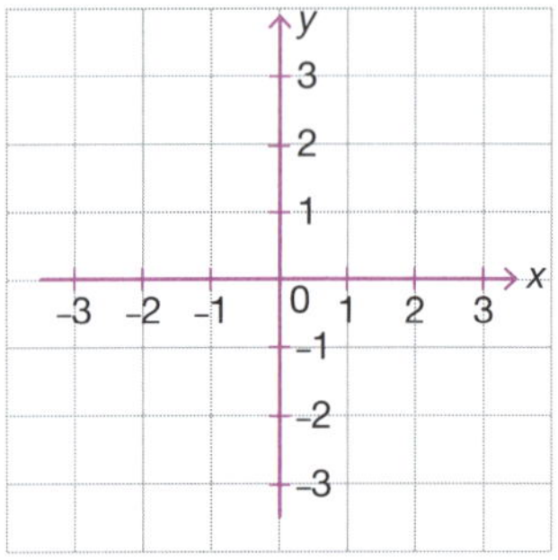

3 On the number plane, plot the points *A*(−3, 3), *B*(2, 3), *C*(2, −2) and *D*(−3, −2).

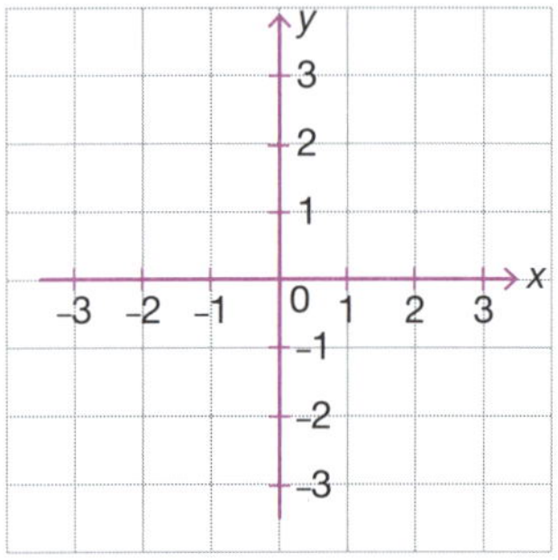

What type of shape is formed?

4 The points *A*, *B* and *C* are located on the number plane.

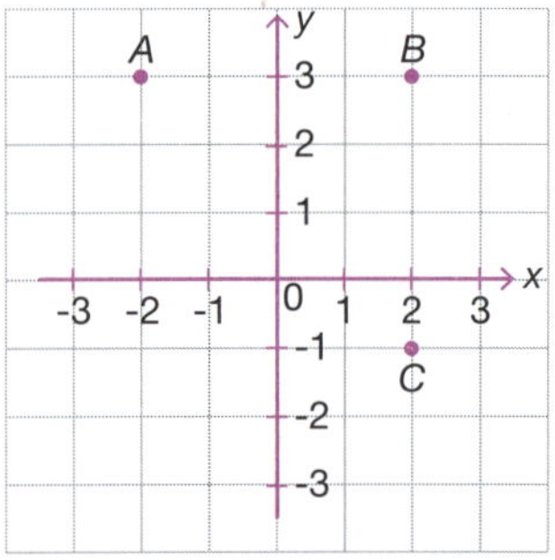

What are the coordinates of *D* if *ABCD* is a square?

5 From *X* on the number plane, move east 4 units, south 5 units and east 1 unit to *Y*. Locate *Y* on the number plane.

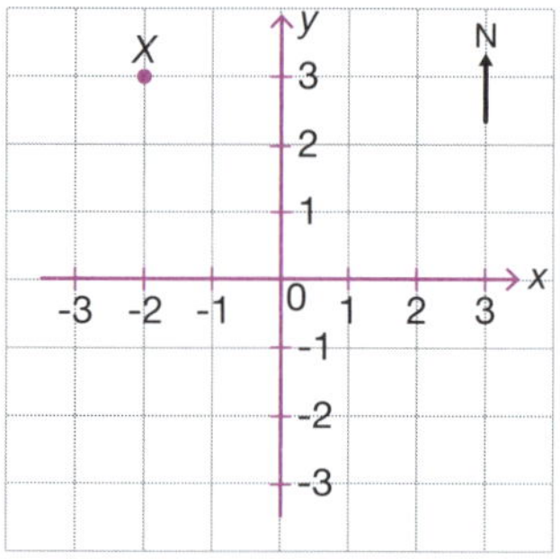

6 Complete: The shape has been translated .... units down and .... units right.

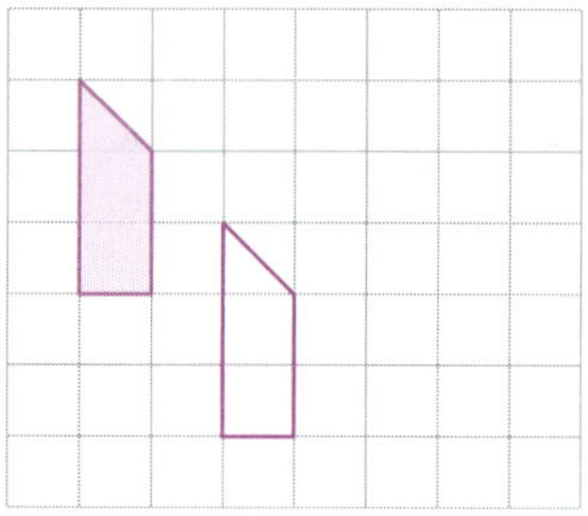

7 Reflect the shape in the line *L*.

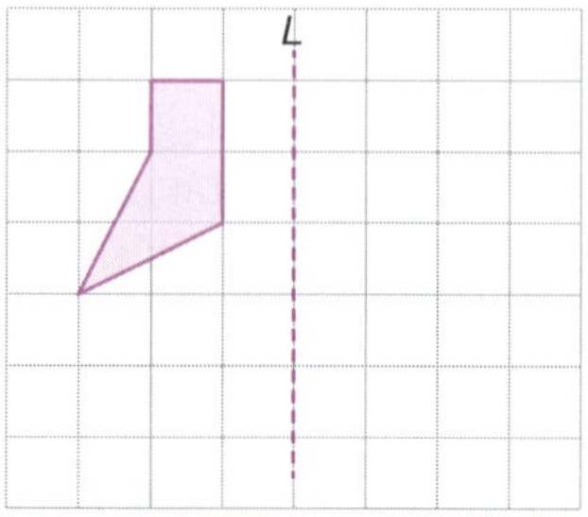

8 Translate the shape 3 units to the left and then reflect it in line *L*.

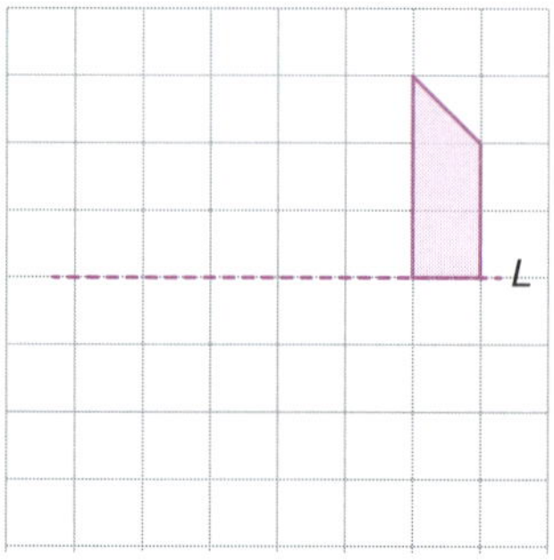

9 Rotate the shape 90° clockwise about *O*.

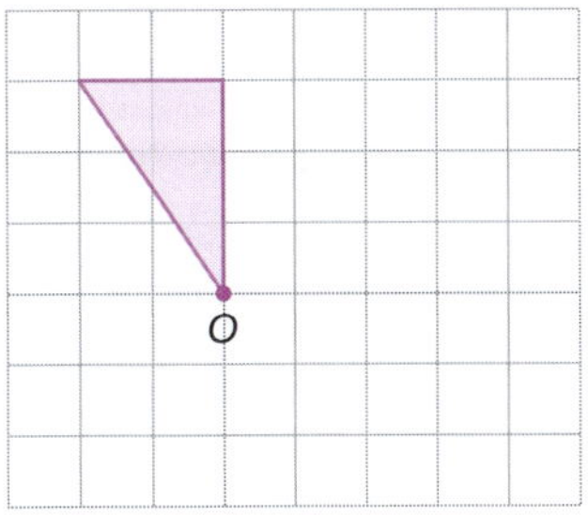

10 Rotate the shape 90° anticlockwise about *O*.

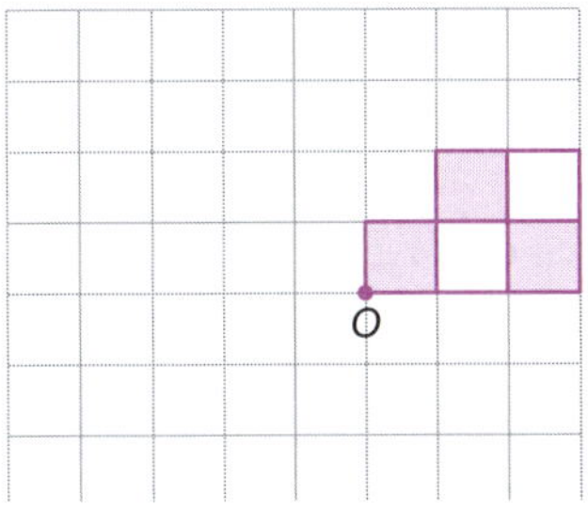

11 What is the size of the angle marked as *?

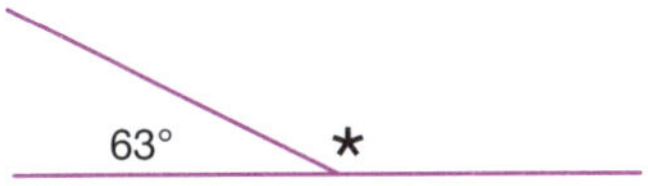

12 What is the size of the angle marked as *?

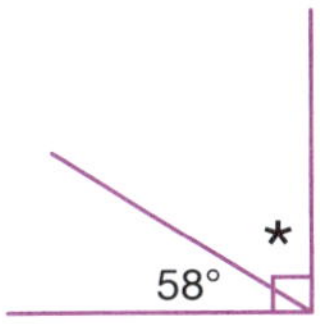

13 What is the size of the angle marked as *?

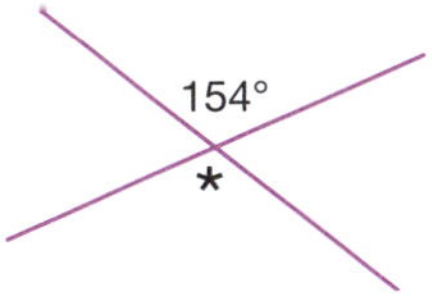

14 What is the value of the angle marked as *?

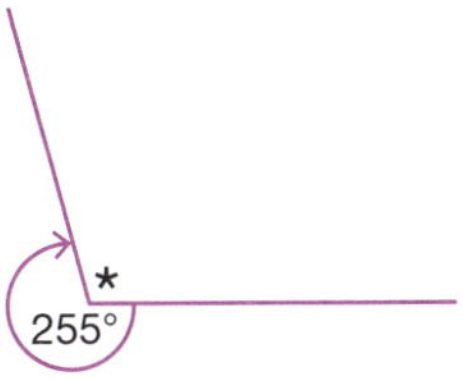

15 What is the value of the angle marked as *?

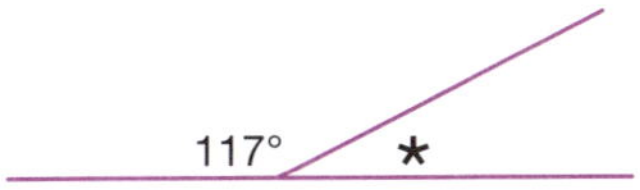

16 What is the size of the angle marked as *?

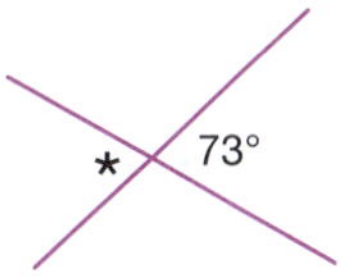

17 What is the size of the angle marked as *?

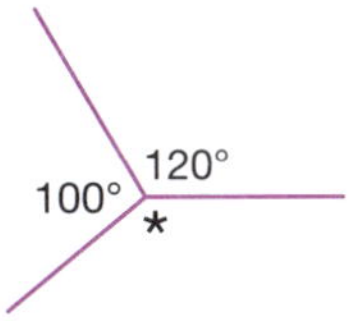

18 What is the size of the angle marked as *?

19 What is the size of the angle marked as *?

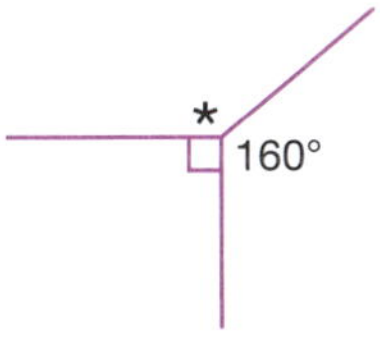

20 What is the size of the angle marked as *?

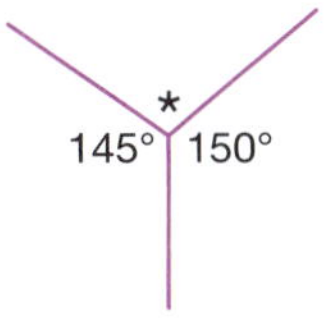

21 What is the size of the angle marked as *?

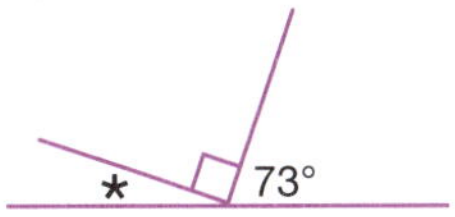

22 What is the size of the angle marked as *?

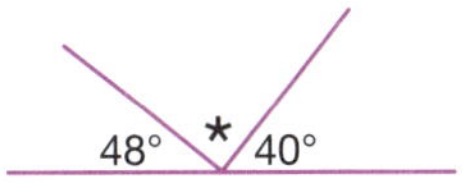

FOCUS ON SHAPE, LOCATION, TRANSFORMATIONS AND GEOMETRIC REASONING

1 On the number plane, plot the point $X(-1, -3)$ and $Y(-1, 2)$. Draw another line through $Z(2, 1)$ which is parallel to XY.

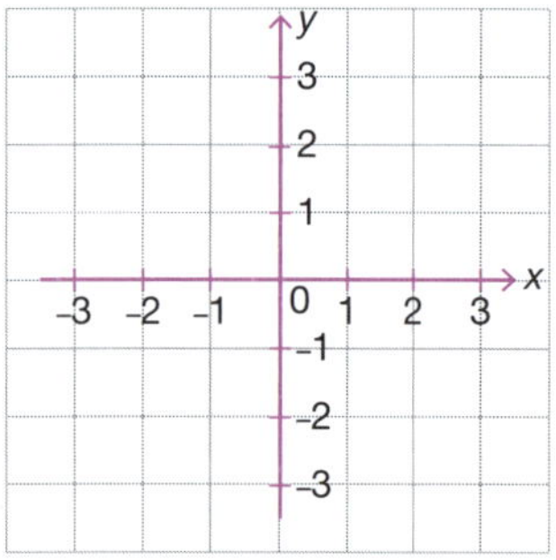

2 On a number plane, Eleni plots the points $(-1, 3)$ and $(2, -3)$.

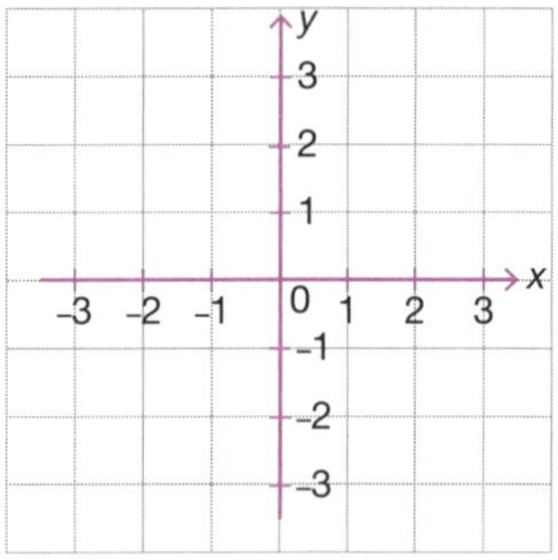

A line is drawn through the two points. Circle any of these points which the line has passed through.

(1, 0) origin (0, 1)

3 The points $P(-2, 1)$, $Q(3, 1)$, $R(3, -2)$ and S form a rectangle. Plot the points, find the coordinates of S and calculate the area of $PQRS$.

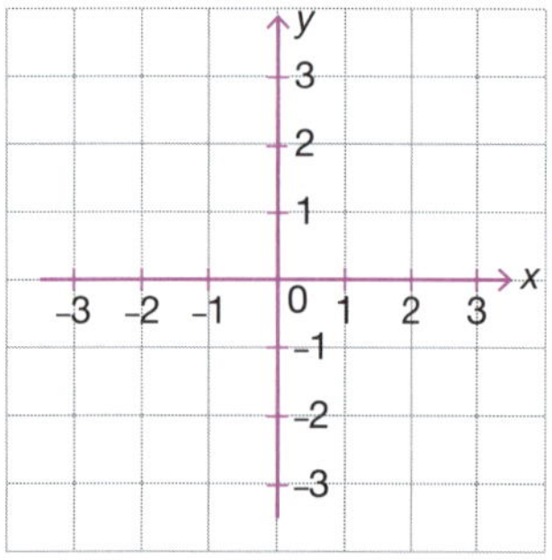

4 Plot the points $Q(2, 2)$, $R(3, -3)$ and $S(-1, -3)$ on the number plane.

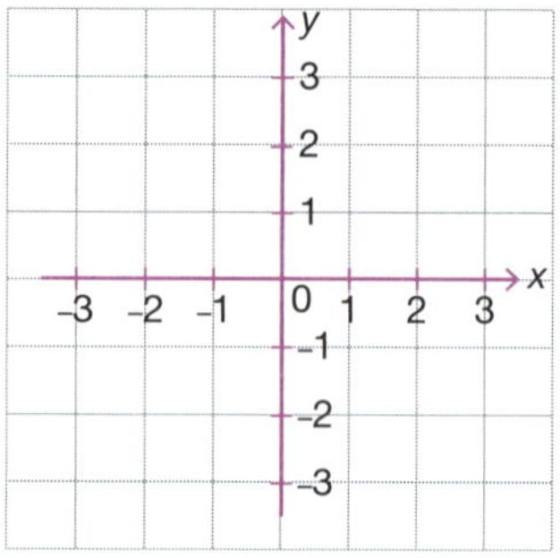

If $PQRS$ forms a parallelogram, what are the coordinates of P?

5 Find the area of XYZ if $X(-2, 2)$, $Y(2, -2)$ and $Z(-2, -2)$.

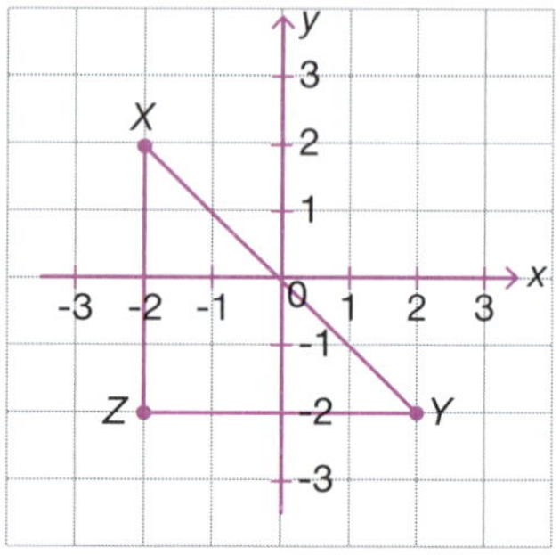

6 A is 5 units north of $B(-2, -2)$ and is north-west of C. If C is east of B, what are the coordinates of C?

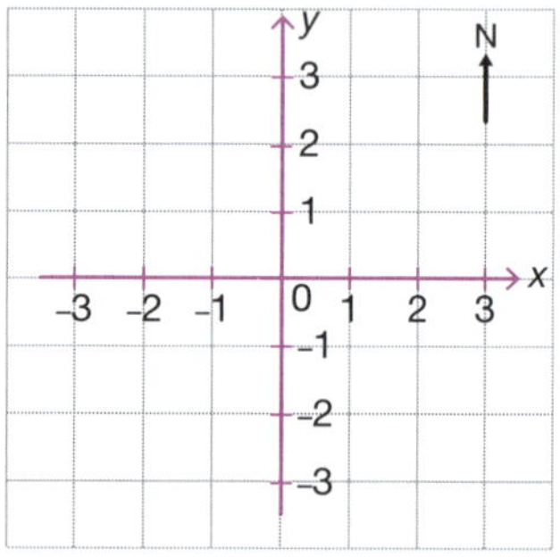

7 Translate the triangle down 2 units and then to the right 3 units.

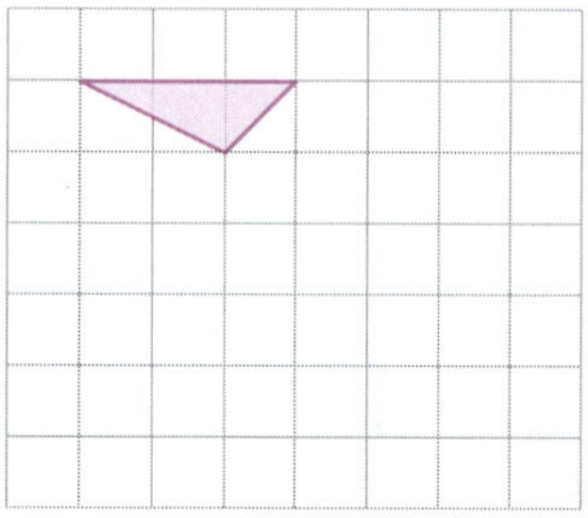

8 Reflect the shape in the line L_1, then in L_2.

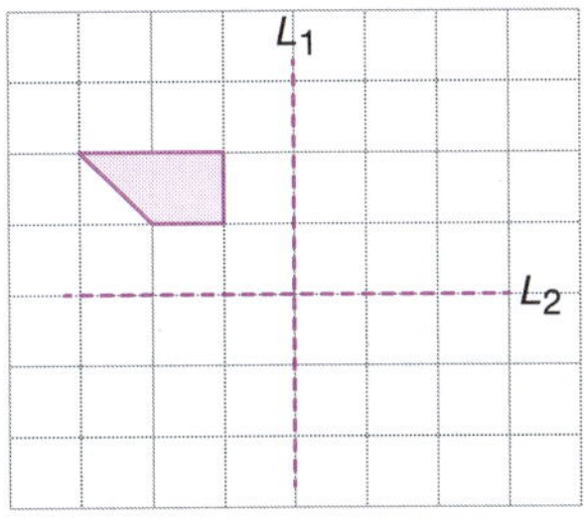

9 What are the two transformations used?

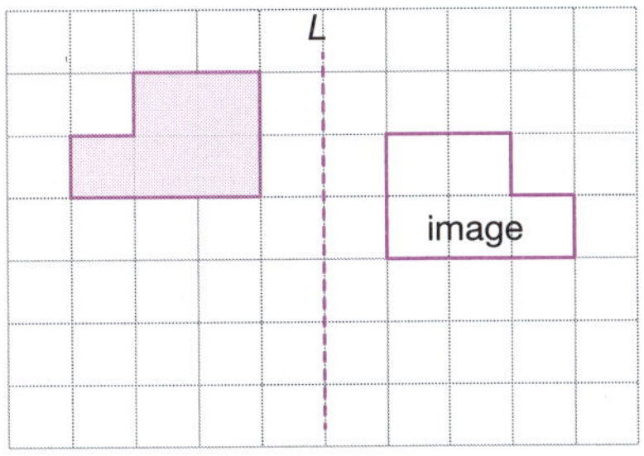

10 Rotate the shape 90° clockwise about *O* and then translate 2 units down.

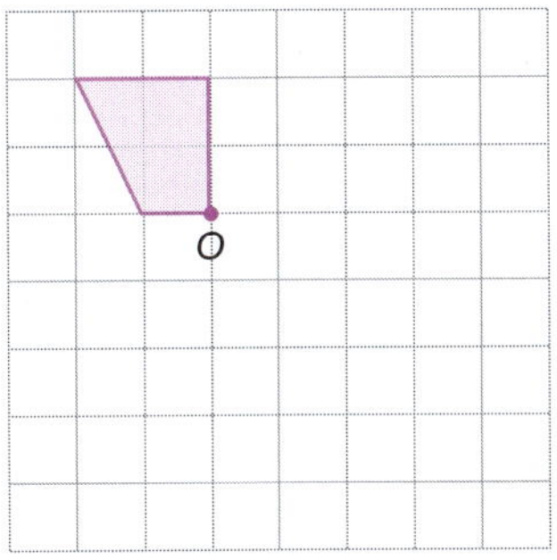

11 Rotate the shape 90° clockwise about *O* and then reflect in line *L*.

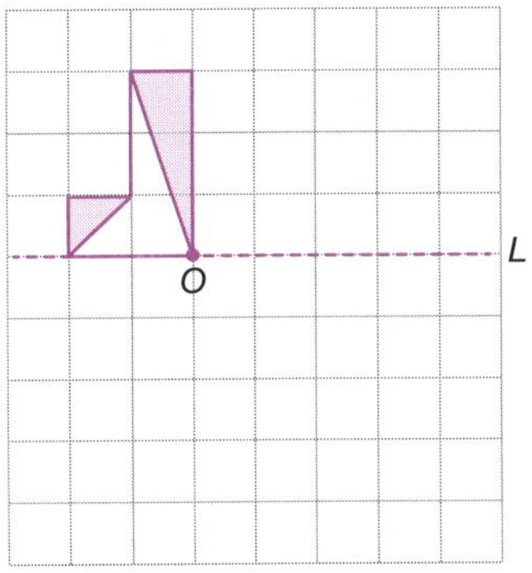

12 What is the size of the angle marked as *?

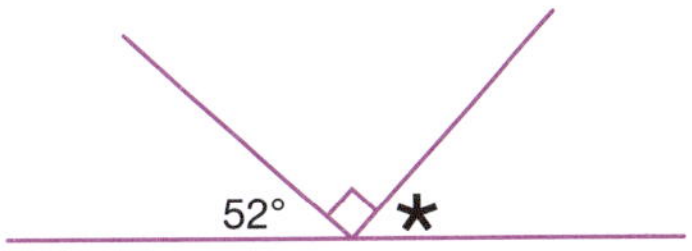

13 What is the size of the angle marked as *?

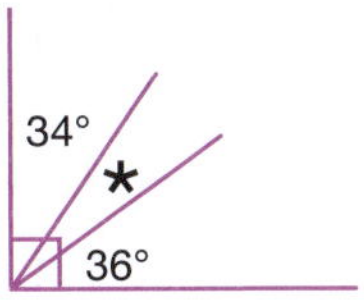

14 What is the value of *x*?

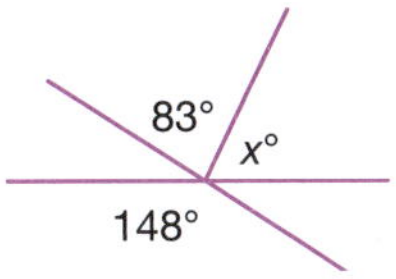

15 What is the value of *x*?

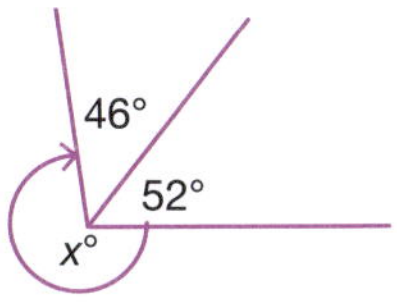

16 What is the value of *x*?

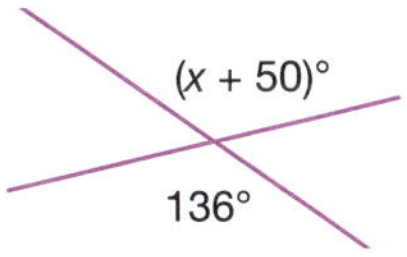

17 What is the value of *x*?

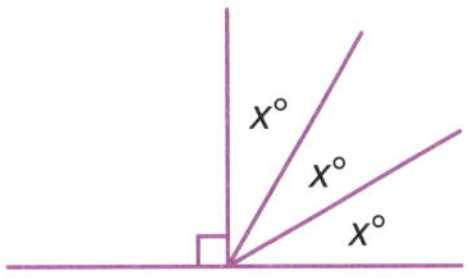

18 What is the value of *x*?

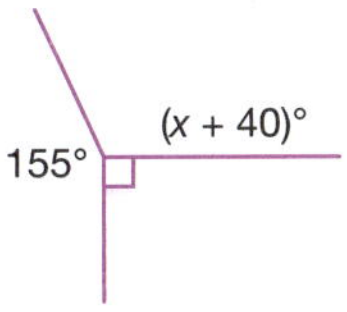

19 What is the value of *x*?

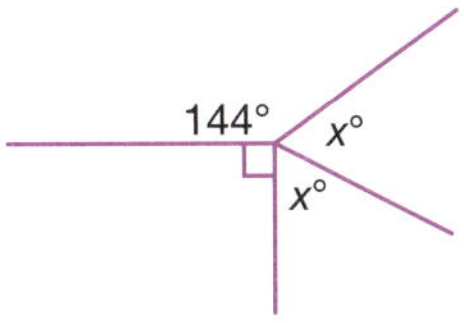

20 What is the value of *x*?

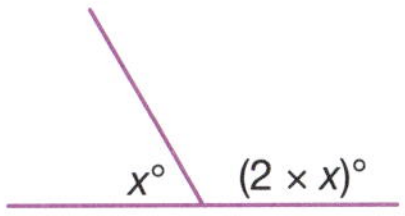

21 What is the value of *x*?

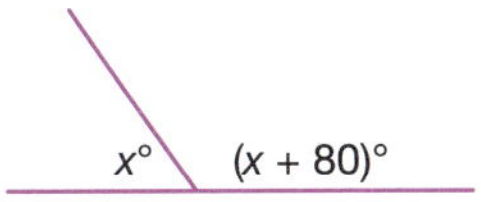

FOCUS ON CHANCE

1 A fair coin is tossed 30 times. What is the expected number of heads?

2 A bag contains four black balls and a white ball. If a ball is selected, what is the probability that it is white?

3 Of the 30 students on a bus, 20 are boys. If a student is chosen at random, what is the probability they are a boy?

4 The table shows the number of different coloured cubes contained in a box. A cube is chosen at random. What is the probability it is red?

Colour	Number
Red	5
Blue	9
Green	6

5 The probabilities of three events are recorded. Circle the probability that represents the event most likely to occur.

0.4 $\frac{1}{4}$ 35%

6 A normal dice is rolled ☐ times and the number 5 appears on 10 occasions. Circle the best estimate of ☐.

50 60 100 120

7 What is the probability of spinning an odd number?

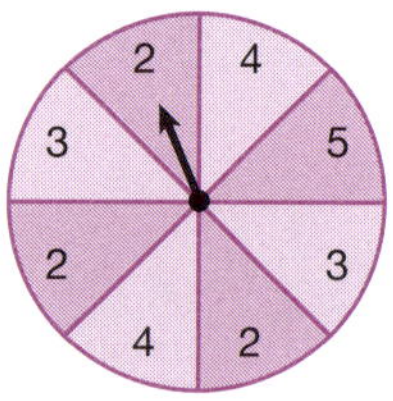

8 Balls numbered 1 to 20 are placed into a bag. What is the probability of selecting number 19, expressed as a decimal?

9 Two normal dice are rolled and their scores multiplied. What is the highest possible result?

10 The probability of selecting a black ball from this box is 0.6. Shade the correct number of black balls.

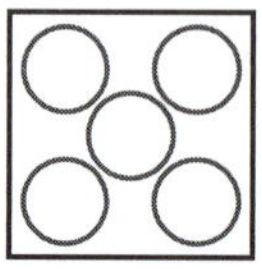

11 The spinner is spun 8 times. What is the expected number of times it lands on 2?

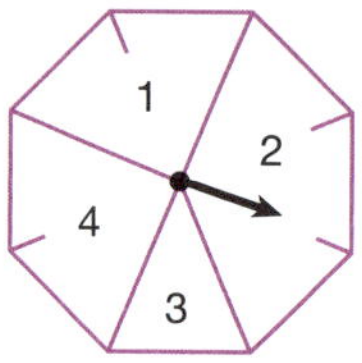

12 The weather forecast says there is a 40% probability of rain on Sunday. What is the probability of no rain?

13 A ball is chosen at random from a box. What is the probability, as a percentage, that the ball is black?

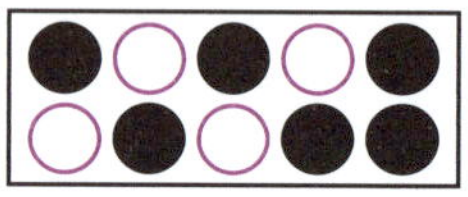

14 A raffle has 200 numbered tickets. Cameron buys one ticket. What is the probability that his ticket is the winning ticket?

15 What is the probability of spinning a 5?

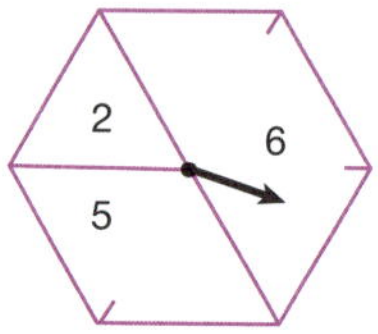

16 There are red, green and blue cards in a box.

The probability of choosing a red card is $\frac{1}{2}$ and choosing a green card is $\frac{1}{4}$.

What is the smallest possible number of cards in the box?

17 The probability of spinning a 3 is the same as spinning a 1 and twice the probability of spinning a 4. Complete the spinner by writing the missing numbers.

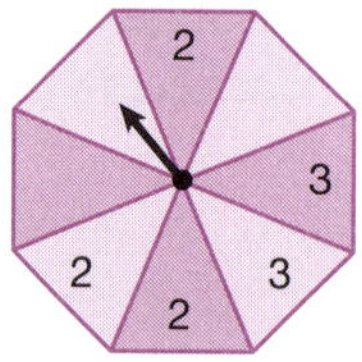

18 The probability of an event occurring is 0.74. What is the probability of the event **not** occurring?

19 John scores a 6 when he rolls a normal dice. What is the probability that he rolls another 6 on his next roll?

20 A letter in the word ADVANCED is chosen at random. What is the probability that it is an A?

FOCUS ON CHANCE

1 A normal dice is rolled 90 times. What is the expected number of times a 2 or a 3 is rolled? ☐

2 A bag contains four black balls and a white ball. A ball is selected and then returned to the bag. If this happens 20 times, what is the expected number of times a black ball is selected? ☐

3 A normal dice is rolled. What is the chance the number rolled is 4 or more? ☐

4 The table shows the number of different coloured cubes contained in a box.

Colour	Number
Red	5
Blue	9
Green	6

Two cubes of each colour are removed. What is now the probability of choosing a blue cube? ☐

5 The probabilities of four events are recorded. Circle the probability that represents the event least likely to occur.

$\frac{2}{5}$ 26% 0.39 $\frac{3}{10}$

6 A normal dice was rolled ☐ times and a prime number appeared 15 times.

Circle the best estimate of ☐.

30 60 90 120

7 The spinner is spun 48 times. What is the expected number of times a 4 is spun?

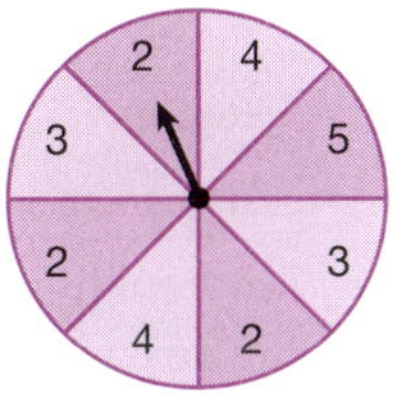

8 Balls numbered 1 to 20 are placed into a bag. What is the probability of selecting a number less than 10, expressed as a decimal? ☐

9 A dice has been numbered 1, 2, 2, 4, 6, 7. What is the probability of rolling an odd number? ☐

10 The probability of selecting a black ball from this box is 40%. Shade the correct number of black balls.

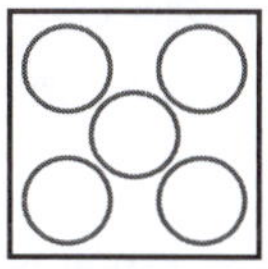

11 Number each of the sectors on the spinner if the probability of a 2 is three times as likely as spinning a 5. The probability of spinning a 4 is the same as spinning a 6.

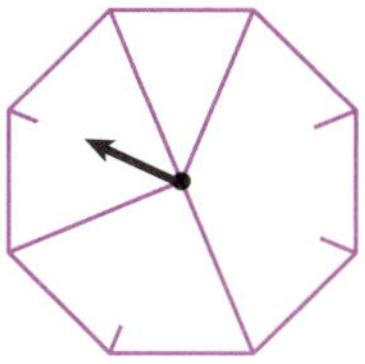

12 In a bag of balls, one-fifth are red and two-fifths are yellow. The rest of the balls are green. If a ball is chosen at random, what is the probability that it is green? ☐

13 The probability of choosing a black ball from the box is 40% and choosing a pink ball is 30%. The remaining balls are white. Represent this on the diagram.

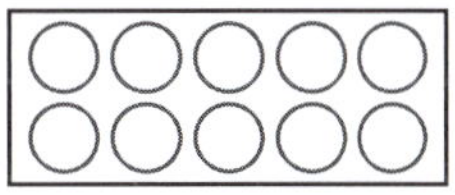

14 A raffle has 1000 numbered tickets. Erica buys 10 tickets. What is the probability that she wins first prize, expressed as a decimal? ☐

15 The spinner is spun 180 times. What is the expected number of times an even number is spun?

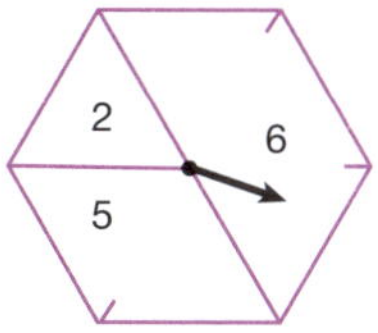

16 A bucket contains green and yellow balls. The probability of selecting a green ball is twice the probability of choosing a yellow ball. If there are 30 green balls, what is the total number of balls in the bucket? ☐

17 There are red, green and blue cards in a box. The probability of choosing a red card is $\frac{1}{3}$ and choosing a green card is $\frac{1}{4}$. What is the smallest possible number of blue cards in the box? ☐

18 A biased coin is tossed 200 times and heads appears 150 times. Estimate the number of times it will land tails in 500 tosses. ☐

FOCUS ON

DATA REPRESENTATION AND INTERPRETATION

1 The colour and style of students' hair is recorded.

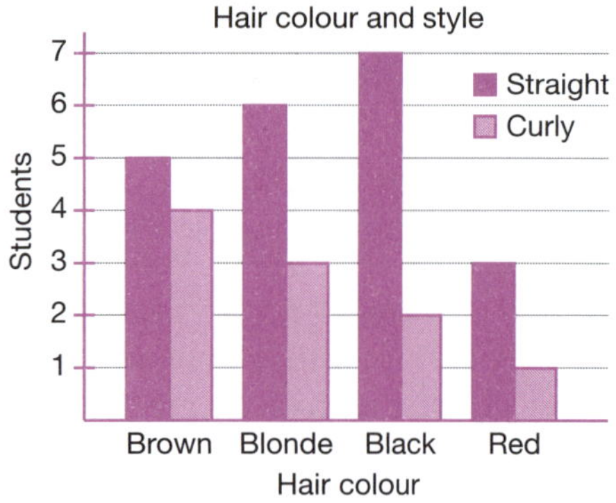

How many students have curly hair?

2 The way students returned home from school last Friday is recorded.

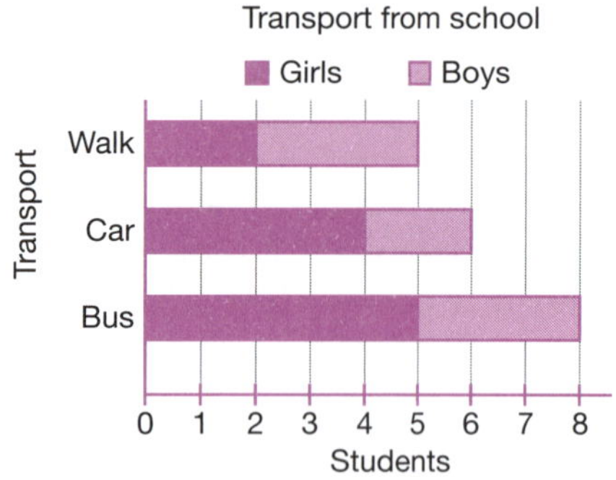

What fraction of the students who walked home were girls?

3 The table shows the number and sex of students in a class who play chess.

	Yes	No
Girls	7	8
Boys	9	4

How many students play chess?

4 The table shows the hot drink preferred by 50 young people.

	Male	Female
Coffee	18	23
Tea	4	2
Other	2	1

How many people preferred coffee?

5 The table shows whether 90 year olds have a driver's licence. How many 90 year olds have a licence?

	Women	Men
Licence	4	11
No licence	38	27

6 The table shows the number of books read by students in Term 3. How many students read at least four books?

	Fewer than 4	At least 4
Girls	3	9
Boys	5	7

7 The table shows the number of high distinctions, distinctions and credits earned by students in a competition.

	Females	Males
High distinction	2	1
Distinction	12	10
Credit	7	9

How many students were awarded a distinction or a credit?

8 The table shows the age of people who have a landline phone at home.

Age	Landline	No landline
40 or more	16	8
Less than 40	4	21

How many people have a landline phone?

9 The table shows the colour of vehicles in a car park.

	White	Blue	Other
Sedans	12	9	13
SUVs	4	4	8

How many sedans are in the car park?

10 The table shows the favourite season of a group of workers.

	Summer	Autumn	Winter	Spring
Male	8	5	6	6
Female	6	3	4	9

How many males liked summer or winter?

11 The table shows whether 6B students played sport this year. Complete the table.

	Yes	No	Total
Girls	10	2	
Boys	6	8	
Total			

12 The table shows favourite summer holiday activities. Complete the table.

	Beach	Pool	Movies	Total
Males	12	7	8	
Females	16	10	12	
Total				

13 The table shows the number of students in two high-school year groups. Complete the table.

	Year 7	Year 12	Total
Males	70	55	
Females	85	65	
Total			

14 The table shows the eye colour of students in Year 6. Complete the table.

	Brown	Blue	Other	Total
Boys	8	4		13
Girls	9	2	1	
Total				

15 The table shows the number and colour of each shape in a box of blocks. Complete the table.

	Red	Green	Blue	Yellow	Total
Prisms	8	7	6	5	
Cylinders	3	2	4	5	
Total					

16 The table shows the favourite overseas holiday destinations of a group of people.

	America	Europe	Asia	Africa
Men	16	21	9	4
Women	12	23	8	7

What was the total number of people who selected Europe or Africa?

17 The table shows the fruit packed in students' lunchboxes today. How many more boys had a banana or an apple than had a mandarin or an orange?

	Banana	Apple	Mandarin	Orange
Girls	4	4	3	1
Boys	3	5	3	2

18 Three boxes of crayons, identified as Box A, Box B and Box C, contain the same four colours.

	Box A	Box B	Box C
Red	4	4	6
Blue	8	6	5
Green	5	3	2
Yellow	6	7	4

What fraction of the crayons in Box B are red or green?

19 The results of a class survey are recorded. How many students in the class have a pet?

	Only child	Has sibling(s)
Has a pet	6	10
No pet	4	8

20 30 students were surveyed to find out if they are left- or right-handed.

	Left-handed	Right-handed
Girls	4	15
Boys	2	9

What fraction of the left-handed students were girls?

21 The table shows how students spent their Saturday.

	Shopping	No shopping
Sport	8	7
No sport	11	4

What fraction of the students went shopping and played sport?

22 30 cards all have a picture of a shape. There are the same number of each shape. Complete the table.

	Square	Triangle	Rectangle
Red	4		5
Blue	2	2	
Yellow		3	1

FOCUS ON **DATA REPRESENTATION AND INTERPRETATION**

1 The colour and style of students' hair is recorded.

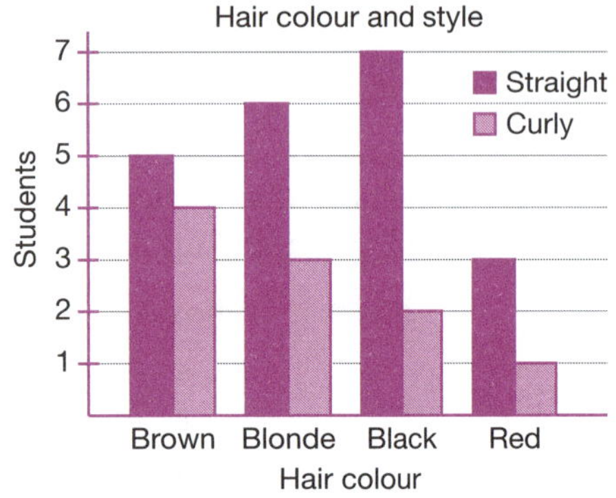

What percentage of the red-haired students have curly hair?

2 The way students returned home from school last Friday is recorded.

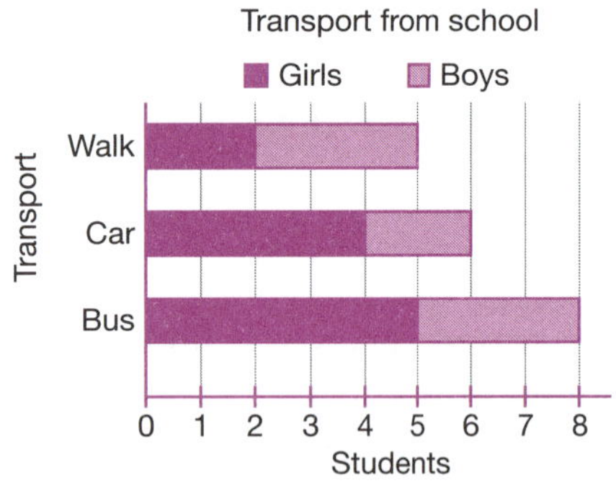

What fraction of the boys were driven home in a car?

3 The table shows the number and sex of students in a class who play chess.

	Yes	No
Girls	7	8
Boys	9	4

What fraction of the class are girls who play chess?

4 The table shows the hot drink preferred by 50 young people.

	Male	Female
Coffee	18	23
Tea	4	2
Other	2	1

How many more females were surveyed than males?

5 The table shows whether 90 year olds have a driver's licence.

	Women	Men
Licence	4	11
No licence	38	27

What fraction of 90 year olds who have a driver's licence are women?

6 The table shows the number of books read by students in Term 3. What percentage of the girls read at least four books?

	Fewer than 4	At least 4
Girls	3	9
Boys	5	7

7 The table shows the number of high distinctions, distinctions and credits earned by students in a competition. If 50 students entered the competition, how many students did **not** receive an award?

	Females	Males
High distinction	2	1
Distinction	12	10
Credit	7	9

8 The table shows the age of people who have a landline phone at home.

Age	Landline	No landline
40 or more	16	8
Less than 40	4	21

What fraction of those people with a landline are less than 40 years old?

9 The table shows the colour of vehicles in a car park.

	White	Blue	Other
Sedans	12	9	13
SUVs	4	4	8

What fraction of the SUVs are white?

10 The table shows the favourite season of a group of workers.

	Summer	Autumn	Winter	Spring
Male	8	5	6	6
Female	6	3	4	9

How much greater is the number of workers who liked spring than the number who liked autumn?

11 The table shows whether 6B students played sport this year. Complete the table.

	Yes	No	Total
Girls	10		15
Boys		7	
Total			28

12 A survey of 60 Year 7 students found the number who play sport and/or an instrument.

	Play instrument	No instrument
Play sport	20	18
No sport		8

How many students play an instrument but no sport?

13 The table shows favourite summer holiday activities. Complete the table.

	Beach	Pool	Movies	Total
Males	6			18
Females		3	8	
Total	17	8		

14 The table shows the number of students in two high-school year groups.

	Year 9	Year 11	Total
Males	85	61	
Females			168
Total		138	

How many females are in Year 9?

15 The table shows the eye colour of students in Years 3 to 6. What percentage of the students were blue-eyed girls?

	Brown	Blue	Other	Total
Boys			4	50
Girls	37			
Total	76	17	7	

16 The table shows the number and colour of shapes in a box of blocks. What fraction of the blocks were red or yellow prisms?

	Red	Green	Blue	Yellow
Prisms	3	2	3	2
Cylinders	2	3	2	3

17 The table shows the favourite overseas holiday destinations of a group of people.
What fraction of women selected America?

	America	Europe	Asia	Africa
Men	16	21	9	4
Women	12	23	8	7

18 Three boxes of crayons, identified as Box A, Box B, and Box C, contain the same four colours.

	Box A	Box B	Box C
Red	4	4	6
Blue	8	6	5
Green	5	3	2
Yellow	6	7	4

What percentage of the green crayons are **not** in Box C?

19 The results of a class survey are recorded.

	Only child	Has sibling(s)
Has a pet	6	10
No pet	4	8

What fraction of students do **not** have a pet or a sibling?

20 30 students were surveyed to find out if they are left- or right-handed. What percentage of the students are right-handed boys?

	Left-handed	Right-handed
Girls	4	15
Boys	2	9

21 The table shows how students spent their Saturday.

	Shopping	No shopping
Sport	8	7
No sport	11	4

What percentage of the students played sport?

22 45 cards all have a picture of a shape. There are the same number of each shape and each colour. Complete the table.

	Square	Triangle	Rectangle
Red	2		6
Blue			1
Yellow		3	

NUMBER AND ALGEBRA

1 Circle the even numbers.

28 441 746 3000

2 Locate and label the number –2 on the number line.

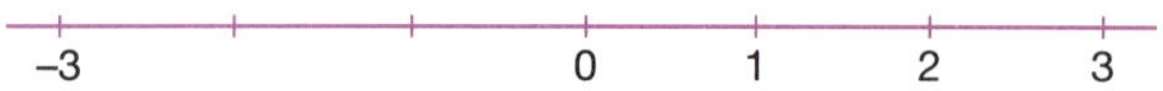

3 The sum of two numbers is 6000. If the smaller number is 2375, what is the larger number?

4 Circle any fractions that represent the shaded part.

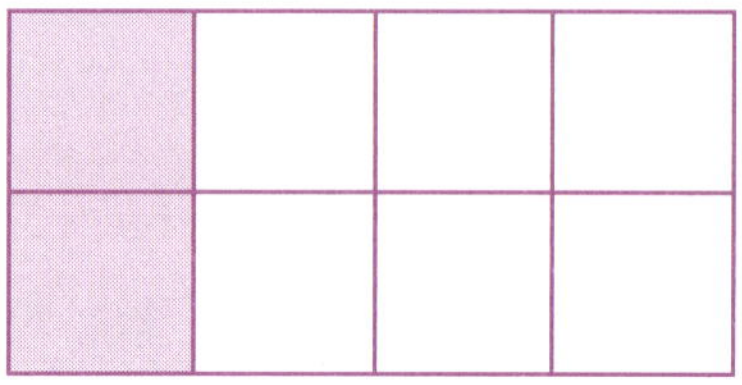

$\frac{1}{4}$ $\frac{1}{2}$ $\frac{6}{8}$ $\frac{2}{8}$

5 $\frac{3}{8} + \frac{1}{8} =$

6 Find the sum of 2.3 and 0.86.

7 Write $\frac{43}{100}$ as a percentage.

8 A wheelbarrow priced at $129 is discounted by $30. What is the new price?

9 What is the next number in the sequence?

4.8, 5.15, 5.5,

10 What is 10 – 3 × 2?

MEASUREMENT AND SPACE

11 Change 3.761 m to millimetres.

12 How many grams are in 3.67 kg?

13 Toby was born in January 2013. Mark his birth as *X* on the timeline.

14 Draw the top view of this solid.

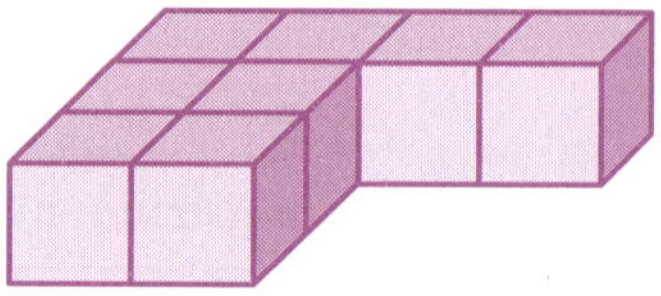

15 What are the coordinates of *A* and *B*?

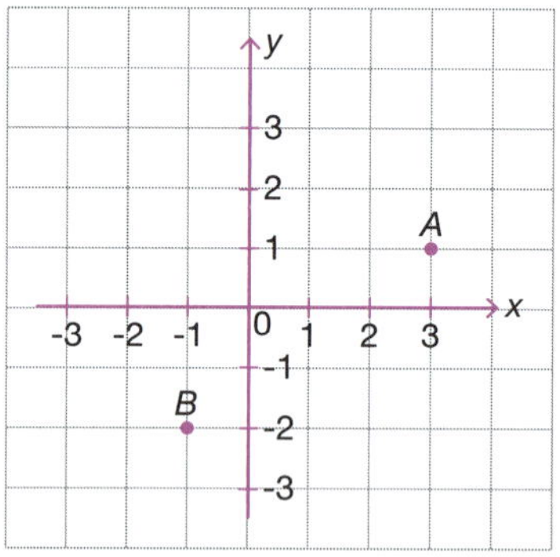

16 Circle any angles that are acute.

202° 96° 133° 65°

STATISTICS AND PROBABILITY

17 A fair coin is tossed 50 times. What is the expected number of heads?

18 The table shows whether students in a class own a pet.

	Pet	No pet
Girls	13	3
Boys	11	1

How many students own a pet?

NUMBER AND ALGEBRA

1 Circle the numbers divisible by 6.

54 609 2400 6661

2 What number is represented by P on the number line?

3 The difference between an unknown number and 3280 is 2865. If the unknown number is more than 3500, what is the number?

4 Circle any fractions that represent the shaded part.

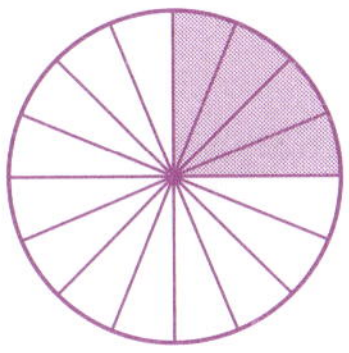

$\frac{1}{4}$ $\frac{4}{20}$ $\frac{4}{16}$ $\frac{2}{8}$

5 $\frac{7}{10} + \frac{9}{10} =$

6 $4.981 + 5 + 0.08 =$

7 Write $\frac{670}{1000}$ as a percentage.

8 Reggie bought 40 L of petrol at 169.9 cents per litre. He used his loyalty card and received a 4 cent per litre discount. How much was the discount?

9 What is the next number in the sequence?

6.43, 6.71, 6.99,

10 What is $16 \div 8 + 4 \times 2$?

MEASUREMENT AND SPACE

11 Change 6 498 000 mm to kilometres.

12 How many kilograms are in 0.65 tonnes?

13 In November 2018 Noah turned 3 years old. Record his birth as X on the timeline.

14 Draw the view of this solid from the right.

15 On the number plane, plot the points $A(-2, 1)$ and $B(3, 1)$ and find the length of AB.

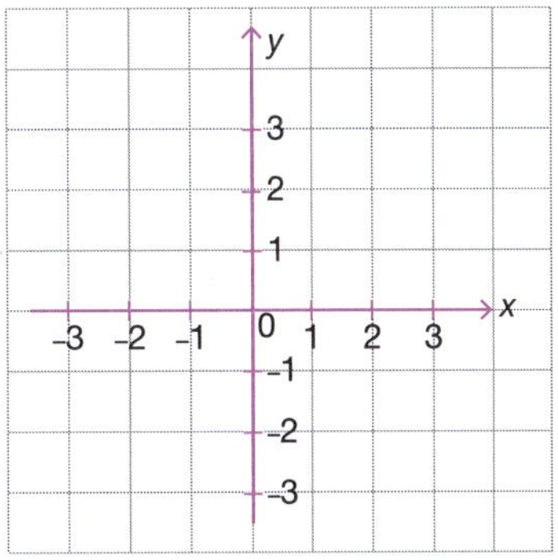

16 True or false? If two angles add to 180°, and one of the angles is acute, the other angle cannot be acute.

STATISTICS AND PROBABILITY

17 A normal dice is rolled 60 times. What is the expected number of times a 5 or a 6 is rolled?

18 The table shows whether students in a class own a pet.

	Pet	No pet
Girls	13	3
Boys	11	1

How many more girls are in the class than boys?

NUMBER AND ALGEBRA

1 Jack adds two odd numbers. He says the answer is even. Is Jack correct?

2 Locate and label the numbers –4 and –2 on the number line.

3 Farmer Frank has 7250 newborn chicks. On Wednesday he sells 2800 chicks and on Thursday he sells another 4200. How many chicks has he remaining?

4 Circle any fractions that represent the shaded part.

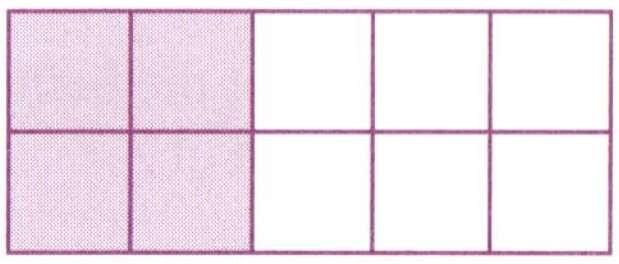

$\frac{1}{4}$ $\frac{2}{3}$ $\frac{4}{10}$ $\frac{2}{5}$

5 $\frac{1}{5} + 2 + \frac{3}{5} =$

6 $12 - 8.6 =$

7 Express 0.57 as a percentage.

8 A diamond ring originally priced at \$1250 is on sale for \$899. What was the amount of discount?

9 What is the next number in the sequence?

0.5, 1.4, 2.3, 3.2,

10 What is the value of $15 - (10 + 3)$?

MEASUREMENT AND SPACE

11 How many centimetres are in 8.3 m?

12 Complete: 6740 g = ... kg.

13 In July 2002 Priya arrived in Australia. Record this event as X on the timeline.

14 Draw the front view of this solid.

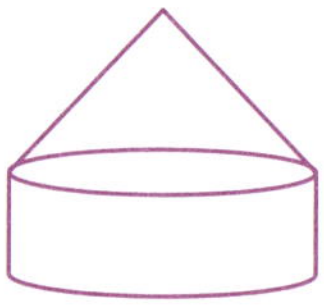

15 On the number plane, plot the points $P(-3, 2)$ and $Q(1, -2)$.

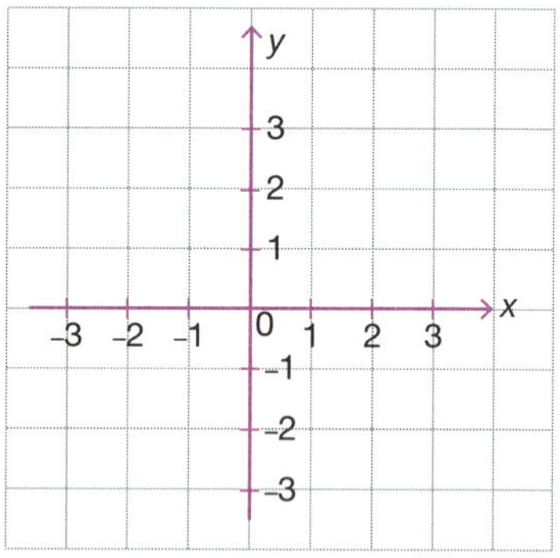

16 Circle any angles that are obtuse.

191° 296° 88° 145°

STATISTICS AND PROBABILITY

17 A bag contains 3 red balls and 2 blue balls. If a ball is selected, what is the probability that it is blue?

18 The table shows the hot drink preferred by a group of adults.

	Men	Women
Coffee	11	15
Tea	8	6
Other	2	1

How many people preferred coffee?

NUMBER AND ALGEBRA

1 If ♥ is an odd number, which of these is the next odd number? Circle the answer.

♥ + 1 ♥ + 2 ♥ × 3

2 What number is represented by Q on the number line?

3 Lara plans to drive from her home in Adelaide to Rockhampton which is 2210 km away. On the first day she drives 800 km and by the end of the second day she still has 810 km remaining. How far did she drive on the second day?

4 Circle any fractions that represent the shaded part.

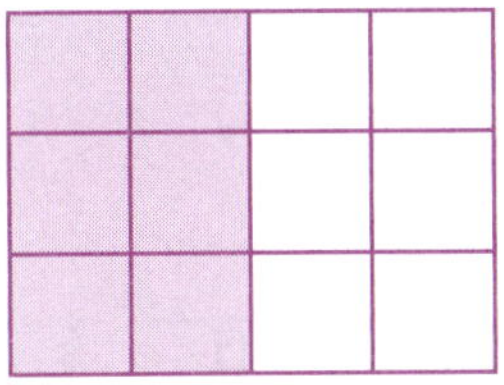

$\frac{1}{6}$ $\frac{6}{12}$ $\frac{1}{2}$ $\frac{2}{4}$

5 $1\frac{2}{5} + 4\frac{1}{5} =$

6 $3 - 1.2 - 0.86 =$

7 Express 3.06 as a percentage.

8 In a store's clearance sale a laptop is priced at $1689. If this was a reduction of $336, what was the original price of the laptop?

9 What is the missing number in the sequence?

0.47, 1.4, ______, 3.26, 4.19, ...

10 What is the value of $3.6 - (5.2 - 3.8)$?

MEASUREMENT AND SPACE

11 How many centimetres are in 7.9 mm?

12 Complete: 5.43 kg = ... mg

13 In December 2009 Mia's parents celebrated their twelfth wedding anniversary. Record their wedding day as X on the timeline.

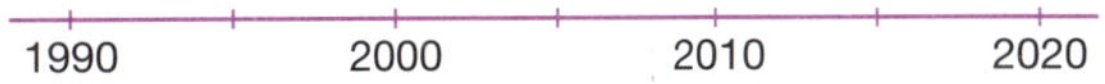

14 Draw the top view of this solid.

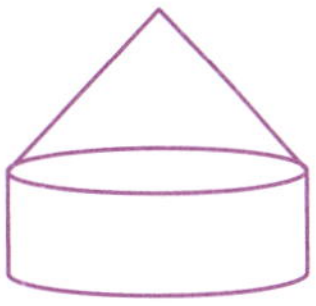

15 The points $X(2, -3)$ and $Y(-1, -3)$ are plotted on a number plane. What is the length of XY?

16 True or false? If three angles add to 360°, it is possible they can all be obtuse angles.

STATISTICS AND PROBABILITY

17 A bag contains 3 red balls and 2 blue balls. A ball is selected and then returned to the bag. If this happens 50 times, what is the expected number of times a red ball is selected?

18 The table shows the hot drink preferred by a group of adults.

	Men	Women
Coffee	11	15
Tea	8	6
Other	2	1

What was the total number of women who preferred coffee or tea?

NUMBER AND ALGEBRA

1 Ella calls out all the counting numbers less than 20. How many of the numbers are odd?

2 What numbers are represented by *A* and *B* on the number line?

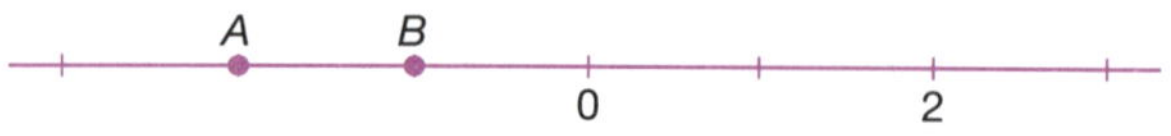

3 There are 58 passengers on a bus. Sixteen are men, 28 are women and the rest are children. How many children are on the bus?

4 Circle the fraction that is the same as $\frac{2}{5}$.

$\frac{2}{15}$ $\frac{4}{10}$ $\frac{21}{51}$

5 $\frac{1}{10} + \frac{3}{10} + \frac{3}{10} =$

6 Round 3.476 to two decimal places.

7 Shade 50% of the shape.

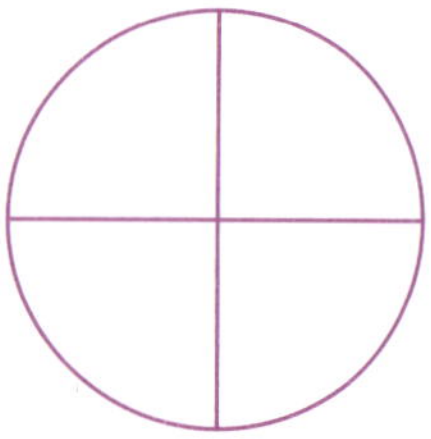

8 After a discount of $180, Christian pays $2250 for a television. What was the original price of the television?

9 What is the next number in the sequence?

0.03, 0.3, 3,

10 Complete: 30 + 6 ÷ 3 = ...

MEASUREMENT AND SPACE

11 Convert 20 000 m² to hectares.

12 What fraction of a litre is 600 mL?

13 Neil Armstrong walked on the moon in 1969. Record the event as *A* on the timeline.

14 Draw the front view of this solid.

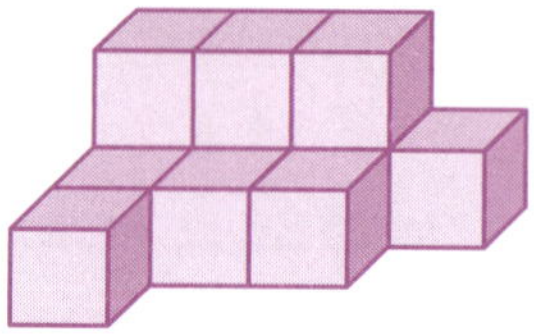

15 On the number plane, plot the points *P*(3, 0) and *Q*(0, −3).

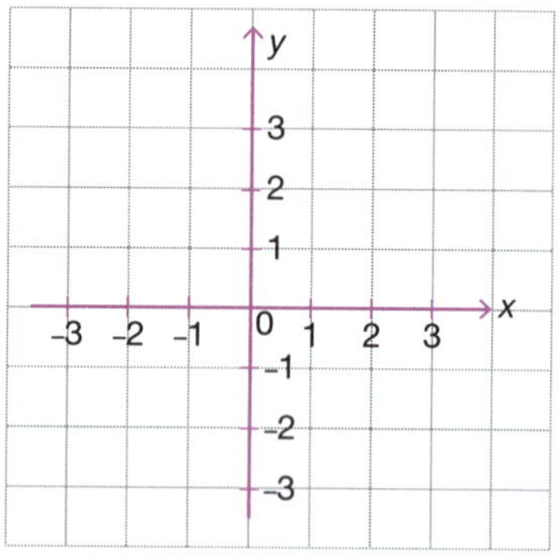

16 Circle any angles that are reflex.

322° 183° 73° 101°

STATISTICS AND PROBABILITY

17 The 25 students on a bus include 15 girls. If a student is chosen at random, what is the probability he or she is a girl?

18 The table shows the number of 18 year olds who have a driver's licence.

	Female	Male
Licence	24	36
No licence	18	12

How many 18 year olds have a licence?

NUMBER AND ALGEBRA

1 If ☺ is an even number, which of these is **not** an even number? Circle the answer.

☺ + ☺ ☺ × ☺ ☺ + 20 ☺ + 7

2 What number is represented by X on the number line?

3 The sum of two numbers is 276. The smaller number is 76. What is the product of the two numbers?

4 Which two of these fractions are equivalent to $\frac{2}{3}$?

$\frac{4}{6}$ $\frac{12}{13}$ $\frac{20}{30}$ $\frac{4}{9}$

5 $\frac{3}{8} + \frac{7}{8} + \frac{1}{8} =$

6 Round 8.995 to two decimal places.

7 Shade 75% of the shape.

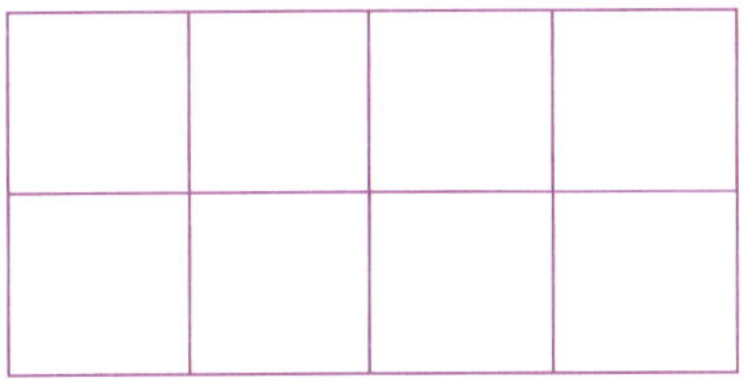

8 This week the price of a golf set falls to $1200. If the new price is three-quarters of its original price, what was the price last week?

9 What is the next number in the sequence?

28, 14, 7, 3.5,

10 Find the value of 400 ÷ 100 × 2 ÷ 2.

MEASUREMENT AND SPACE

11 How many square metres are in 3.75 ha?

12 What fraction of 5 kg is 100 g?

13 Brock's dad was 34 years old when Brock was born in 2012. Record Brock's birth as X and his dad's birth as Y.

14 Draw the top view of this solid.

15 On a number plane, Faith plots the point (2, 2) and (−3, −3). A line is drawn through the two points.

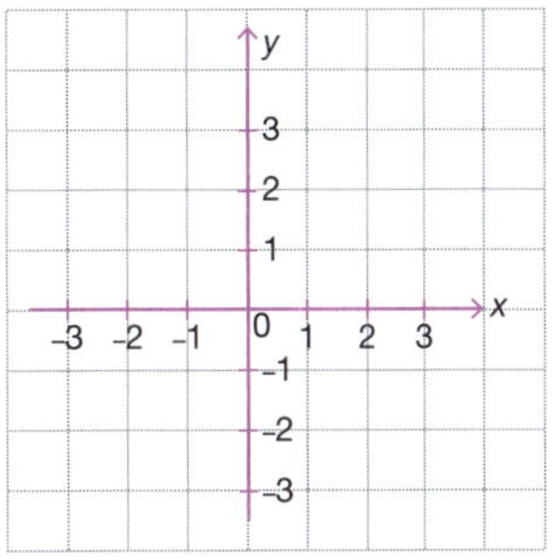

Circle the points which the line has passed through.

(2, −3) origin (−3, 2)

16 True or false? If three angles add to 360° and one angle is reflex, the other two angles must be acute.

STATISTICS AND PROBABILITY

17 A normal dice is rolled. What is the probability of rolling a number that is at least 2?

18 The table shows the number of 18 year olds who have a driver's licence.

	Female	Male
Licence	24	36
No licence	18	12

What fraction of 18 year old males have a driver's licence?

NUMBER AND ALGEBRA

1 Write the first six prime numbers.

2 Yesterday's temperature was 3 °C. Today it is 5 degrees colder. What is today's temperature?

3 Dan and Adam have a total of 100 comic books. If Dan has 40 more than Adam, how many should he give to Adam so that they have the same number?

4 Find the missing number:

$\frac{6}{8} = \frac{\square}{4}$

5 $\frac{1}{2} + \frac{1}{3} = \square$

6 What is 3.6 – 0.2 + 0.4?

7 Shade 50% of the shape.

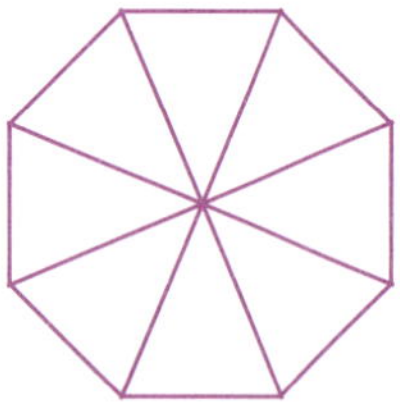

8 A pair of shoes priced at $80 is discounted by 10%. What is the new price of the shoes?

9 What is the next number in the pattern?

$\frac{1}{5}, \frac{4}{5}, 1\frac{2}{5}, \square$

10 Find the value of 24 ÷ 6 + 6.

MEASUREMENT AND SPACE

11 Complete: $\frac{1}{2}$ metre = ... mm

12 From a 2-litre bottle of water, 300 mL is poured into a glass. What amount remains in the bottle?

13 Record on the timeline Kamala's wake-up time (6 am) as *X* and her arrival home after work (7 pm) as *Y*.

14 Draw the view of this solid from the top.

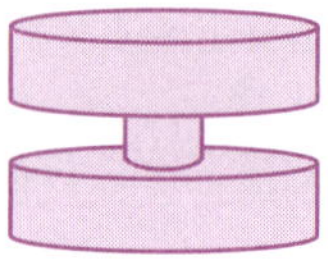

15 Here is a pattern of points (–3, –1), (–2, 0), (–1, $\square$), (0, 2), …

What is the missing value?

16 What is the size of the angle marked as *?

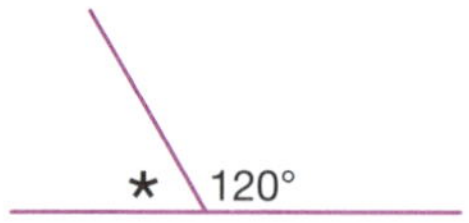

STATISTICS AND PROBABILITY

17 If a fair coin is tossed 1000 times, which of these is the most likely number of times a tail is tossed?

50 100 500 600

18 The table shows the source of news used by two age groups.

Media	Under 30	30 and over
Television	12	18
Radio	9	14
Newspaper	4	10
Internet	14	12

How many under 30 year olds were surveyed?

NUMBER AND ALGEBRA

1 How many composite numbers lie between 11 and 23?

2 This morning at 6 am the temperature was –3 °C. By 10 am the temperature had risen by 7 degrees. What was the temperature at 10 am?

3 Edna was comparing her age with that of her granddaughter Ebony. Edna was 12 times Ebony's age when Ebony celebrated her fifth birthday. How old will Ebony be when Edna is 70 years old?

4 Find the missing number:

$\frac{3}{\square} = \frac{12}{16}$

5 $\frac{2}{3} + \frac{3}{4} =$

6 Find the answer:

3 – 1.07 + 2.9

7 Shade 25% of the shape.

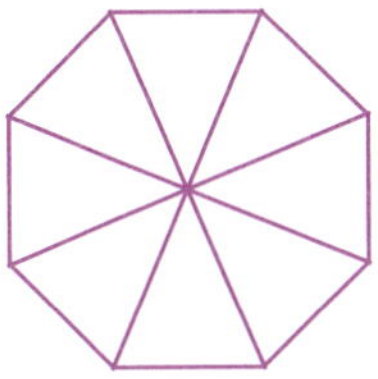

8 A furniture store is having a 20% discount sale. What is saved on a table originally priced at $900?

9 What is the next number in the pattern?

$5\frac{3}{4}, 5\frac{1}{4}, 4\frac{3}{4}, 4\frac{1}{4},$

10 What is $15 \times 2 \div 6 - 2 \times 2$?

MEASUREMENT AND SPACE

11 Complete: $5\frac{3}{4}$ m = ... mm

12 Jack completely fills his 50-litre petrol tank. On Monday he uses 16.3 L, on Tuesday 4.8 L and on Wednesday 18.9 L. What amount of petrol remains in his petrol tank?

13 Record on the timeline the departure of a train (5 am) as *P* and its arrival (9 pm) as *Q*.

14 Draw the view of this solid from the left.

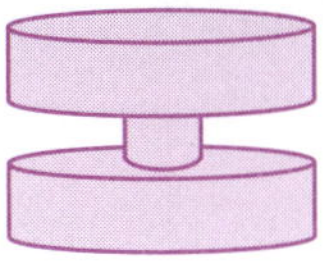

15 What is the area of *ABCD*?

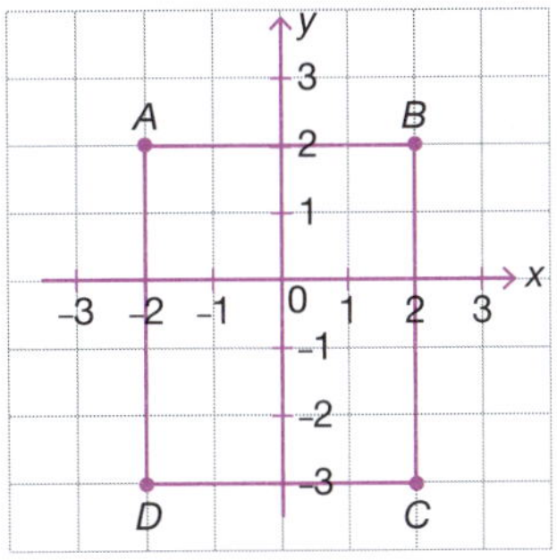

16 What is the size of the angle marked as *?

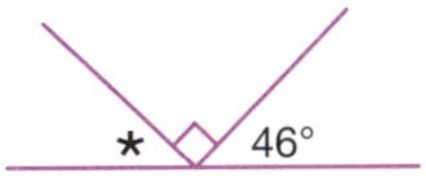

STATISTICS AND PROBABILITY

17 If a normal dice is rolled 6300 times, which of these is the most likely number of times it lands on a 4?

400 1050 1500 4000

18 The table shows the source of news used by age groups.

Media	Under 30	30 and over
Television	12	18
Radio	9	14
Newspaper	4	10
Internet	14	12

How many more people used the internet than the number who used the radio?

NUMBER AND ALGEBRA

1 What are the prime numbers between 20 and 30?

2 Write the word **cooler** or **warmer**:

−4 °C is .... than 2 °C .

3 What is the average of 4, 12 and 11?

4 Circle the fraction of the shape that is shaded.

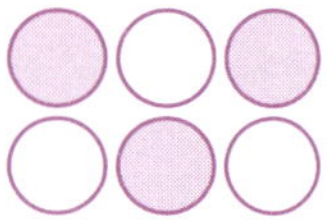

$\frac{1}{3}$ $\frac{3}{5}$ $\frac{1}{2}$

5 $1 - \frac{2}{3} =$

6 $3.65 \times 3 =$

7 Shade 30% of the shape.

8 A DVD is reduced in price from \$20 to \$18. What is the discount as a percentage?

9 What is the missing number in this sequence?

4.6, 5.8, 7, ☐ , 9.4

10 What is half the sum of 12 and 28?

MEASUREMENT AND SPACE

11 Convert 6700 cm to metres.

12 How many cubic centimetres are in 2 L?

13 Joshua purchased a house (shown as P) and sold it again (Q). Estimate the number of years he owned the house?

14 Liana built a model of a hexagonal prism using straws. How many straws were used?

15 On the number plane, plot $P(-3, 0)$ and $Q(2, -1)$.

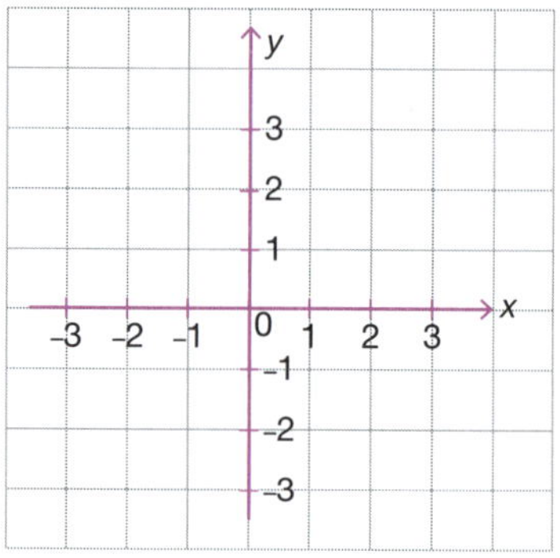

16 What is the size of the angle marked as *?

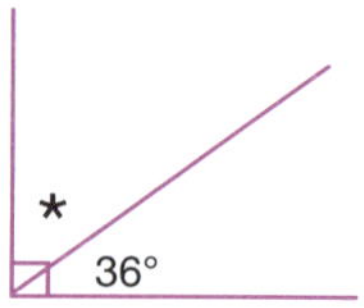

STATISTICS AND PROBABILITY

17 The table shows the number of different coloured cubes contained in a box.

Colour	Number
Red	8
Blue	7
Green	5

A cube is chosen at random.
What is the probability it is green?

18 The table shows a car yard's monthly vehicle sales.

	Sedans	SUVs	Utility
Weekdays	12	17	3
Weekends	3	9	4

How many vehicles were sold on the weekends?

NUMBER AND ALGEBRA

1 How many composite numbers are between 0 and 10?

2 Insert < or > to make the statement correct:

−8 ☐ 3

3 The average height of three friends is 158 cm. If Aiden is 164 cm tall and he is 3 cm taller than Sam, how tall is Carter?

4 Circle the fraction of the shape that is shaded.

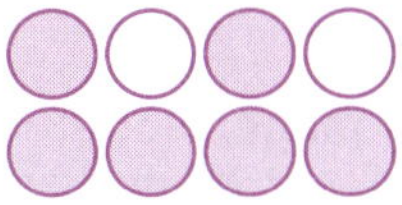

$\frac{1}{6}$ $\frac{3}{4}$ $\frac{1}{3}$

5 $2 - \frac{3}{5} =$

6 $7.32 \times 23 =$

7 Shade 50% of the shape.

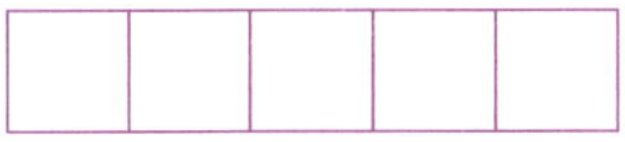

8 An airline's price for a return flight from Sydney to Perth is advertised as $600. In a sale, the price was reduced to $450. What was the discount as a percentage?

9 What is the missing number in this sequence?

10, 5, 2.5, 1.25, ☐, 0.3125

10 Find three-quarters of the difference between 48 and 28.

MEASUREMENT AND SPACE

11 Convert 42 mm to metres.

12 Find the number of litres in 6530 cm^3.

13 Abigail completed this timeline. If *A* represents her birth, what letter represents when Abigail started high school?

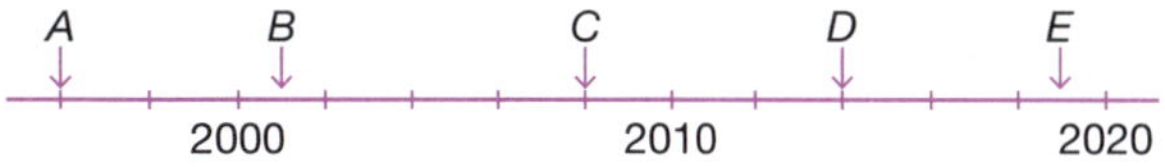

14 Michelle built a model of a hexagonal pyramid using straws. How many straws were used?

15 Join the points to form a rectangle *PQRS*. Find the perimeter.

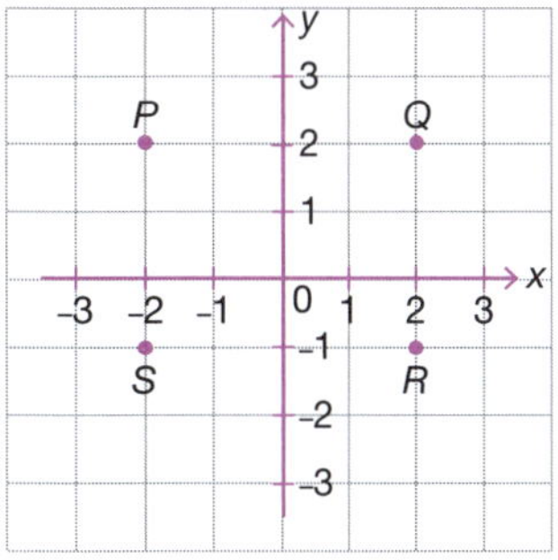

16 What is the size of the angle marked as *?

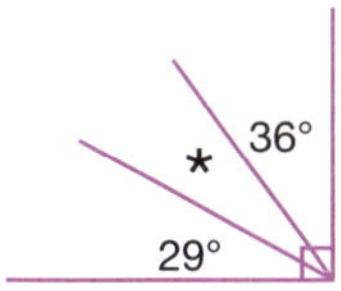

STATISTICS AND PROBABILITY

17 The table shows the number of different coloured cubes contained in a box.

Colour	Number
Red	8
Blue	7
Green	6

Four cubes of each colour are removed. What is now the probability of choosing a blue cube?

18 The table shows a car yard's monthly vehicle sales.

	Sedans	SUVs	Utility
Weekdays	12	17	3
Weekends	3	9	4

What was the total number of vehicles sold?

NUMBER AND ALGEBRA

1 Here are four triangular numbers. Circle the numbers that are composite.

55 1 36 3

2 Circle the words that can be represented with a positive (+) sign.

lose profit decrease over below

3 Three friends went bowling. Emily scored 100, and Alex and Mia 110 each. What was the total score?

4 Shade $\frac{1}{4}$ of the shape.

5 $\frac{7}{10} - \frac{3}{10} =$

6 What is the cost of 1.85 kg of tomatoes at $4 per kg?

7 Complete: 0.35 = ... %

8 A jewellery store is closing down and is selling all items at a discount of 50%.
What is the new price of a watch originally priced at $174?

9 Write the first four numbers in this pattern:

'Start with 3.7 and subtract 0.4 each time.'

10 What is the sum of 10 and the product of 4 and 3?

MEASUREMENT AND SPACE

11 Add these lengths: 760 mm and 1.4 m, writing your answer in millimetres.

12 Find the volume of the solid made from cubic-centimetre blocks.

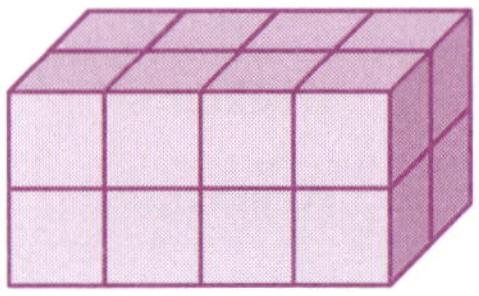

13 Here is a list of bands playing at a local venue. Each band plays for 40 min and there is a 20-minute break between bands for set-up. If Me & Him starts at 7 pm, what time does Postscript finish?

Me & Him
Postscript
Cheerleader
Emerson
La Roma

14 Draw the front view of this solid.

15 On the number plane, plot the points $A(-2, 2)$, $B(2, 2)$, $C(2, -2)$ and $D(-2, -2)$.

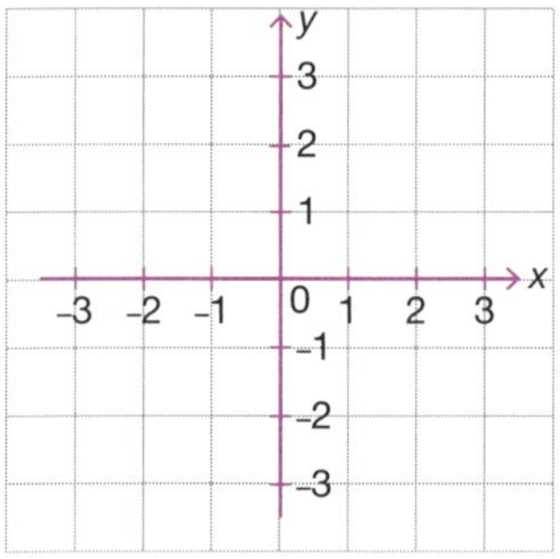

What type of shape is formed?

16 What is the size of the angle marked as *?

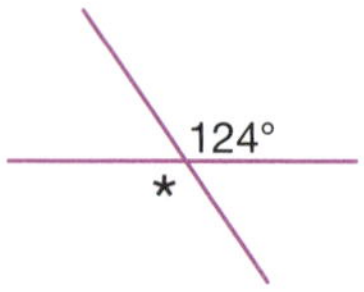

STATISTICS AND PROBABILITY

17 The probabilities of three events are recorded. Circle the probability that represents the event most likely to occur.

$\frac{1}{4}$ 0.3 24%

18 The table shows the number of prizes, distinctions and credits earned by students in a competition.

	Females	Males
Prize	4	3
Distinction	16	18
Credit	10	10

How many students were awarded a distinction?

NUMBER AND ALGEBRA

1 What is the square of the fifth prime number?

2 Write the opposite of winning $20.

3 Ethan has 16 model cars and Noah has 20 model cars. How many cars should Noah give Ethan so that Ethan will have twice as many model cars as Noah?

4 Shade $\frac{3}{4}$ of the shape.

5 From a 2-kg container of flour, Isaiah uses $1\frac{1}{3}$ kg to make muffins. How much flour remains in the container?

6 Robyn bought three magazines at $7.75 each. What was her change from a $50 note?

7 Complete: 1.6 = ... %

8 An office chair is originally priced at $199. At a sale, the price drops to $149.25. Circle the best estimate of the discount as a percentage.

5% 15% 25% 35%

9 Write the first four numbers in this pattern:

'Start with 4.5 and add 0.65 each time.'

10 What is the difference between the sum of 23 and 16 and the sum of 17 and 9?

MEASUREMENT AND SPACE

11 What is the sum of 24 cm, 1.3 m and 890 mm, writing your answer in metres?

12 Find the volume of the solid made from cubic-centimetre blocks.

13 Here is a list of bands playing at a local venue. Each band plays for 40 min and there is a 15-minute break between bands for set-up. If Postscript started at 2010, what time did La Roma start?

Me & Him
Postscript
Cheerleader
Emerson
La Roma

14 Draw the view of this solid from the right.

15 Join the points to form rectangle *ABCD*.

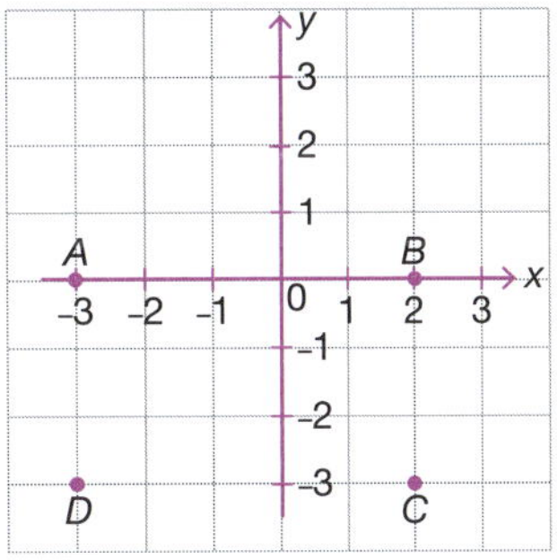

Find the area.

16 What is the size of the angle marked as *?

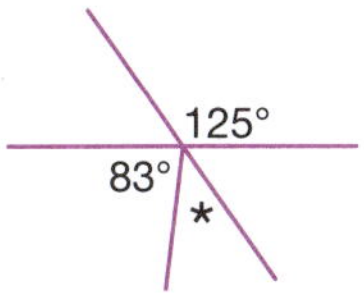

STATISTICS AND PROBABILITY

17 The probabilities of four events are recorded. Circle the probability that represents the event least likely to occur.

$\frac{2}{5}$ 32% 0.35 $\frac{12}{40}$

18 The table shows the number of prizes, distinctions and credits earned by students in a competition.

	Females	Males
Prize	4	3
Distinction	16	18
Credit	10	10

What fraction of those who were awarded a credit were males?

NUMBER AND ALGEBRA

1 There are 13 players in a rugby league team wearing numbers 1 to 13. How many players are wearing prime numbers?

2 Circle the words that can be represented with a negative (–) sign.

win loss decrease under above

3 Kalyn cycles 16 km on Monday, 35 km on Tuesday, 28 km on Wednesday and 41 km on Friday. What is the average distance he cycles each day?

4 What is half of 176?

5 $\frac{5}{6} - \frac{1}{3} =$

6 Complete: $4.673 \times 100 =$ ....

7 What percentage of the circles are shaded?

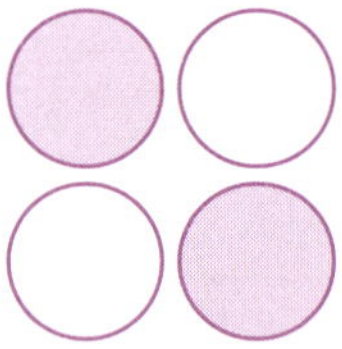

8 A clothing store is having a closing-down sale and everything is half price. What was the original price of a jacket which has a discounted price of $130?

9 Write the first four numbers in this pattern: 'Start with $\frac{3}{4}$ and add $\frac{1}{4}$ each time.'

10 Find $2.6 + 1.2 \times 2$.

MEASUREMENT AND SPACE

11 Jasmine removed 1670 mm from a 30-metre ball of string. What length remained on the ball?

12 A jar containing chocolate sultanas has a mass of 520 g. If the mass of the empty jar is 125 g, what is the total mass of the chocolate sultanas?

13 The timetable shows two buses that travel the same route at the same speed each morning.

Benloch	0817	0931
Dunolly	0853	?
Logan	0934	1048
Marnoo	1016	1130

What is the missing time?

14 Draw a sketch of a hemisphere.

15 Find the length of AB.

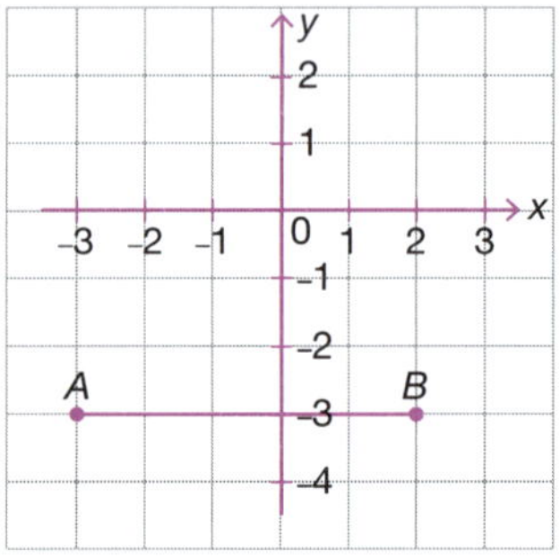

16 What is the size of the angle marked as *?

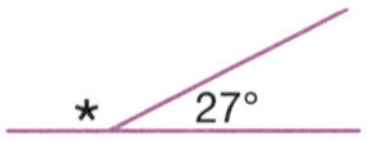

STATISTICS AND PROBABILITY

17 There are 3 black balls in a box containing 5 balls. Record on the number line the probability of selecting a black ball.

18 The table shows the number of students who own a phone.

	Phone	No phone
Boys	8	6
Girls	11	3

How many students own a phone?

NUMBER AND ALGEBRA

1 Jacob looked at the calendar for July. How many prime numbers are on the calendar?

2 Write the opposite of being 15 m below sea level.

3 In four tests Zoey scored an average of 83. What score does she need in her next test to increase her average to 86?

4 What is $\frac{3}{4}$ of 24?

5 Levi and Skylar went to an orchard. Levi picked $1\frac{1}{4}$ buckets of oranges while Skylar picked $2\frac{1}{2}$ buckets. What was the total amount of oranges picked?

6 What is the missing number?

$3.287 \times \square = 3287$

7 What percentage of the shape is shaded?

8 Headphones are reduced in price by 20%. What will be the savings on a set of headphones priced at $135?

9 Write the first four numbers in this pattern:

'Start with $\frac{1}{2}$ and add $\frac{1}{3}$ each time.'

10 Find $3.5 \div 5 + 16.8 \div 4$.

MEASUREMENT AND SPACE

11 Taylor swam 850 m, rode 16.3 km and ran 9.45 km. What was the total distance, in kilometres?

12 Here is the mass of each of four students: 37.2 kg, 42.7 kg, 41.3 kg, 38.8 kg. What is the average mass?

13 The timetable shows one of the many buses that travel the same route at the same speed each day. If another bus arrived in Marnoo at 1253, what time had it arrived in Dunolly?

Benloch	0817
Dunolly	0853
Logan	0934
Marnoo	1016

14 Draw a sketch of a pentagonal prism.

15

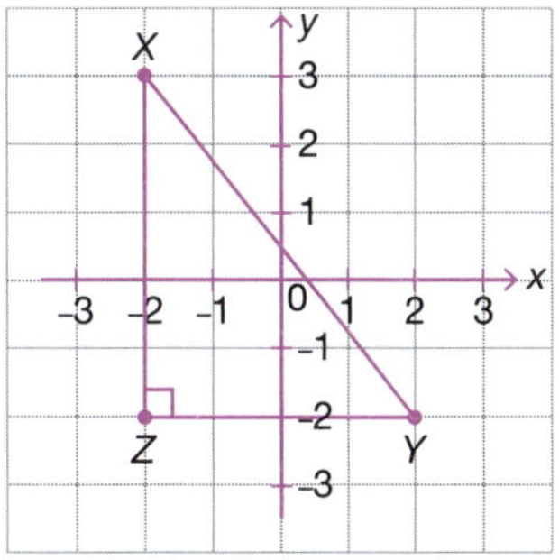

Find the area of the triangle.

16 What is the size of the angle marked as *?

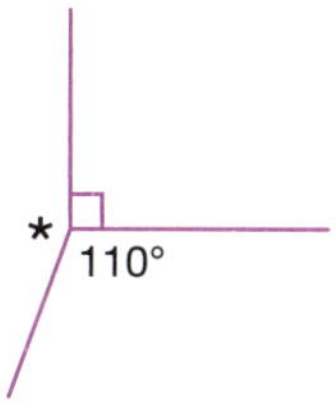

STATISTICS AND PROBABILITY

17 A bag contains 2 red balls, 2 blue balls and a yellow ball. Record on the number line, as a decimal, the probability of selecting a blue ball.

18 The table shows the number of students who own a phone.

	Phone	No phone
Boys	8	6
Girls	11	3

What fraction of the students are boys?

NUMBER AND ALGEBRA

1 Candice wrote this two-digit prime number: 3☐. Circle all the possible digits.

0   1   7   8

2 Rewrite this list of numbers in order from smallest to largest:

4   −1   3   −2

☐

3 Bella View has a population of 10 000 living in three housing estates. 5600 live in Bella Vista, while 2700 live in Bella Grove. How many people live in Bella Heights? ☐

4 Find $\frac{1}{4}$ of 40. ☐

5 $\frac{3}{4} - \frac{2}{5} =$ ☐

6 Find 5.32 × 7. ☐

7 Insert either < or > to make the statement true:

5% ☐ $\frac{1}{10}$

8 A haircut usually costs $25 but a discount of 10% is available for students. What is the saving on a student's haircut? ☐

9 Wyatt wrote a sequence starting with 4.2 and adding 0.6 each time. Circle the number that is in the sequence.

5.0   5.2   5.4   5.5

10 What is $\frac{7}{10} - (\frac{2}{10} + \frac{4}{10})$? ☐

MEASUREMENT AND SPACE

11 Ingrid is 165 cm tall. Her sister Phoebe is 1.73 m tall. What is the difference in their heights, in centimetres? ☐

12 Use a decimal to find the missing number:

7 L 200 mL = ☐ L.

13 The timetable shows two buses that travel the same route at the same speed each morning.

Wigram	0919	1028
Sockburn	0943	?
Edgeware	1028	1137
Ferrymead	1107	1216

What is the missing time? ☐

14 A cylinder is placed on top of a cylinder with a larger radius. Draw a sketch of the solid.

15 Plot the points $A(-3, 1)$, $B(2, 1)$ and $C(2, -3)$.

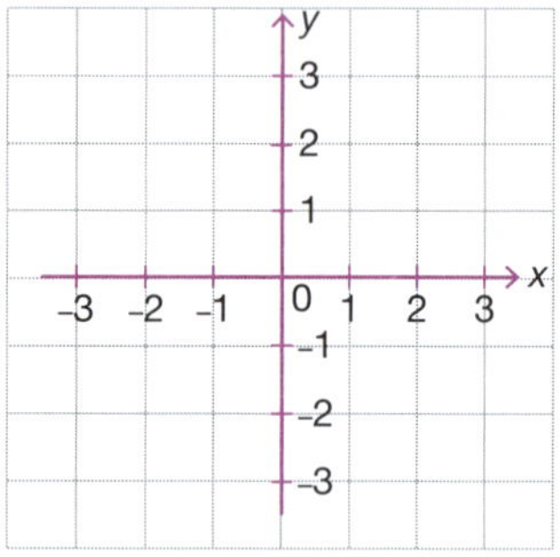

What type of shape is formed? ☐

16 What is the size of the angle marked as *?

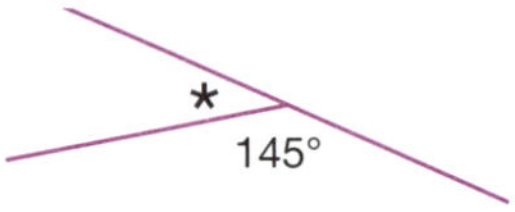

☐

STATISTICS AND PROBABILITY

17 A normal dice is rolled ☐ times and the number 2 appears on 10 occasions. Circle the best estimate of ☐.

12   20   60   120

18 The table shows the colour of vehicles in a car park.

	White	Red	Other
Cars	26	5	15
Vans	4	0	0

How many cars are in the car park? ☐

NUMBER AND ALGEBRA

1 Ethan wrote this three-digit composite number:

12☐. Circle all the possible digits.

0 1 3 7

2 Rewrite this list of numbers in ascending order:

−5 −11 2 −2

3 The average age of three cousins is 12. If Rosie is 9 and Eliza is 16, how old is Peyton?

4 What is $\frac{7}{10}$ of 60?

5 Claire had $\frac{9}{10}$ of a metre of ribbon. She used $\frac{2}{5}$ of a metre to wrap a present. What length of ribbon remains?

6 Find 30 × 2.35.

7 Rewrite in ascending order:

40% $\frac{8}{100}$ 0.37 9%

8 Ellie works as a waitress and is paid $21 per hour. If she is to receive a 20% pay rise, what will be her new hourly rate?

9 Emma wrote a sequence starting with 8.3 and subtracting 0.7 each time. Circle the number that was in the sequence.

3.7 4.1 4.6 5.1

10 Find the value of $\frac{3}{4} - (\frac{1}{2} - \frac{1}{4})$.

MEASUREMENT AND SPACE

11 Tom bought a timber plank 3.5 m long. Josie also bought a timber plank which was 640 mm longer than Tom's plank. How long was Josie's plank, in metres?

12 Use a decimal to find the missing number:

20 kg 30 g = ☐ kg

13 The timetable shows one of the many buses that travel the same route at the same speed each day. If another bus arrived in Ferrymead at 1419, what time had it arrived in Sockburg?

Wigram	0919
Sockburn	0943
Edgeware	1028
Ferrymead	1107

14 A cone is placed on top of a cylinder. Both shapes have the same diameter. Draw a sketch of the solid.

15 Use the number plane to draw a shape formed by all the points 2 units from the origin.

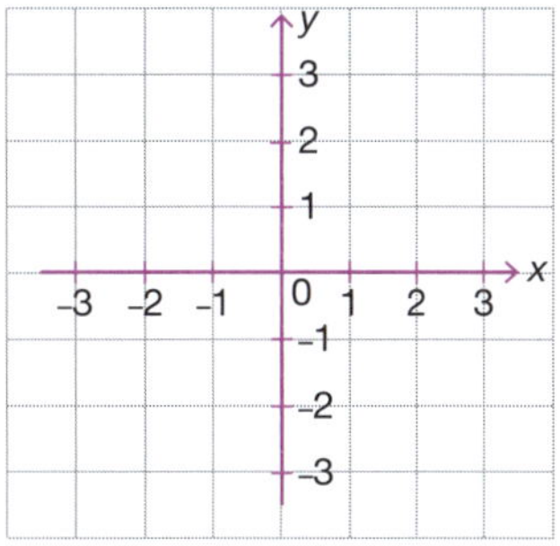

16 What is the size of the angle marked as *?

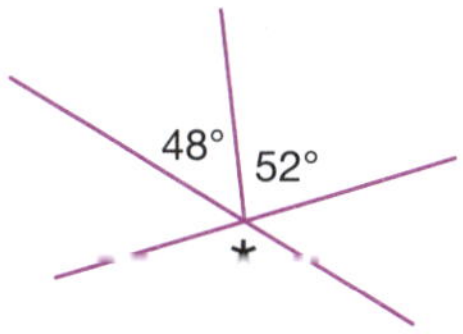

STATISTICS AND PROBABILITY

17 A normal dice is rolled ☐ times and a prime number appears 60 times. Circle the best estimate of ☐.

60 90 120 180

18 The table shows the colour of vehicles in a car park.

	White	Red	Other
Cars	26	5	15
Vans	4	0	0

What fraction of the vehicles are white?

NUMBER AND ALGEBRA

1 Jonathon wrote this four-digit number: 376☐. If the number is divisible by 5, write the two possible four-digit numbers.

2 Rewrite this list of numbers in order from largest to smallest:

$-5 \quad 8 \quad 0 \quad -2$

3 Find the answer $3487 \times 9 =$

4 $\frac{1}{6}$ of $48 =$

5 $\frac{5}{8} - \frac{3}{8} + \frac{1}{8} =$

6 $5\overline{)3.75}$

7 Change 85% to a decimal.

8 A guitar is priced at $360. Nathan buys the guitar after receiving a discount of 10%. What price does Nathan pay for the guitar?

9 Write the first four numbers in this pattern:

'Start with 11.4 and add 0.21 each time.'

10 Find the value of $\frac{3}{4} + (\frac{5}{8} + \frac{3}{8})$.

MEASUREMENT AND SPACE

11 Michael is building a fence. The total length of the fence will be 17.4 m. He has already completed half the length. What distance remains to be built?

12 A container, when full, holds 240 L. What amount of water is in the container when it is two-thirds filled with water?

13 A train timetable is shown below.

Woodside	1348
Prospect	1406
Norwood	1451
Moana	1533

How long does it take to travel from Woodside to Norwood?

14 Keeley uses plasticine to build a triangular prism. How many faces has the solid?

15 From X on the number plane, move south 3 units and then west 5 units to Y. Locate Y on the number plane.

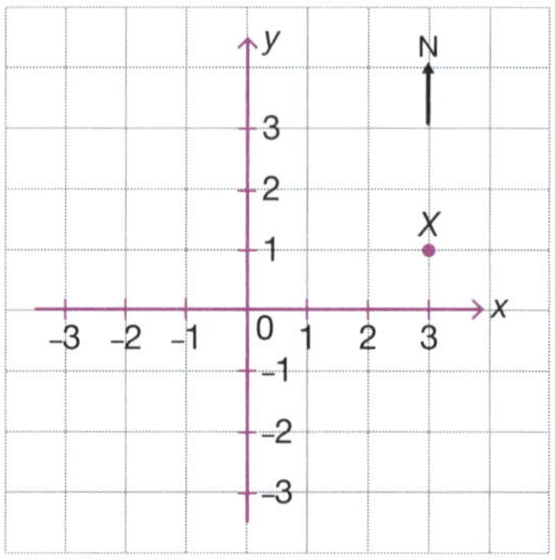

16 What is the size of the angle marked as *?

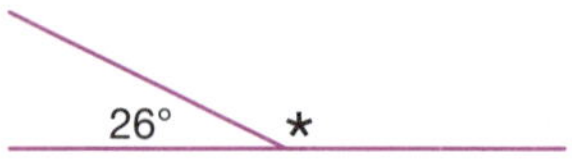

STATISTICS AND PROBABILITY

17 James either rides or catches a bus to work five mornings a week. On any day the probability that he rides to work is 0.6. What is the probability that he catches a bus?

18 The table shows the favourite seasons of a group of students.

	Summer	Autumn	Winter	Spring
Girls	8	5	4	6
Boys	4	3	9	1

How many boys liked summer or spring best?

NUMBER AND ALGEBRA

1 Jonathon wrote this four-digit number: 54 ☐ 2. If the number is divisible by 3, write all possible four-digit numbers.

2 Rewrite this list of numbers in descending order:

−7 3 −12 6 −1

3 Find the answer $963 \times 28 =$

4 A box contains 24 balls. If $\frac{2}{3}$ of the balls are red, how many are **not** red?

5 Andrew had a bag of marbles. He gave one-quarter of the marbles to Jack and one-third of the marbles to Aaron. He gave the rest to Daniel. What fraction of the marbles did Daniel receive?

6 $6\overline{)84.18}$

7 Change 5.2% to a decimal.

8 A boat is priced at $32 800 but, as there is a new model coming soon, the salesperson reduces the price by 25%. What is the new price?

9 Write the first four numbers in this pattern:

'Start with 120 and divide by 4 each time.'

10 Find the value of $\frac{3}{4} \times (3\frac{3}{10} + \frac{7}{10})$.

MEASUREMENT AND SPACE

11 Laura's pace is 85 cm long. How far has she walked after 4000 steps. Give your answer in kilometres.

12 A fuel tank is showing one-quarter full. If 36 L of fuel will completely fill the tank, what is the total capacity of the tank?

13 The timetable of one of many trains that travel the same route at the same speed each day is shown.

Woodside	1348
Prospect	1406
Norwood	1451
Moana	1533

If another train arrives at Norwood at 1704, what time does it arrive at Moana?

14 A square-based pyramid is placed on top of a cube. The pyramid's base and the cube's face are identical. If the solid is painted, how many faces are painted?

15 From *A*, move 5 units north, 3 units west and 2 units south to *B*. What are the coordinates of *B*?

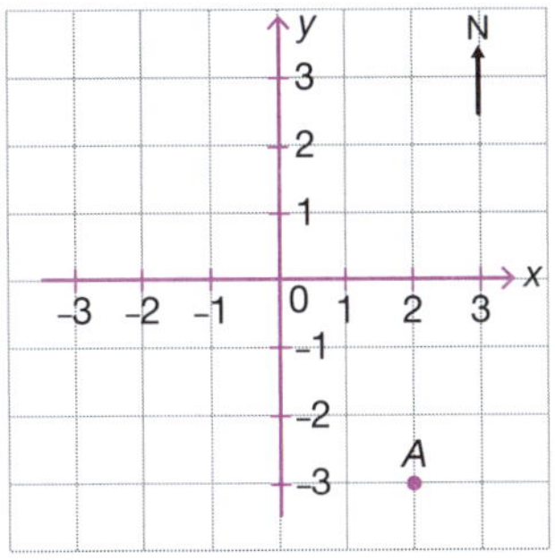

16 What is the size of the angle marked as *?

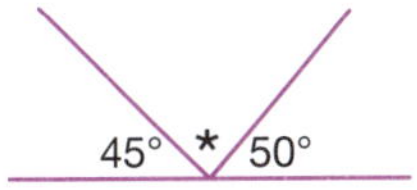

STATISTICS AND PROBABILITY

17 Each morning Layla either runs, cycles or swims. The probability of Layla cycling is $\frac{2}{7}$. How many times will Layla cycle in 5 weeks?

18 The table shows the favourite seasons of a group of students.

	Summer	Autumn	Winter	Spring
Girls	8	5	4	6
Boys	4	3	9	1

How much greater is the number of students who liked winter than the number who liked autumn?

NUMBER AND ALGEBRA

1 Below are some numbers. Circle the prime numbers.

9 13 17 28 35

2 Here are four temperatures. Circle the coldest.

7 °C −3 °C −6 °C −0.5 °C

3 How many 9s are in 3627?

4 What is $\frac{1}{10}$ of 60?

5 Find the sum of $\frac{1}{4}$ and $\frac{1}{3}$.

6 $4\overline{)4.12}$

7 What is 10% of 90?

8 Nora's electricity bill is $700. If she pays the bill by a certain date, she receives a discount of 10%. How much will Nora pay?

9 What is the missing number in the sequence?

7, 7.35, 7.7, ____, 8.4 …

10 Insert grouping symbols to make the number sentence correct:

$4 \times 6 + 2 = 32$

MEASUREMENT AND SPACE

11 Sarah plans to swim 2.4 km. She has already swum 1250 m. How far does she have to swim to complete her distance?

12 If a litre of water has a mass of 1 kg, what amount of water has a mass of 1 tonne?

13 A train timetable is shown below. How long does it take to travel from Miramar to Newlands?

Miramar	1348
Brooklyn	1406
Newlands	1441
Seaview	1533

14 Lara drew this shape to represent the net of a cube which does not have a lid. Is she correct?

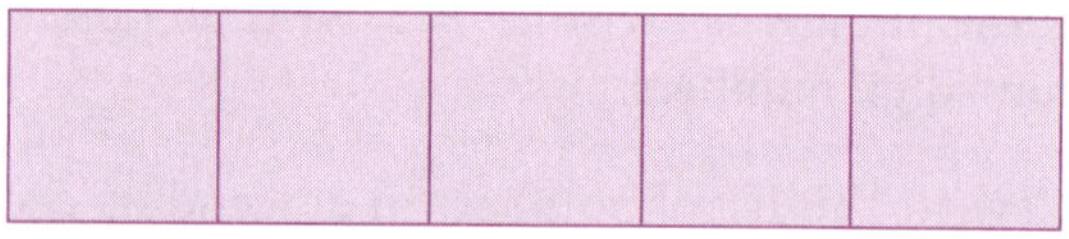

15 From X on the number plane, move south 4 units and then east 2 units to Y. Locate Y on the number plane.

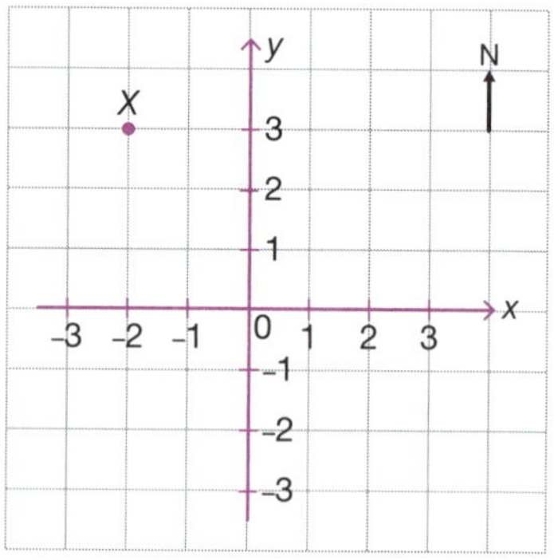

16 What is the size of the angle marked as *?

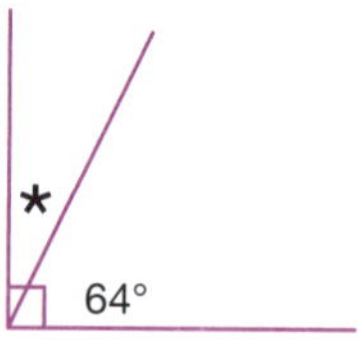

STATISTICS AND PROBABILITY

17 What is the probability of spinning an even number?

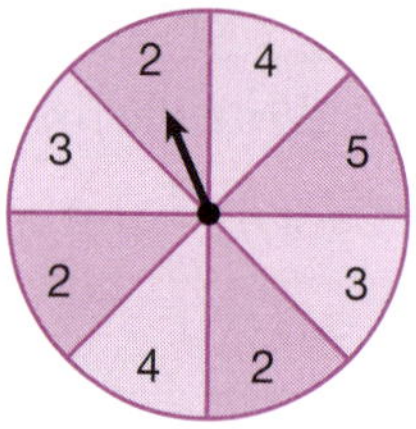

18 The table shows the way students travelled to school this morning.

	Bus	Car	Other
Boys	46	37	15
Girls	38	41	12

How much greater is the number of boys who travelled by bus than the number of girls who arrived in a car?

NUMBER AND ALGEBRA

1 Write down the prime numbers between 40 and 60.

2 Here are three temperatures. Rearrange them from coldest to warmest.

2.5 °C   −2.5 °C   −4.5 °C   −1.5 °C

3 A multiplex has five cinemas. The number of seats in the cinemas are 360, 280, 260, 180 and 160. What is the average number of seats in each cinema?

4 Two-thirds of a class are members of the choir. If there are 27 students in the class, how many are in the choir?

5 Mila worked for $6\frac{3}{4}$ h on Saturday and $5\frac{1}{2}$ h on Sunday. What was the total number of hours worked across the weekend?

6 $8\overline{)183.92}$

7 What is 70% of 60?

8 Circle the greatest discount.

10% of \$640   25% of \$280   50% of \$138

9 What is the missing number in the sequence?

6.4, 1.6, ____, 0.1, 0.025, …

10 Insert grouping symbols to make the number sentence correct:

20 − 4 × 3 + 2 = 0.

MEASUREMENT AND SPACE

11 From edge to edge, a 50-cent coin measures 31.65 mm. Andrew placed \$50 of the coins alongside each other to make a line. How long is the line of coins, in metres?

12 A bucket has a total capacity of 9 L. When empty, the bucket has a mass of 350 g. If 1 L of water has a mass of 1 kg, what is the total mass when the bucket is exactly a quarter full?

13 The timetable of one of many trains that travel the same route at the same speed each day is shown. If another train arrives in Seaview at 1639, what time does it leave Miramar?

Miramar	1348
Brooklyn	1406
Newlands	1441
Seaview	1533

14 A cube is made without a lid. Which of these could **not** be the net?

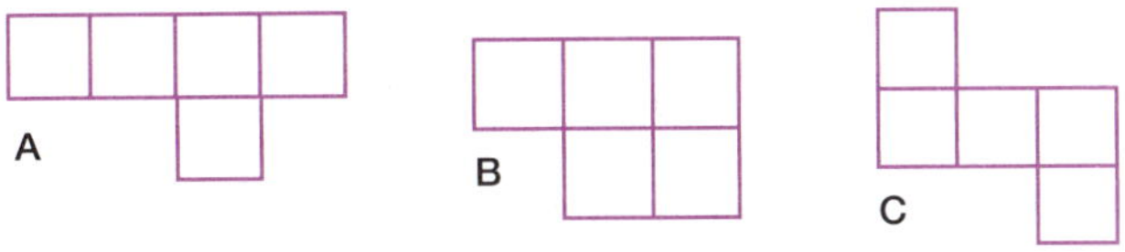

15 Q is 4 units east of $P(-2, -3)$ and south-east of R. If R is north of P, what are the coordinates of R?

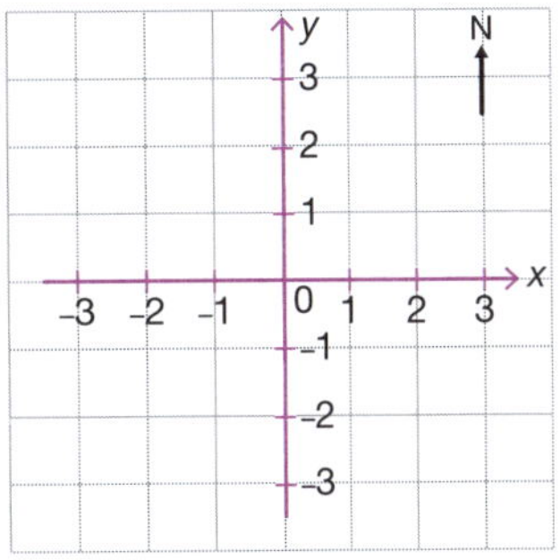

16 What is the value of x?

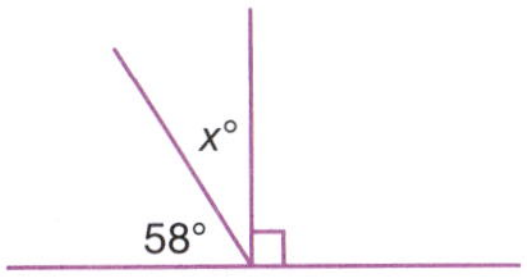

STATISTICS AND PROBABILITY

17 The spinner is spun 40 times. What is the expected number of times a 3 is spun?

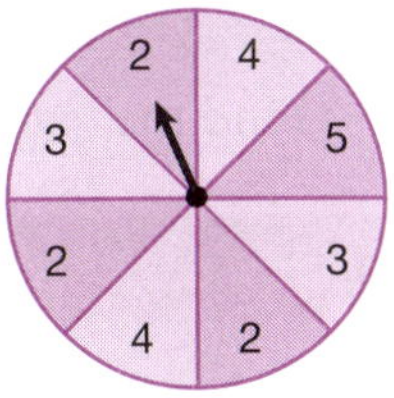

18 The table shows the way students travelled to school this morning. How many more students travelled by bus than the number who went by car?

	Bus	Car	Other
Boys	46	37	15
Girls	38	41	12

NUMBER AND ALGEBRA

1 Write the square numbers more than 10 but less than 50.

2 What is the opposite of positive 10?

3 $140 \div \square = 20$

What is the missing number?

4 There are eight marbles in a bag. If $\frac{1}{4}$ of the marbles are red, how many red marbles are in the bag?

5 What is $1\frac{1}{2} + 2\frac{1}{2}$?

6 $15.67 \div 10 =$

7 100 cars were driven into a car park by 8 am. By 5:30 pm only 27 cars remained. What percentage of the cars had departed the car park?

8 What is the percentage discount if a pot reduces in price from \$10 to \$6?

9 What is the missing number in the sequence, as a mixed numeral?

$\frac{3}{4}, \frac{5}{4}, \square, \frac{9}{4}, \frac{11}{4} \ldots$

10 Find the value of $16 \div 4 \times 2$.

MEASUREMENT AND SPACE

11 A side of a regular hexagon is 9.4 cm. What is the perimeter of the hexagon?

12 What is the capacity, in litres, of a container that can hold 20 000 cm^3?

13 Part of a train timetable is shown. It takes 29 min to travel from Pasadena to Woodside.

Pasadena	1518
Woodside	?
Millbrook	1602
Birdwood	1639

What is the missing time?

14 What solid is formed using this net?

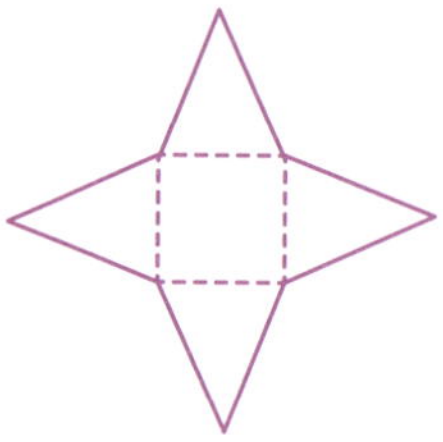

15 Complete: B is .... units north of A and .... units east of A.

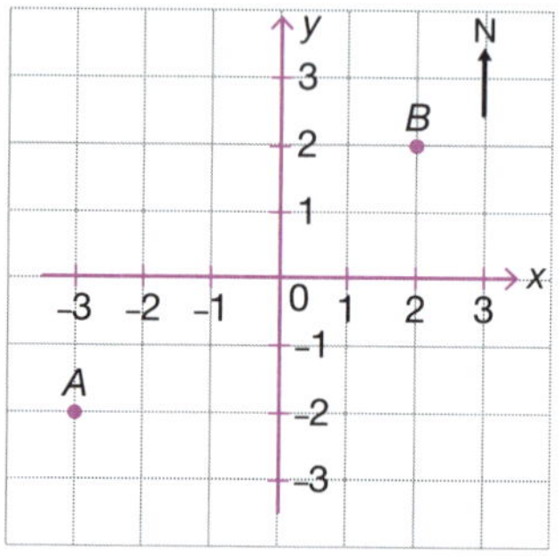

16 What is the size of the angle marked as *?

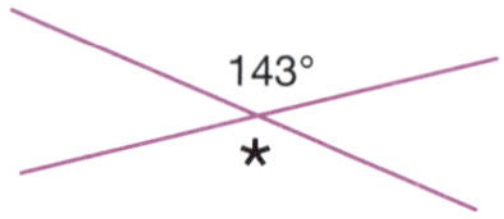

STATISTICS AND PROBABILITY

17 Balls numbered 1 to 50 are placed into a bag. What is the probability of selecting the number 37, expressed as a decimal?

18 The table shows the 6P students who have and have not represented the school in sport this year. Complete the table.

	Yes	No	Total
Boys	9	4	
Girls	12	3	
Total			

NUMBER AND ALGEBRA

1 Complete the pattern of triangular numbers:

1, 3, 6, 10, ..., ..., ..., ...

2 What is the opposite of negative 8.4?

3 15 760 ÷ ☐ = 40.

What is the missing number?

4 Andrew is reading a book which has 200 pages.

He has read $\frac{2}{5}$ of the book.

How many pages has he read?

5 On Saturday Ross dug a trench $6\frac{4}{5}$ m long. If the total length of the trench at the end of Sunday was 10 m, what was the length of the trench dug on Sunday?

6 What is the missing number?

124 ÷ ☐ = 1.24

7 Write the fraction $\frac{168}{200}$ as a percentage.

8 The price of a caravan drops from $80 000 to $60 000. What is the percentage discount?

9 What is the missing number in the sequence?

$7, 6\frac{1}{6},$ ☐ $, 4\frac{1}{2}, 3\frac{2}{3}$ …

10 What is the value of 28 − 12 × 2 ÷ 6?

MEASUREMENT AND SPACE

11 The perimeter of a regular octagon is 61.6 cm. What is the length of each side?

12 Rewrite these masses from lightest to heaviest.

125 g   0.2 kg   115 000 mg   0.025 kg

13 Part of a train timetable is shown. It takes 37 minutes to travel from Millbrook to Birdwood.

Pasadena	1753
Woodside	1822
Millbrook	**?**
Birdwood	1924

What is the missing time?

14 This net is used to form a solid. How many edges has the solid?

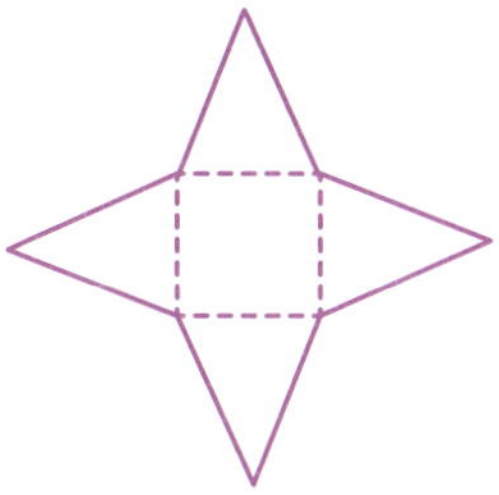

15 Complete: Q is .... units .... of P and .... units .... of P.

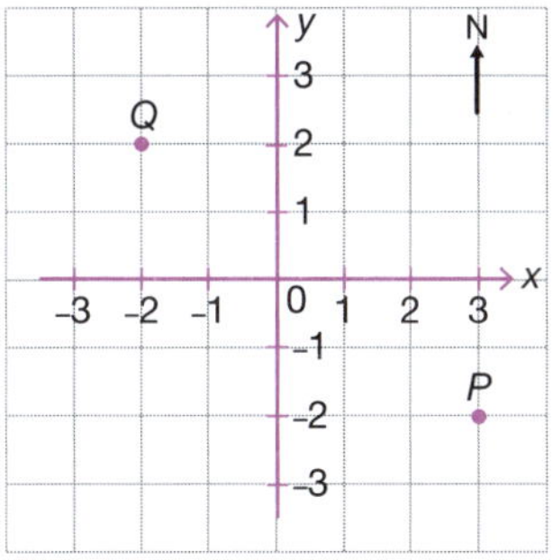

16 What is the value of x?

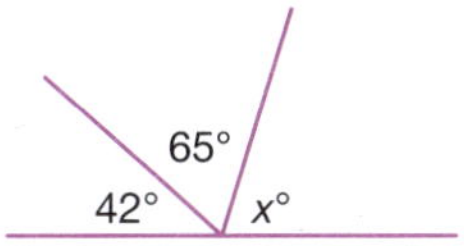

STATISTICS AND PROBABILITY

17 Balls numbered 1 to 25 are placed into a bag. What is the probability of selecting an odd number, expressed as a decimal?

18 The table shows the 6K students who had represented the school in sport this year. Complete the table.

	Yes	No	Total
Boys		3	15
Girls	10	5	
Total			

NUMBER AND ALGEBRA

1 What is $2^2 + 3^2$?

2 What is the opposite of +5?

3 The product of a number and 20 is 240. What is the number?

4 Twelve bananas are in a fruit bowl. Two of the bananas are ripe. What fraction of the bananas are ripe?

5 On Saturday Leah ran $4\frac{1}{4}$ km followed by a $15\frac{1}{4}$ km cycle.

What was the total distance?

6 Divide 27 by 5, writing your answer as a decimal.

7 What is $\frac{2}{5}$ as a decimal?

8 A gym set is usually priced at $199.90. If it is discounted by $23.40, what is the new price?

9 Every year the price of netball registration increases by $2.50. If last year it was $87.50, what will be the cost of registration next year?

10 Insert grouping symbols to make the number sentence correct:

$$15 - 5 \times 2 = 20$$

MEASUREMENT AND SPACE

11 A square has a side length of $3\frac{1}{2}$ cm. What is the perimeter of the square?

12 What is the volume of a rectangular prism with dimensions 12 cm, 10 cm and 8 cm?

13 Part of the train timetable is shown. It takes 24 min to travel from Henderson to Manurewa. What is the missing time?

Albany	1711
Henderson	1739
Manurewa	?
Pokeno	1826

14 Draw all the diagonals of the pentagon.

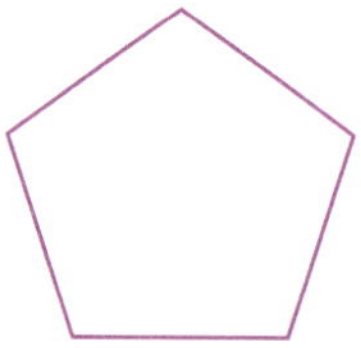

15 From the list, circle any point west of X.

(−3, −2) (2, 3) (2, −3) (3, −2)

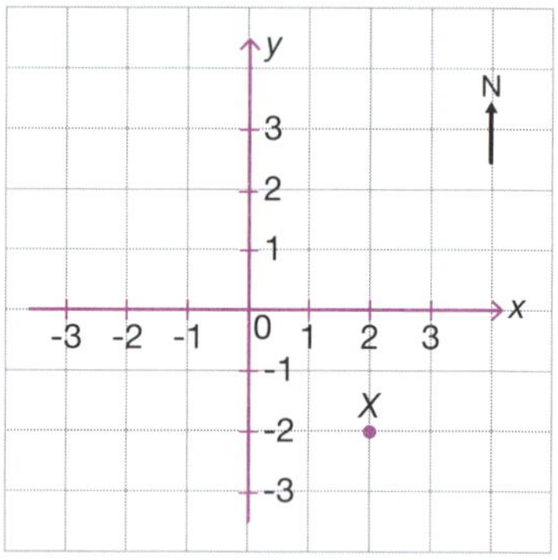

16 What is the size of the angle marked as *?

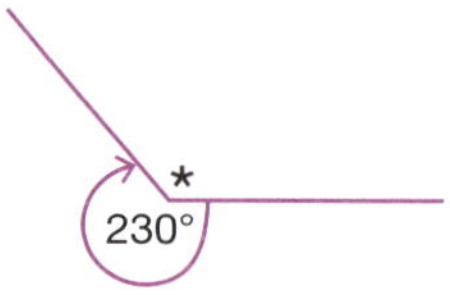

STATISTICS AND PROBABILITY

17 A normal dice is thrown. What is the probability of rolling a square number?

18 The table shows the results of a survey into sport and work for 16 year olds. Complete the table.

	Work	No work	Total
Sport	14	12	
No sport	10	6	
Total			

NUMBER AND ALGEBRA

1 What two positive numbers less than 100 are both a square number and a triangular number?

2 What is the opposite of −11?

3 What number divided by 16 is equal to 30?

4 There are 16 seats in a waiting room. If 6 seats are occupied, what fraction of the seats are empty?

5 Ely received a big box of chocolates for his birthday. After one week he had eaten half the chocolates. By the end of the second week he had eaten two-thirds of the chocolates and by the end of the third week he had eaten five-sixths of the chocolates. What total fraction of the box had he eaten during the second and third weeks after his birthday?

6 What is 348.645 divided by 5 to the nearest whole?

7 What is $\frac{5}{8}$ as a decimal?

8 Owen buys two tins of paint at $64.90 each. If he receives a trade discount of 10%, what total amount will he pay?

9 Monica is training for a fun-run and runs an extra 2.6 km each week. If she runs 19.3 km this week, how far will she run in 3 weeks time?

10 Insert grouping symbols to make the number sentence correct:

$16 \div 2 + 6 \times 3 + 1 = 7$

MEASUREMENT AND SPACE

11 A rectangle measures $2\frac{1}{2}$ cm by $1\frac{1}{2}$ cm.

What is the perimeter of the rectangle?

12 Find the volume of a rectangular prism which has dimensions 25 cm by 12 cm by 9 cm.

13 Part of the train timetable is shown. It takes 1 h 23 min to travel from Manurewa to Pokeno. What is the missing time?

Albany	2043
Henderson	2111
Manurewa	?
Pokeno	2305

14 How many diagonals has a hexagon?

15 From the list, circle the point(s) north-east of *A*.

(−3, −3) (−1, 4) (2, 3) (−2, −1)

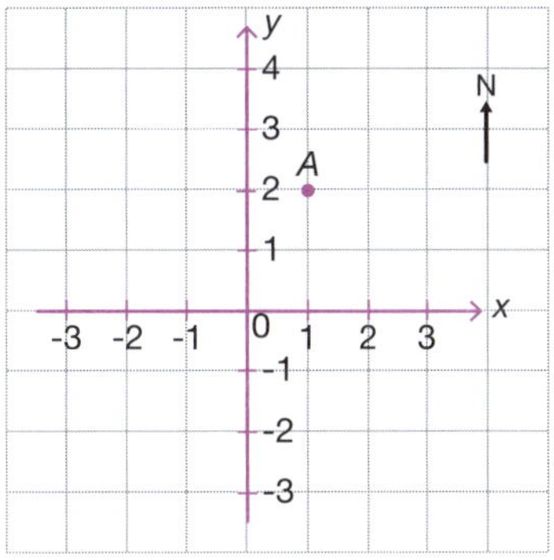

16 What is the value of *x*?

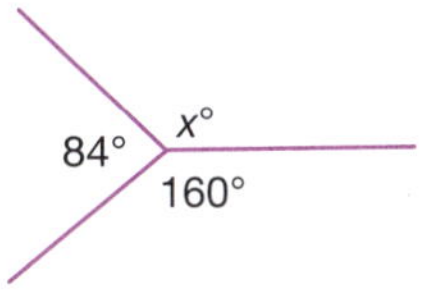

STATISTICS AND PROBABILITY

17 420 normal dice are thrown at the same time. What is the expected number of dice that land on a 2?

18 The table shows the results of a survey into sport and work for 18 year olds. Complete the table.

	Work	No work	Total
Sport			17
No sport	12	9	
Total	23		

NUMBER AND ALGEBRA

1 What is the difference between 7^2 and 3^2?

2 On a number line, what two numbers are 5 units from 0?

3 Of 2485 drivers who applied for their driver's licence, 1170 were female. How many males applied?

4 In a deck of 52 cards, 26 are red and the rest are black. What fraction of the cards are red?

5 What is the difference between $\frac{7}{10}$ and $\frac{2}{5}$?

6 When he was 2 years old, Logan's dad measured Logan's height at 0.87 m. On his 21st birthday his height was measured again, and he had doubled his 2-year-old height. How tall was Logan on his 21st birthday?

7 Circle the largest amount.

$\frac{1}{4}$ 0.18   20%

8 A store has all office furniture discounted by 20%. What will be paid for a desk priced at $150?

9 Here is a pattern of three shapes made of matchsticks.

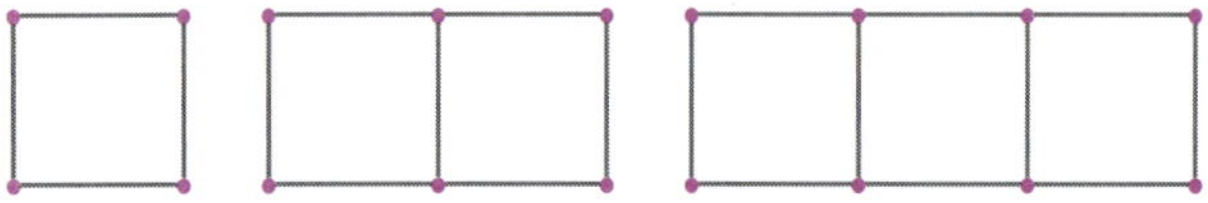

How many matchsticks would be used to make the fourth shape in the pattern?

10 Jack works 14 h one week and 16 h the next week. If he is paid $12 per hour, what is his total pay?

MEASUREMENT AND SPACE

11 The perimeter of a square is 7.2 cm. What is the length of each side?

12 Four sweet potatoes have these masses: 870 g, 1.1 kg, 950 g and 1.05 kg. What is the total mass of the sweet potatoes, in kilograms?

13 A train timetable is shown.

Jandacot	11:48 am
Cannington	12:16 pm
Coogee	1:02 pm
Oakford	1:33 pm

How long does it take to travel from Jandacot to Coogee?

14 Circle any shape which has diagonals of equal length.

15 Points *A*, *B* and *C* are plotted on the number plane. What are the coordinates of *D* to form square *ABCD*?

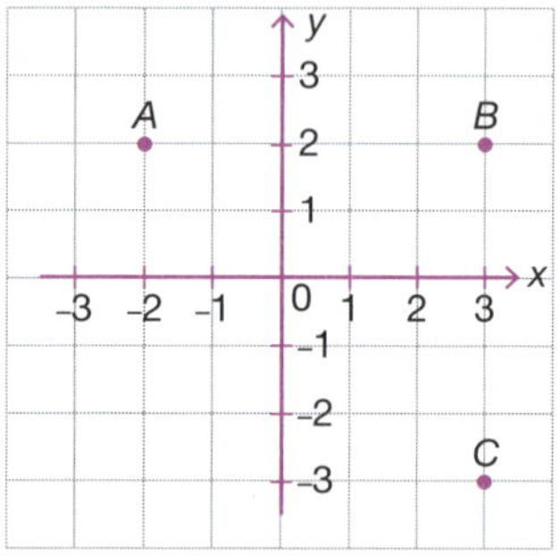

16 What is the size of the angle marked as *?

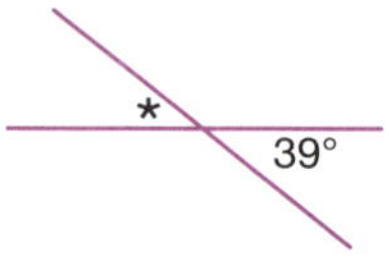

STATISTICS AND PROBABILITY

17 Three normal dice are rolled and their scores totalled. What is the highest possible total?

18 The table shows people's favourite winter sport. Complete the table.

	AFL	League	Netball	Other
Males	16	11	4	10
Females	11	6	12	18
Total				

NUMBER AND ALGEBRA

1 The sum of a square number and a triangular number is 44. What are the two numbers?

2 On a number line, what two numbers are 6 units from 2?

3 The total population of a city is 3 389 981 people. If 657 894 residents were born overseas, how many people were **not** born overseas?

4 A bag contains 12 balls. Six of the balls are red, three are blue and the remainder green. What fraction of the balls are green?

5 A rectangle is split into equal squares. Gary shades $\frac{1}{4}$ of the squares and Audrey shades $\frac{2}{5}$ of the squares. What fraction of the rectangle remains unshaded?

6 Oranges are priced at \$2.49/kg and apples at \$3.89/kg. Kim bought 1 kg of oranges and 1 kg of apples. What is the total cost to the nearest 10 cents?

7 Circle the fractions or decimals that equal 50%.

$\frac{1}{5}$ 0.5 0.05 $\frac{4}{8}$

8 An optometrist sells glasses for \$190, with any second set discounted by 50%. What will Jack pay for two sets of glasses?

9 Here is a pattern of three shapes made of matchsticks.

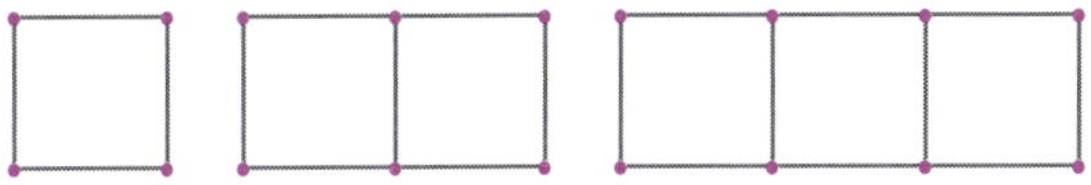

How many matchsticks would be used to make the sixth shape in the pattern?

10 Ella walks dogs for her part-time job. She charges \$14 to walk each dog. On Monday she walked 5 dogs, on Wednesday 8 dogs, on Thursday 9 dogs and on Friday 7 dogs. What is her total pay?

MEASUREMENT AND SPACE

11 A rectangle has a perimeter of 42 cm. If the length is 16 cm, what is the width?

12 Ken bought three bags of firewood with a total mass of 42 kg. One bag had a mass of 14.5 kg, which was 1.2 kg heavier than a second bag. What was the mass of the third bag?

13 A train timetable is shown. The train is held up for 56 minutes between Cannington and Coogee. If no time was made up, what time did it arrive in Oakford?

Jandacot	11:48 am
Cannington	12:16 pm
Coogee	1:02 pm
Oakford	1:33 pm

14 Circle any shape which has diagonals of equal length.

rhombus kite
regular octagon equilateral triangle

15 Points P, Q and R are plotted on the number plane. What are the coordinates of S to form parallelogram $PQRS$?

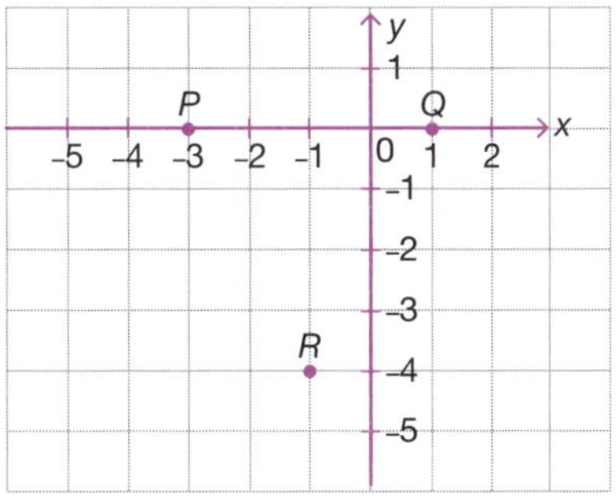

16 What is the value of x?

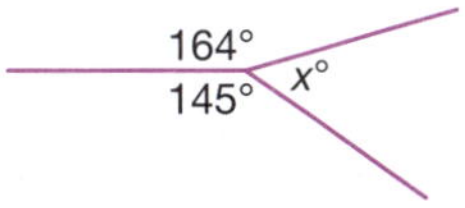

STATISTICS AND PROBABILITY

17 Two normal dice are rolled and their difference recorded. What is the largest possible difference?

18 The table shows 100 people's favourite winter sport. Complete the table.

	AFL	League	Netball	Other
Males	21	14	6	
Females	12		15	11
Total				16

NUMBER AND ALGEBRA

1 Find the answer:

$3^2 + 4^2 =$

2 On a number line, what two numbers are 4 units from 4?

3 What is 1188 divided by 11?

4 Al's Car Sales had 72 cars on site. If $\frac{1}{6}$ of the cars are sold, what number of cars are sold?

5 What is $1\frac{2}{3} + \frac{1}{3}$?

6 Find the answer: 0.054×1000.

7 Rewrite $\frac{7}{10}$ as a percentage.

8 What is the discount on a smartwatch priced at $600 at a sale of '25% off the price of all wearable technology'?

9 Here is a pattern of three shapes made of dots.

How many dots would be in the fifth shape?

10 What is the sum of 10 and the product of 3 and 8?

MEASUREMENT AND SPACE

11 A square has a perimeter of 48 cm. What is the length of each side?

12 How many kilolitres are in 3750 L?

13 A train timetable is shown. How long does it take to travel from Antioch to Stockton?

Richmond	10:17 am
Oakland	11:21 pm
Antioch	12:53 pm
Stockton	2:11 pm

14 On the circle, draw and identify a chord and the circumference.

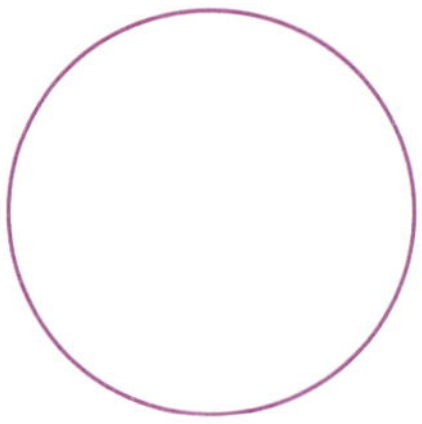

15 What is the length of the diameter of the circle?

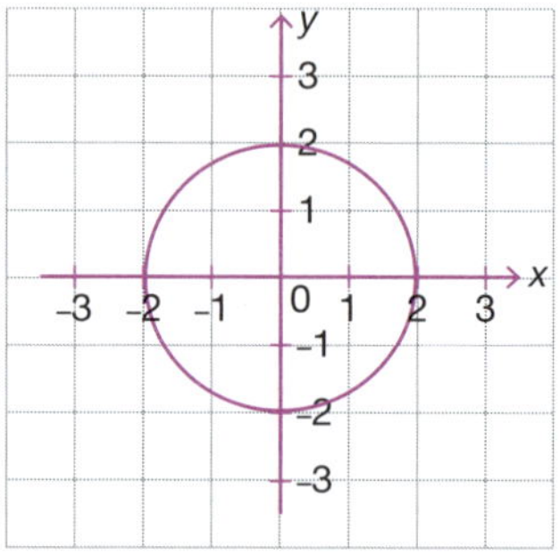

16 What is the size of the angle marked as *?

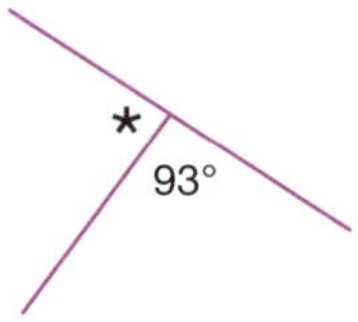

STATISTICS AND PROBABILITY

17 The probability of selecting a black ball from this box is 0.2. Shade the correct number of black balls.

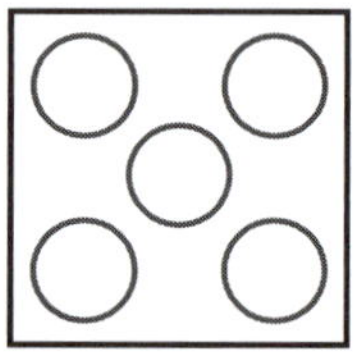

18 The table shows favourite summer holiday activities. Complete the table.

	Beach	Pool	Movies	Total
Males	13	10	11	
Females	17	15	8	40
Total	30			74

NUMBER AND ALGEBRA

1 Here are some consecutive triangular numbers: 820, 861, 903, 946, ...

What is the next number?

2 On a number line, what two numbers are 4 units from −6?

3 An egg farmer has 13 152 eggs to be packed into cartons that hold a dozen eggs. How many cartons will be used?

4 What fraction of the positive numbers less than 15 are prime?

5 $1\frac{1}{4} - \frac{3}{4} =$

6 $25 \times 3.871 \times 4 =$

7 Express $\frac{13}{20}$ as a percentage.

8 At a sale at Lyndon's Pool Shop, the prices of pool equipment are discounted by 5%. What is the saving on a chlorinator priced at $1680?

9 Here is a pattern of three shapes made of dots.

Which shape is made from 45 dots?

10 What is the product of 5 and the sum of 1.5 and 4.5?

MEASUREMENT AND SPACE

11 A rectangle has dimensions 1.75 m by 94 cm. What is the perimeter, in metres?

12 Rewrite these capacities from least to greatest.

4050 mL 4.15 L 0.005 kL 4 L

13 A train timetable is shown. The train is held up for 36 min between Richmond and Oakland. If 19 minutes had been made up by the time it arrived in Stockton, what was the arrival time?

Richmond	10:17 am
Oakland	11:21 pm
Antioch	12:53 pm
Stockton	2:11 pm

14 On the circle, draw and identify a segment and a sector.

15 Draw a circle on the number plane with centre at (3, −3) and radius 2 units.

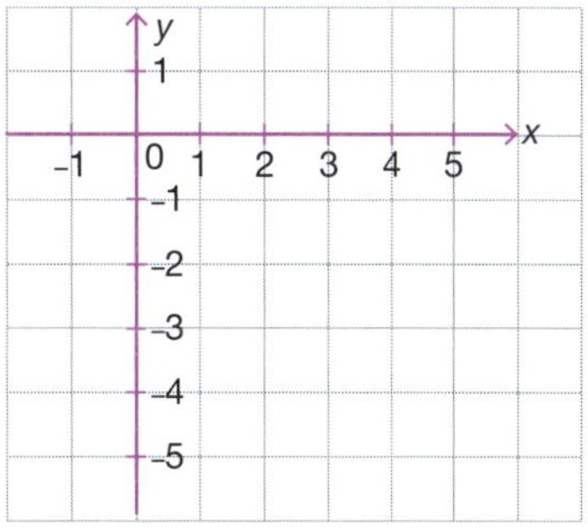

16 What is the value of x?

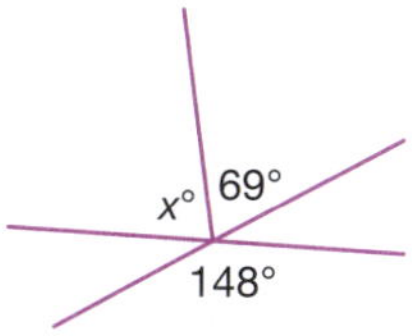

STATISTICS AND PROBABILITY

17 The probability of selecting a black ball from this box is 80%. Shade the correct number of black balls.

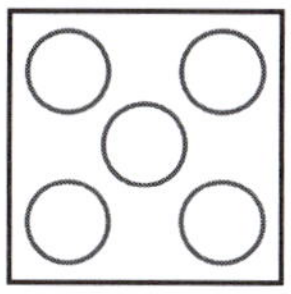

18 The table shows favourite summer holiday activities. Complete the table.

	Beach	Pool	Movies	Total
Males	10	11		28
Females	9		8	
Total				50

NUMBER AND ALGEBRA

1 What is the difference between 10^2 and 8^2?

2 What is the difference between P and Q?

3 A fun run had 65 000 starters. At the end of the run, only 61 400 had finished. How many starters did **not** finish the fun run?

4 Ava buys a dozen eggs and uses three in a recipe. What fraction of eggs has she used?

5 Find the missing number:

$\frac{4}{5} + \frac{3}{5} = 1\frac{\square}{5}$

6 A syndicate of 100 people share a lotto win. If the prize was $238 735, about how much will each person receive, to the nearest dollar?

7 What is 50% of 160?

8 A hardware store claims it will beat any competitor's price by 10%. If Shelby can buy a bag of fertiliser for $14.50 at another store, what discount will be given by this hardware store?

9 Here is a pattern of three shapes made of matchsticks.

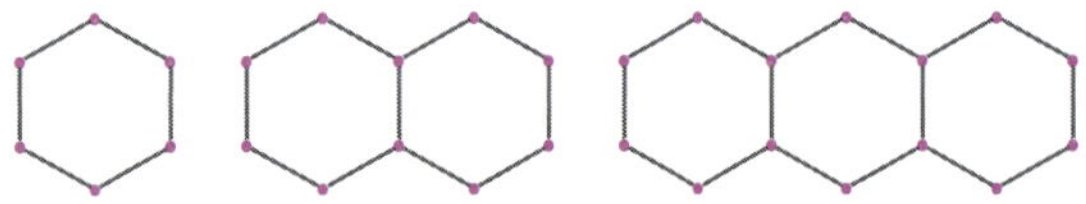

How many matchsticks would be used to make the fifth shape in the pattern?

10 What is 80 – 9 – 9 – 9 – 9 – 9?

MEASUREMENT AND SPACE

11 How many kilometres are in 3 650 000 mm?

12 A tin of olive oil in the shape of a rectangular prism is 15 cm long by 10 cm wide and 20 cm tall. What is the capacity of the tin, in litres?

13 Part of a bus timetable is shown. All buses throughout the day travel at the same speed. What time does the second bus arrive in Malaga?

Landsdale	1117	1423
Malaga	1156	?
Bayswater	1221	?
Midland	1254	?

14 A circle has a radius of $2\frac{1}{2}$ cm. What is the diameter of the circle?

15 Complete: The triangle has been translated .... units down and .... units right.

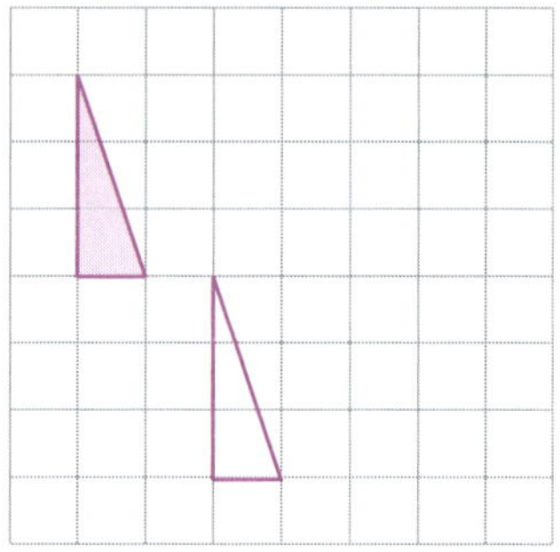

16 What is the size of the angle marked as *?

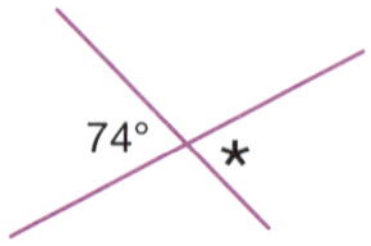

STATISTICS AND PROBABILITY

17 The table shows the quiz results of students. If a student is chosen at random, what is the probability that they scored 7?

Quiz results	7	8	9	10
No. of students	3	9	8	4

18 The table shows the number of students in two high-school year groups. Complete the table.

	Year 7	**Year 8**	**Total**
Males	78	80	
Females	79	85	164
Total	157		322

NUMBER AND ALGEBRA

1 Coen wrote the first 20 square numbers bigger than zero. Here are the first four numbers: 1, 4, 9, 16. What is the sum of Coen's tenth and twentieth numbers?

2 What is the difference between the temperatures −4 °C and −9 °C?

3 Subtract six million two hundred and three thousand from five billion.

4 Jacob starts a 16-km fun run. After 20 min he has completed $\frac{1}{4}$ of the course. What distance has Jacob yet to complete?

5 Find the missing number:
$\frac{3}{8} + \frac{11}{12} = 1\frac{\square}{24}$

6 The mass of a $2 coin is 6.6 g. Vihaan has $100 in two-dollar coins. What is the total mass of the coins?

7 Find 20% of 360.

8 In a toy sale the price of Lego is reduced by 20%. What will be saved on a box normally priced at $140?

9 Here is a pattern of three shapes made of matchsticks.

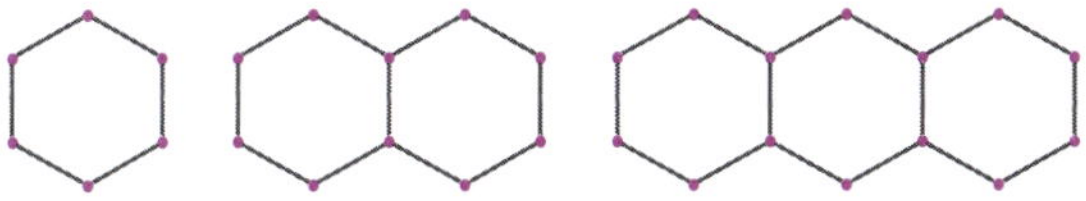

How many matchsticks would be used to make the tenth shape in the pattern?

10 What is the value of $16 + 13 + 13 + 13 + 13 + 13$?

MEASUREMENT AND SPACE

11 Convert 0.004 52 km to metres.

12 From a 2-litre bottle of soft drink, 320 mL is poured into each of five glasses. What amount of soft drink remains in the bottle?

13 Part of a bus timetable is shown.

Landsdale	1117	?
Malaga	1156	?
Bayswater	1221	?
Midland	1254	1407

All buses throughout the day travel at the same speed. What time does the second bus leave Landsdale?

14 The diameter of a circle is 15.07 cm long. What is the radius of the circle?

15 Translate the triangle 3 units to the right and 4 units down.

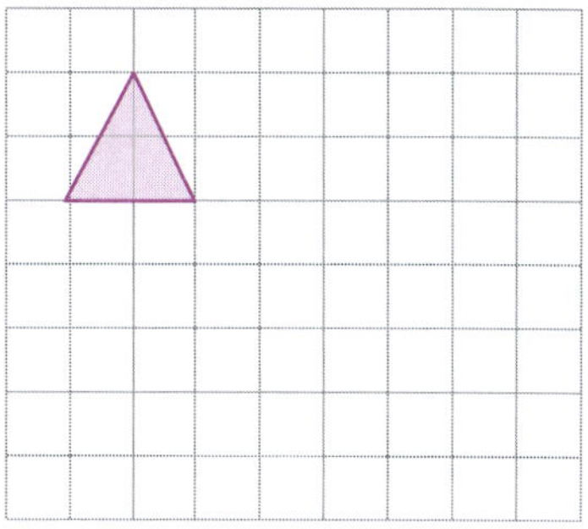

16 What is the value of x?

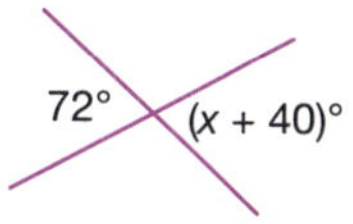

STATISTICS AND PROBABILITY

17 The table shows the quiz results of students. If a student is chosen at random, what is the probability that they scored at least 9?

Quiz results	7	8	9	10
No. of students	3	9	8	4

18 The table shows the number of students in two high-school year groups.

	Year 9	**Year 10**	**Total**
Males			160
Females	80		
Total		145	310

How many males are in Year 10?

NON-CALCULATOR

1 Michelle empties six jugs of milk into a large container.
Each jug contains 1.5 L.

She then uses the container to fill glasses.

Each glass holds 200 mL.

How many glasses can Michelle fill? [ ]

2 A fundraising dance costs $1600 to organise and tickets cost $20.

If 110 tickets are sold, how much profit is made? $ [ ]

3 The temperature at Mt Buller at 0630 was –3.5 °C.

By 1300 it had risen 7 degrees and by 1845 it had dropped 9 degrees.

What was the temperature at 1845?

A	B	C	D
1.5 °C	–1.5 °C	–4.5 °C	–5.5 °C

4 What is the missing number?

$$8 + 4 \times (2 + 3) - \square = 10$$

A	B	C	D
9	17	18	50

CALCULATOR ALLOWED

5 Which of these expressions has a value of 0.77?

A 0.077 × 100 B 0.000 077 × 1000 C 77 ÷ 100 D 7.7 ÷ 1000

6 For a limited time, a restaurant chain served soft drink in coloured glasses.
The table shows the first 50 glasses used.

Colour	Number
red	12
yellow	10
green	?
blue	8
purple	9

What percentage of the glasses were green? [ ] %

7 The cost of an adult ticket to the cinema is $16.

The cost of a child's ticket is three-quarters of the price of an adult ticket.

What is the cost of tickets for an adult and two children? $ ☐

8 The sum of the opposite faces on a standard dice is always 7.

Shirlee rolls five dice. The sum of the top faces was 16.

What is the sum of the five bottom faces? ☐

9 In Ms Dann's class today there are three empty chairs. When all her students are present, all the chairs are taken.

If 10% of the students are absent today, how many students make up her entire class? ☐

10 Denis is 5 years older than Justin. In 10 years, their combined ages will be 45.

How old is Justin now? ☐

11 Which of the following is closest to $\frac{1}{2}$?

$\frac{7}{12}$	$\frac{5}{6}$	$\frac{4}{9}$	$\frac{0}{1}$
A	B	C	D

12 Packets of small flags are on sale for Australia Day.

Packet A contains 5 flags for $12. Packet B contains 3 flags for $8.

Elise wants to buy 30 flags to decorate her front yard.

How much will she save if she buys Packet As instead of Packet Bs? $ ☐

13 Bill drives at an average speed of 90 km/h for 2 h 20 min.

What distance has Bill travelled? ☐ km

14 An empty swimming pool is being filled at the rate of 30 L per minute.

It takes 5 hours to fill the pool a quarter full.

How many litres does the pool hold when full? ☐ L

15 Sam is posting a Christmas present in a cardboard box that is a rectangular prism.

The net of the box is shown below.

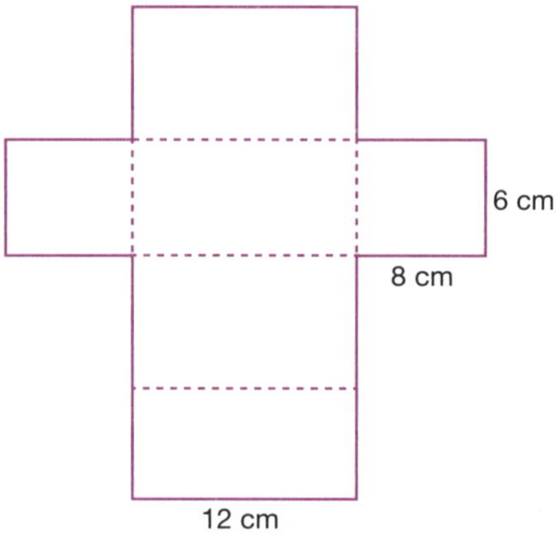

What is the area of cardboard, in square centimetres, required for Sam's box? $\square$ cm^2

16 Twenty students in a class brought cans of food to school to support a Winter Appeal.

The dot plot shows the number of cans brought in by the students.

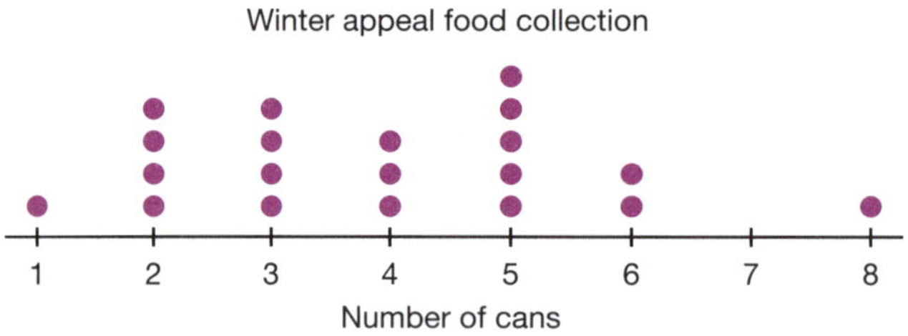

What was the total number of cans collected? $\square$

17 Which of the following describes the transformation of the original shape onto the image?

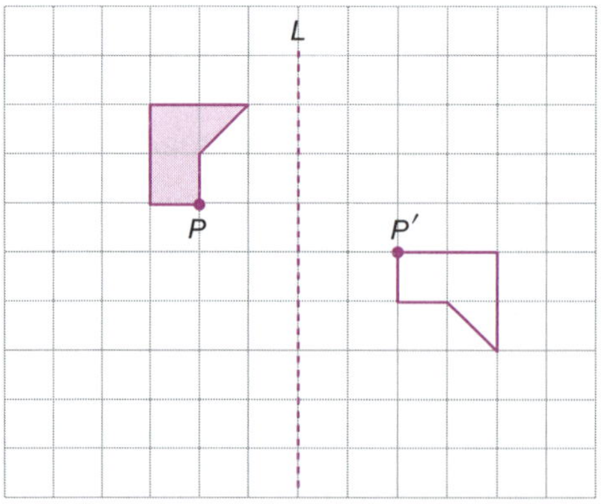

A Translate 5 units to right, then translate 2 units down.

B Reflect about line *L*, then translate 2 units down.

C Rotate 90° in a clockwise direction about *P*, then translate 1 unit down.

D Rotate 90° in a clockwise direction about *P*, translate 4 units right, then translate 1 unit down.

18 A box contains identically sized balls. There are 4 green, 6 yellow, 8 blue, 10 orange and 12 red balls in the box. A ball is chosen at random.

Which colour has a 0.25 probability of being chosen?

green	yellow	blue	orange	red
A	B	C	D	E

19 What is the value of x in this diagram?

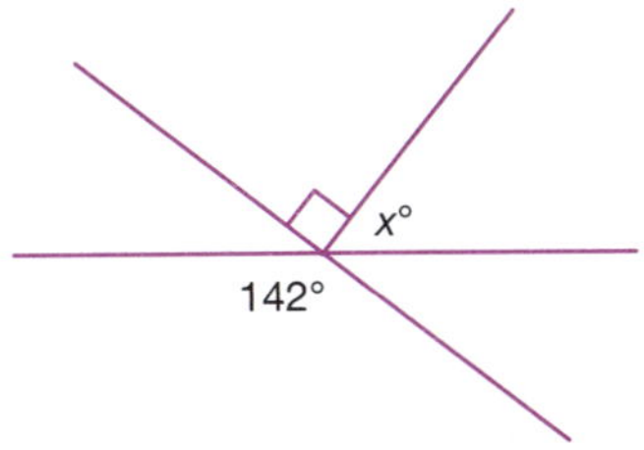

20 The square *ABCD* is drawn with dimensions shown. All dimensions are in centimetres.

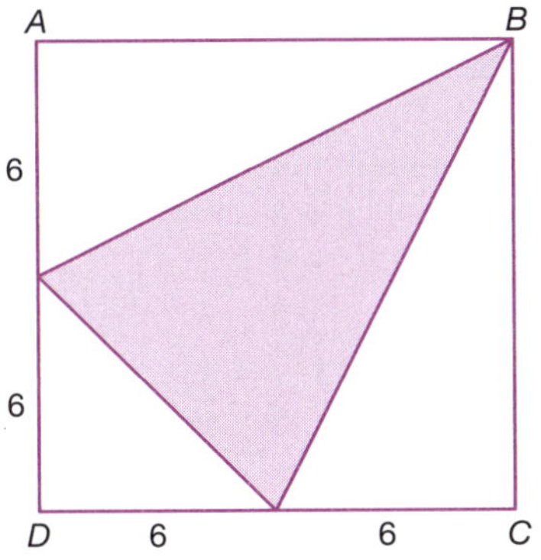

What is the area of the shaded triangle? ______ cm^2

NUMBER AND ALGEBRA

1 What factors of 100 are square numbers?

2 What is the difference between *A* and *B*?

3 What is the product of 74, 5 and 2?

4 Complete the equivalent fractions:

$\frac{12}{15} = \frac{\square}{5}$

5 When a party ended, there was still $\frac{5}{24}$ of the cake uneaten. Grandma took $\frac{1}{12}$ of the original cake home. What fraction of the cake remained?

6 A box of muesli has a mass of 0.825 kg. What is the total mass of 100 boxes?

7 Brett is flying 750 km between two towns. He has flown 10% of the distance. How far has he flown?

8 All jewellery is discounted by 50% at an 'End of Year Sale'. Daniel buys a necklace for his wife and pays $645. What was the normal price of the necklace?

9 Find the missing number in this sequence.

10, 3, ☐, −11, −18

10 Find the value of 43 − (17 + 15).

MEASUREMENT AND SPACE

11

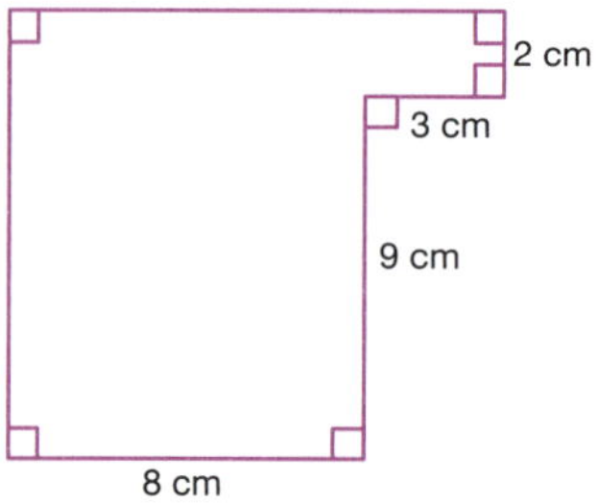

Find the area of the shape.

12 A box of cereal has a mass of 420 g. The side panel on the box advises there are 10 servings in the box. What is the mass of each serving?

13 Part of a bus timetable is shown. All buses throughout the day travel at the same speed. What time does the second bus arrive in Vista?

Ventura	1036	1227
Riverside	1108	?
Vista	1147	?
Pine Valley	1225	?

14 What is the name of a sector which has an angle of 90°.

15 Complete: The shape has been translated .... units left and .... units down.

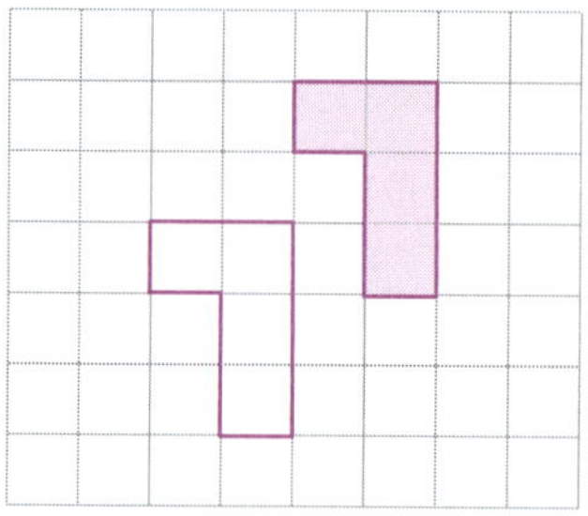

16 What is the size of the angle marked as *?

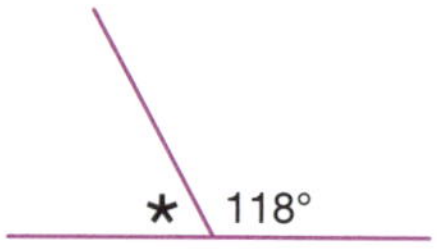

STATISTICS AND PROBABILITY

17 The spinner is spun 24 times. What is the expected number of times it lands on 1?

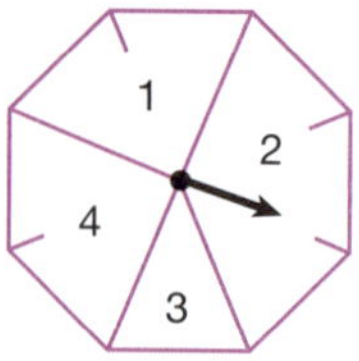

18 The table shows students' eye colour. Complete the table.

	Brown	Blue	Other	Total
Males	38	6	6	
Females	32	4		
Total				100

NUMBER AND ALGEBRA

1 What is the sum of the first five positive square numbers?

2 What is the difference between the temperatures 8 °C and −3 °C?

3 A carton holds 36 boxes of tissues. Each box contains 100 tissues. How many tissues are contained in 24 cartons?

4 Complete: $2\frac{6}{8} = \frac{\square}{4}$

5 Josh and Nora are sharing the driving on their road trip north, planning to stop exactly halfway overnight. During the first day Josh drove $\frac{3}{4}$ of the distance. On the second day he drove $\frac{1}{5}$ of the distance. Who drove the greater distance across the two days?

6 Find the value of $17 \div 10^2$.

7 In a survey of 60 students, 40% of students said they had flown overseas. What number of students had **not** flown overseas?

8 All luggage is reduced in price by 30% in a sale. A carry-on bag is usually priced at $130. What will be the new price?

9 Find the tenth number in this sequence

16, 13, 10, 7 …

10 Find the value of $17 - (16 - 72 \div 6)$.

MEASUREMENT AND SPACE

11 Find the area of the shape.

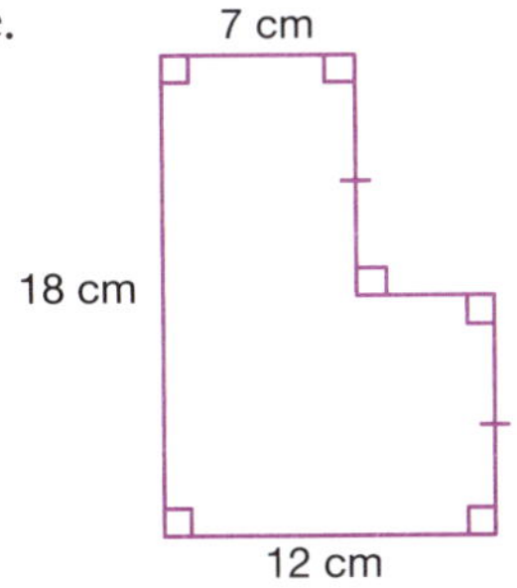

12 A machine pours 240 mL of juice every 4 s. How many litres of juice does the machine pour every minute?

13 Part of a bus timetable is shown. All buses throughout the day travel at the same speed. What time does the second bus leave Ventura?

Ventura	1036	?
Riverside	1108	?
Vista	1147	?
Pine Valley	1225	1503

14 A circle is cut into 12 equal sectors. What is the size of each sector's angle?

15 Translate the shape 2 units left and rotate 90° anticlockwise at the point *X*.

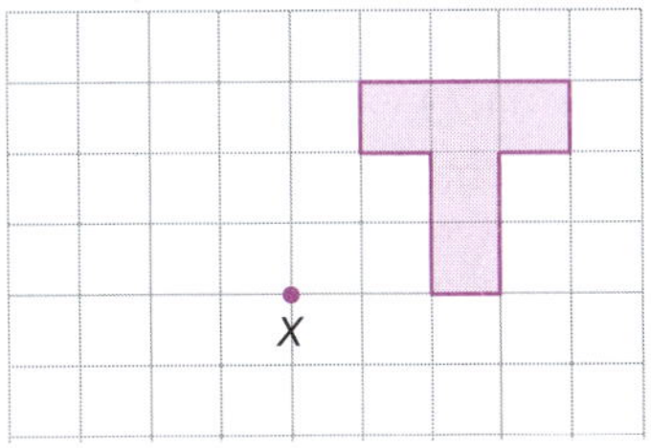

16 What is the value of *x*?

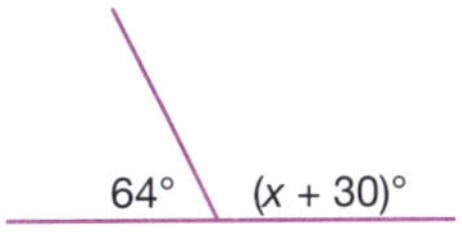

STATISTICS AND PROBABILITY

17 The probability of spinning 1 or 2 is the same. The probability of 4 is three times as likely as 3. Use this information to label the spinner.

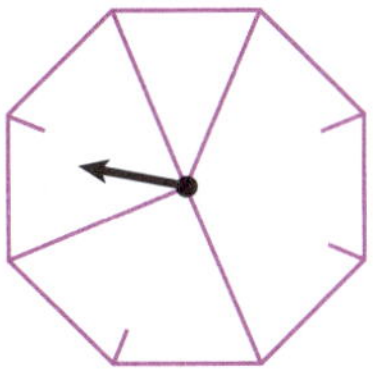

18 The table shows students' eye colour.

	Brown	Blue	Other	Total
Males			2	
Females	43	6	3	
Total		10		100

What percentage of the students were brown-eyed males?

NUMBER AND ALGEBRA

1 Circle the numbers that are factors of 48.

3 9 12 20

2 Put a cross (**X**) on the number which is 5 less than 2.

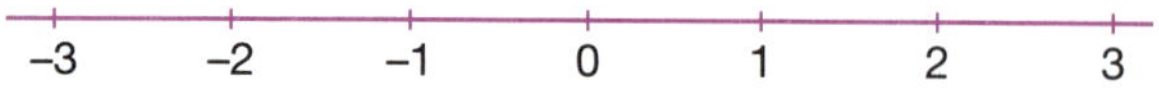

3 Luke travelled 675 km in 9 h. What is his average speed in km/h?

4 Complete the equivalent fractions:

$\frac{18}{24} = \frac{\square}{4}$

5 Subtract the sum of $\frac{2}{7}$ and $\frac{3}{7}$ from one whole.

6 What is the sum of 4.76 + 34.9 + 0.023, to the nearest tenth?

7 From a carton of a dozen eggs, Geoff used three eggs for an omelette. What percentage of the eggs has been used?

8 In a sale, the price of a $4200 lounge drops by 25%. What is the amount of the discount?

9 Here is a pattern of three shapes made of dots.

How many dots would be in the sixth shape?

10 What is $\frac{12 + 16}{4}$?

MEASUREMENT AND SPACE

11 What is the perimeter of a rectangular paddock with side lengths of 482 m and 391 m?

12 A box of crackers has a mass of 170 g. What is the total mass of 30 boxes, in kilograms?

13 A bus timetable is shown.

Rocklea	1418	1601	1713
Taringa	1453	1636	1748
Coorinda	1516	1659	1811
Camira	1531	1714	1826

Heath needs to catch a bus to arrive at Camira before 6 pm. What is the latest he can leave Rocklea?

14 The radius of the circle is 12 cm. Which of these is the best estimate for the length of chord *AB*?

20 cm 24 cm 28 cm

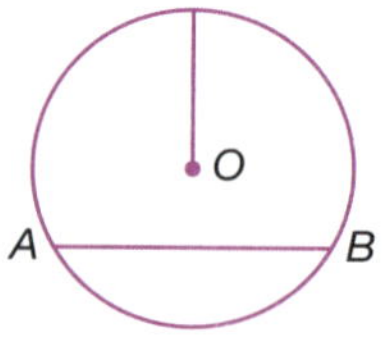

15 Reflect the shape in the line *L*.

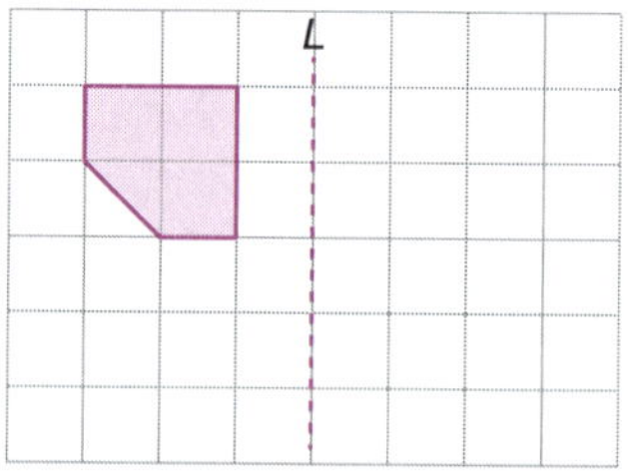

16 What is the size of the angle marked as *?

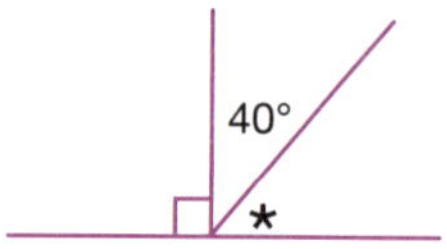

STATISTICS AND PROBABILITY

17 The weather forecast says there is an 80% probability of rain on Sunday. What is the probability of no rain?

18 The table shows the number of shapes in a box of blocks. Complete the table.

	Red	Green	Blue	Yellow	Total
Prisms	8	7		8	
Cylinders		3	7		20
Total	14				50

NUMBER AND ALGEBRA

1 A bag contains between 40 and 50 lollies. The lollies can be shared equally between 3 boys or 5 girls. Exactly how many lollies are in the bag?

2 Put a cross (**X**) on the number which is 10 less than 4.

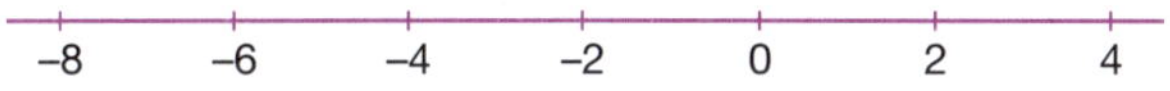

3 Chloe's plane took off at 8 am and flew north for 7740 km. If she arrived at her destination at 5 pm, what was the average speed of the plane?

4 What are the missing numbers?

$\frac{20}{80} = \frac{\square}{20} = \frac{1}{\square}$

5 Dylan filled a bucket of water. He spilled $\frac{1}{10}$ of the water as he walked across his lawn. He poured $\frac{2}{3}$ of a bucket of water around a shrub. What fraction of the water remained in the bucket?

6 What is the difference between 87.05 and 31.861, to the nearest tenth?

7 There are 20 students in a class. 70% of the students have brought their lunch from home today. How many students have **not** brought lunch from home?

8 The price of a T-shirt is $20. If the price is to be discounted by 20%, how much will Steve pay for five T-shirts?

9 Here is a pattern of three shapes made of dots.

How many dots would be in the 30th shape?

10 What is $\frac{60 - 12 \times 3}{4 + 4}$?

MEASUREMENT AND SPACE

11 A rectangular paddock has an area of 2 ha. If the width of the paddock is 80 m, what is the length?

12 A can of tomatoes has a mass of 410 g. In one week, a supermarket sells 15 cartons of cans of tomatoes. If each carton holds 12 cans, what is the total mass sold?

13 A bus timetable is shown. Skye arrived at the Taringa bus stop at 4:45 pm. What is the earliest she can arrive in Coorinda?

Rocklea	1418	1601	1713
Taringa	1453	1636	1748
Coorinda	1516	1659	1811
Camira	1531	1714	1826

14 The shaded sector *AOB* is shown on the circle. If the area of the circle is 24 cm^2, what is the area *AOB*?

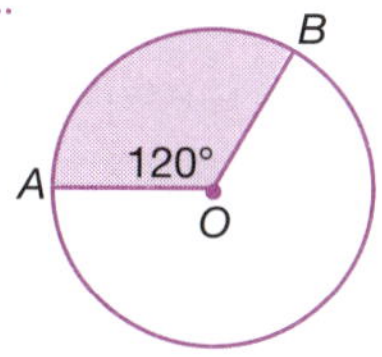

15 Reflect the shape in the line L_1, then in L_2.

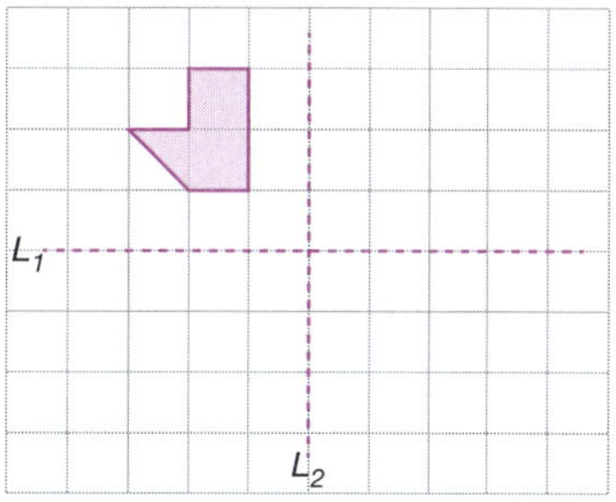

16 What is the value of *x*?

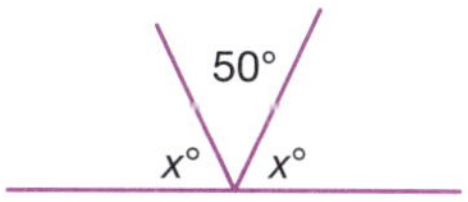

STATISTICS AND PROBABILITY

17 In a bag of balls, half are red and a third are yellow. The rest of the balls are green. If a ball is chosen at random, what is the probability that it is green?

18 The table shows the number of shapes in a box of blocks. What fraction of the blocks are cylinders?

	Red	Green	Blue	Yellow
Prisms	9	6	8	9
Cylinders	5	4	5	4

NUMBER AND ALGEBRA

1 What is the largest number that is a factor of 16 and 40?

2 Put a cross (**X**) on the number 4 more than –3.

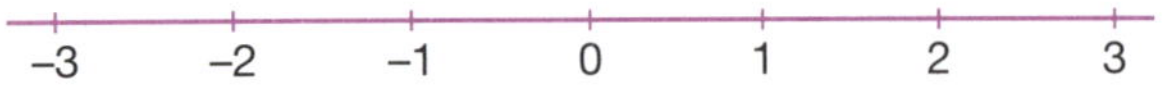

3 Find 26 780 ÷ 5.

4 Reduce $\frac{10}{12}$ to its simplest form.

5 A jug contains $\frac{1}{4}$ L of juice. Another $\frac{1}{2}$ L of juice is added to the jug. What amount of juice is now in the jug?

6 What is the average of 6, 8, 3 and 4, written as a decimal?

7 There are 5000 spectators at a footy match. Only 10% of the spectators support the Tigers. How many Tigers supporters are at the game?

8 A coffee shop offers a Seniors Discount of 10% on all drinks. A regular cappuccino usually costs $5. How much will a senior save if she orders a cappuccino each morning for 5 days?

9 Here is a pattern of three shapes made of matchsticks.

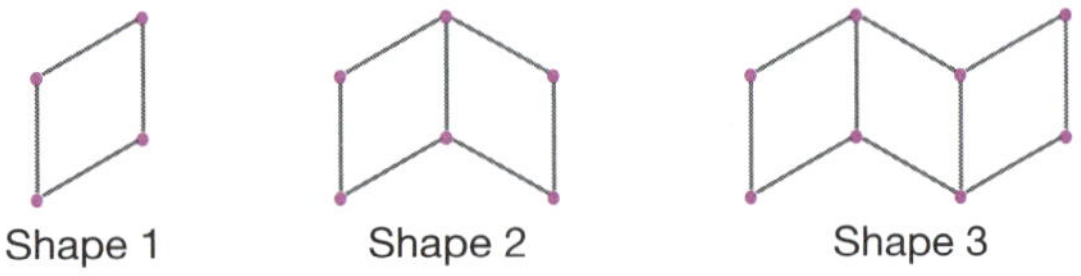

How many matchsticks would be used to make the sixth shape in the pattern?

10 Find the value of $6^2 - 3 \times 8 + 5$.

MEASUREMENT AND SPACE

11 Find the area of the triangle.

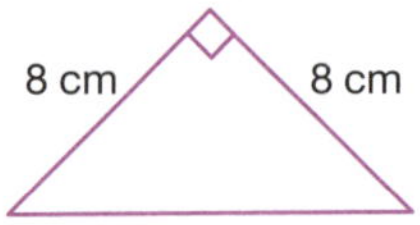

12 Six students are following the same cake recipe. If each cake requires 125 g of butter, what is the total amount of butter used, in kilograms?

13 A bus timetable is shown. Samantha needs to catch a bus to arrive at Chesterton before 4 pm. What is the latest she can leave Hammond?

Aurora	1217	1348	1501
Hammond	1255	1426	1539
Shorewood	1329	1500	1613
Chesterton	1402	1533	1646

14 What solid is formed using this net?

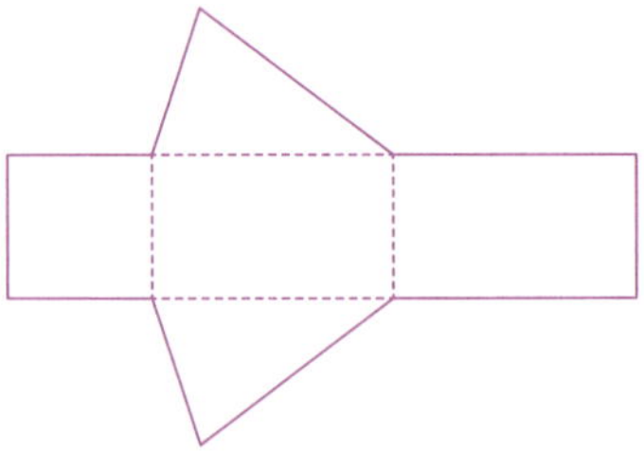

15 Translate the shape 2 units to the right and then reflect it in line *L*.

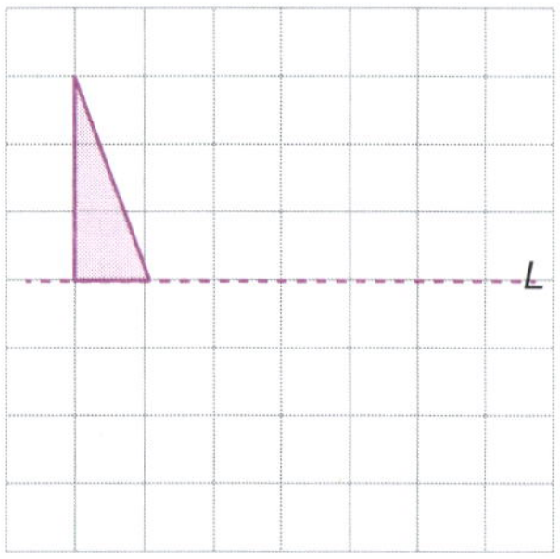

16 What is the size of the angle marked as *?

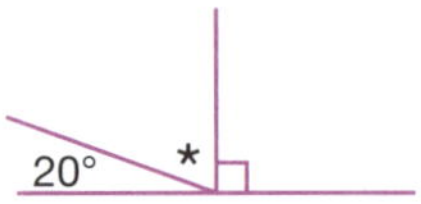

STATISTICS AND PROBABILITY

17 A ball is chosen at random from a box. What is the probability, as a percentage, the ball is white?

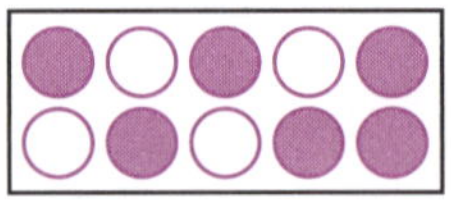

18 The table shows the favourite overseas holiday destinations of a group of people. What was the total number of people who selected Asia or Africa?

	America	Europe	Asia	Africa
Women	10	17	8	5
Men	16	11	6	7

NUMBER AND ALGEBRA

1 Here are four numbers. Circle those numbers that are composite.

425 173 681 8009

2 Put a cross (**X**) on the number 6 more than −10.

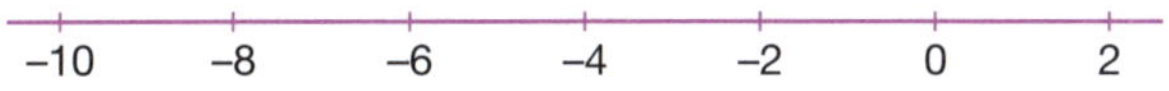

3 At an assembly, students are arranged into 26 groups of 15 students. If there are nine students left over, how many students are at the assembly?

4 Reduce $\frac{45}{135}$ to its simplest form.

5 On a cruise ship, $\frac{1}{4}$ of the passengers are men and $\frac{1}{3}$ are children. What fraction of the passengers are women?

6 The temperatures (in Celsius) at noon on five consecutive days were 21.7°, 23.9°, 18.4°, 22.5° and 27.2°. What was the average temperature?

7 Aria has read 75% of the 240 pages in her novel. How many pages has she yet to read?

8 A restaurant offers a 20% discount on all meals every Tuesday. If six people ordered meals priced at $30 each, what will be saved by dining on Tuesday instead of Thursday?

9 Here is a pattern of three shapes made of matchsticks.

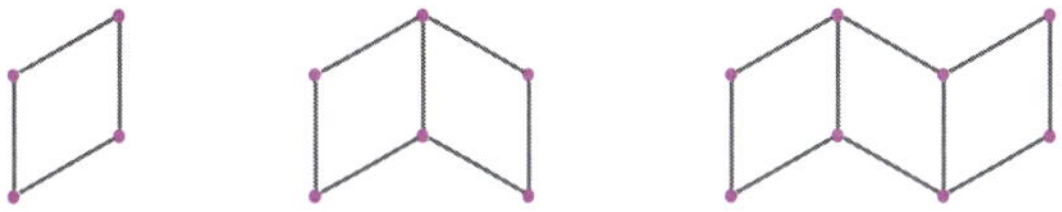

How many matchsticks would be used to make the 12th shape in the pattern?

10 Find the value of $(4 + 3 \times 2)^2$.

MEASUREMENT AND SPACE

11 A right-angled triangle has side lengths 5 cm, 12 cm and 13 cm. What is the area of the triangle?

12 How many grams are in 6 tonnes?

13 A bus timetable is shown. Caleb arrived at the Aurora bus stop at 2:25 pm. What is the earliest he can arrive in Shorewood?

Aurora	1217	1348	1501
Hammond	1255	1426	1539
Shorewood	1329	1500	1613
Chesterton	1402	1533	1646

14 What solid is formed using this net?

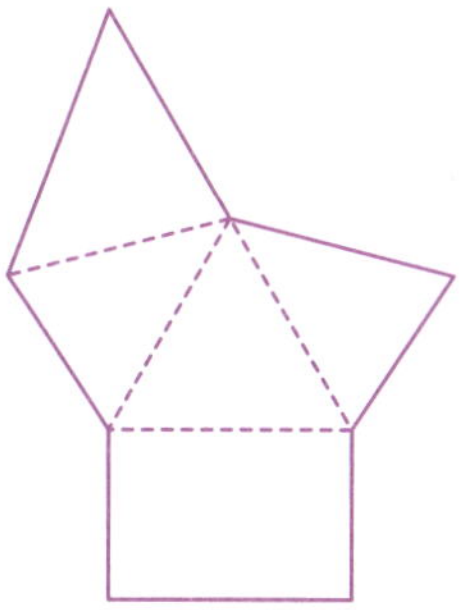

15 What are the two transformations used?

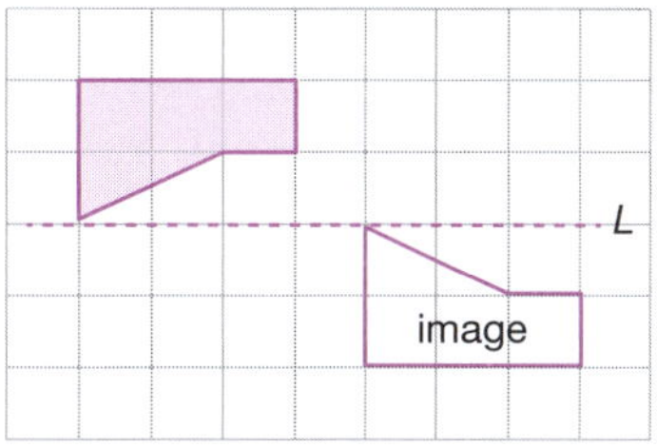

16 What is the value of x?

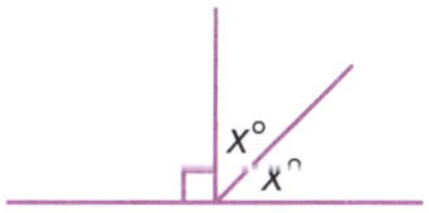

STATISTICS AND PROBABILITY

17 The probability of choosing a black ball from a box of 10 balls is 50% and choosing a white ball is 30%. The remaining balls are shaded. Represent this on a diagram.

18 The table shows the favourite overseas holiday destinations of a group of people. What fraction of women selected Asia?

	America	Europe	Asia	Africa
Women	10	17	8	5
Men	16	11	6	7

NUMBER AND ALGEBRA

1 What is the smallest prime number larger than 32?

2 What is the combined effect of riding a lift down three floors and then up five floors?

3 How many seconds are in 3 h?

4 Complete the equivalent fractions:

$\frac{2}{3} = \frac{\square}{12}$

5 Pavel trained for $2\frac{1}{2}$ h on Wednesday and $1\frac{1}{4}$ h on Thursday. What is the total amount of training in the two days?

6 Last week Amanda earned $386.70 and this week she earned $438.15. How much more did she earn this week compared to last week?

7 When full, a water tank has a capacity of 12 000 L. If the tank is 25% full of water, how much water is in the tank?

8 Members of a golf club receive a 20% discount on all purchases from the golf shop. What will be saved on the purchase of a golf set priced at $1470?

9 Here is a pattern of three shapes made of dots. How many dots would be in the sixth shape?

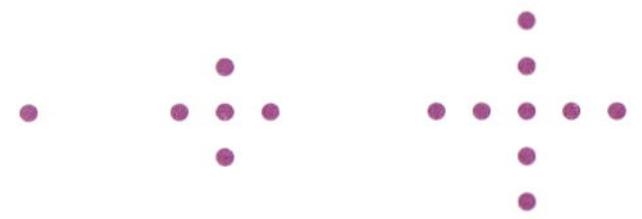

10 Andrew is playing a game. He has 6753 points and is given another 500 bonus points. How many points away is he from scoring 10 000 points?

MEASUREMENT AND SPACE

11 What is the perimeter of the rectangle?

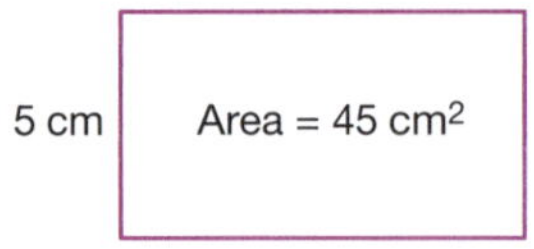

12 An egg producer has 2400 eggs with an average mass of 70 g. What is the total mass of the eggs?

13 A bus timetable is shown. Jane needs to catch a bus to arrive at Nulkaba before 3:40 pm. What is the latest she can leave Fletcher?

Fletcher	1226	1407	1653
Chisholm	1254	1435	1721
Cliftleigh	1333	1514	1800
Nulkaba	1401	1542	1828

14 What solid is formed using this net?

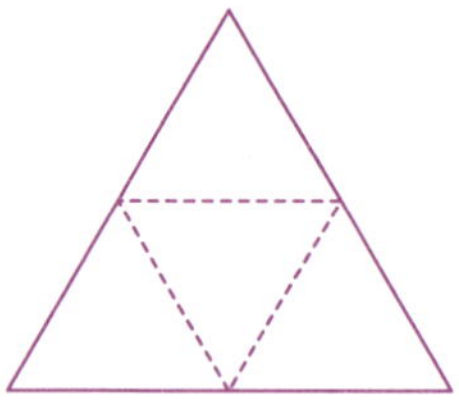

15 Reflect the shape in line L and then translate 3 units to the right.

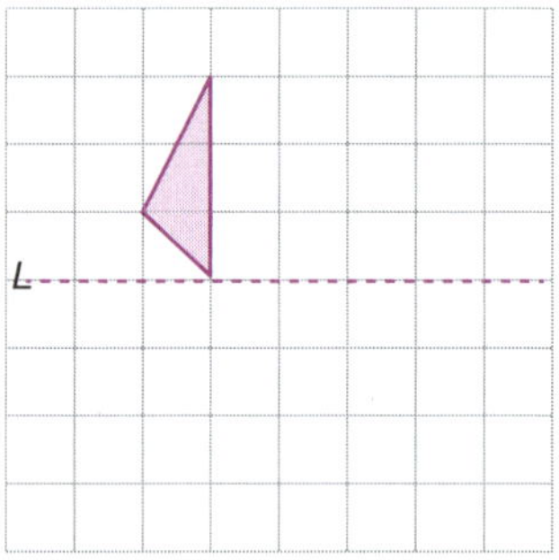

16 What is the size of the angle marked as *?

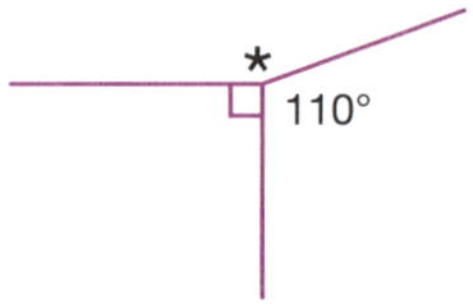

STATISTICS AND PROBABILITY

17 A raffle has 100 numbered tickets. Sam buys one ticket. What is the probability that his ticket is the winning ticket?

18 The table shows students' favourite science strand.

	Physics	Chemistry	Biology	Earth
Females	12	10	18	10
Males	14	12	16	8

How many more students selected Biology than the number who selected Physics?

NUMBER AND ALGEBRA

1 Sharlene wants to make a square using rectangular cards that measure 6 cm by 4 cm. What is the smallest number of cards she needs?

2 What is the combined effect of a temperature fall of 10 °C and then a rise of 3 °C?

3 Ella was born at midday on 15 June. How many hours had she lived by midday on 15 October?

4 What fraction is in the middle of $\frac{1}{2}$ and $\frac{3}{5}$?

5 On her three javelin throws, Layla threw a total distance of 64 m. For her first two throws she threw $21\frac{1}{2}$ m and $27\frac{1}{4}$ m. How far did she throw on her third attempt?

6 What is 4.5 ÷ 1000?

7 Noah usually cycles 120 km each week. Next week he plans to increase the distance by 20%. How far does Noah plan to ride?

8 A coat is priced at $180. What is the reduced price if it is sold at a discount of 15%?

9 Here is a pattern of three shapes made of dots. Which shape would be made from 37 dots?

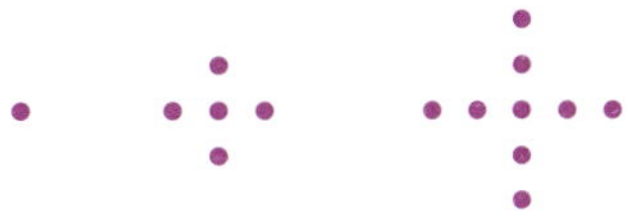

10 Thor has five discs with a mass of 8 kg each and three discs with a mass of 12 kg each. What is the average mass of the discs?

MEASUREMENT AND SPACE

11 What is the area of the rectangle?

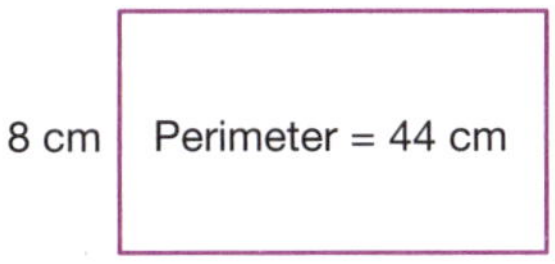

12 Change 7.2 gigalitres into kilolitres.

13 A bus timetable is shown. Ely arrives at the Chisholm bus stop at 2:23 pm. What is the earliest he can arrive in Nulkaba?

Fletcher	1226	1407	1653
Chisholm	1254	1435	1721
Cliftleigh	1333	1514	1800
Nulkaba	1401	–	1828

14 What solid is formed using this net?

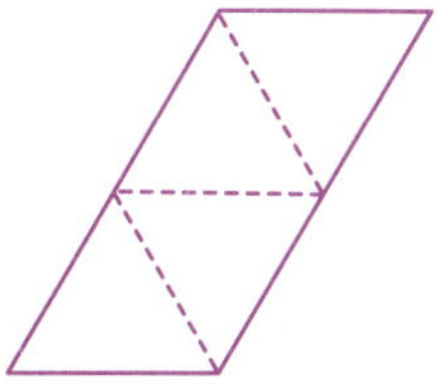

15 What are the two transformations used?

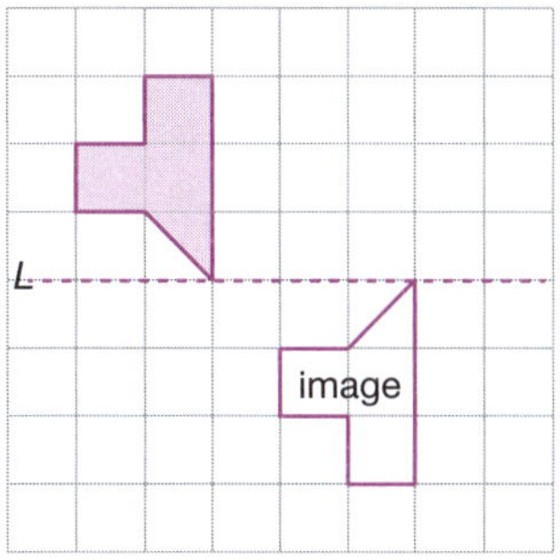

16 What is the value of x?

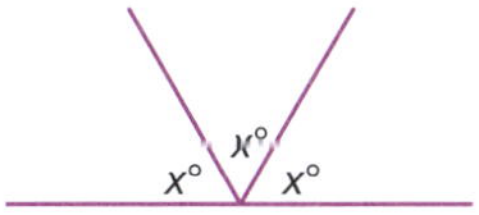

STATISTICS AND PROBABILITY

17 A raffle has 100 numbered tickets. Sam buys five tickets. What is the probability that he wins first prize expressed as a decimal?

18 The table shows students' favourite science strand.

	Physics	Chemistry	Biology	Earth
Females	12	10	18	10
Males	14	12	16	8

What percentage of students selected Chemistry?

NUMBER AND ALGEBRA

1 What is the 10th prime number?

2 What is the combined effect of travelling 3 km north then 7 km south?

3 ☐ ÷ 8 = 7264

4 What fraction of an hour is 12 minutes?

5 $\frac{3}{8} +$ ☐ $= 1$

6 Three friends had a restaurant meal which cost a total of $220.20. They decided to split the bill evenly. How much did each person pay?

7 In his maths quiz, Grayson scored 16 marks out of 20. What is this result as a percentage?

8 An outdoor setting originally priced at $2000 is discounted by $200. What is the discount as a percentage of the original price?

9 Here is a pattern of three shapes made of matchsticks. How many matchsticks would be used to make the fifth shape in the pattern?

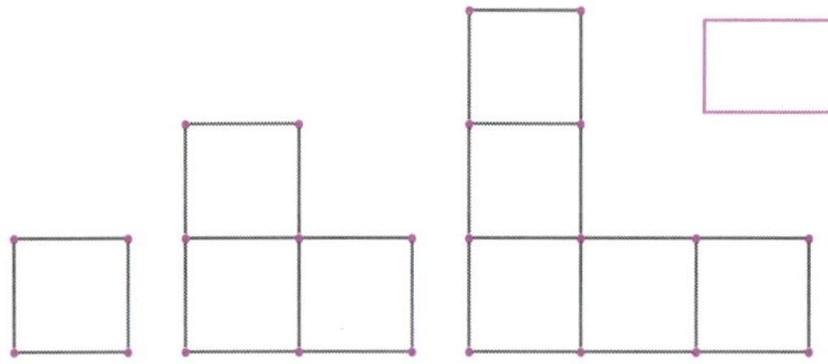

10 Find $1 - (\frac{1}{2} + \frac{1}{3})$.

MEASUREMENT AND SPACE

11 The perimeter of a square is 24 cm. The diagram shows three of the squares joined to make a new shape. What is the perimeter of the new shape?

12 Chapman Valley Horse Riding Centre requires no rider to weigh more than one-fifth of the mass of a horse. Glory has a mass of 520 kg. What is the maximum weight of a person who can ride him?

13 A bus timetable is shown. Jamal needs to catch a bus to arrive at Bethany before 1:20 pm. What is the latest he can leave Weston, in 12-hour time?

Weston	0953	1118	1502
Lawson	–	1213	1557
Bethany	1141	1328	1712
Davis City	1255	–	1826

14 How many diagonals in a rectangle are also lines of symmetry?

15 Rotate the shape 90° clockwise about O.

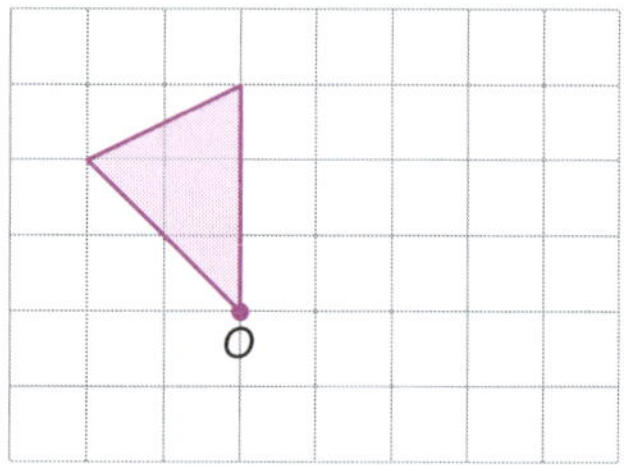

16 What is the size of the angle marked as *?

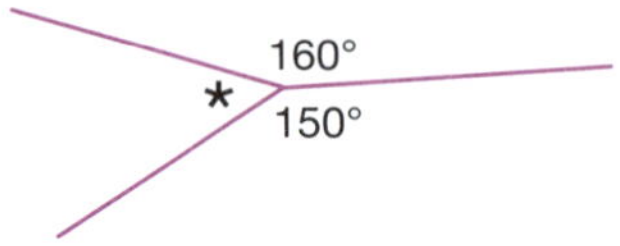

STATISTICS AND PROBABILITY

17 Here are some balls. If a ball is chosen at random, what is the probability it is **not** black?

18 The table shows the fruit packed in students' lunchboxes today.

	Banana	Apple	Mandarin	Grapes
Females	9	8	6	4
Males	6	7	5	5

How many more students had a banana than had a mandarin?

NUMBER AND ALGEBRA

1 Lee used rectangular prisms measuring 4 cm by 3 cm by 2 cm to make a cube. What was the number of prisms used to make the smallest possible cube?

2 What is the combined effect of winning $10, losing $15 and then losing $20?

3 $\square \div 34 = 5712$

4 What fraction of a day is 15 hours?

5 $\square + \frac{2}{3} = 1\frac{1}{6}$

6 Ely mailed two packages. One package had a mass of 1.86 kg, and the second weighed half as much as the first package. What was the total mass of the two packages?

7 On his retirement, the father of three girls decided to give a total of $100 000 to his daughters. He gave $36 500 to Hannah and $28 500 to Audrey. If the remainder was given to Mila, what percentage of the total amount did Mila receive?

8 To calculate the amount of discount he will receive when buying a floor rug, Jack divided the original price by 10 and then multiplied the answer by 4. What is the percentage discount?

9 Here is a pattern of three shapes made of matchsticks. Which shape would be made using 52 matchsticks?

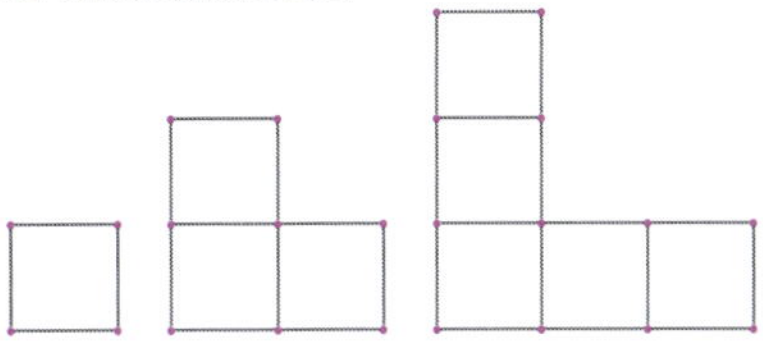

10 Find the value of $2\frac{1}{2} - (1\frac{1}{2} + \frac{1}{4})$.

MEASUREMENT AND SPACE

11 The diagram shows four squares joined to make a new shape. The area of each square is 100 cm^2. What is the perimeter of the new shape?

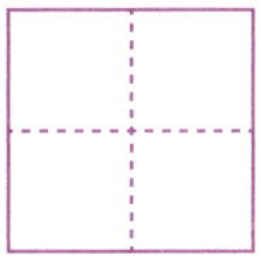

12 There are 240 passengers on a flight from Melbourne to Tokyo. The average mass of each passenger's check-in baggage is 22.1 kg. What is the total mass of check-in baggage?

13 A bus timetable is shown. Françoise arrives at the Lawson bus stop at 9:30 am. What is the earliest she can arrive at Davis City, in 12-hour time?

Weston	0953	1118	1502
Lawson	–	1213	1557
Bethany	1141	1328	1712
Davis City	1255	–	1826

14 How many diagonals in a regular octagon are also lines of symmetry?

15 Rotate the shape 90° clockwise about *O* and then translate 1 unit down.

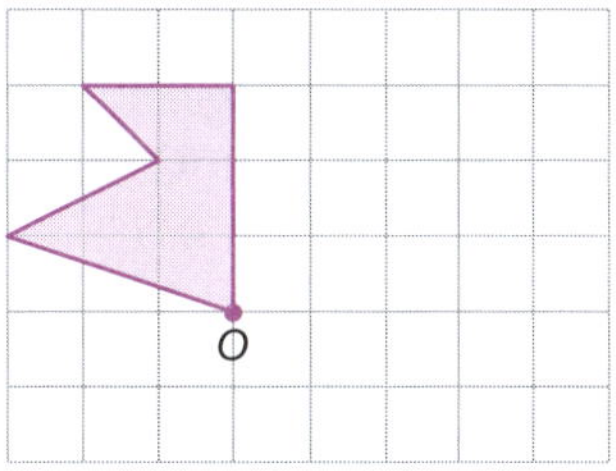

16 What is the value of *x*?

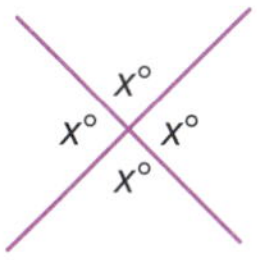

STATISTICS AND PROBABILITY

17 Here are some balls. If a ball is chosen at random, what is the probability, as a percentage, that it is black?

18 The table shows the fruit packed in students' lunchboxes today. What percentage of students had packed an apple?

	Banana	Apple	Mandarin	Grapes
Females	9	8	6	4
Males	6	7	5	5

NUMBER AND ALGEBRA

1 How many composite numbers are between 7 and 19?

2 The arrows on the number line are used to write a number sentence. Complete the number sentence:

4 + ... = ...

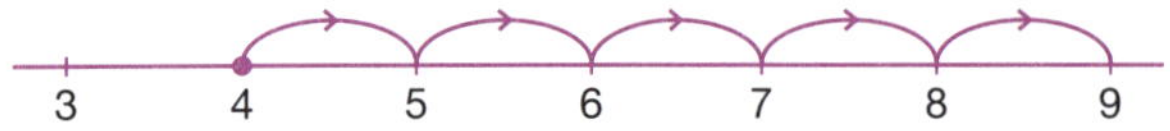

3 Sebastian is 12 years old. His father is 44 and his grandfather is 67. What is the average age of the three males?

4 By changing these fractions to eighths, rewrite them from smallest to largest:

$\frac{5}{8}$ $\frac{1}{2}$ $\frac{3}{4}$

5 ☐ $- \frac{7}{10} = \frac{3}{10}$

6 The temperature at Gundagai at 7 am was 3.6 °C. By 2 pm it had risen by 18.8 °C, and then by 5 pm it had dropped by another 11.9 °C. What was the temperature at 5 pm?

7 Arthur had 48 marbles and gave 25% of the marbles to Theo. How many marbles did he give to Theo?

8 A bed priced at $1500 is reduced in price by 20%. Which of these would be the amount of the discount? Circle your answer.

$100 $200 $300 $500

9 Here is a pattern of three shapes made of matchsticks. How many matchsticks would be used to make the sixth shape in the pattern?

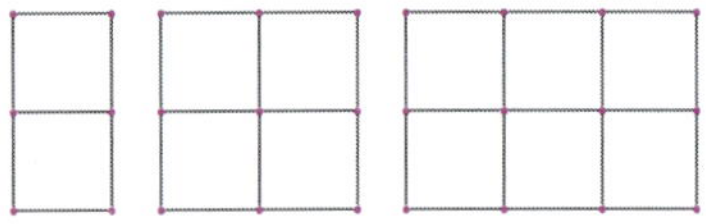

10 True or false? (10 – 4) × 3 + 3 = 36

MEASUREMENT AND SPACE

11 Rewrite these lengths from longest to shortest.

1.32 m 123 cm 1430 mm 1.023 m

12 A skydiving company has a weight limit of 115 kg for customers. George has a mass of 123 kg. How much weight on average must he lose over each of 4 weeks to be allowed to jump?

13 A bus timetable is shown. Lincoln arrives at the Shell Cove bus stop at 5:30 pm. How long does he need to wait for the bus to arrive?

Berkeley	1706
Oak Flats	1740
Shell Cove	1804
Bombo	1823

14 Here is the net of a triangular prism.

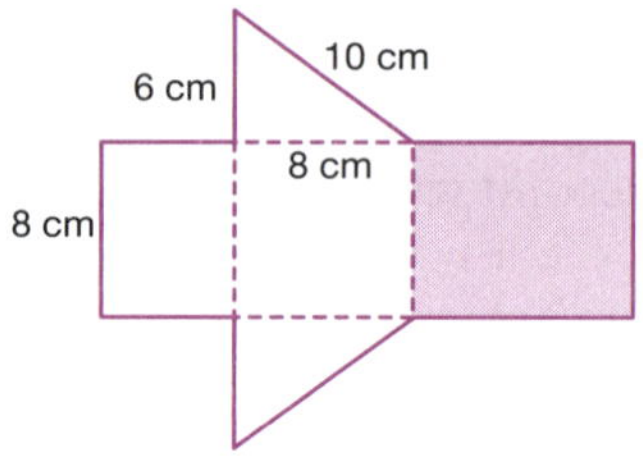

What is the area of the shaded rectangle?

15 Rotate the shape 90° anticlockwise about *O*.

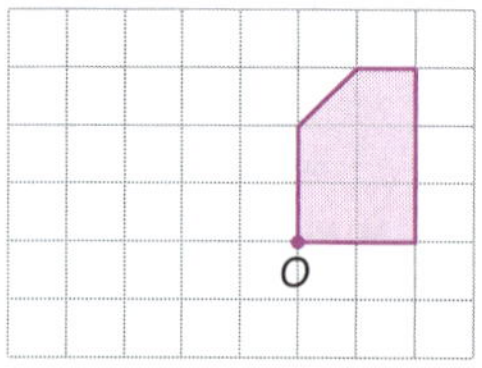

16 What is the size of the angle marked as *?

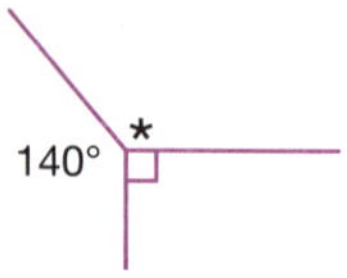

STATISTICS AND PROBABILITY

17 What is the probability of spinning an even number?

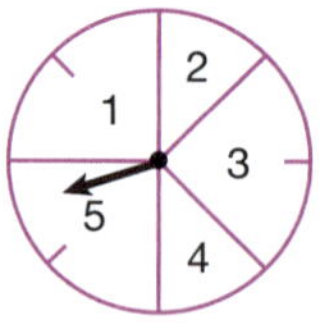

18 The colour and style of students' hair is recorded.

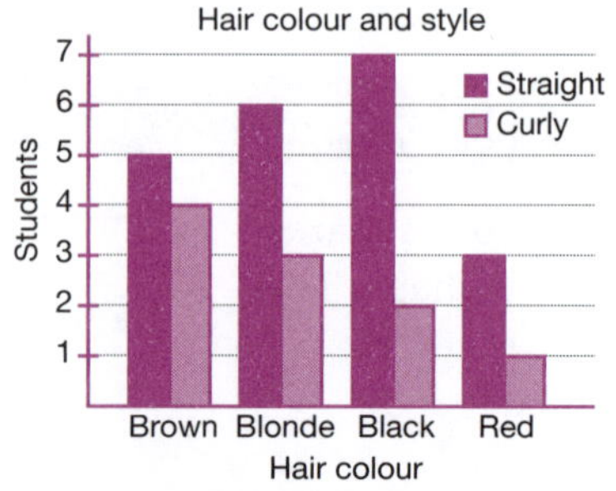

How many students have straight hair?

NUMBER AND ALGEBRA

1 What is the square of the sum of the positive triangular numbers less than 12?

2 The arrows on the number line are used to write a number sentence. Complete the number sentence:

.... + ... = ...

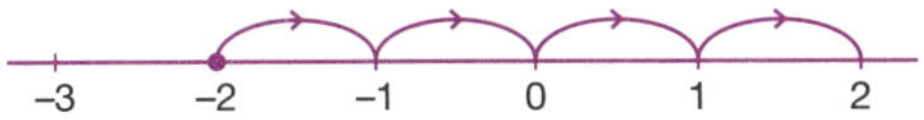

3 A garage sells bags of ice. On Christmas Eve 436 bags were sold, on Christmas Day 981 and on Boxing Day 728. What was the average number of bags sold in the three days?

4 Express these fractions in ascending order:

$\frac{3}{5}$ $\frac{11}{20}$ $\frac{3}{4}$ $\frac{7}{10}$

5 $\square - \frac{2}{3} = 1\frac{1}{2}$

6 At Perisher the temperature at 0540 this morning was –3.6 °C. By 1300 it had risen 2.9 °C and by 2150 it had dropped another 1.7 °C. What was the temperature at 2150?

7 Bonnie was paid $120 last month working as a babysitter. She spent 40% of the money on a T-shirt and 35% on a meal and saved the remainder. How much did Bonnie save?

8 A jacket is priced at $200 but is discounted by 10%. As Jordie notices a stain on the jacket he is offered another 10% discount, on top of the original discount. How much will he pay for the jacket?

9 Here is a pattern of three shapes made of matchsticks. How many matchsticks would be used to make the first six shapes in the pattern?

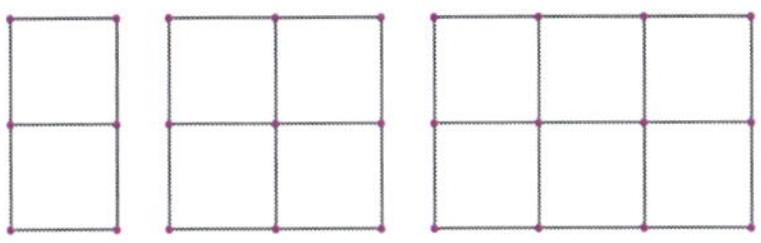

10 Find the value of $(40 - 4) \div 6 + 3 \times (8 - 3 \times 2)$.

MEASUREMENT AND SPACE

11 Rearrange these lengths in descending order.
2.86 cm 0.028 m 29 mm 2.89 cm

12 At a theme park, the combined mass of two riders permitted on a slide is 180 kg. Ada has a mass of 89 kg, Ben 92 kg, Cam 97 kg and Dana 86 kg. How many different pairs of riders are allowed?

13 A bus timetable is shown. Ellie arrives at the Berkeley bus stop at 4:41 pm. How long does she need to wait for the bus to arrive, if it is 16 minutes late?

Berkeley	1706
Oak Flats	1740
Shell Cove	1804
Bombo	1823

14 Here is the net of a triangular prism.

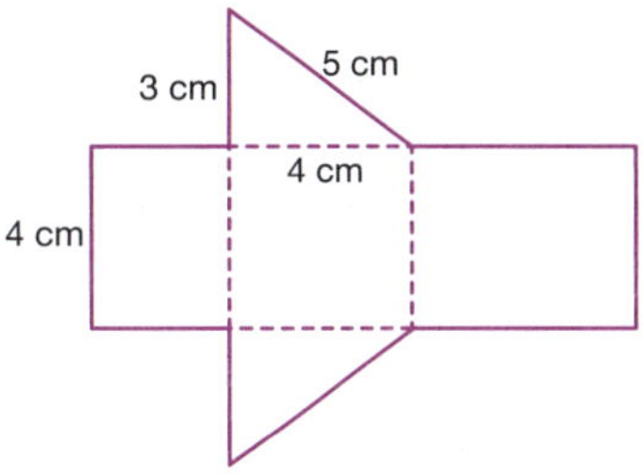

What is the area of the net?

15 Rotate the shape 90° anticlockwise about *O* and then translate 2 units left.

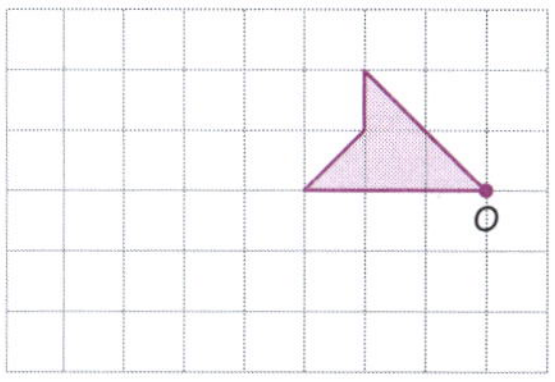

16 What is the value of *x*?

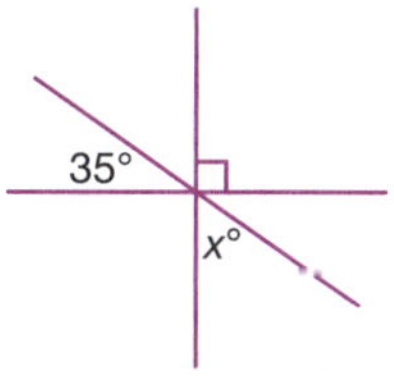

STATISTICS AND PROBABILITY

17 The spinner is spun 160 times. What is the expected number of times a number less than 4 is spun?

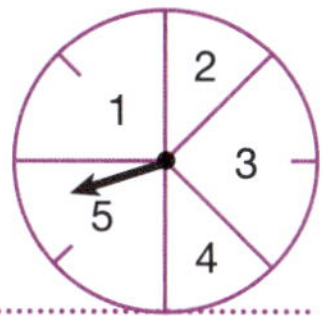

18 The colour and style of students' hair is recorded.

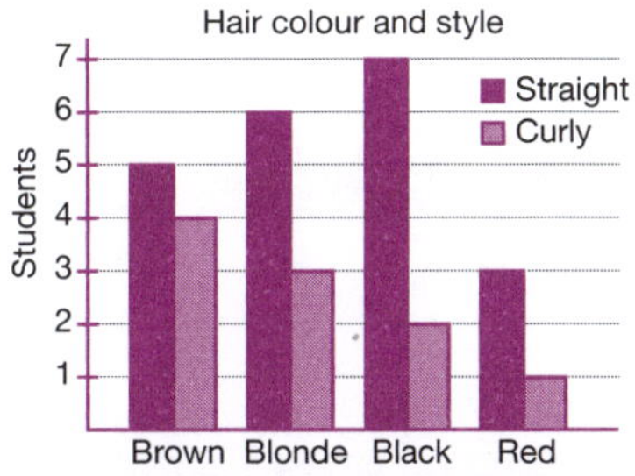

What fraction of the blonde-haired students have straight hair?

NUMBER AND ALGEBRA

1 How many square numbers are also prime numbers?

2 The arrows on the number line are used to write a number sentence. Complete the number sentence:

4 – .... = ...

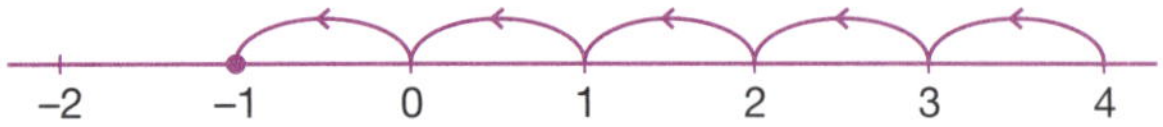

3 A wedding function venue has 18 tables which can seat 12 people each. How many people can be seated?

4 By changing these fractions to sixths, rewrite them from smallest to largest:

$\frac{1}{2}$ $\frac{5}{6}$ $\frac{2}{3}$

5 Find the missing number: $\frac{7}{10} - \square = \frac{1}{5}$

6 Lewis drove 4.8 km from his home to a shopping centre. He then drove 7.3 km to a hardware store and 5.3 km back home. What was the total distance travelled?

7 How many years are in 20% of a decade?

8 A movie ticket usually costs $20. Megan buys two tickets and uses her loyalty card to receive a 10% discount. What will be the total cost of the tickets?

9 Here is a pattern of three shapes made of matchsticks. How many matchsticks would be used to make the eighth shape in the pattern?

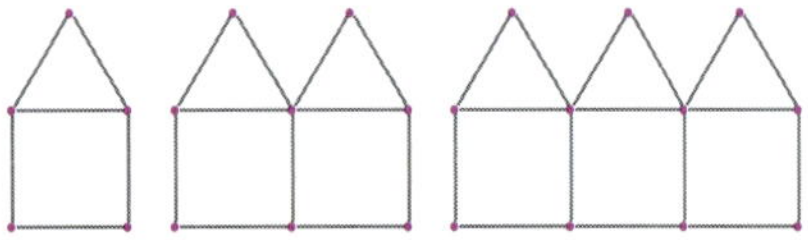

10 What is the missing number in this number sentence?

$24 - 4 \times \square = 12$

MEASUREMENT AND SPACE

11 A patio is to be tiled. The dimensions are 5 m by 3.6 m. What is the area of the patio?

12 Every cubic centimetre of this metal block has a mass of 2 g. What is the mass of the block?

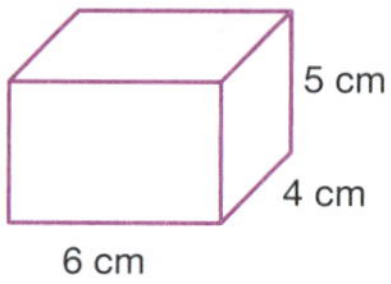

13 A bus timetable is shown. Leila arrives at the Lakeland bus stop at 7:53 am. How long does she need to wait for the bus to arrive?

Clearwater	0751
Lakeland	0843
Avon Park	0928
Sebastian	0953

14 The net of a square pyramid is shown. The height of each triangle is 6 cm. Circle a possible area of the square shown on the net.

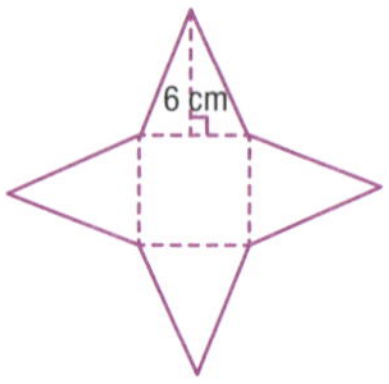

64 cm²

144 cm²

200 cm²

15 Name the transformation used.

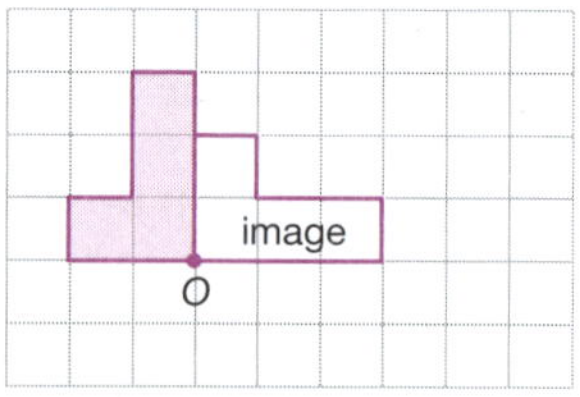

16 What is the size of the angle marked as *?

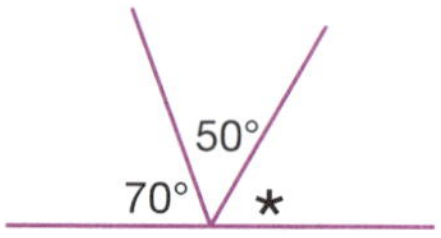

STATISTICS AND PROBABILITY

17 A coin is biased so that it is twice as likely to land on heads as tails. What is the probability of tossing a tail?

18 The way students returned home from school yesterday is recorded.

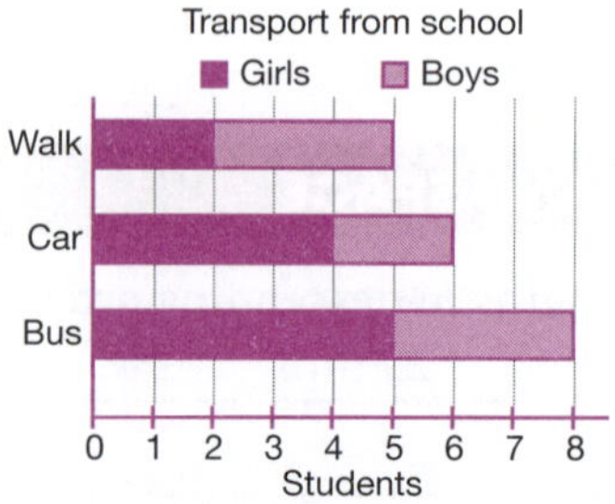

What is the total number of boys who walked home?

NUMBER AND ALGEBRA

1 What is the smallest odd number that is the sum of a composite number and a prime number?

2 The arrows on the number line are used to write a number sentence. Complete the number sentence:

.... – .... = ...

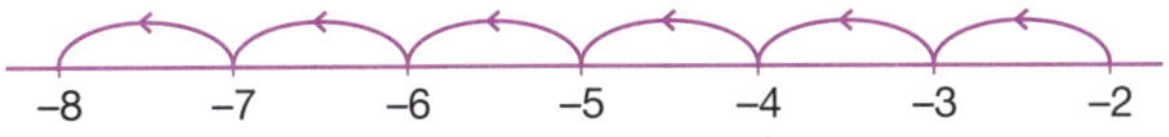

3 A box contains trays of oranges. There are 20 oranges on a tray. There are four trays in a box. A supermarket sells 36 boxes of oranges. How many oranges were sold by the supermarket?

4 Express these fractions in descending order:

$\frac{3}{4}$ $\frac{5}{6}$ $\frac{2}{3}$ $\frac{1}{2}$

5 $2\frac{1}{4}$ – ☐ = $1\frac{1}{2}$

6 16.92 – ☐ + 3.08 = 19.541

7 Bodhi is walking 15 km for charity. If she has walked 60% of the distance, how far has Bodhi to walk to finish?

8 The cost of a season pass ticket to a theme park is normally $420. Late in the year the price is discounted by 80%. What will be the discounted price of the season pass?

9 Here is a pattern of three shapes made of matchsticks. How many matchsticks would be used to make the 20th shape in the pattern?

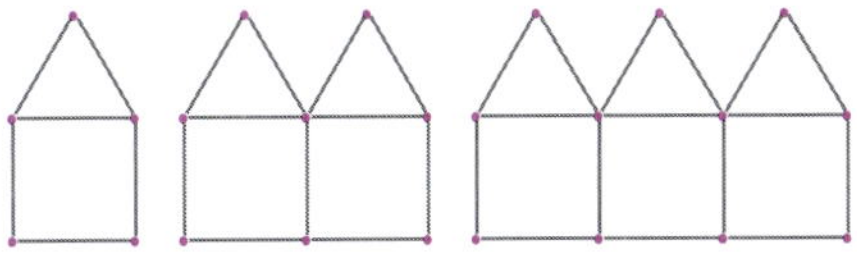

10 65 – 15 + 100 ÷ (☐ + 4) = 55

MEASUREMENT AND SPACE

11 A rectangle has side lengths in whole-number dimensions. The area is 24 cm^2. What is the largest possible perimeter of the rectangle?

12 The diagram shows the net of a solid which has a capacity of 64 mL. What is the area of the shaded section?

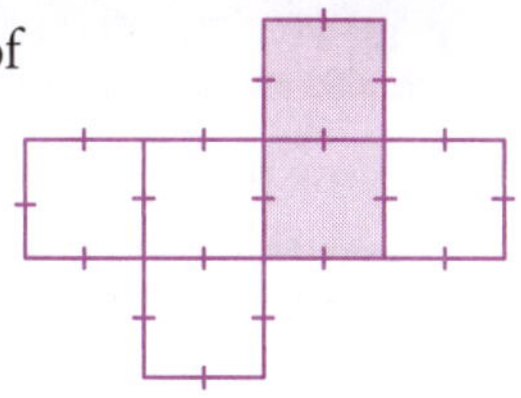

13 A bus timetable is shown. Fatima arrives at the Avon Park bus stop at 8:50 am.

Clearwater	0751
Lakeland	0843
Avon Park	0928
Sebastian	0953

How long does she need to wait for the bus to arrive, if it is 3 min early?

14 The net of a square pyramid is shown. The height of each triangle is 12 cm and the area of the base of the pyramid is 100 cm^2. What is the area of the net?

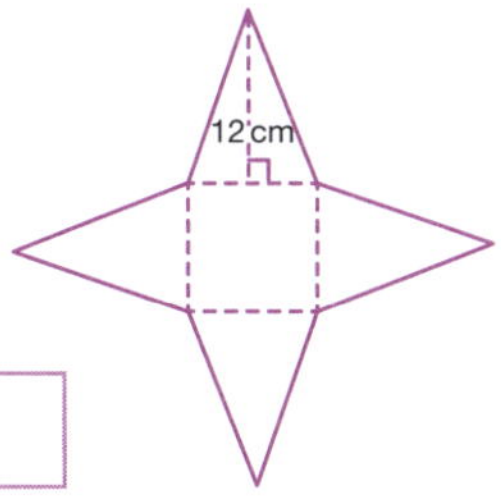

15 Name the two transformations used.

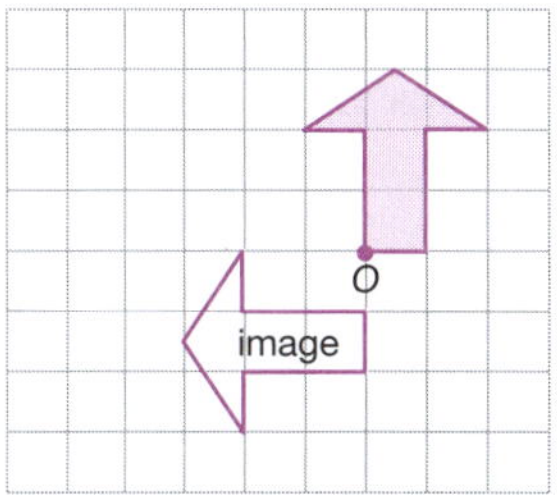

16 What is the value of x?

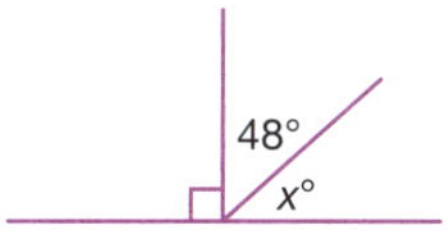

STATISTICS AND PROBABILITY

17 A coin is biased so that it is three times as likely to land on heads as tails. If the coin is tossed 24 times, what is the expected number of heads?

18 The way students returned home from school yesterday is recorded.

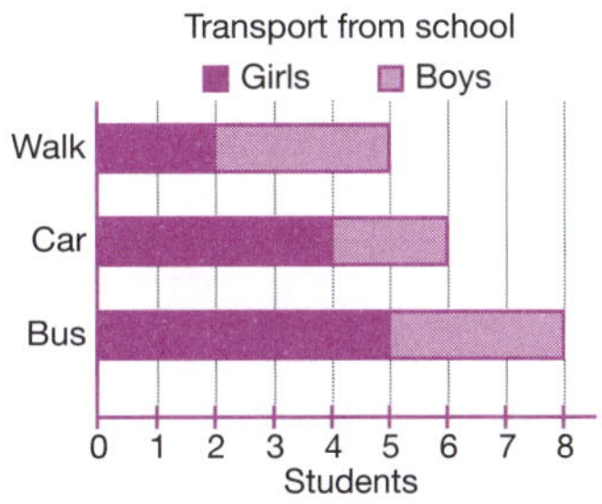

What fraction of the boys travelled by car?

NUMBER AND ALGEBRA

1 How many prime numbers less than 12 are also triangular numbers?

2 Write the whole numbers between –9 and –5.

3 Which two numbers multiply to give six hundred thousand? Circle the two numbers.

20 30 200 300 2000

4 Insert either <, = or > to make a true statement:

$\frac{2}{3}$ ☐ $\frac{3}{4}$

5 Christopher spent $\frac{2}{5}$ of his birthday money on a computer game and $\frac{1}{2}$ on a football. What fraction of his money was spent?

6 Gail drove 370 km in 4 h. What was her average speed?

7 What is 90% of 800?

8 What will be the cost of a washing machine priced at $1600 after a discount of 25%?

9 Here is a pattern of three shapes made of matchsticks.

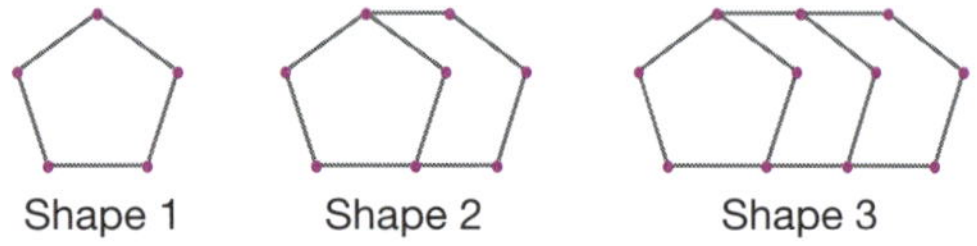

Which shape is made from 21 matchsticks?

10 What is the difference between the average of 14 and 26 and the average of 10 and 18?

MEASUREMENT AND SPACE

11 An isosceles triangle has a perimeter of 40 cm. If the longest side is 18 cm, what is the length of each of the other two sides?

12 What is the volume of a cube with side length 8 cm?

13 A bus timetable is shown. How much quicker is the second bus from Moonah to Risdon than the first bus?

Moonah	0703	0739	0803
Rosny	0732	–	0832
Lindisfarne	0802	0812	0902
Risdon	0843	0853	0943

14 The area of the net of a cube is 24 cm^2. When the cube is formed, what is the volume of the cube?

15 The shape is rotated 90° clockwise about *O*. Draw the image.

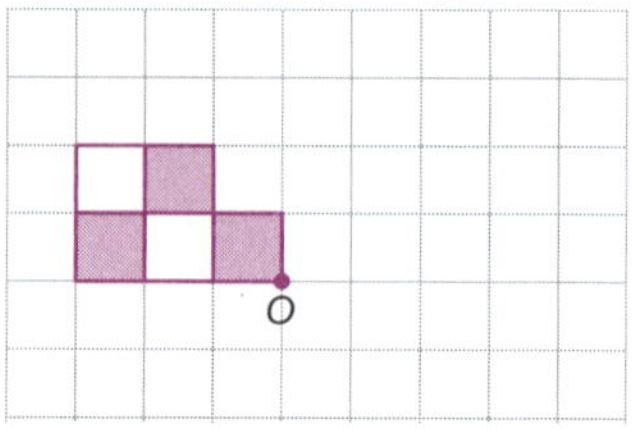

16 What is the size of the angle marked as *?

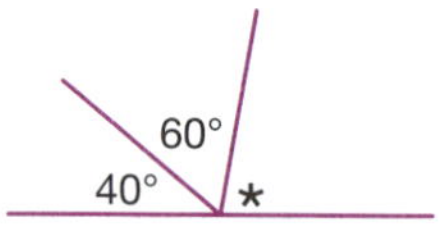

STATISTICS AND PROBABILITY

17 Using this spinner, the probability of spinning a 3 is twice the probability of spinning a 5. Complete the labelling of the spinner.

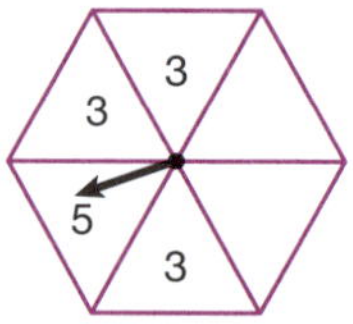

18 The votes for a member of the school's SRC are shown. How many Year 6 students voted for Arlo or Maeve?

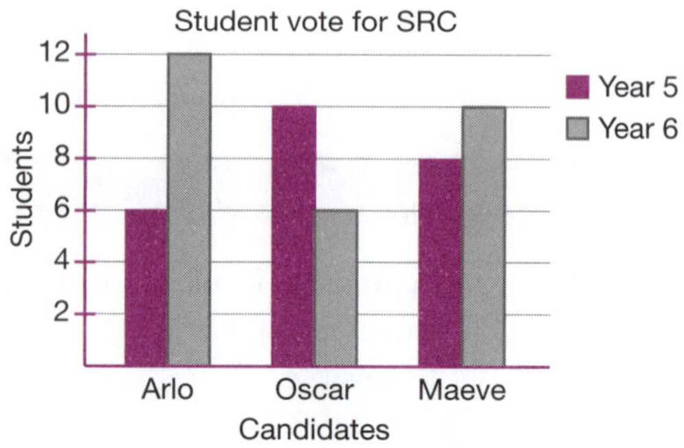

NUMBER AND ALGEBRA

1 Colin picked oranges from his backyard tree. If he gave an equal share of oranges to 4 friends, he would have 3 left over. If he gave an equal share to 6 friends, he would also have 3 left over. What is the smallest number of oranges?

2 How many whole numbers are between –5 and 2?

3 Find the value of 250 × 64 × 17.

4 Insert either <, = or > to make a true statement: $\frac{10}{3}$ ☐ $\frac{13}{4}$

5 Scarlett bought a pizza. She ate $\frac{3}{8}$ of the pizza and her friend Lily ate $\frac{1}{4}$ of the pizza. What fraction of the pizza remained?

6 Kendra left her home at 7 am and drove at an average speed of 80 km/h. If she arrived at her destination at 2:30 pm, what was the total distance travelled?

7 Indiana is 160 cm tall. Rose is 10% taller. How tall is Rose?

8 A supermarket usually sells a brand of laundry powder for $14.90. If the price drops by 10%, what is the new price?

9 Here is a pattern of three shapes made of matchsticks. Mollie has 100 matchsticks to copy the pattern of shapes. How many shapes can she make?

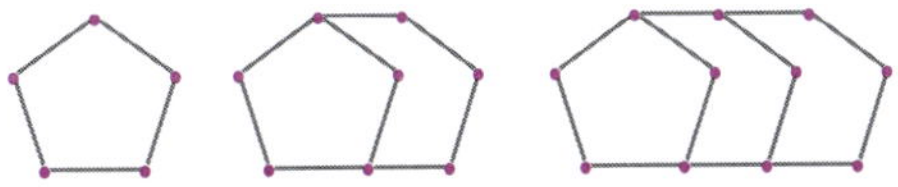

10 In the first eight games of a season, a team scored an average of 3 goals each game. In the next 12 games the average was 2 goals each game. What is the average number of goals scored in all games?

MEASUREMENT AND SPACE

11 A rectangle has side lengths in whole-number dimensions. What is the largest possible area if the perimeter is 32 cm?

12 A rectangular prism has a volume of 680 cm^3. If the width is 8 cm and the height is 10 cm, what is the length of the prism?

13 A bus timetable is shown. Audrey lives in Rosny and misses the 0732 bus. What is the earliest she can arrive in Lindisfarne?

Moonah	0703	0739	0803
Rosny	0732	–	0832
Lindisfarne	0802	0812	0902
Risdon	0843	0853	0943

14 The net of a pyramid is comprised of isosceles triangles and a square, and the perimeter of the net is 120 cm. If the area of the base of the pyramid is 64 cm^2, what is the sum of the lengths of the edges when the pyramid is formed?

15 The shape is reflected about line *L*. Draw the image.

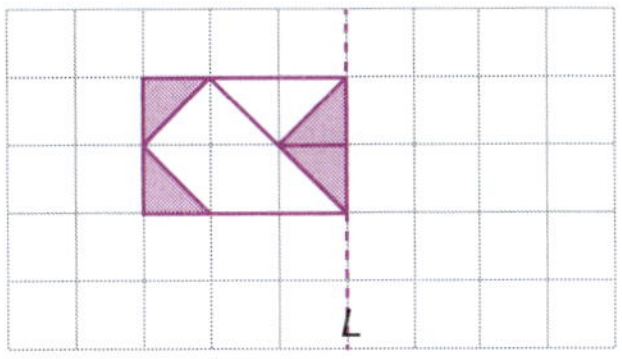

16 What is the value of *x*?

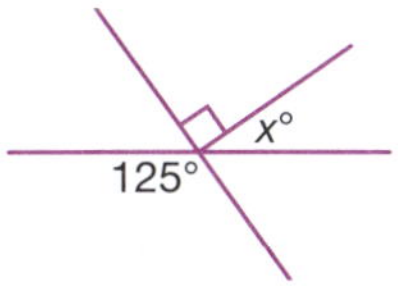

STATISTICS AND PROBABILITY

17 On this spinner, the probability of spinning a 1 is $\frac{1}{3}$, the probability of a 2 is $\frac{1}{4}$, the probability of a 3 is $\frac{1}{6}$ and the remaining sections are numbered 4. Label the spinner.

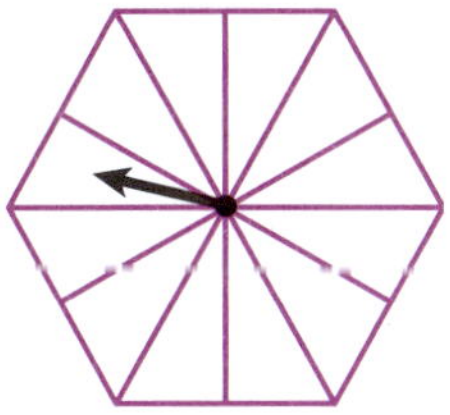

18 The votes for a member of the school's SRC are shown. What fraction of the Year 5 students voted for Oscar?

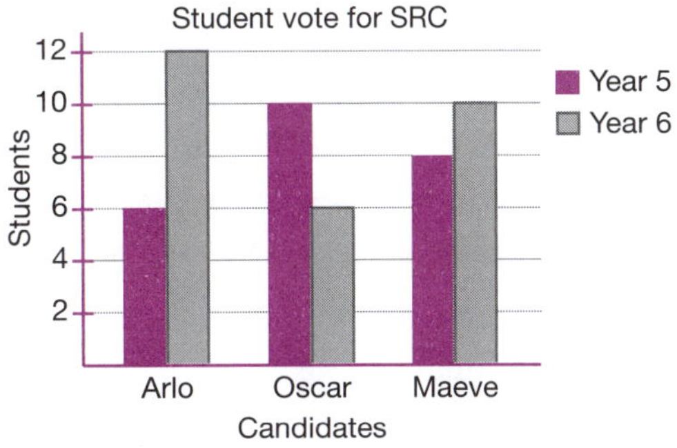

NUMBER AND ALGEBRA

1. How many even numbers less than 20 have more than two factors?

2. What is the difference between the temperatures 6 °C and –2 °C?

3. Eighty-four people attended Michael's art exhibition on Friday, 162 on Saturday and 81 on Sunday. What was the average daily attendance?

4. On the number line, locate and label $\frac{1}{4}$ and $\frac{5}{6}$.

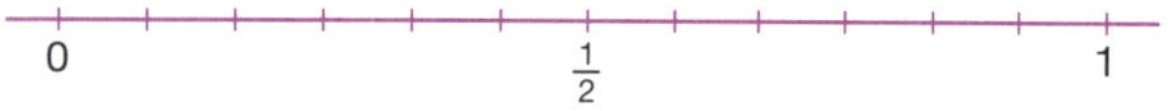

5. Lily surveyed the way students travelled to school. $\frac{1}{4}$ of the students walked and $\frac{1}{3}$ travelled by car. What total fraction walked or travelled by car?

6. Joanne received a pay rise of $1.27 per hour. If she works 40 hours each week, what will be the increase in her weekly pay?

7. 50% of the tickets for a concert were sold in the first hour of sales. If 3500 tickets were sold, how many tickets are still available?

8. To celebrate a birthday, a pizza shop manager reduces the price of a small pizza from $16 to $12. The same percentage discount also applies to a large pizza with a usual price of $24. What will be the new price of a large pizza?

9. Agnes has the rule 'starting with 4, add 1 and double' to write this sequence: 4, 10, 22, 46 …

   What is the sixth number?

10. Paul has 80 golf balls. He keeps 30 balls and shares the remaining balls between five friends. How many golf balls does he give to each of his friends?

MEASUREMENT AND SPACE

11. Find the area of the rectangle, in square m.

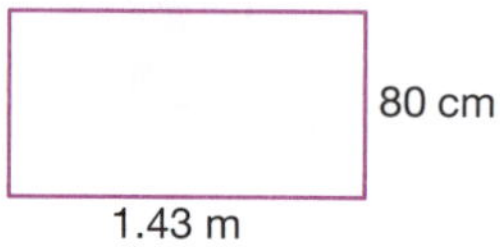

12. What is the total of 340 mL, 967 mL and 1.8 L, expressed in litres.

13. A bus timetable is shown. How much quicker is the second bus from Allendale to Kingstree than the first bus?

Allendale	1121	1408	1727
Ridgeville	1157	–	1803
Kingstree	1248	1512	–
Beaufort	1335	1559	1928

14. How many edges are on the solid formed using this net?

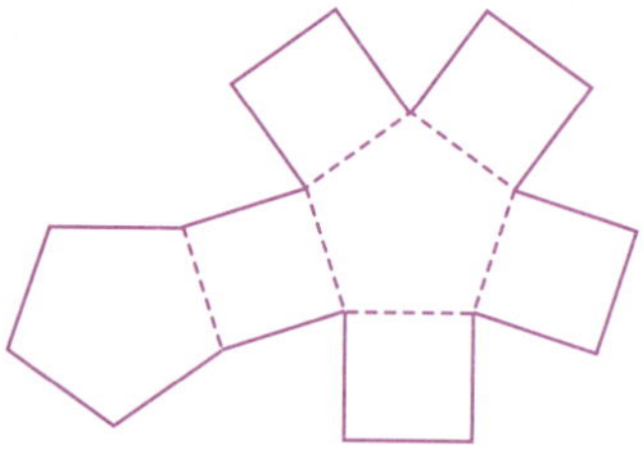

15. The shape is rotated 180° about O. Draw the image.

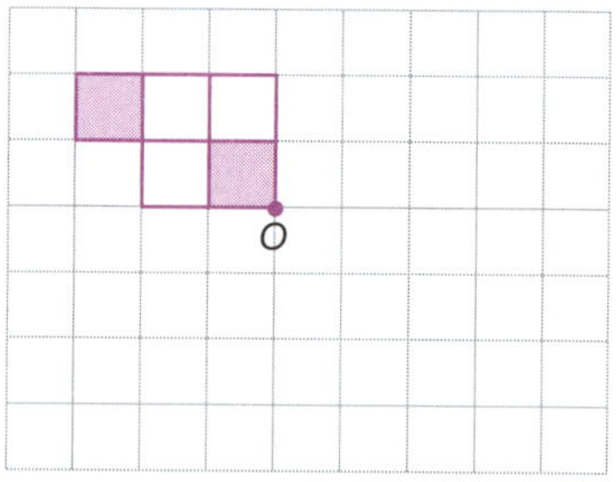

16. What is the size of the angle marked as *?

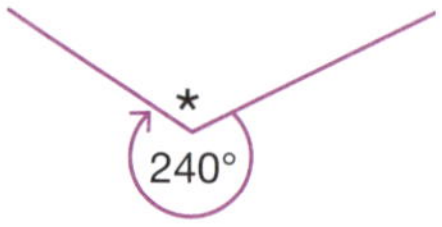

STATISTICS AND PROBABILITY

17. The probability of an event happening is $\frac{36}{50}$. Express this as a decimal.

18. The table shows the number of students who visited the library over four lunchtimes.

	Monday	Tuesday	Thursday	Friday
Girls	16	24	18	14
Boys	8	12	16	12

How many students visited on Tuesday or Friday?

NUMBER AND ALGEBRA

1 Mr Jaxson can arrange all the chairs in the library into rows of 8, 12 or 16 chairs for a parent meeting. What is the smallest number of chairs in the library?

2 What is the difference between the temperatures −4 °C and −10 °C?

3 In 2019, 2550 people attended an annual market day at the showground. In 2020 the number had increased by 1761. In 2021 the attendance had increased by another 1263. What was the average attendance in the three years?

4 On the number line, locate and label $2\frac{1}{3}$ and $2\frac{3}{4}$.

5 One-sixth of a circle is coloured red and two-fifths of the circle is coloured blue. What fraction of the circle has **not** been coloured?

6 Sarah earns 2.5 times more money each hour than her brother Craig. If Craig earns $12 per hour, what will Sarah earn for 18.5 h work?

7 What number is 30% more than 60?

8 A shopkeeper increases the price of a pair of shoes by 50% and then discounts this new price by 50%. If the original price was $60, what is the discounted price?

9 Phil has the rule 'starting with 0.5, add 0.3 and double' to write this sequence: 0.5, 1.6, 3.8, 8.2 …

What is the seventh number?

10 Grace has made 16 blueberry muffins, 14 chocolate muffins and 18 lemon muffins. She keeps a dozen muffins and places the remaining muffins evenly into nine paper bags. How many muffins are in each bag?

MEASUREMENT AND SPACE

11 Find the area of the rectangle, in square centimetres.

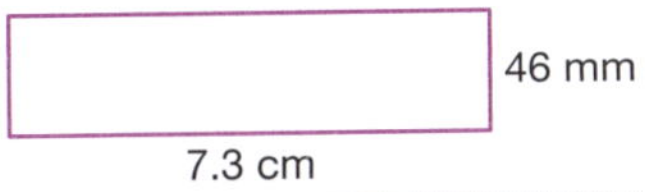

12 Water is poured from a full 5-litre container into eight glasses. If 2.88 L of water remains in the container, what is the average amount in each glass?

13 A bus timetable is shown. Arianne lives in Ridgeville and needs to travel to Kingstree. What time will she arrive in Kingstree?

Allendale	1121	1408	1727
Ridgeville	1157	–	1803
Kingstree	–	1512	1854
Beaufort	1316	1559	1941

14 Circle the net(s) that form a square pyramid.

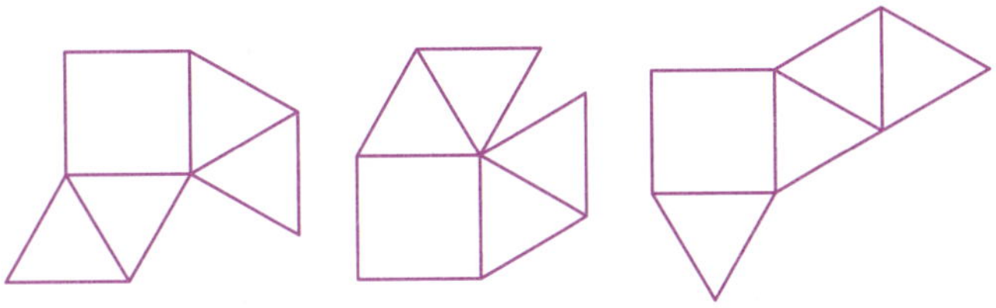

15 The shape is rotated 180° about O. Draw the image.

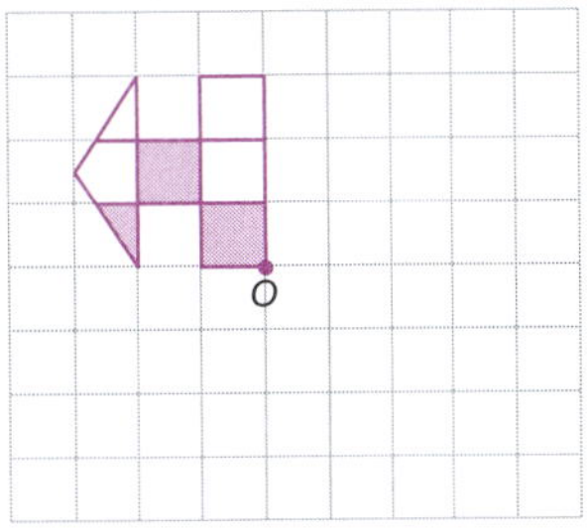

16 What is the value of x?

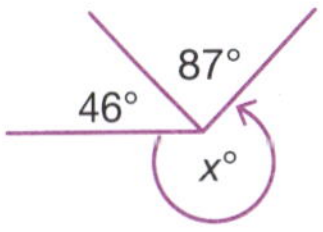

STATISTICS AND PROBABILITY

17 The probability of selecting a blue ball from a box is 60%. What is the smallest number of balls in the box?

18 The table shows the number of students who visited the library over four lunchtimes.

	Monday	Tuesday	Thursday	Friday
Girls	16	24	18	14
Boys	8	12	16	12

What percentage of the boys who visited the library went on Friday?

NUMBER AND ALGEBRA

1 Find the prime numbers that multiply to give 66.

2 Here is a pattern of numbers.

−6, −4, −2, 0, ☐

What is the missing number?

3 How long would it take Aubrey to drive 720 km at an average speed of 80 km/h?

4 On the number line, locate and label $\frac{1}{2}$ and $\frac{2}{3}$.

5 Joe has read 62 pages, which is one-fifth of his novel. What is the total number of pages in the novel?

6 Isabelle bought four paintbrushes. If she paid $67.40 for the brushes, what was the cost of each paintbrush?

7 Circle the smallest amount.

7%   0.6 $\frac{8}{100}$ 3

8 Pamela is offered a discount of either $180, or 10%, on the purchase of a refrigerator. If the price is $1740, which offer gives the greater discount?

9 Here is a pattern of three shapes made of matchsticks. How many matchsticks would be used to make the seventh shape in the pattern?

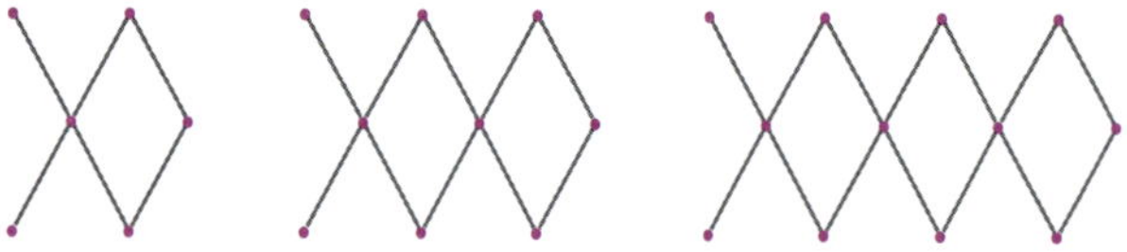

10 Find the value of $(10 - 3 \times 2)^2$.

MEASUREMENT AND SPACE

11 An equilateral triangle has a perimeter of 14.04 cm. What is the length of each side?

12 A rectangular tank measuring 40 cm by 20 cm by 10 cm is half filled with water. How many more litres are needed to fill the tank?

13 The table shows the times of sunrise and sunset in Melbourne for different dates. What time was sunset on 19/11/2020, in 12-hour time?

18/11/2020	0557	2013
19/11/2020	0557	2014
20/11/2020	0556	2015

14 What solid is formed using this net?

15 The shape is reflected in line *L*. Draw the image.

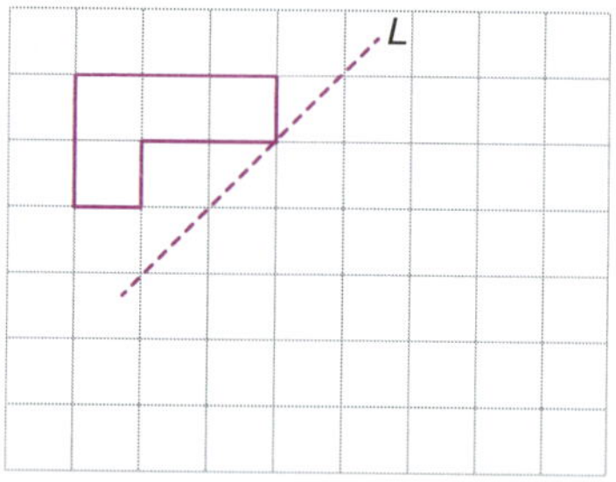

16 What is the size of the angle marked as *?

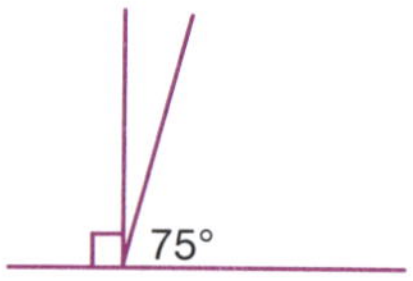

STATISTICS AND PROBABILITY

17 At the end of the season it was found that the probability of the Tigers winning a game was $\frac{1}{3}$. If the team had played 18 games, how many games did they win?

18 The results of a class survey are recorded. How many students in the class do **not** have siblings?

	Only child	Has sibling(s)
Has a pet	7	9
No pet	4	6

NUMBER AND ALGEBRA

1 Hunter multiplied four prime numbers and the result was even. Which of these must be one of his numbers? Circle it. 1 2 3 5

2 Here is a pattern of numbers: 6, 4, 2, 0, –2, ☐

What is the missing number?

3 Andrew leaves home at 10:00 am and drives a distance of 600 km. If his average speed is 75 km/h, at what time will he arrive at his destination?

4 On the number line, locate and label $3\frac{4}{5}$ and $4\frac{1}{10}$.

5 Layla has travelled 150 km, which is $\frac{3}{8}$ of a trip. How much further does she need to travel to reach her destination?

6 Complete: 18.6 ÷ 0.25 = ... ÷ 1 = ...

7 What is 25% of the sum of 0.2 and $\frac{3}{5}$, written as a decimal?

8 The Great Gals store offers a storewide discount sale. The price of a television reduces from \$2000 to \$1600. If the same percentage discount is applied, what will be the price of a laptop originally priced at \$1200?

9 Here is a pattern of three shapes made of matchsticks.

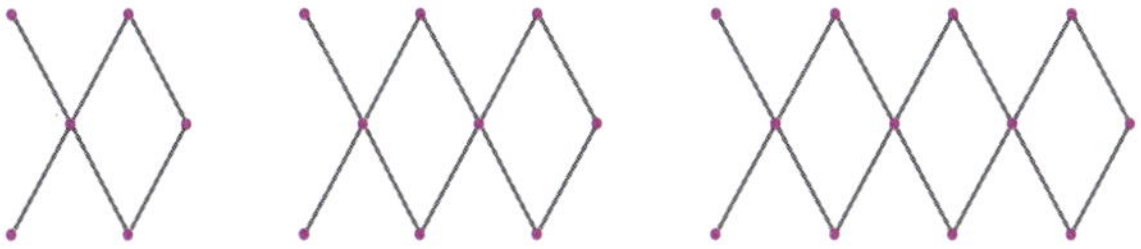

Which shape is made from 50 matchsticks?

10 $24 \times (\frac{1}{2} + \frac{1}{4} - \frac{1}{3}) =$ ....

MEASUREMENT AND SPACE

11 The length of a rectangle is 2 cm longer than its width. If the perimeter is 28 cm, what is the area?

12 A box has a square base and a height of 24 cm. If the perimeter of the base is 80 cm, what is the capacity of the box, in litres?

13 The table shows the times of sunrise and sunset in Melbourne for different dates. What was the length of daylight on 20/11/2020?

18/11/2020	0557	2013
19/11/2020	0557	2014
20/11/2020	0556	2015

14 Draw a sketch of the solid formed using this net, labelling the side of length *A*.

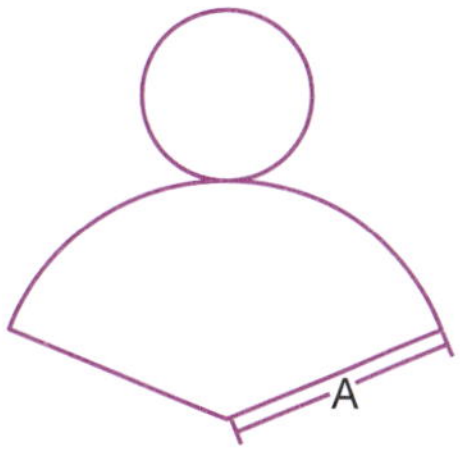

15 The shape is reflected in line *L*. Draw the image.

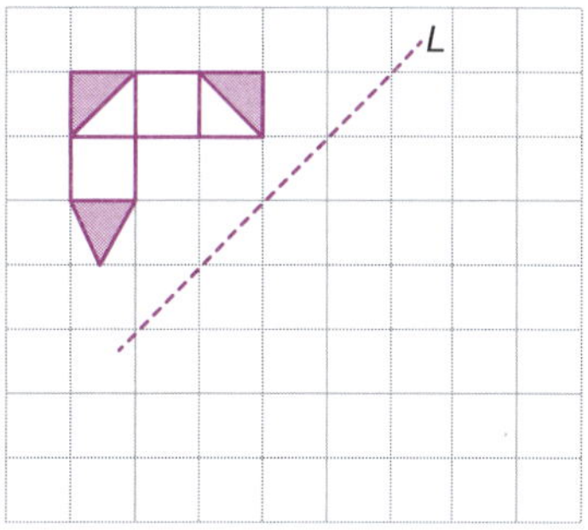

16 What is the value of *x*?

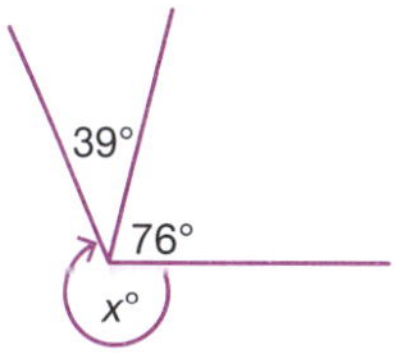

STATISTICS AND PROBABILITY

17 At the end of the season it was found that the probability of the Tigers winning a game was 0.4. If the team had won eight games, how many games did they **not** win?

18 The results of a class survey are recorded. What percentage of the students who do not have a pet have at least one sibling?

	Only child	Has sibling(s)
Has a pet	7	9
No pet	4	6

NUMBER AND ALGEBRA

1 What are the only two consecutive prime numbers?

2 Here is a pattern of numbers.

−5, −2, 1, 4, ☐

What is the missing number?

3 What is 67 500 ÷ 500?

4 On the number line, locate and label $\frac{5}{8}$ and $1\frac{1}{4}$.

5 Camilla needs 2 cups of flour for a recipe. When she checks her pantry she only has $1\frac{1}{4}$ cups, so she borrows the remainder from her neighbour. How much flour did she have to borrow?

6 At the athletics carnival Gladys won her 200-m race in a time of 23.71 s. Emilee came second with a time 0.4 s slower than Gladys's. In what time did Emilee run?

7 A new subdivision consists of 200 housing blocks. If 90% of the blocks have been sold, how many blocks are **not** sold?

8 This weekend the cost of a room at a Melbourne hotel is discounted by 25%. If the price is usually $480, what will be the new price?

9 A table uses a rule to link two numbers.

First number	1	2	3	4	5
Second number	4	8	12	16	?

What is the missing number?

10 What is half the sum of 18 and 32?

MEASUREMENT AND SPACE

11 A regular pentagon has a perimeter of 40.2 cm. What is the length of each side?

12 The solid below is formed using cubes, each with a mass of 0.8 kg. What is the total mass of the solid?

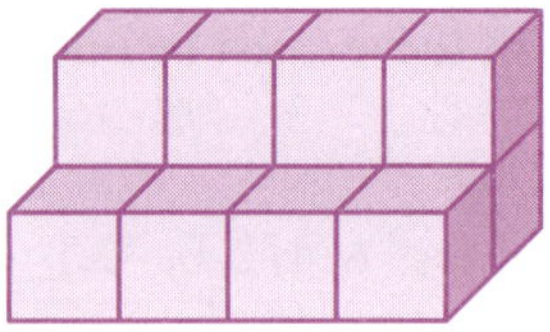

13 The table shows movies showing at a multiplex cinema. Hannah arrives at the cinema at 3:40. How long does she wait until the start of *Game Change*?

Film	Session Times		
High Living	11:15	1:20	3:35
The End	11:35	2:05	4:05
Game Change	11:55	1:55	4:25

14 Naomi drew the net of a cube. The volume of the constructed cube is 8 cm^3. What is the area of the net?

15 The shape is reflected in line *L*. Draw the image.

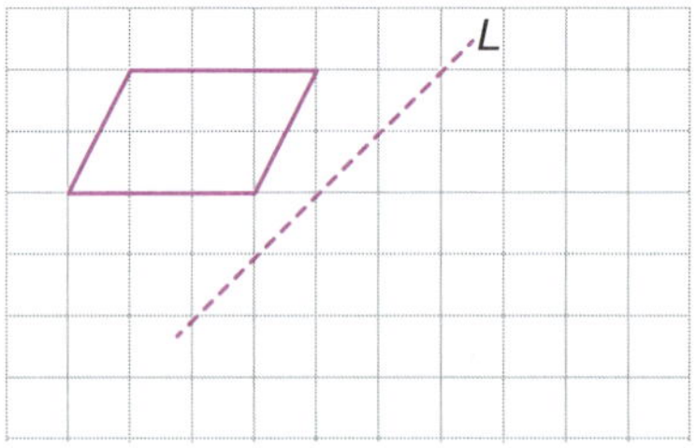

16 What is the size of the angle marked as *?

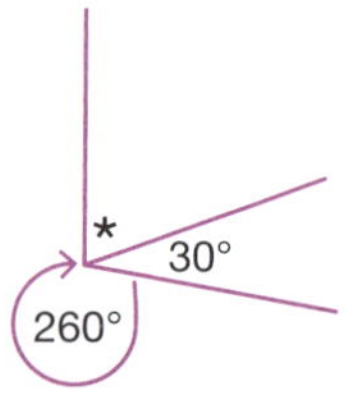

STATISTICS AND PROBABILITY

17 The probability of an event occurring is 0.54. What is the probability of the event **not** occurring?

18 The results of a student survey on hand preference are recorded. What fraction of the left-handed students were boys?

	Left-handed	Right-handed
Girls	3	11
Boys	2	9

NUMBER AND ALGEBRA

1 To celebrate its opening, a hardware store gave hats to the first 200 customers. Every fifth person in line also received a paintbrush, every eighth person a bag of potting mix and every twelfth person a $50 voucher. Which person in line received all four items?

2 −6, ______, 4, 9, 14

3 A pallet holds 12 boxes of tins of paint. Each box contains six 4-litre tins of paint. If a hardware store ordered a shipment of 10 pallets, how many litres of paint are in the shipment?

4 On the number line, locate and label $-\frac{2}{3}$ and $-1\frac{1}{2}$.

5 Jacinta has a box of chocolates. She gives $\frac{1}{4}$ of the chocolates to each of her two friends and eats $\frac{1}{3}$ herself. What fraction of the chocolates remain?

6 The average of two decimals is 16.73. If the smaller decimal is 14.8, what is the larger number?

7 300 people applied for jobs when a fast food restaurant was about to open. Only 8% of the people were given jobs. How many people were employed?

8 A microwave is purchased for $384 after a discount of $96. What would have been the price if instead it had been discounted by 10%?

9 A table uses a rule to link two numbers.

First number	1	2	3	...	?
Second number	7	14	21	...	147

What is the missing number?

10 What is the value of $\frac{1}{4} \times (8 + 16 \div 4)$?

MEASUREMENT AND SPACE

11 Carmen has 4 pieces of timber measuring 320 mm, 40 cm, 1.2 m and 2.6 m. What is the average length of the pieces?

12 The solid shown is formed using cubes. If the solid has a mass of 1.2 tonnes, what is the mass of each cube, in kilograms?

13 The table shows movies showing at a multiplex.

Film	Session Times		
High Living	11:15	1:20	3:35
The End	11:35	2:05	4:05
Game Change	11:55	1:55	4:25

Simon arrived 25 min early to watch the 1:20 showing of *High Living* but it was sold out. He decided to watch *The End* instead. How long did he have to wait?

14 What would be the area of the net of this rectangular prism?

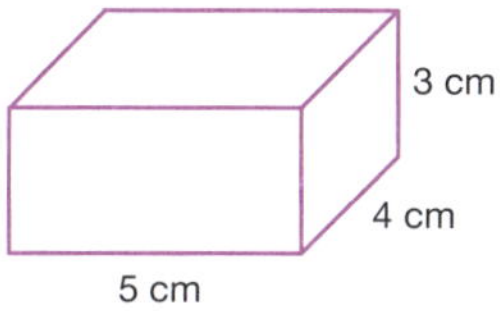

15 The shape is reflected in line L. Draw the image.

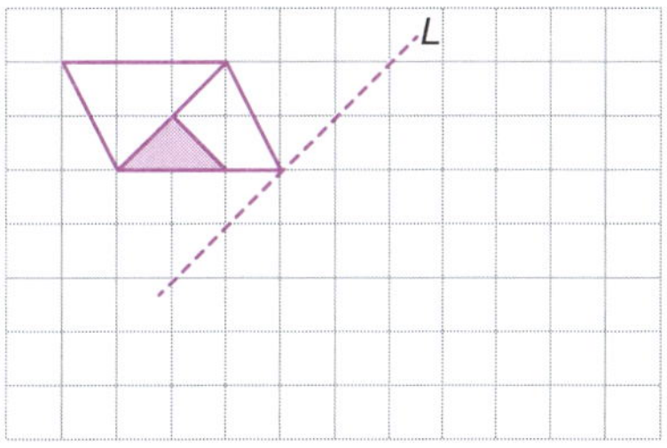

16 What is the value of x?

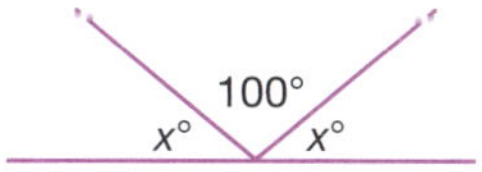

STATISTICS AND PROBABILITY

17 Tickets are numbered 1 to 20. What is the probability of randomly selecting a ticket with an even number greater than 10?

18 The results of a student survey on hand preference are recorded. What percentage of the students were right-handed girls?

	Left-handed	Right-handed
Girls	3	11
Boys	2	9

NUMBER AND ALGEBRA

1 Mrs Thomas gave each of her 30 students a number from 1 to 30. When she asked those students with a prime number to stand, how many stood up?

2 Here is a pattern of numbers. What is the missing number?

5, 3, 1, –1, ☐

3 Find the missing number: ☐ ÷ 21 = 12

4 Circle any of these fractions that are less than $\frac{1}{3}$:

$\frac{1}{4}$ $\frac{9}{30}$ $\frac{7}{15}$

5 One-quarter of the students have represented the school this year. If 58 students have represented the school, what is the total number of students enrolled?

6 In two days, Jarrod ran a total of 11.65 km. If he ran 6.86 km on the first day, how far did he run on the second day?

7 Rewrite 40% as a decimal and a fraction (in simplest form).

8 The cost of a maths workbook in a department store has been reduced by 20%. What will be the price if the workbook usually costs $25?

9 A table uses a rule to link two numbers.

First number	2.4	2.8	3.2	3.6	4
Second number	4.1	4.5	4.9	5.3	?

What is the missing number?

10 Find the value of (0.56 + 0.24) ÷ 2.

MEASUREMENT AND SPACE

11 A right-angled triangle has an area of 48 cm^2. If the base of the triangle is 16 cm, what is the height of the triangle?

12 A carton of almond milk has dimensions 20 cm by 5 cm by 10.5 cm. Which of these is closest to the capacity of the carton?

600 mL 1 L 1.5 L

13 The table shows flights from Sydney to Melbourne, which all have the same flight time.

	Sydney to Melbourne flight schedule			
Sydney	0735	0815	0930	1050
Melbourne	0900	0940	1055	1215

How long is the flight?

14 The perimeter of this net is 42 cm. When the net is used to make a cube, what is the volume of the cube?

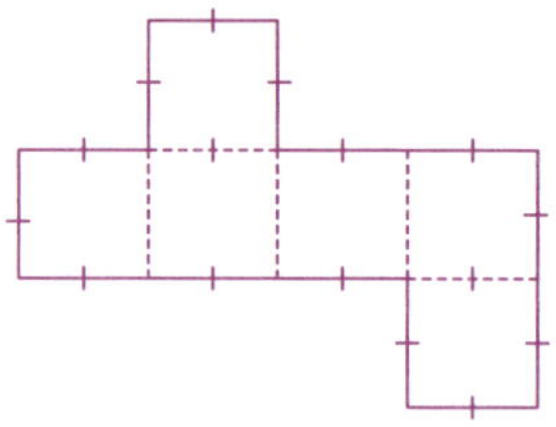

15 The triangle *ABC* is translated 4 units right. What are the coordinates of *B* on the image?

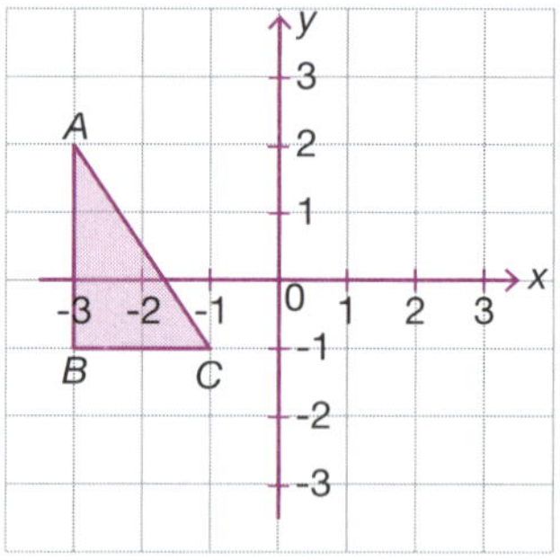

16 What is the size of the angle marked as *?

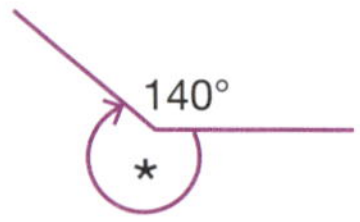

STATISTICS AND PROBABILITY

17 A bag contains red, blue and pink balls. The probability of choosing a red ball is 0.3 and a blue ball 0.5. What is the probability of choosing a pink ball?

18 There are 29 students in the class. There are 14 girls and half of them are at least 150 cm tall. There are six boys who are less than 150 cm. Complete the table.

	Boys	Girls
Less than 150 cm		
At least 150 cm		

NUMBER AND ALGEBRA

1 There are 300 students in the hall for an assembly. Every student has been given a numbered ticket from 1 to 300. Which of these is the best estimate of the number of students who have a ticket with a composite number? Circle your answer.

120 150 170 230

2 −16, −22, [ ], −34, −40

3 [ ] ÷ 36 = 126 × 18

4 What is the fraction that is in the middle of $\frac{1}{4}$ and $\frac{1}{2}$?

5 A water tank is $\frac{2}{5}$ full of water. During a heavy thunderstorm, 1500 L of water flows into the tank and it is completely filled. How much water is in the tank when it is full?

6 The cost of petrol is 169.9 cents per litre. What is the cost of 40 L of petrol?

7 Express $2\frac{1}{2}$% as a decimal and a fraction (in simplest form).

8 A beach towel was originally priced at $60. It was reduced in price by 25% and then a further 10% discount was applied. How much is paid for the beach towel?

9 A table uses a rule to link two numbers. What is the missing number?

First number	10.5	8.8	7.1	5.4	3.7
Second number	5.25	4.4	3.55	?	1.85

10 Find the value of $4 + (\frac{2}{3}$ the sum of 12 and 15).

MEASUREMENT AND SPACE

11 A square and a regular hexagon have the same perimeter. If a side of the hexagon is 12 cm, find the area of the square.

12 Each sprinkler on a sports field sprays 80 L of water every minute. If six sprinklers are flowing at the same time, how much water, in kilolitres, is released every hour?

13 The table shows flights from Sydney to Melbourne, which all have the same flight time. An afternoon flight arrives in Melbourne at 4:05 pm. At what time did the flight leave Sydney?

	Sydney to Melbourne flight schedule			
Sydney	0735	0815	0930	1050
Melbourne	0900	0940	1055	1215

14 The diagram shows a triangular prism where the area of the triangle is 6 cm^2. What would be the area of the net of the prism?

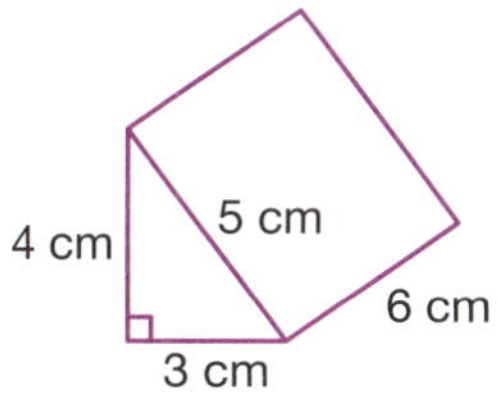

15 The triangle *PQR* is translated 3 units down and 2 units left.

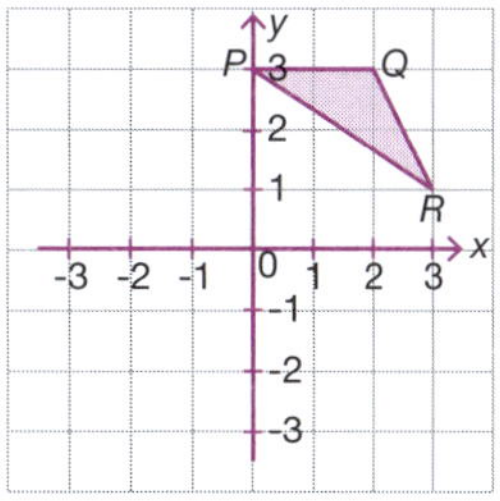

What are the coordinates of *R* on the image?

16 What is the value of *x*?

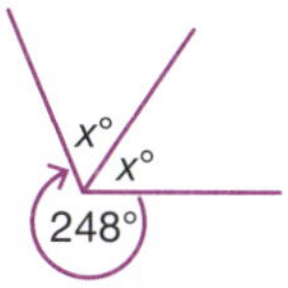

STATISTICS AND PROBABILITY

17 The probability of selecting a blue marble from a bag is 0.3. There are 20 red marbles in the bag and the probability of selecting a red or blue marble is 0.7. How many blue marbles are in the bag?

18 There are 28 students in the class. One-quarter of the students are girls who are less than 150 cm tall. There are two more boys in the class than girls and three-fifths of the boys are at least 150 cm tall. Complete the table.

	Boys	Girls
Less than 150 cm		
At least 150 cm		

NUMBER AND ALGEBRA

1 What are the first three consecutive numbers that are all composite numbers?

2 It was minus four degrees at 6 am. By 10 o'clock the temperature had risen by 12°. What was the new temperature?

3 Leah measured the heights of four tomato plants in her garden. The heights were 165 cm, 148 cm, 171 cm and 156 cm. What was the average height of the plants?

4 Circle the largest fraction.

$\frac{2}{3}$ $\frac{5}{6}$ $\frac{3}{4}$

5 $\frac{5}{8}$ of the stamps in John's collection are Australian and $\frac{1}{4}$ are from Europe. What fraction of his stamps are Australian or European?

6 Three friends divided equally the cost of petrol on a trip from Wollongong to Byron Bay and back. If the cost was $138.75, how much did each person pay?

7 What is 10% of 140?

8 When a bracelet is discounted by 10%, the price drops by $40. What would have been the drop in price if the bracelet had been discounted by 15%?

9 A table uses a rule to link two numbers. Complete the rule: Bottom number = Top number ....

Top number	6	8	10	12
Bottom number	3	4	5	6

10 How much greater is the sum of 12 and 18 than the product of 8 and 3?

MEASUREMENT AND SPACE

11 The dimensions of a square are doubled. The area of the enlarged square is 100 cm^2. What was the perimeter of the original square?

12 A cube and a rectangular prism have the same volume. A side length of the cube is 10 cm. The rectangular prism has a length of 20 cm and width 10 cm. What is the height of the prism?

13 A timetable shows the journeys of two buses that travel the same route at the same speed. What is the missing time?

Chantilly	1531	1728
Columbia	1658	?
Pasadena	1743	1940
Wayne	1819	2016

14 What is the area of the net of the rectangular prism?

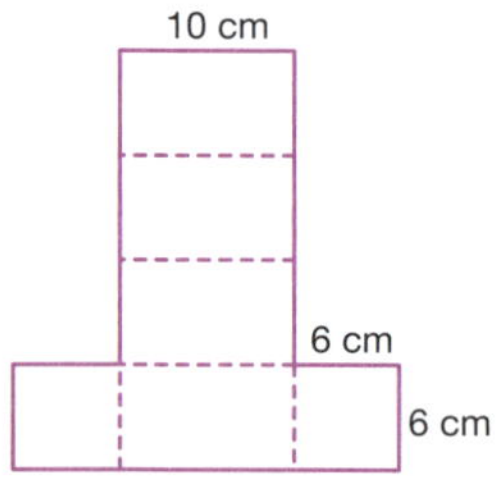

15 Use the y-axis to reflect the shape.

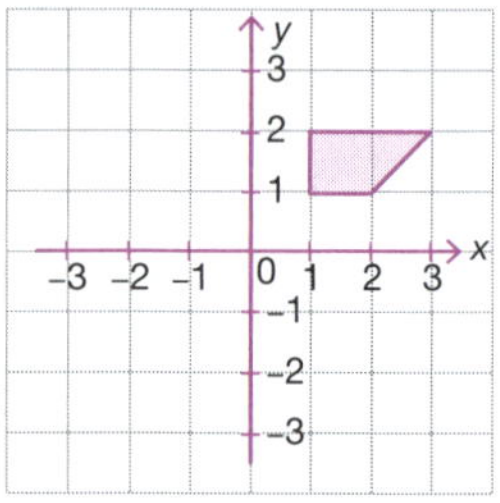

16 What is the size of the angle marked as *?

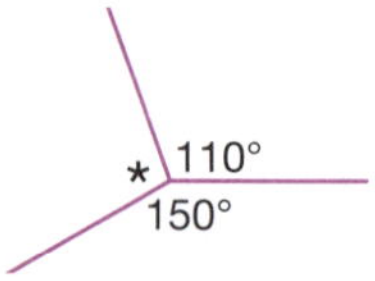

STATISTICS AND PROBABILITY

17 Students at a Brisbane school were asked whether they had travelled to Melbourne and the results are in the table. A student is chosen at random. What is the probability that the student is a girl who has been to Melbourne?

	Melbourne	No Melbourne
Girls	8	16
Boys	6	20

18 There are 40 students surveyed and half of them are boys. Half the boys and one-quarter of the girls can swim 200 m. Complete the table.

	Can swim 200 m	Cannot swim 200 m
Girls		
Boys		

NUMBER AND ALGEBRA

1 How many prime numbers less than 100 have a digit of 9?

2 The temperature at the bottom of a mountain on a winter's morning was –2.5 °C. The temperature at the top was three degrees colder. What was the temperature at the top of the mountain?

3 The average number of goals scored by Riley's team in six netball games was 24. In each of the next two games the team scored 16 goals. What is the average of goals scored in all games?

4 Allison and Lincoln brought identical cakes to a class party. Allison cut her cake into 12 equal pieces and Lincoln cut his into eight equal pieces. At the end of the party Allison's cake had five pieces left and Lincoln's cake had three pieces left. Which cake had more pieces eaten?

5 $\frac{3}{4}$ of a number is 40 more than $\frac{1}{3}$ of the same number. What is half the number?

6 A school purchased 60 calculators at a total cost of $1137. What was the cost of each calculator?

7 There are 500 people watching a movie. 60% of the people are male. 20% of the females are under 18 years old. How many females are **not** under 18 years old?

8 Tom buys a saxophone for $810, at a discount of 10% of the usual price. What was the usual price of the saxophone?

9 A table uses a rule to link two numbers. Complete the rule: Bottom number = Top number ....

Top number	4	6	8	10
Bottom number	16	36	64	100

10 Complete: $2.1 \times 8 - 6.8 \div 4 =$ ....

MEASUREMENT AND SPACE

11 A square tile has an area of 400 cm^2. A rectangular tile has a length 8 cm longer and a width 5 cm shorter than the square tile. Find the area of the rectangular tile.

12 When full, a can contains one litre of water. All the water from the can is poured into a cube with side length 20 cm. How deep is the water in the new cube?

13 A timetable shows the journeys of two buses that travel the same route at the same speed. What are the times at *A* and *B*?

Chantilly	1626	1754
Columbia	1701	1829
Pasadena	*A*	1927
Wayne	1836	*B*

14 What is the capacity when this net is used to make a solid?

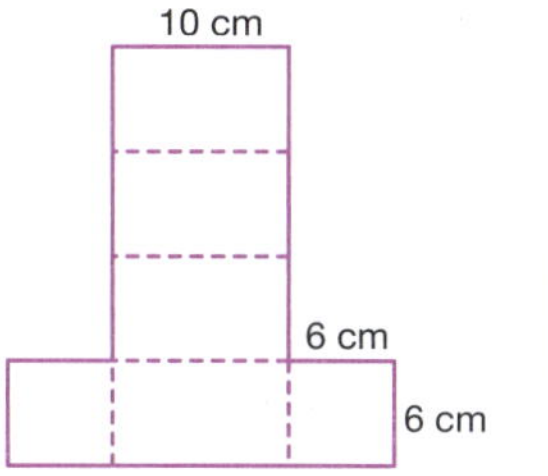

15 Reflect the shape in the *x*-axis and then in the *y*-axis.

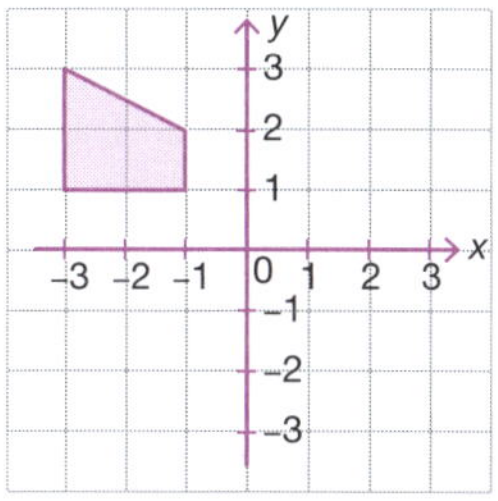

16 What is the value of *x*?

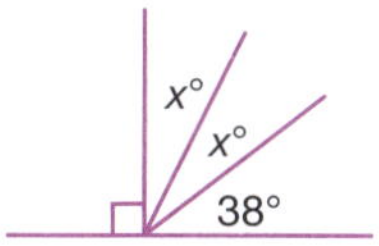

STATISTICS AND PROBABILITY

17 Students at a Brisbane school were asked whether they had travelled to Melbourne and the results are in the table. A boy is chosen at random. What is the probability that he has **not** been to Melbourne?

	Melbourne	No Melbourne
Girls	8	16
Boys	6	20

18 50 students are surveyed and 40% of them are boys. One-third of the girls can swim 200 m and 50% of the boys cannot swim 200 m. Complete the table.

	Can swim 200 m	Cannot swim 200 m
Girls		
Boys		

NUMBER AND ALGEBRA

1 What are the prime factors of 165?

2 Cora places a counter on the number 1 on a number line. She moves the counter 3 units to the left. What is the new position of the counter?

3 Mrs Dann handed 15 small pieces of cardboard to each of her 25 students. How many pieces did she hand out?

4 Which of these is larger?

$2\frac{3}{4}$ $\quad \frac{21}{8}$

5 Owen is one-sixth the age of his grandfather and one-quarter the age of his father. If Owen is 10 years old, what is the age difference between his grandfather and father?

6 $5\overline{)72.8}$

7 Our team played 10 games this season and won 40% of the games. How many games did our team win?

8 A clothes dryer is priced at \$440. The price is discounted by 25%. What will be the discounted price?

9 A table uses the rule 'Bottom number = 3 × top number + 1'. Use the rule to complete the table.

Top number	2	3	4	5
Bottom number	7			

10 Find the value of 60 ÷ (36 – 12 × 2).

MEASUREMENT AND SPACE

11 The perimeter of a square is 48 cm. What is the area of the square?

12 A box contains 2.4 kg of washing powder. Eloise uses 60 g of powder for each load. If she uses all the powder in the box, find the number of loads.

13 A timetable shows the journeys of three buses that travel the same route at the same speed.

Hicksville	1420	1611	?
Harrison	1532	?	?
Milford	1550	?	?
Guilford	1709	?	2016

There are times missing on the timetable. What time will the second bus arrive in Milford?

14 The perimeter of the net is 70 cm. When the net is used to make a cube, what is the total length of edges on the cube?

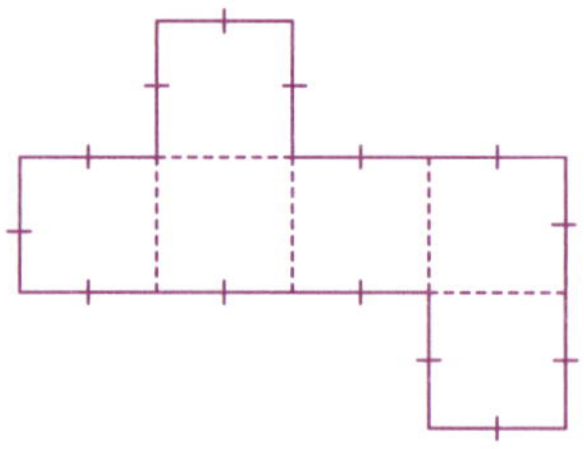

15 The shape is rotated 180° about the origin. Draw the image.

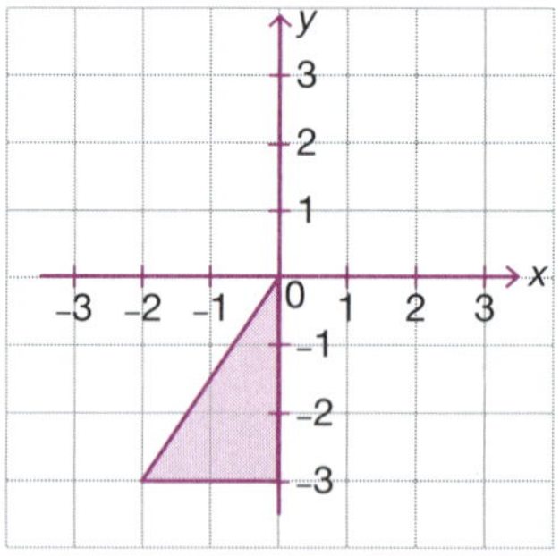

16 What is the size of the angle marked as *?

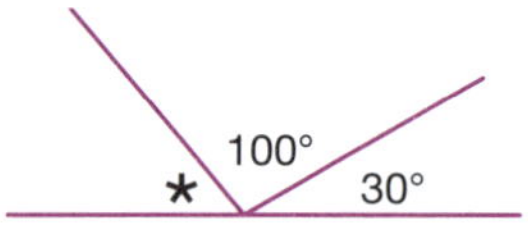

STATISTICS AND PROBABILITY

17 A number is chosen from a bag of balls numbered 1 to 24. What is the probability of selecting a ball that is a prime?

18 A new release movie has three screenings and the table shows the number of customers at each.

	1410	**1705**	**1815**
Adults	35	48	88
Children	53	78	98

How many were at the 1705 screening?

NUMBER AND ALGEBRA

1 Below is a sequence of square numbers. By considering the differences between the numbers, what is the next number?

784, 841, 900, 961,

2 Golf scores can be positive or negative where the person with the 'highest negative number' score wins. Here are four scores: Phil –8, Scott –10, Simon +4 and Tommy –3. Who came third?

3 Brooklyn's car uses petrol at an average rate of 8 L for every 100 km travelled. How far has she driven if she uses 144 L?

4 Arrange these in ascending order:

$3\frac{5}{6}$ $-3\frac{1}{2}$ $\frac{10}{3}$ $-\frac{15}{4}$

5 A man shared a sum of money between his wife and his four children. His wife received $\frac{1}{3}$ of the money and his four children receive equal shares of the remainder. What fraction did each child receive?

6 If Joseph spends \$50 each day, his money will last a week. If he only spends \$37.50 each day, how much money will he have remaining after the week?

7 Three-quarters of the balls in a box are red and one-fifth are blue. The rest of the balls are green. What percentage of balls in the box are green?

8 A frypan is priced at \$200. It was discounted by 25% last week and then by another 20% this week. What single discount percentage is represented by the two discounts?

9 A table uses the rule 'Bottom number = 2 × Top number – 9'. Use the rule to complete the table.

Top number	6	8		
Bottom number			11	15

10 Find the value of $(6 + 3) \times 4 - 4 \div (12 - 10)$.

MEASUREMENT AND SPACE

11 The area of a rectangle is 64 cm. If the width is 4 cm, what is the perimeter?

12 A cube has a side length 20 cm. Three 2-L bottles of water are poured into the empty cube. What fraction of the cube is full?

13 A timetable shows the journeys of three buses that travel the same route at the same speed.

Hicksville	1429	1611	?
Harrison	1532	?	?
Milford	1616	?	?
Guilford	1709	?	2016

There are times missing on the timetable. What time will the third bus leave Harrison?

14 The total length of edges on a cube is 720 cm. What is the capacity of the cube, in litres?

15 The shape is rotated 90° clockwise about the origin. Draw the image.

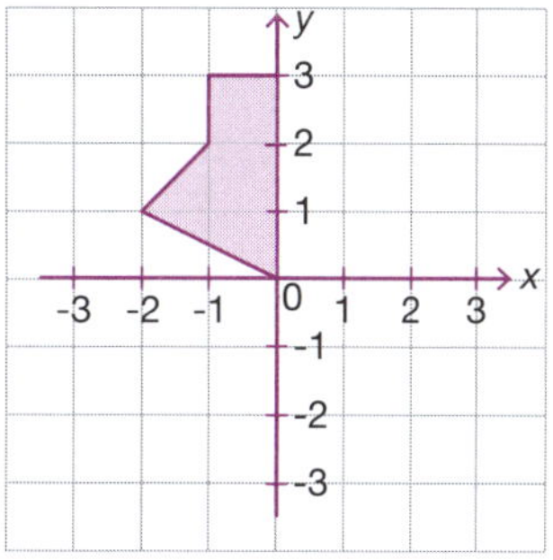

16 What is the value of x?

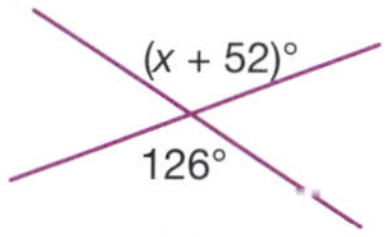

STATISTICS AND PROBABILITY

17 The probability of choosing a red marble from a bag of marbles is $\frac{1}{4}$. If 15 of the marbles are not red, how many red marbles are in the bag?

18 A new release movie has three screenings and the table shows the number of customers. What percentage of the total number of customers in the three screenings were adults at the 1815 screening?

	1410	1705	1815
Adults	35	48	88
Children	53	78	98

NUMBER AND ALGEBRA

1 How many composite numbers less than 100 are square numbers?

2 Georgia's fridge is set at 4 °C while her freezer is set at a temperature of –15 °C. How much warmer is the fridge compared to the freezer?

3 Fiona is making face masks during a pandemic. She uses 30 cm of elastic for each mask. What length of elastic is needed to make 24 masks?

4 On a number line, what fraction is halfway between $\frac{3}{4}$ and 1?

5 What is the sum of $\frac{1}{2}$, $\frac{1}{3}$ and $\frac{1}{4}$?

6 Ingrid used a website to buy two pairs of jeans priced at $69.95 each. Postage for the two pairs cost a total of $9.95. What was the total cost?

7 Find 40% of 600.

8 Entry for each adult into a museum costs $36. The price of a child is the adult price discounted by 50%. What is the total cost of an adult and two children?

9 A table uses the rule 'Bottom number = top number ÷ 4'. Use the rule to complete the table.

Top number	4	8	12	
Bottom number	1			4

10 Find the value of 3.5 – (1.2 + 1.8).

MEASUREMENT AND SPACE

11 Two rectangles have the same area. One rectangle has dimensions of 12 cm by 4 cm. If the other rectangle has a length of 6 cm, what is the difference in their perimeters?

12 A rectangular prism has dimensions 120 cm by 100 cm by 80 cm. What is the capacity of the prism, in kilolitres?

13 Part of a timetable of three trains is shown. Lola lives in Harrow and has an appointment in Maidstone at 6:00 pm. What is the latest time she can catch the train?

Harrow	1516	1624	–
Dartford	1604	1712	1725
Brentwood	1626	1734	–
Maidstone	1630	–	1748

14 Draw the solid that is formed using this net.

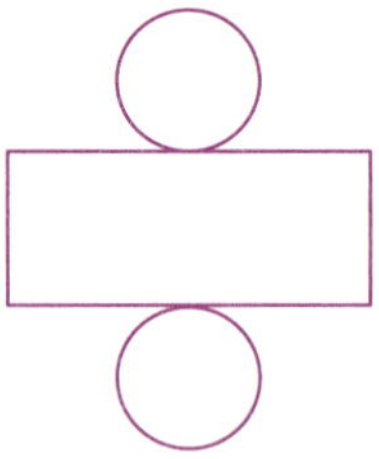

15 The shape is reflected about the y-axis and then translated 4 units down. Draw the image.

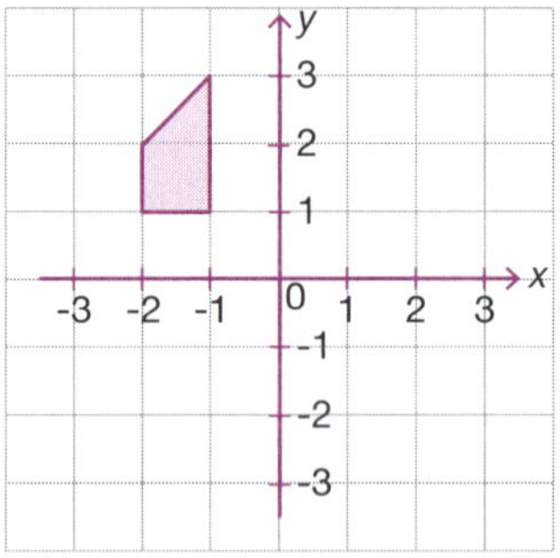

16 What is the size of the angle marked as *?

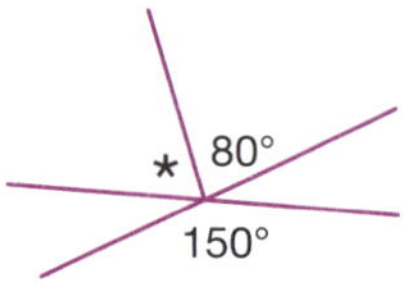

STATISTICS AND PROBABILITY

17 In a bucket of balls there are eight red balls. If the probability of selecting a red ball is $\frac{1}{3}$, how many balls are in the bucket?

18 A survey found the number of students who went to the beach and saw a movie last weekend. Complete the transfer of data from the diagram to the two-way table.

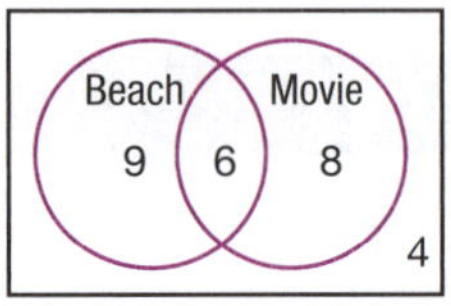

	Beach	No beach
Movie	6	
No movie		4

NUMBER AND ALGEBRA

1 What is the first prime number larger than 200?

2 Tom's bank allows him to 'overdraw' money from his account. Today he has \$35 in the account and he withdraws \$120. What is his balance now?

3 From a roll of electrical cable Aaron removes 16 lengths of cable which have an average length of 4 m. If 28 m of cable remain, what was the original length of cable on the roll?

4 On a number line, what number is halfway between $1\frac{2}{3}$ and $2\frac{1}{2}$?

5 A petrol tank gauge is showing three-quarters full. After using 20 L of petrol, the gauge shows one-third full. How much petrol is needed to fill the petrol tank?

6 The average height of three boys and two girls is 1.47 m. The average height of the three boys is 1.51 m. What is the average height of the two girls?

7 When George stopped for a rest-break he had driven 120 km, which was 30% of the distance he planned to drive. What distance does he still need to drive?

8 On Monday the price of a diamond ring in a store is \$2500. On each subsequent day, the price is discounted by 20%. If the ring is not sold, what is the price of the ring on Friday?

9 A table uses the rule 'Bottom number = (top number)^2'. Use the rule to complete the table.

Top number	5	8		
Bottom number			121	196

10 Find the value of $[(48 - 24) \div 8 + 2] \times (3 + 4 \times 2)$.

MEASUREMENT AND SPACE

11 A rectangle has a perimeter of 36 cm. The rectangle is to be enlarged by a factor of 2. If the original rectangle had a length of 10 cm, what is the area of the new rectangle?

12 A container is in the shape of a rectangular prism with a length of 20 cm and width of 15 cm. If it has a capacity of 5.4 L, how high is the container?

13 Part of a timetable of three trains is shown. Kareem arrives at the Harrow station at 3:10 pm. What is the earliest he can arrive in Maidstone?

Harrow	1516	–	1703
Dartford	1604	1725	1751
Brentwood	–	–	1811
Maidstone	–	1748	1827

14 The length of the rectangle is twice the width and its area is 18 cm^2. What is the perimeter of the net?

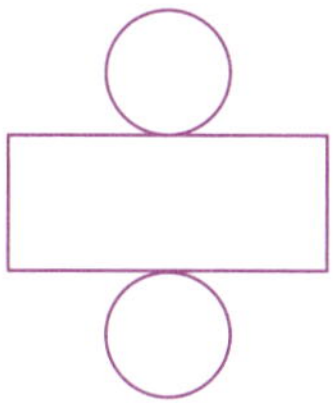

15 The shape is reflected about the x-axis and then rotated 90° clockwise about the origin. Draw the image.

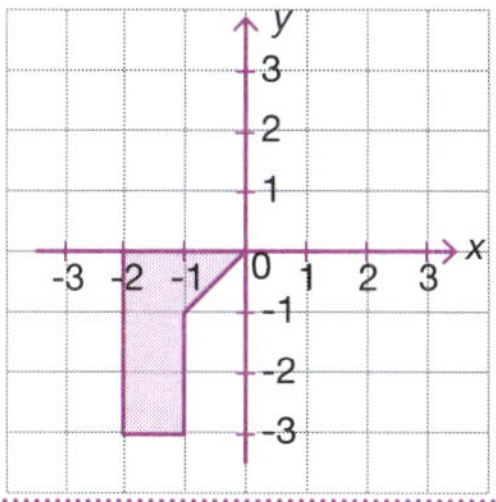

16 What is the value of x?

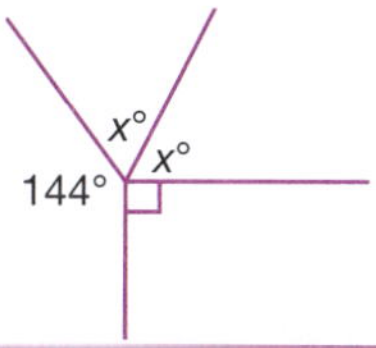

STATISTICS AND PROBABILITY

17 The probability of drawing a red card from a pile is 0.7. The probability of drawing a blue card is 0.1. The only other cards in the pile are 24 green cards. How many blue cards are in the pile?

18 A survey of 28 students found that 12 students went to the beach **and** saw a movie. A total of 18 students went to the beach and 3 students did **not** go to the beach or see a movie. Complete the table and diagram with the student numbers.

	Beach	No beach
Movie		
No movie		

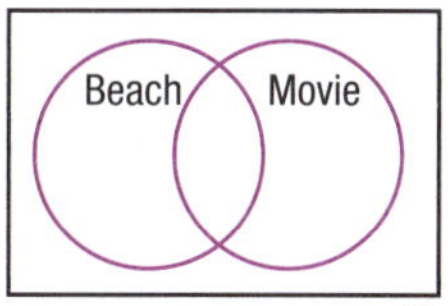

NON-CALCULATOR

1 Lyenna scored 75% in a history test. She scored the same result in a maths test. Which of these could be her result in the maths test? Select **all** the correct answers.

A	B	C	D	E
$\frac{40}{50}$	$\frac{30}{40}$	$\frac{75}{90}$	$\frac{35}{50}$	$\frac{15}{20}$

2 The diagram shows part of a compass rose.

Lines are also drawn to form angles. What is the size of the shaded angle?

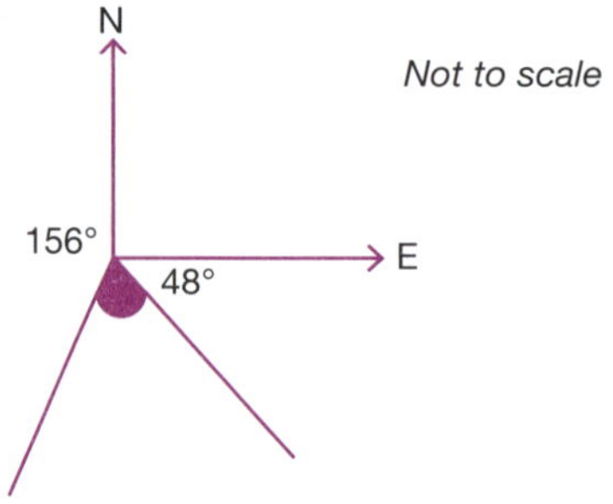

3 Remy, Harriet and Maddie enter the high jump event at the athletics carnival.

Remy jumped 1.25 m.

Harriet jumped 0.3 m less than Remy.

Maddie jumped 0.15 m higher than Harriet.

What was the average height jumped by the three girls?

4 What is the value of $20 - (4 + 6 \div 2 \times 3) + 8 \div (8 - 4)$?

A	B	C	D	E
1	3	9	7	10

CALCULATOR ALLOWED

5 The prices of two grades of petrol are listed.

Regular: 179.9 c/L
Premium: 191.9 c/L

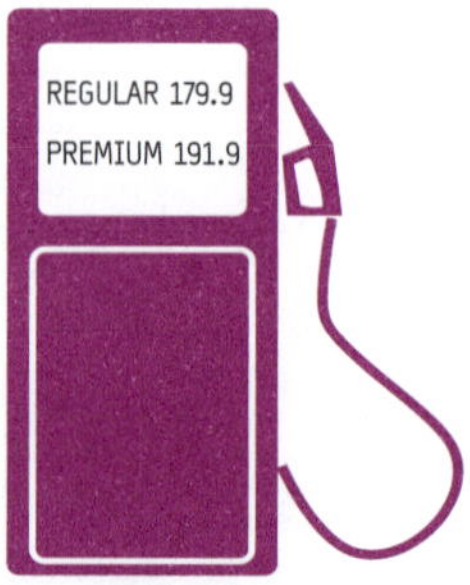

Gabrielle bought 40 L of petrol. How much more does she pay if she buys Premium grade rather than Regular?

6 On Monday, entries opened for a golf charity day. Sixteen men and four women registered on Monday. On Tuesday another 14 men and some women registered.

If twice as many men than women have now registered, how many women registered on Tuesday?

A	B	C	D
7	10	11	15

7 Points X and Y are located on the number plane at (2, 1) and (–2, –3) respectively.

Z is located north-west of X and north of Y.

What is the area of triangle XYZ?

☐ units²

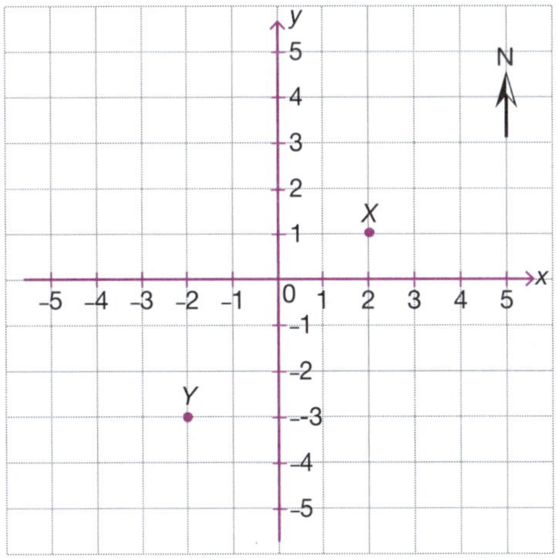

8 Sarah buys a 2-litre container of milk.
She has an empty rectangular prism with dimensions 20 cm by 10 cm by 5 cm.
If Sarah fills this container with milk, how much remains in the container?

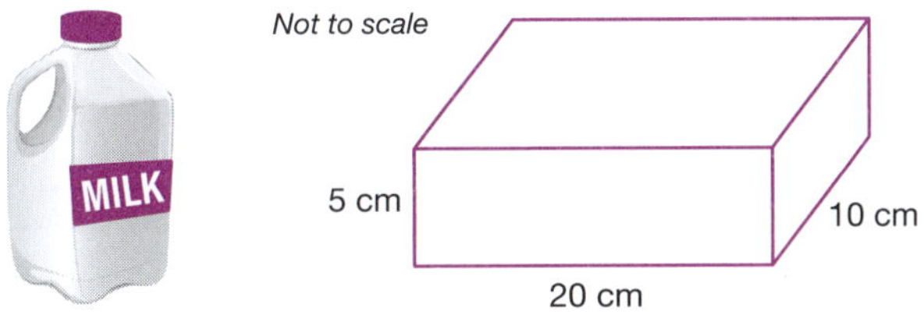

A 250 mL **B** 500 mL **C** 1000 mL **D** 1250 mL

9 A rectangle has a perimeter of 36 cm. If the length is 10 cm, what is the area of the rectangle?

A 80 cm² **B** 84 cm² **C** 180 cm² **D** 360 cm²

10 A bag contains six red balls and three blue balls.

Thomas randomly chooses balls from the bag and gives one to each of nine friends.

The results of the balls given to the first four friends are recorded in the table below.

Name	Lily	Oliver	Zoey	Jacob
Colour	red	blue	red	blue

What is the probability that the next ball Thomas chooses is red?

A 0.2 **B** 0.5 **C** 0.8 **D** 1

11 What is the value of X?

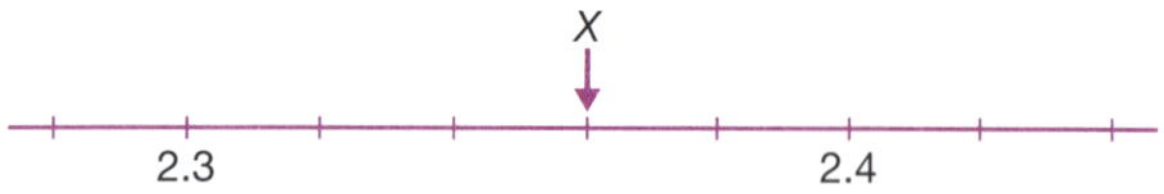

12 Here is a pattern of three shapes made of matchsticks.

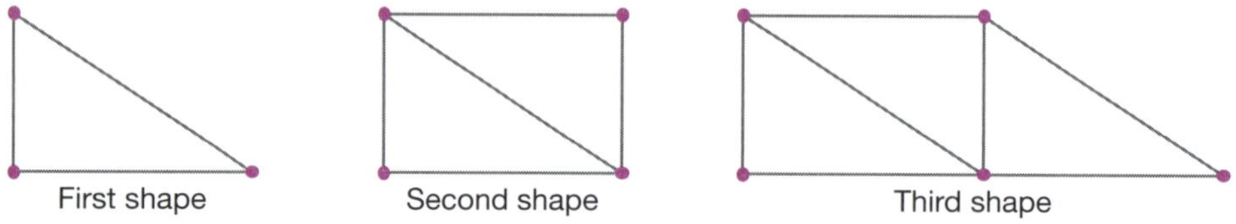

How many matchsticks are needed to make the eighth shape?

13 A pair of jeans priced at $89 is discounted by 10%.
What is the new price of the jeans?

14 Chloe, Clare and Carolyn compare their ages. The total of their ages is 60.
Carolyn is 28 years old. Clare is 4 years older than Chloe.

How old is Chloe?

15 The graph shows the way students in Years 5 and 6 usually travel to school.

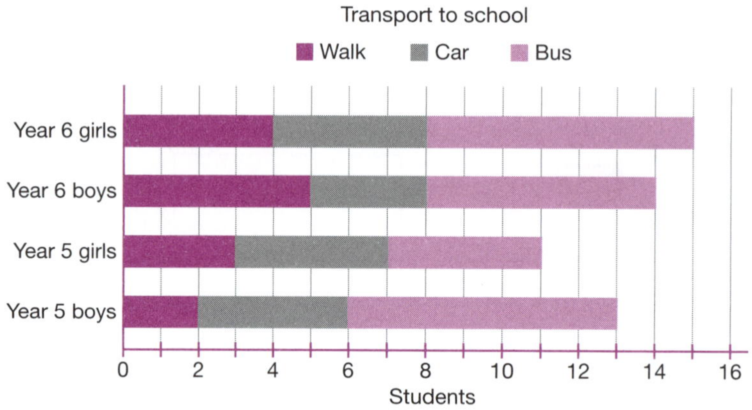

How many girls catch the bus?

16 A red light flashes every 6 seconds and a blue light flashes every 8 seconds.

If both lights flash at the same instant at 8 pm, how many **more** times will they flash at the same instant in the next 3 minutes?

17 Paul places seven identical hexagonal tiles side by side to form this larger shape.

Each hexagonal tile has a perimeter of 24 cm.
What is the perimeter of the larger shape?

18 A bag contains 12 balls.

Four of the balls are red, three are green and the remainder are blue.

Violet randomly selects a ball from the bag, notes its colour and returns it to the bag.

Violet does this a total of 60 times.

How many times does she expect to select a blue marble?

19 Here is a pattern of numbers. What is the twelfth number in the sequence?

$2\frac{1}{2}, 2\frac{3}{4}\ 3, 3\frac{1}{4} \ldots$

20 The shape is to be reflected about the y-axis and then translated down 6 units.

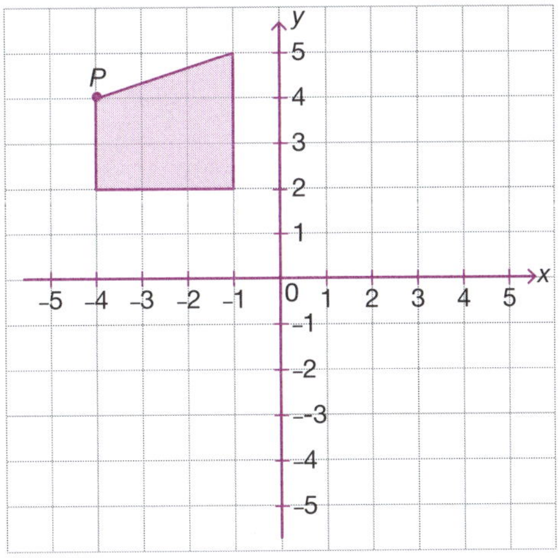

What will be the coordinates of the image of point P?

A	B	C	D	E
(1 , –2)	(4 , –2)	(1 , –1)	(4 , –1)	(2 , –5)

WORKED SOLUTIONS & ANSWERS

Section 1

Unit 1A PAGE 10

1. 2, 3, 5, 7, 11, 13, 17, 19, 23, 29

A prime number has only two factors. This means the numbers are 2, 3, 5, 7, 11, 13, 17, 19, 23 and 29.

2. 3, 9

The four options represent the numbers 23, 25, 27 and 29. Of these, the prime numbers are 23 and 29. The possible digits are 3 and 9.

3. 1, 4, 9, 16, 25, 36, 49, 64, 81

$1^2 = 1$, $2^2 = 4$, $3^2 = 9$, $4^2 = 16$, $5^2 = 25$, $6^2 = 36$, $7^2 = 49$, $8^2 = 64$ and $9^2 = 81$. The square numbers are 1, 4, 9, 16, 25, 36, 49, 64 and 81.

4. 72

11^2 is 121 and 7^2 is 49. $11^2 - 7^2$ is 121 − 49 which is 72.

5. 8 and 9

Composite numbers are 4, 6, 8, 9, 10 … This means that 8 and 9 are the first two consecutive numbers that are composite.

6. 7

The square numbers under 80 are 0, 1, 4, 9, 16, 25, 36, 49 and 64. Of these numbers, all are composite except 0 and 1. There are 7 numbers.

7. 2, 3, 5 and 7

210 is divisible by 3: 210 ÷ 3 is 70. Also, 70 ÷ 7 is 10, and 10 ÷ 5 is 2. As 210 = 3 × 7 × 5 × 2, the prime factors are 2, 3, 5 and 7.

8. 4

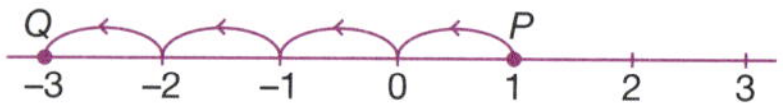

There are 4 jumps from *P* to *Q*. This means the difference between 1 and −3 is 4.

9. −6, −4, 1, 3

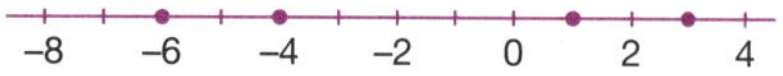

When reading the numbers on the number line from left to right, the numbers are in ascending order. The order is −6, −4, 1, 3.

10. −1

Starting at 3, subtracting 3 gives 0 and then subtracting another 1 gives −1.

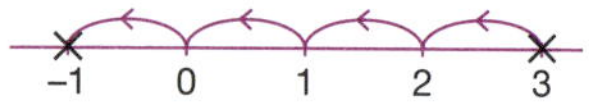

11. up 3 floors (+3)

Going down 4 floors is −4 and then going up is +7. From −4 counting on 7 gives 3 so there is a combined effect of going up 3 floors.

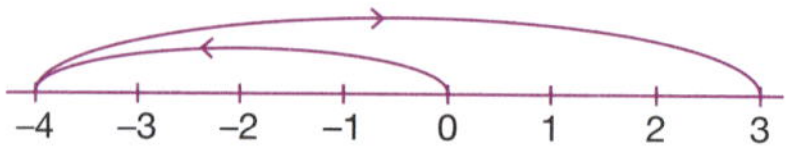

12. south 2 km (−2)

Going north for 4 km is +4 and then going south for 6 km is −6. From 4 counting backwards by 6 gives −2. This means a combined effect of travelling south for 2 km, which can be written as −2.

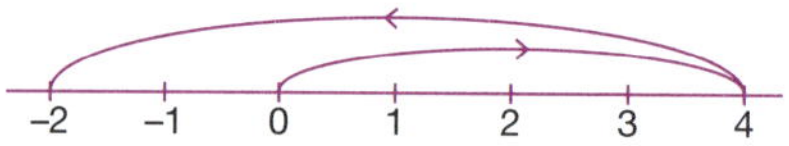

13. 5, 3

From −2, moving to the right 5 units takes you to 3. This means −2 + 5 = 3.

14. −5, −4, −3

The numbers are −5, −4 and −3.

15. 5 °C

Think of a number line. From −1 to 0 is 1 and then from 0 to 4 is 4. As 1 + 4 is 5, the difference in temperatures is 5 °C.

16. 4

The pattern is adding 3. As 1 + 3 is 4, the missing number is 4.

17. −4

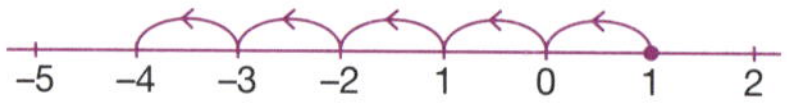

Starting at 1 and moving to the left 5 units takes you to −4.

18. 6

As 27 + 18 is 45, and 51 − 45 is 6, there are 6 children on the bus.

19. 14

8 + 11 + 16 + 21 is 56. As 56 ÷ 4 is 14, the average is 14.

20. 69

The missing number is the answer to 345 ÷ 5. This has the same answer as 690 ÷ 10 which is 69.

21. 92 km/h

$$7\overline{)\,64^{1}4}\quad\text{quotient } 92$$

Sofia's average speed was 92 km/h.

22. 200, 400

Eighty thousand is written as 80 000. This has four zeros so use 200 × 400 which is 80 000.

23. 405

The missing number is found using 9 × 45.

```
   45
×   9
  405
```

The missing number is 405.

24. 173

69 200 ÷ 400 is the same as 692 ÷ 4.

$$4\overline{)\,6^{2}9^{1}2}\quad\text{quotient } 173$$

This means 69 200 ÷ 400 is 173.

Unit 1B PAGE 11

1. 15

A composite number has more than two factors. The numbers are 18, 20, 21, 22, 24, 25, 26, 27, 28, 30, 32, 33, 34, 35 and 36. This means there are 15 numbers.

2. 5, 6, 9

The four options represent the numbers 125, 126, 127 and 129. Of these, the composite numbers are 125, 126 and 129 (which is divisible by 3). The possible digits are 5, 6 and 9.

3. 55

Triangular numbers have differences that are increasing by 1s. The numbers are 1, 3, 6, 10, 15, 21, 28, 36, 45, 55 … The tenth triangular number is 55.

4. 25 and 6

Here are some square numbers: 1, 4, 9, 16, 25, 36 … Here are some triangular numbers: 1, 3, 6, 10, 15, 21, 28, 36 … As 25 × 6 is 150, the numbers are 25 and 6.

5. 10

Students with prime numbers and 1 remained seated. The prime numbers are 2, 3, 5, 7, 11, 13, 17, 19 and 23. As 9 + 1 is 10, then 10 students remained seated.

6. 61

53 is the first prime after 50, then 59 then 61. The third prime is 61.

7. 784

The differences are 625 − 576 = 49, 676 − 625 = 51, 729 − 676 = 53. As the sequence of differences is 49, 51, 53, the next difference is 55. The missing number is 729 + 55 = 784.

8. 9 degrees

The difference between −11 and −2 is the same as the difference between 2 and 11. As 11 − 2 is 9, then the difference between the two temperatures is 9 °C.

9. 3, 1, −2, −5, −7

When reading the numbers on the number line from right to left, the numbers are in descending order. The order is 3, 1, −2, −5, −7.

10. −10

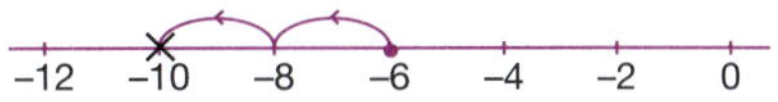

Using the number line, starting at −6 and subtracting 4 results in −10.

11. fall 4 degrees (−4)

Going down 6 degrees is −6 and then going up is +2. From −6 counting on 2 gives −4 which is a combined effect of a fall of 4 degrees, which can be written as −4.

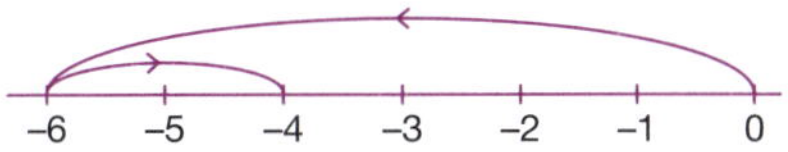

12. losing $30 (−30)

Winning $30 and then losing $50 means losing $20: 30 − 50 = −20. Losing another $10 means −20 − 10 which is −30, or losing $30.

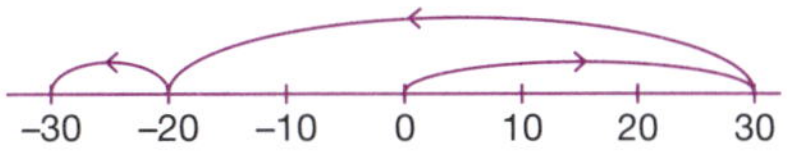

13. −7, 4, −11

From −7, move to the left 4 units to −11. This means −7 − 4 = −11.

14. 7

The numbers are −2, −1, 0, 1, 2, 3 and 4. There are 7 whole numbers between −3 and 5.

15. 7 °C

As the difference between 6 and 13 is 7, then the difference between −6 and −13 is also 7. The difference in temperatures is 7 °C.

16. −20 °C

The pattern is temperatures that are getting colder by 4 °C. The missing temperature would be −20 °C.

17. Dustin

The order is −6, −4, −2, +5. Dustin's score of −2 means he is coming third.

18. 13 392

$$\begin{array}{r} 237 \\ -\ \ 93 \\ \hline 144 \end{array}$$

The two numbers are 144 and 93.

$$\begin{array}{r} 144 \\ \times\ \ 93 \\ \hline 432 \\ 12\,960 \\ \hline 13\,392 \end{array}$$

The product is 13 392.

19. 150 cm

If the average height is 146 cm then the total height will be 146 × 3 or 438 cm. Zoe is 141 cm and Amelia is 147 cm. As 141 + 147 = 288, and 438 − 288 = 150, Claire is 150 cm tall.

20. 196

The missing number is the answer to 11 760 ÷ 60. This is the same answer as 1176 ÷ 6.

$$6\overline{)11^{5}7^{3}6}\ = 196$$

The missing number is 196.

21. 620 km/h

From 10 am to 5 pm is 7 hours.

$$7\overline{)43^{1}40}\ = 620$$

The average speed was 620 km/h.

22. 276 000

As 48 is 4 × 12 then the product is 250 × 4 × 12 × 23, which is 1000 × 12 × 23 or 12 000 × 23.

$$\begin{array}{r} 23 \\ \times\ \ 12 \\ \hline 276 \end{array}$$

As 23 × 12 is 276, then 12 000 × 23 is 276 000.

23. 78 336

$$\begin{array}{r} 68 \\ \times\ \ 48 \\ \hline 544 \\ 2720 \\ \hline 3264 \end{array}$$

The missing number is found using 3264 × 24.

$$\begin{array}{r} 3264 \\ \times\ \ 24 \\ \hline 13\,056 \\ 65\,280 \\ \hline 78\,336 \end{array}$$

The missing number is 78 336.

24. 1920 L

The number of litres is 12 × 8 × 4 × 5. As 12 × 8 is 96 and 4 × 5 is 20, the calculation needed is 96 × 20. As 96 × 2 is 192, then 96 × 20 is 1920. The shipment contains 1920 L of oil.

Unit 2A PAGE 12

1. $\frac{1}{2}$

4 out of 8 circles are shaded.

$\frac{4}{8} = \frac{4 \div 4}{8 \div 4} = \frac{1}{2}$

2. 245

$\frac{1}{3}$ of 735 is 735 ÷ 3.

$$3\overline{)7^{1}3^{1}5}\ = 245$$

One-third is 245.

3. 103

$\frac{1}{6}$ of 618 is 618 ÷ 6.

$$6\overline{)618}\ = 103$$

This means $\frac{1}{6}$ of 618 is 103.

4. $\frac{2}{3}$

Sixteen out of 24 is $\frac{16}{24} = \frac{16 \div 8}{24 \div 8}$ which is $\frac{2}{3}$. This means $\frac{2}{3}$ of the students borrowed a book from the library.

5. $\frac{1}{4}$

As 8 − 4 − 2 is 2, then 2 out of the 8 balloons are pink. As $\frac{2}{8} = \frac{2 \div 2}{8 \div 2} = \frac{1}{4}$, then $\frac{1}{4}$ of the balloons are pink.

6. $\frac{3}{5}$

Sebastian has 24 out of 40 cards. As $\frac{24}{40} = \frac{24 \div 8}{40 \div 8} = \frac{3}{5}$, he has $\frac{3}{5}$ of the set.

7. 5

Compare the denominators: 18 has been divided by 3 to give 6.

$\frac{15}{18} = \frac{15 \div 3}{18 \div 3} = \frac{5}{6}$

The missing number is 5.

8. 12

Compare the numerators: 56 has been divided by 8 to give 7.

$\frac{56}{96} = \frac{56 \div 8}{96 \div 8} = \frac{7}{12}$

The missing number is 12.

9. $\frac{4}{6}, \frac{3}{6}$

$\frac{2}{3} = \frac{2 \times 2}{3 \times 2} = \frac{4}{6}$

Also, $\frac{1}{2} = \frac{1 \times 3}{2 \times 3} = \frac{3}{6}$

The two fractions are $\frac{4}{6}$ and $\frac{3}{6}$.

10. $\frac{3}{8}, \frac{1}{2}, \frac{3}{4}$

$\frac{3}{4} = \frac{3 \times 2}{4 \times 2} = \frac{6}{8}, \frac{1}{2} = \frac{4}{8}, \frac{3}{8}$

The numerators are 6, 4, 3.

This means the order of fractions is $\frac{3}{8}, \frac{1}{2}, \frac{3}{4}$.

11. **>**

Rewrite the fractions with a denominator of 24: $\frac{2}{3} = \frac{2 \times 8}{3 \times 8} = \frac{16}{24}$ and $\frac{5}{8} = \frac{5 \times 3}{8 \times 3} = \frac{15}{24}$.

As 16 > 15, then $\frac{2}{3} > \frac{5}{8}$

12. The number line is marked in twelfths. $\frac{1}{4} = \frac{3}{12}$ and $\frac{2}{3} = \frac{8}{12}$

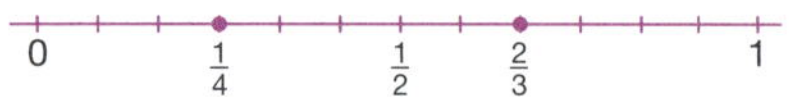

13. $\mathbf{\frac{9}{10}}$

As $\frac{2}{10}$, $\frac{4}{10}$ and $\frac{3}{10}$ have the same denominator, and 2 + 4 + 3 is 9, then $\frac{2}{10} + \frac{4}{10} + \frac{3}{10} = \frac{9}{10}$.

14. $\mathbf{\frac{1}{10}}$

Use a related denominator. As 2 and 5 are factors of 10, rewrite the fractions as tenths. $\frac{1}{2} = \frac{1 \times 5}{2 \times 5} = \frac{5}{10}$ and $\frac{2}{5} = \frac{2 \times 2}{5 \times 2} = \frac{4}{10}$.

This means $\frac{1}{2} - \frac{2}{5} = \frac{5}{10} - \frac{4}{10} = \frac{1}{10}$.

15. $\mathbf{1\frac{7}{15}}$

Use a related denominator. As 3 and 5 are factors of 15, rewrite the fractions as fifteenths. $\frac{2}{3} = \frac{2 \times 5}{3 \times 5} = \frac{10}{15}$ and $\frac{4}{5} = \frac{4 \times 3}{5 \times 3} = \frac{12}{15}$. This means $\frac{2}{3} + \frac{4}{5}$ is $\frac{10}{15} + \frac{12}{15} = \frac{22}{15}$, which is $1\frac{7}{15}$.

16. $\mathbf{1\frac{1}{2}}$

First consider $\frac{3}{4} - \frac{1}{4} = \frac{2}{4}$ which is $\frac{1}{2}$.

This means $1\frac{3}{4} - \frac{1}{4}$ is $1\frac{1}{2}$.

17. **5**

$\frac{7}{8} + \frac{6}{8} = \frac{13}{8}$, which can be rewritten as $1\frac{5}{8}$. The missing number is 5.

18. $\mathbf{\frac{2}{5}}$

The missing number is $1 - \frac{3}{5}$, which is $\frac{5}{5} - \frac{3}{5} = \frac{2}{5}$.

19. $\mathbf{\frac{7}{12}}$

You need to find $\frac{1}{4} + \frac{1}{3}$. Use a related denominator. As 4 and 3 are factors of 12, rewrite the fractions as twelfths.

$\frac{1}{4} = \frac{1 \times 3}{4 \times 3} = \frac{3}{12}$ and $\frac{1}{3} = \frac{1 \times 4}{3 \times 4} = \frac{4}{12}$

$\frac{1}{4} + \frac{1}{3} = \frac{3}{12} + \frac{4}{12} = \frac{7}{12}$, so Michaela has drunk $\frac{7}{12}$ of her water bottle.

20. **27**

To find $\frac{3}{5}$ of 45, find one-fifth and then multiply by 3. 45 ÷ 5 × 3 is 9 × 3 which equals 27. This means $\frac{3}{5}$ of 45 is 27.

21. **8 m**

As $1 - \frac{2}{3} = \frac{1}{3}$, then $\frac{1}{3}$ of the fence needs to be built. As $\frac{1}{3}$ of 24 is 24 ÷ 3 which is 8, Pearl has 8 m to complete.

22. $\mathbf{\frac{2}{3}}$ **cup**

$2 - 1\frac{1}{3}$ is $2 - 1 - \frac{1}{3}$, which is $1 - \frac{1}{3}$.

As $1 = \frac{3}{3}$, then $\frac{3}{3} - \frac{1}{3}$ is $\frac{2}{3}$. Jacinta borrowed $\frac{2}{3}$ of a cup.

23. **60**

You need to find $\frac{3}{5}$ of 100 which is 100 ÷ 5 × 3. This is 20 × 3 which is 60. This means 60 teapots come from Europe.

24. **18 km**

The distance is $2\frac{1}{4} + 2\frac{1}{4} + 2\frac{1}{4} + 2\frac{1}{4}$, which is $8 + \frac{4}{4} = 9$. Chloe walks a distance of 9 km to work and 9 km home. This is a total of 18 km.

Unit 2B PAGE 13

1. $\mathbf{\frac{1}{4}}$

2 out of 8 circles are not shaded.

$\frac{2}{8} = \frac{2 \div 2}{8 \div 2} = \frac{1}{4}$.

2. **270**

$\frac{3}{4}$ of 360 is 360 ÷ 4 × 3.

This is 90 × 3 = 270.

3. **34**

If $\frac{3}{5}$ of the bananas are ripe then $\frac{2}{5}$ are not ripe. $\frac{2}{5}$ of 85 is 85 ÷ 5 × 2 which is 17 × 2 = 34. This means 34 bananas are not ripe.

4. $\mathbf{\frac{2}{25}}$

As 200 – 184 is 16, then 16 students out of 200 were late to school.

As $\frac{16}{200} = \frac{16 \div 8}{200 \div 8} = \frac{2}{25}$, then $\frac{2}{25}$ of the students were late.

5. $\mathbf{\frac{1}{10}}$

As 20 – 12 – 6 = 2, then 2 out of 20 are white chocolate. This means $\frac{2}{20}$, or $\frac{1}{10}$, are white chocolate.

6. $\mathbf{\frac{10}{19}}$

The composite numbers less than 20 are 4, 6, 8, 9, 10, 12, 14, 15, 16 and 18.

As there are 19 positive numbers less than 20 the fraction is $\frac{10}{19}$.

7. **7**

$1\frac{9}{12} = \frac{21}{12}$. The question is $\frac{21}{12} = \frac{\square}{4}$.

Compare the denominators: 12 has been divided by 3 to give 4.

$\frac{21}{12} = \frac{21 \div 3}{12 \div 3} = \frac{7}{4}$

The missing number is 7.

8. $\mathbf{\frac{1}{6}}$

$\frac{24}{144} = \frac{24 \div 12}{144 \div 12} = \frac{2}{12} = \frac{2 \div 2}{12 \div 2} = \frac{1}{6}$

9. $\mathbf{\frac{27}{12}, \frac{44}{12}}$

The denominators are 4 and 3 so use 12 as the related denominator.

$2\frac{1}{4} = \frac{9}{4} = \frac{9 \times 3}{4 \times 3} = \frac{27}{12}$

Also, $3\frac{2}{3} = \frac{11}{3} = \frac{11 \times 4}{3 \times 4} = \frac{44}{12}$. The two improper fractions are $\frac{27}{12}$ and $\frac{44}{12}$.

10. $\mathbf{\frac{5}{8}, \frac{2}{3}, \frac{3}{4}, \frac{5}{6}}$

Rewrite each fraction with a denominator of 24.

$\frac{5}{6} = \frac{20}{24}$, $\frac{2}{3} = \frac{16}{24}$, $\frac{5}{8} = \frac{15}{24}$, $\frac{3}{4} = \frac{18}{24}$

Comparing the numerators of 20, 16, 15 and 18, the order is $\frac{5}{8}, \frac{2}{3}, \frac{3}{4}, \frac{5}{6}$.

11. **>**

Rewrite each fraction with a denominator of 12: $\frac{15}{4} = \frac{15 \times 3}{4 \times 3} = \frac{45}{12}$ and $\frac{11}{3} = \frac{11 \times 4}{3 \times 4} = \frac{44}{12}$. As 45 > 44, then $\frac{15}{4} > \frac{11}{3}$.

12. The number line is marked in eighths.

$2\frac{1}{2} = 2\frac{4}{8}$ and $3\frac{1}{4} = 3\frac{2}{8}$

13. $\mathbf{2\frac{1}{6}}$

$\frac{5}{6}$, $\frac{3}{6}$ and $\frac{5}{6}$ have the same denominator, and 5 + 3 + 5 is 13.

$\frac{5}{6} + \frac{3}{6} + \frac{5}{6} = \frac{13}{6}$, which is $2\frac{1}{6}$.

14. $\mathbf{\frac{13}{24}}$ **L**

The question is $\frac{7}{8} - \frac{1}{3}$. Use a related denominator. As 8 and 3 are factors of 24, rewrite the fractions as twenty-fourths.

As $\frac{7}{8} = \frac{21}{24}$ and $\frac{1}{3} = \frac{8}{24}$,

then $\frac{7}{8} - \frac{1}{3} = \frac{21}{24} - \frac{8}{24} = \frac{13}{24}$.

Indira has $\frac{13}{24}$ L remaining.

15. **$10\frac{3}{4}$ hours**

The question is $4\frac{1}{2} + 6\frac{1}{4}$. Use a related denominator. As 2 and 4 are factors of 4, rewrite the fractions as quarters.

$\frac{1}{2} = \frac{2}{4}$. As $4\frac{2}{4} + 6\frac{1}{4} = 10\frac{3}{4}$, Levi worked $10\frac{3}{4}$ hours.

16. $\frac{2}{5}$

$1\frac{1}{5}$ is $\frac{6}{5}$.

This means $1\frac{1}{5} - \frac{4}{5} = \frac{6}{5} - \frac{4}{5} = \frac{2}{5}$.

17. **1**

Use a related denominator. As 8 and 6 are factors of 24, rewrite the fractions as twenty-fourths.

$\frac{7}{8} = \frac{21}{24}$ and $\frac{1}{6} = \frac{4}{24}$

This means $\frac{7}{8} + \frac{1}{6} = \frac{21}{24} + \frac{4}{24} = \frac{25}{24}$, which can be rewritten as $1\frac{1}{24}$.

The missing number is 1.

18. $\frac{2}{5}$ **or** $\frac{4}{10}$

The missing number is $1\frac{1}{10} - \frac{7}{10}$. As $1\frac{1}{10} = \frac{11}{10}$, then $1\frac{1}{10} - \frac{7}{10} = \frac{11}{10} - \frac{7}{10} = \frac{4}{10}$, which can be rewritten as $\frac{2}{5}$.

19. $\frac{1}{8}$

The question is $1 - \frac{5}{8} - \frac{1}{4}$. Use a related denominator. As 8 and 4 are factors of 8, rewrite the fractions as eighths. As $1 = \frac{8}{8}$ and $\frac{1}{4} = \frac{2}{8}$, then $1 - \frac{5}{8} - \frac{1}{4}$ is $\frac{8}{8} - \frac{5}{8} - \frac{2}{8} = \frac{1}{8}$. This means $\frac{1}{8}$ of the novel remains.

20. **18**

As $1 - \frac{5}{8} = \frac{3}{8}$, then $\frac{3}{8}$ of the people are men. $\frac{3}{8}$ of 18 is 18 ÷ 8 × 3 which is 6 × 3 or 18. This means 18 men were surveyed.

21. **225 km**

$\frac{3}{5}$ of the total distance is 135 km. As 135 ÷ 3 = 45, then $\frac{1}{5}$ of the distance is 45 km, and so 45 × 5 = 225. The total distance is 225 km.

22. $\frac{2}{5}$

The question is $1 - \frac{3}{10} - \frac{3}{10}$, which is $1 - \frac{6}{10}$. As $1 = \frac{10}{10}$, then $1 - \frac{6}{10} = \frac{10}{10} - \frac{6}{10} = \frac{4}{10}$. This can be rewritten as $\frac{2}{5}$.

23. **2560 L**

As 1600 × 2 is 3200, the tank contains 3200 L of water when full. As $\frac{4}{5}$ of 3200 is 3200 ÷ 5 × 4 = 640 × 4 which is 2560, the tank has 2560 L of water when it is $\frac{4}{5}$ full.

24. $\frac{7}{20}$

As $2 \times \frac{1}{5}$ is $\frac{2}{5}$, Bruce receives $1 - \frac{2}{5} - \frac{1}{4}$ of the estate. Using a related denominator of 20, then $1 - \frac{2}{5} - \frac{1}{4} = \frac{20}{20} - \frac{8}{20} - \frac{5}{20}$, which is $\frac{7}{20}$. Bruce is given $\frac{7}{20}$ of the estate.

Unit 3A

PAGE 14

1. **20.97**

Rewrite 12.9 as 12.90.

$$\begin{array}{r} 12.90 \\ +\ \ 8.07 \\ \hline 20.97 \end{array}$$

2. **8.6**

Rewrite with 1 decimal place.

$$\begin{array}{r} 18.0 \\ -\ \ 9.4 \\ \hline 8.6 \end{array}$$

3. **17.79**

Look at the digit in the third decimal place: as it is 6, then round the 8 up to 9. The answer is 17.79.

4. **10.7**

First, 12.7 – 5 is 7.7. Now add 3 to get 10.7.

5. **40.15**

$$\begin{array}{r} 803 \\ \times\ \ 5 \\ \hline 4015 \end{array}$$

As there are 2 decimal places in the question, then the answer has 2 decimal places. This means 8.03 × 5 = 40.15.

6. **2387.2**

Multiplying by 100 moves the decimal point 2 places to the right. This means 23.872 × 100 = 2387.2.

7. **4.77**

$$5\overline{)23.{}^{3}8{}^{3}5} = 4.77$$

8. **0.4886**

Dividing by 100 moves the decimal point 2 places to the left. This means 48.86 ÷ 100 = 0.4886.

9. **6.8**

$$5\overline{)34.{}^{4}0} = 6.8$$

10. **4.8 m**

You need to find 1.6 × 3.

$$\begin{array}{r} 16 \\ \times\ \ 3 \\ \hline 48 \end{array}$$

As there is 1 decimal place in the question, then the answer has 1 decimal place. Fiona needs 4.8 m of material.

11. **73**

As 20 × 5 is 100, the question is 0.73 × 100. Multiplying by 100 moves the decimal point 2 places to the right. This means 0.73 × 100 = 73.

12. **112.48 kg**

$$\begin{array}{r} 1406 \\ \times\ \ \ \ 8 \\ \hline 11248 \end{array}$$

As there are 2 decimal places in the question, then the answer has 2 decimal places. This means 14.06 × 8 is 112.48. The total mass is 112.48 kg.

13. **0.7**

The missing number is 2.3 – 1.6, which is 0.7.

14. **31.12**

$$\begin{array}{r} 12.780 \\ 0.239 \\ +\ 18.096 \\ \hline 31.115 \end{array}$$

In 31.115, the digit in the third place is a 5, so the answer is 31.12.

15. **801 g**

26.7 × 10 × 3 = 267 × 3 = 801

The total mass is 801 g.

16. **1467.1**

As 10^2 is 100, then 14.671 × 100 is 1467.1

17. **193**

The total is 38.6 × 5.

$$\begin{array}{r} 386 \\ \times\ \ \ 5 \\ \hline 1930 \end{array}$$

As 386 × 5 = 1930, then 38.6 × 5 = 193.0. Jason completed 193 push-ups.

18. **$197.25**

$$\begin{array}{r} 6575 \\ \times\ \ \ \ 3 \\ \hline 19725 \end{array}$$

As 6575 × 3 = 19725, then 65.75 × 3 = 197.25. The total cost was $197.25.

19. **13.9 °C**

$$\begin{array}{r} 23.5 \\ -\ \ 9.6 \\ \hline 13.9 \end{array}$$

The minimum temperature was 13.9 °C.

20. **0.84 m**

$$5\overline{)4.2{}^{2}0} = 0.84$$

Each piece was 0.84 m long.

21. **65.6 m**

As 36 × 4 is 144, then 3.6 × 4 is 14.4. You need to find 80 – 14.4.

```
  80.0
– 14.4
  65.6
```

There was still 65.6 m of string on the ball.

22. **421 km**

The distance is 84.2 × 5.

```
  842
×   5
 4210
```

As 842 × 5 = 4210, then 84.2 × 5 = 421.0. Max drove 421 km.

23. **0.023 25**

```
  0.023 25
2)0.0465¹0
```

24. **26.16 s**

```
  24.90
+  1.26
  26.16
```

Linus's time was 26.16 s.

25. **2 m**

20 cm = 0.2 m and
0.8 + 0.2 × 6 = 0.8 + 1.2 = 2.
The shrub will be 2 m tall.

26. **8.49**

Any number greater than or equal to 7.5, but less than 8.5, rounds to 8. This means the largest number is 8.49.

27. **2.9 m**

As 50 + 20 = 70 and 70 cm = 0.7 m, you need to find 3.6 – 0.7.
As 3.6 – 0.6 – 0.1 = 2.9, the length remaining is 2.9 m.

Unit 3B PAGE 15

1. **22.778**

Rewrite each decimal with 3 decimal places.

```
   9.280
   0.098
+ 13.400
  22.778
```

2. **1.62**

First, work out 4 – 1.8:

```
  4.0
– 1.8
  2.2
```

Now 2.2 – 0.58:

```
  2.20
– 0.58
  1.62
```

3. **43.60**

Look at the digit in the third decimal place: as it is 8, then increase the 9 to 0 which then increases the 5 to a 6. The answer is 43.60.

4. **7.815**

```
  9.00
– 4.26
  4.74
```

Now, add 4.74 and 3.075:

```
  4.740
+ 3.075
  7.815
```

5. **3506.4**

```
    974
×    36
   5844
 29 220
 35 064
```

As there is 1 decimal place in the question, then the answer has 1 decimal place. This means 97.4 × 36 = 3506.4.

6. **100**

Comparing 9.481 and 948.1, the decimal point has moved 2 places to the right.
This means 9.481 × 100 = 948.1.
The missing number is 100.

7. **0.789**

```
  0.7 8 9
4)3.1³5³6
```

8. **100**

Comparing 64 (which is 64.0) and 0.64, the decimal point has moved 2 places to the left. This means 64 ÷ 100 = 0.64. The missing number is 100.

9. **37**

```
   3 6.6
4)14²6.²4
```

146.4 ÷ 4 is 36.6, which rounds to 37, the nearest whole.

10. **$8.90**

```
  2.69
  2.69
+ 3.49
  8.87
```

The cost is $8.87, which is $8.90 to the nearest 10 cents.

11. **37.8**

Rewrite the question as 0.0378 × 250 × 4, which is 0.0378 × 1000. As multiplying by 1000 moves the decimal point 3 places to the right, then 0.0378 × 1000 = 37.8.

12. **33.7**

As 17 × 5 is 85, and 42 × 6 is 252, then 1.7 × 5 + 4.2 × 6 = 8.5 + 25.2.

```
   8.5
+ 25.2
  33.7
```

13. **32.8**

As 1.672 × 100 is 167.2, you need to find 200 – 167.2.

```
  200.0
– 167.2
   32.8
```

The missing number is 32.8.

14. **3.17**

As dividing by 100 moves the decimal point 2 places to the left, then 316.814 ÷ 100 = 3.16814. Rounding off to the nearest hundredth is leaving it to 2 decimal places. As there is an 8 is in the third decimal place, the answer is 3.17.

15. **7**

The sum of 3.9, 12.8, 6.1 and 5.2 is 28.0. As 28 ÷ 4 is 7, the average is 7.

16. **1.783**

As 10^2 is 100, then $\frac{178.3}{10^2}$ is 178.3 ÷ 100 which is 1.783.

17. **24.1 °C**

```
  236
×   4
  944
```

As 236 × 4 = 944, then 23.6 × 4 = 94.4.
Now as 94.4 + 26.1 = 120.5, you need to find 120.5 ÷ 5.

```
  2 4.1
5)12²0.5
```

The average temperature is 24.1 °C.

18. **86.4**

The missing number is found by multiplying 36 × 2.4.

```
   36
×  24
  144
  720
  864
```

As 36 × 24 = 864, then 36 × 2.4 = 86.4.
The missing number is 86.4.

19. **7.25 kg**

```
  2.15
+ 0.80
  2.95
```

The heavier package had a mass of 2.95 kg.

```
  2.15
  2.15
+ 2.95
  7.25
```

The total mass was 7.25 kg.

20. **40.7 mm**

```
   43.1
+  32.9
   76.0
  116.7
–  76.0
   40.7
```

40.7 mm fell in August.

21. 7.5 °C

You need to find 2.9 + 16.4 – 11.8.

```
  2.9
+ 16.4
  19.3
```

Now work out 19.3 – 11.8.

```
  19.3
– 11.8
   7.5
```

The temperature was 7.5 °C.

22. $675

```
   1875
×    36
  11250
  56250
  67500
```

As 1875 × 36 is 67 500 then 18.75 × 36 is 675.00. Jasmine will be paid $675.

23. 4.65

You need to find 6.2 ÷ 4 × 3.

```
   1.5 5
4)6.²2²0
```

Now, work out 1.55 × 3.

```
  155
×   3
  465
```

As 155 × 3 is 465, then 1.55 × 3 is 4.65.

24. 21.635

You need to add 17.8 and 25.47 and divide the total by 2.

```
  17.80
+ 25.47
  43.27
```

```
  21.635
2)43.¹27¹0
```

The middle is 21.635.

25. 1.25

There are 4 units between 4 and 5 which means each unit represents 0.25. Between *A* and *B* there are 5 units. As 0.25 × 5 = 1.25, the value of *B* – *A* is 1.25.

26. 2.5 kg

As 3.2 × 3 = 9.6 and 9.6 – 4.6 = 5, the total mass of the other two packages is 5 kg. As half of 5 is 2.5, the average mass is 2.5 kg.

27. 0.57 s

```
  59.38
–  0.68
  58.70
```

As 70 – 13 = 57, the time between 58.70 and 58.13 is 0.57. Jack finished 0.57 s ahead of Thomas.

Unit 4A PAGE 16

1. $\frac{3}{6}$, $\frac{50}{100}$

As 50% = $\frac{1}{2}$, then look for fractions that can be simplified to $\frac{1}{2}$. As $\frac{3}{6} = \frac{1}{2}$, and $\frac{50}{100} = \frac{1}{2}$, the fractions are $\frac{3}{6}$ and $\frac{50}{100}$.

2. 50%

4 out of 8 squares are shaded.

Writing as a fraction, $\frac{4}{8} = \frac{1}{2}$, which is 50%.

3. 75% is $\frac{3}{4}$, which means 3 out of 4 columns should be shaded.

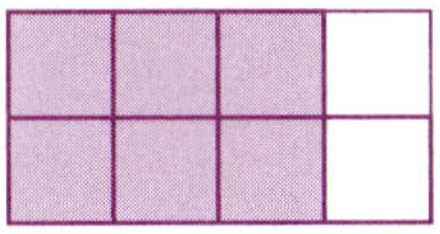

4. 0.8

Express each as a percentage:

0.8 = 80%, 60%, $\frac{65}{100}$ = 65%, $\frac{3}{4}$ = 75%.

The largest percentage is 80%, so the largest is 0.8.

5. 80%

16 out of 20 is $\frac{16}{20} = \frac{16 \times 5}{20 \times 5} = \frac{80}{100}$, which is 80%.

6. 40%

$\frac{2}{5} = \frac{2 \times 20}{5 \times 20} = \frac{40}{100}$

This is 40%.

7. 218

50% is $\frac{1}{2}$, and $\frac{1}{2}$ of 436 is 436 ÷ 2 = 218.

50% of 436 is 218.

8. 9000 L

25% is the same as $\frac{1}{4}$. You need to find $\frac{1}{4}$ of 36 000, which is 36 000 ÷ 4. As 36 ÷ 4 is 9, then 36 000 ÷ 4 is 9000. There is 9000 L of water in the tank.

9. 75%

As 6 out of 24 rolls have been used then $\frac{6}{24} = \frac{1}{4}$ = 25% of the rolls have been used. As 100 – 25 = 75, then 75% of the rolls remain.

10. $\frac{9}{20}$

45% can be rewritten as

$\frac{45}{100} = \frac{45 \div 5}{100 \div 5} = \frac{9}{20}$.

This means 45% = $\frac{9}{20}$.

11. 20%

As 1 – $\frac{4}{5}$ is $\frac{1}{5}$, Charlotte has one-fifth of the book to read. $\frac{1}{5} = \frac{1 \times 20}{5 \times 20} = \frac{20}{100}$, which is the same as 20%.

12. 6

As 100 – 80 = 20, then 20% of the 30 students do not have their ears pierced. As 20% is $\frac{1}{5}$, and 30 ÷ 5 = 6, then 6 girls do not have their ears pierced.

13. $585

```
  860
– 275
  585
```

The new price is $585.

14. $7800

One-third of 23 400 is 23 400 ÷ 3.

```
  7800
3)23²400
```

Cooper sold the bike for $7800.

15. $443

```
  378
+  65
  443
```

The original price was $443.

16. $2061

As 10% is $\frac{1}{10}$, then 2290 ÷ 10 is 229.

```
  2290
–  229
  2061
```

The discounted price is $2061.

17. $133.50

Half of $89 is $44.50.

```
   89.00
+  44.50
  133.50
```

Zoe will pay $133.50.

18. 35%

As 100 – 65 is 35, the discount is $35. As a fraction the discount is 35 out of 100, which is $\frac{35}{100}$ = 35%.

19. $24

Half is 50% and equals $48. 25% will be $48 ÷ 2 which is $24. The pool toy cost $24.

20. 20%

As 200 – 160 is 40, the discount fraction is $\frac{40}{200} = \frac{20}{100}$, which is 20%.

The discount is 20%.

21. $65.19

As 10% is $\frac{1}{10}$, you need to divide 651.90 by 10. As division by 10 means the decimal point moves 1 place to the left, 651.90 ÷ 10 is 65.19. Loki will save $65.19.

22. $475

If 20% is $95 and 100% is the usual price, you need to multiply 95 × 5 which is 475. The usual price is $475.

23. $30 800

As 10% is $\frac{1}{10}$ then 28 000 ÷ 10 is 2800. As 28 000 + 2800 is 30 800, Thomas sells the painting for $30 800.

24. $720 000

As 10% is $\frac{1}{10}$, then 800 000 ÷ 10 = 80 000 which means the price has dropped by $80 000.

As 800 – 80 is 720, the new price is $720 000.

Unit 4B PAGE 17

1. 0.25, $\frac{3}{12}$

As 25% = $\frac{1}{4}$ = 0.25, and $\frac{3}{12} = \frac{1}{4}$, the answers are 0.25 and $\frac{3}{12}$.

2. 70%

Seven out of 10 columns are shaded. As $\frac{7}{10} = \frac{70}{100}$, then 70% is shaded.

3. There are 2 rows of 10 squares, which means 20 squares.

As 35% = $\frac{35}{100} = \frac{35 \div 5}{100 \div 5} = \frac{7}{20}$, then shade 7 squares.

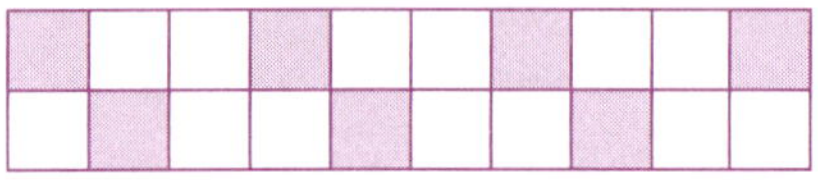

4. 35%, 0.4, $\frac{9}{20}$, $\frac{23}{50}$

Express each as a percentage:

$\frac{9}{20} = \frac{9 \times 5}{20 \times 5} = \frac{45}{100}$ = 45%, 0.4 = 0.40 = 40%, $\frac{23}{50} = \frac{23 \times 2}{50 \times 2} = \frac{46}{100}$ = 46%, 35%.

The order of numbers is 35, 40, 45, 46.

In ascending order, 35%, 0.4, $\frac{9}{20}$, $\frac{23}{50}$.

5. 36%

$\frac{72}{200} = \frac{72 \div 2}{200 \div 2} = \frac{36}{100}$, which is 36%.

6. 37.5%

You need to work out 3 ÷ 8.

$8\overline{)3.0^{6}0^{4}0}$ = 0.375

This means $\frac{3}{8}$ = 0.375, which is 37.5%.

7. 128

As 20% is $\frac{1}{5}$, you need to divide 640 ÷ 5.

As $5\overline{)6^{1}4^{4}0}$ = 128, then 20% of 640 is 128.

8. 575 km

25% is the same as $\frac{1}{4}$. You need to find $\frac{1}{4}$ of 460.

$4\overline{)46^{2}0}$ = 115

As 460 + 115 is 575, Colton plans to ride 575 km next week.

9. 5

As 100 – 80 is 20, then 20% of the students have not handed in the note.

As 20% is $\frac{20}{100} = \frac{1}{5}$, you need to find $\frac{1}{5}$ of 25. As 25 ÷ 5 is 5, then 5 students have not handed in the note.

10. 0.075

$7\frac{1}{2}$% is 7.5%, and can be rewritten as $\frac{7.5}{100} = \frac{7.5 \times 10}{100 \times 10} = \frac{75}{1000}$, which is 0.075.

11. $\frac{2}{5}$

As 50 + 10 is 60, and 100 – 60 is 40, then 40% of the balls are blue. 40% can be written as $\frac{40}{100} = \frac{40 \div 20}{100 \div 20} = \frac{2}{5}$, so $\frac{2}{5}$ of the balls are blue.

12. 255

As 30% is $\frac{3}{10}$ you need to find $\frac{3}{10}$ of 850. As 850 ÷ 10 × 3 is 85 × 3 = 255, then 255 people in the audience were opera first-timers.

13. $203.99

```
  138.99
+  65.00
  203.99
```

The original price was $203.99.

14. $11 700

One-quarter of 15 600 is 15 600 ÷ 4 = 3900. Now work out 15 600 – 3900.

```
  15 600
–  3 900
  11 700
```

The new price is $11 700.

15. $60 000

As $1 - \frac{1}{5}$ is $\frac{4}{5}$, then $48 000 is $\frac{4}{5}$ of the original price. You need to divide 48 000 by 4 to find $\frac{1}{5}$ and then multiply by 5 to find $\frac{5}{5}$, which is the whole amount. As 48 ÷ 4 is 12 and 12 × 5 is 60, then the original price was $60 000.

16. $1335

As 25% is $\frac{1}{4}$, then 1780 ÷ 4, which is 445. As 1780 – 445 is 1335, the new price is $1335.

17. $79.80

As 20% is $\frac{1}{5}$, find 399 ÷ 5.

$5\overline{)39^{4}9^{4}.00}$ = 79.80

The saving is $79.80.

18. $25.20

First, 10% is $\frac{1}{10}$, which is 24 ÷ 10 = 2.4. As 5% is half of 10%, then half of 2.4 is 1.2. The pay rise of $1.20 means Sarah's new hourly rate is $25.20.

19. 50%

As 2500 – 1200 is 1300, the discount is $1300. 1300 out of 2500 is $\frac{1300}{2500} = \frac{13}{25}$, which is close to $\frac{1}{2}$, or 50%. The best estimate of the discount is 50%.

20. 30%

Consider $\frac{1}{3}$ as a decimal.

$3\overline{)1.000\ldots}$ = 0.333…

This means $\frac{1}{3}$ = 0.3333…. which means $\frac{1}{3}$ is a little more than 33%.

The best estimate is 30%.

21. $3.12

As 4% is 0.04, you need to multiply 0.04 by 78.

```
   78
×   4
  312
```

4 × 78 is 312. 0.04 × 78 is 3.12 as there are 2 decimal places in the question. This means 4% of $78 is $3.12.

22. $12.

50% is half price. This means the normal price is twice the price paid. As 24 × 2 is 48 and 48 ÷ 4 is 12, the normal price is $12.

23. $43

First, 10% is $\frac{1}{10}$, which is 860 ÷ 10 = 86. Now half of 10% is 5%, and 86 ÷ 2 = 43. Chloe saves $43.

24. $162

10% of 200 is 200 ÷ 10 = 20. The price drops to $180. Now, 10% of 180 is 180 ÷ 10 = 18. As 180 – 18 is 162, the final price is $162.

Unit 5A PAGE 18

1. 6.05

Check the difference between the numbers:

```
  3.55
– 2.30
  1.25
```

The pattern is increasing by 1.25.

```
  4.80
+ 1.25
  6.05
```

The next number is 6.05.

2. **0.12**

The pattern is dividing by 10, which means the decimal point moves 1 place to the left. As 1.2 ÷ 10 is 0.12, the missing number is 0.12

3. **0.12**

The pattern is dividing by 5.

$5\overline{)0.60}$ = 0.12

The next number is 0.12.

4. $\mathbf{1\frac{4}{5}}$

The pattern is adding $\frac{2}{5}$.

The next number is $1\frac{2}{5} + \frac{2}{5}$, which is $1\frac{4}{5}$.

5. **2.4, 2.1, 1.8, 1.5**

2.4 – 0.3 is 2.1. 2.1 – 0.3 is 1.8.
1.8 – 0.3 is 1.5.
The pattern is 2.4, 2.1, 1.8, 1.5.

6. $\mathbf{2\frac{2}{3}, 2\frac{5}{6}, 3, 3\frac{1}{6}}$

As $2\frac{2}{3}$ can be written as $2\frac{4}{6}$, then the sequence is $2\frac{2}{3}, 2\frac{5}{6}, 3, 3\frac{1}{6}$.

7. **5.6**

The sequence is 8, 7.4, 6.8, 6.2, 5.6 …
The number is 5.6.

8. **11**

Counting the matchsticks, the pattern is 3, 5, 7 which is adding 2. As 7 + 2 + 2 is 11, there will be 11 matchsticks in the fifth shape.

9. **25**

Counting the dots, the pattern is 1, 5, 9 which is adding 4. The seventh shape will be made using 9 + 4 + 4 + 4 + 4 which is 25. There will be 25 dots in the seventh shape.

10. **45**

The numbers in the first row are multiplied by 9 to give the corresponding numbers in the second row. As 5 × 9 is 45, the missing number is 45.

11. **9.1**

6.3 – 3 is 3.3. The rule is to add 3.3 to numbers in the first row to give the corresponding numbers in the second row. 5.8 + 3.3 is 9.1.

12. **2**

5 × 2 is 10, and 12 – 5 × 2 is 12 – 10 = 2.

13. **4**

As 4 + 8 is 12, then 16 – 12 is 4.

14. **14**

36 ÷ 4 is 9, so 36 ÷ 4 + 6 – 1 = 9 + 6 – 1 which is 14.

15. **5**

The number sentence is $\frac{1}{4} \times (8 + 12)$.

As 8 + 12 is 20, then $\frac{1}{4}$ of 20 = 20 ÷ 4 = 5.

16. **66**

The number sentence is 6 × (8 + 3). As 8 + 3 is 11, and 6 × 11 is 66, then 6 × (8 + 3) = 66.

17. **3.7**

As 2.8 × 3 is 8.4, then
12.1 – 2.8 × 3 = 12.1 – 8.4 = 3.7.

18. $\mathbf{\frac{3}{10}}$

As $\frac{1}{10} + \frac{5}{10} = \frac{6}{10}$, then $\frac{9}{10} - (\frac{1}{10} + \frac{5}{10}) = \frac{9}{10} - \frac{6}{10}$, which is $\frac{3}{10}$.

19. **(12 – 3) × 4 = 36**

12 – 3 is 9 and 9 × 4 is 36. The number sentence is (12 – 3) × 4 = 36.

20. **$1000**

The number sentence to be used is (28 + 22) × 20. As 28 + 22 is 50, and 50 × 20 is 1000, Corey will be paid $1000.

21. **40**

There are five 4s to be subtracted. The question can be rewritten as 60 – 5 × 4 which is 60 – 20 = 40.

22. **4**

$\frac{24 - 16}{2}$ can be rewritten as (24 – 16) ÷ 2.

24 – 16 is 8, so $\frac{24 - 16}{2} = 8 \div 2 = 4$.

23. **4**

As 30 – 20 is 10, then 5 × ☐ = 20.
This means the missing number is 4.

24. **3**

As 6^2 is 36 and 6 + 6 is 12, then
$6^2 \div (6 + 6) = 36 \div 12 = 3$.

Unit 5B PAGE 19

1. **18.22**

$$\begin{array}{r} 13.66 \\ -\ 11.38 \\ \hline 2.28 \end{array}$$

The pattern is adding 2.28.

$$\begin{array}{r} 15.94 \\ +\ 2.28 \\ \hline 18.22 \end{array}$$

The next number is 18.22.

2. **3.7**

As 37 000 ÷ 370 is 100, the pattern is multiplying by 100, which means the decimal point moves 2 places to the right. As 0.037 × 100 is 3.7, the missing number is 3.7.

3. **320**

Look at the pattern of numbers in reverse. 0.8 is multiplied by 20 to get 16. This means the first number is 16 × 20 which is 320.

4. $\mathbf{3\frac{1}{4}}$

The pattern is subtracting $\frac{3}{4}$.

The next number is $4 - \frac{3}{4}$, which is $3\frac{1}{4}$.

5. **8.4, 9.77, 11.14, 12.51**

8.4 + 1.37 is 9.77. 9.77 + 1.37 is 11.14.
11.14 + 1.37 is 12.51.

6. $\mathbf{8, 6\frac{3}{4}, 5\frac{1}{2}, 4\frac{1}{4}}$

$8 - 1\frac{1}{4}$ is $6\frac{3}{4}$. $6\frac{3}{4} - 1\frac{1}{4}$ is $5\frac{1}{2}$.

$5\frac{1}{2} - 1\frac{1}{4}$ is $4\frac{1}{4}$.

The pattern is 8, $6\frac{3}{4}, 5\frac{1}{2}, 4\frac{1}{4}$.

7. **5.3**

The sequence is 3.5, 3.95, 4.4, 4.85, 5.3 … The number is 5.3.

8. **31**

Counting the matchsticks, the pattern is 4, 7, 10 which is adding 3. The tenth shape will be made from 4 + 9 × 3 = 31 matchsticks.

9. **Shape 8**

The pattern is 4, 7, 10 which is adding 3. Continuing the pattern is 13, 16, 19, 22, 25. This means Shape 8 is made using 25 matchsticks.

10. **22**

The numbers in the second row are divided by 6 to give the corresponding numbers in the first row. As 132 ÷ 6 is 22, the missing number is 22.

11. **12.8**

The numbers in the first row are the corresponding numbers in the second row multiplied by 4. This means the missing number is 3.2 × 4 which is 12.8.

12. **28**

32 ÷ 8 is 4 and 8 × 3 is 24.
32 ÷ 8 + 8 × 3 is 4 + 24 which is 28.

13. **4.5**

First, 4 – 2.7 is 1.3. This means 5.8 – (4 – 2.7) = 5.8 – 1.3 which is 4.5.

14. **34**

As 5 × 6 ÷ 3 is 10 and 12 × 4 ÷ 2 is 24, then 5 × 6 ÷ 3 + 12 × 4 ÷ 2 is 10 + 24 = 34.

15. **12**

The number sentence is $\frac{3}{4} \times (64 - 48)$.

As 64 – 48 is 16, you need to find $\frac{3}{4}$ of 16.

$16 \div 4 \times 3$ is 4×3 which is 12.

$\frac{3}{4} \times (64 - 48)$ is 12.

16. **25**

The number sentence is $8 \times 4 - 63 \div 9$.
8×4 is 32 and $63 \div 9$ is 7.
$8 \times 4 - 63 \div 9 = 32 - 7$ which is 25.

17. **7**

2.3 + 0.7 is 3.

$16 - (2.3 + 0.7)^2 = 16 - 3^2$, which is $16 - 9 = 7$.

18. $\mathbf{\frac{3}{8}}$

First, work out $\frac{3}{4} - \frac{1}{2}$, which is $\frac{3}{4} - \frac{2}{4} = \frac{1}{4} = \frac{2}{8}$. Now $\frac{5}{8} - \frac{2}{8} = \frac{3}{8}$.

19. $\mathbf{16 \div (4 + 3 + 1) = 2}$

As 4 + 3 + 1 is 8, and $16 \div 8$ is 2, the number sentence is $16 \div (4 + 3 + 1) = 2$.

20. **$190**

The number sentence to be used is $5 \times (3 \times 6 + 4 \times 5)$. As $3 \times 6 = 18$ and $4 \times 5 = 20$, the cost is $5 \times (18 + 20) = 5 \times 38$ which is 190. The total cost is $190.

21. **$8**

The number sentence is $200 - (8 \times 9 + 12 \times 10)$.
As $8 \times 9 = 72$ and $12 \times 10 = 120$, then $200 - (72 + 120) = 200 - 192$ which is 8. Kenny has $8 remaining.

22. **2**

$\frac{2 + 3 \times 6}{12 - 8 \div 4}$ can be rewritten as
$(2 + 3 \times 6) \div (12 - 8 \div 4) = (2 + 18) \div (12 - 2)$. This is $20 \div 10$ which is 2.

23. **5**

As 14 – 9 is 5, then $40 \div (\square + 3) = 5$.
This means $\square + 3 = 8$. The missing number is 5.

Unit 6A PAGE 20

1. **2876 mm**

Converting m to mm will mean a bigger number. There are 1000 mm in 1 m. As 2.876×1000 is 2876, then 2.876 m = 2876 mm.

2. **85 m**

Converting cm to m will mean a smaller number. There are 100 cm in 1 m. As $8500 \div 100 = 85$, then 8500 cm = 85 m.

3. **386.2 mm**

Converting cm to mm will mean a larger number. There are 10 mm in 1 cm. As 38.62×10 is 386.2, then 38.62 cm = 386.2 mm.

4. **6 ha**

There are 10 000 m^2 in 1 hectare (ha). As $60\,000 \div 10\,000$ is 6, then 60 000 m^2 = 6 ha.

5. **5580 mm**

There are 1000 mm in 1 m, which means that 5.21 m is 5210 mm.

$$\begin{array}{r} 370 \\ +\ 5210 \\ \hline 5580 \end{array}$$

The total length is 5580 mm.

6. **8.8 m**

There are 1000 mm in 1 m. As $1200 \div 1000$ is 1.2, you need to subtract 10 – 1.2.

$$\begin{array}{r} 10.0 \\ -\ 1.2 \\ \hline 8.8 \end{array}$$

8.8 m remained.

7. **1.56 m**

As there are 100 cm in 1 m, then 16 cm is 0.16 m.

$$\begin{array}{r} 1.72 \\ -\ 0.16 \\ \hline 1.56 \end{array}$$

Morgan is 1.56 m tall.

8. **50 cm**

There are 100 cm in 1 m.
As half of 100 is 50, then $\frac{1}{2}$ metre = 50 cm.

9. **22.55 km**

$$\begin{array}{r} 3.60 \\ 7.10 \\ 6.80 \\ +\ 5.05 \\ \hline 22.55 \end{array}$$

The total length is 22.55 km.

10. **3**

There are 1000 m in 1 km, and so 6000 m in 6 km. As $6000 \div 600$ is $60 \div 6$ which is 10, he needs to walk a total of 10 laps. As 10 – 7 is 3, Josiah has 3 more laps to complete.

11. **5.05 m, 5100 mm, 520 cm**

Change each length to millimetres. 5100 mm, 520 cm is 5200 mm and 5.05 m is 5050 mm. The order of numbers is 5050, 5100 and 5200. The order of lengths is 5.05 m, 5100 mm, 520 cm.

12. **19.6 km**

There are 1000 mm in 1 m and 1000 m in 1 km. This means there are 1 000 000 mm in 1 km. As there will be a smaller number of km than mm, use $19\,600\,000 \div 1\,000\,000$, which is 19.6. There are 19.6 km.

13. **35.4 cm**

A regular hexagon has 6 equal sides.

$$\begin{array}{r} 59 \\ \times\ 6 \\ \hline 354 \end{array}$$

As 59×6 is 354, then 5.9×6 is 35.4. The perimeter is 35.4 cm.

14. **2 m**

The perimeter is $\frac{2}{3} + \frac{2}{3} + \frac{2}{3}$. This is $\frac{6}{3}$, which is 2. The perimeter is 2 m.

15. **2.7 cm**

The length of each side is found using $10.8 \div 4$.

$$\begin{array}{r} 2.7 \\ 4\overline{)10.{}^{2}8} \end{array}$$

The length of each side is 2.7 cm.

16. **1.44 m**

As 36×4 is 144, the perimeter is 144 cm, which is 1.44 m.

17. **108 cm^2**

The top missing length is 12 – 8 = 4. The shape can be split into 2 rectangles. $12 \times 7 + 6 \times 4$ is 84 + 24, which is 108. The area is 108 cm^2.

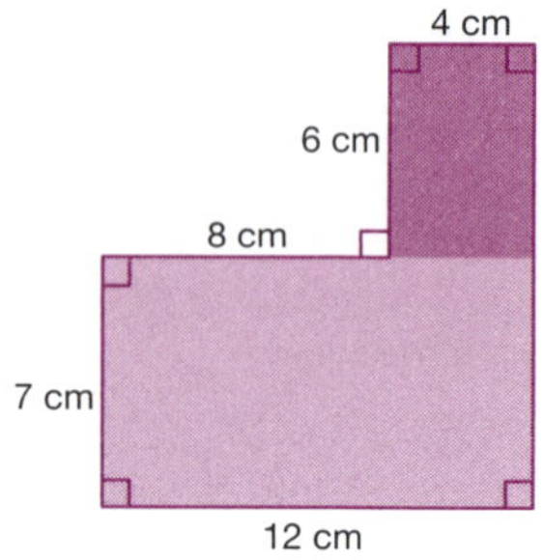

18. **2.04 km**

The perimeter is found using $2 \times (640 + 380)$.

$$\begin{array}{r} 640 \\ +\ 380 \\ \hline 1020 \end{array}$$

This means $2 \times (640 + 380) = 2 \times 1020$ which is 2040. The perimeter is 2040 m, or 2.04 km.

19. **9 m**

As 100 cm is 1 m, then 150 cm is 1.5 m. Now as 1.5 + 1.5 is 3, and 3 + 3 + 3 = 9, the perimeter is 9 m.

20. **25 cm**

First, 24 + 7 is 31. As 56 – 31 is 25, the longest and missing side is 25 cm long.

21. **12 cm**

As 17 + 13 is 30 and 54 – 30 is 24, the two missing sides add to 24 cm. As the sides are equal, each side is 12 cm.

22. **4 m²**

$8 \times \frac{1}{2}$, or $\frac{1}{2} \times 8$ is 4. The area is 4 m².

23. **14 cm**

The length is found by dividing 112 by 8.

$$\begin{array}{r} 14 \\ 8\overline{)11^{3}2} \end{array}$$

The length is 14 cm.

24. **28 cm**

As area = length × width, then 48 = 8 × width. This means the width is 48 ÷ 8 which is 6. The perimeter is 2 × (8 + 6) = 2 × 14 which is 28. The perimeter is 28 cm.

25. **19.2 m²**

The area is found using 6 × 3.2.

$$\begin{array}{r} 32 \\ \times \quad 6 \\ \hline 192 \end{array}$$

There is 1 decimal place in the question, so 6 × 3.2 = 19.2. The area is 19.2 m².

26. **80 cm²**

The area of a triangle is $\frac{1}{2}$ × base × height. As $\frac{1}{2} \times 16 \times 10$ is 8 × 10 = 80, the area is 80 cm².

27. **81 cm²**

As 36 ÷ 4 is 9 then the square has side length 9 cm. As 9 × 9 is 81, the area of the square is 81 cm².

28. **8 cm**

If the sides were all equal the perimeter would be 20 + 4 = 24. As 24 ÷ 3 = 8, the side is 8 cm.

29. **240 cm²**

As length × 5 is 60, the length is 12 cm. If the dimensions are doubled to 24 cm by 10 cm, and 24 × 10 = 240, the area is 240 cm².

30. **108 cm²**

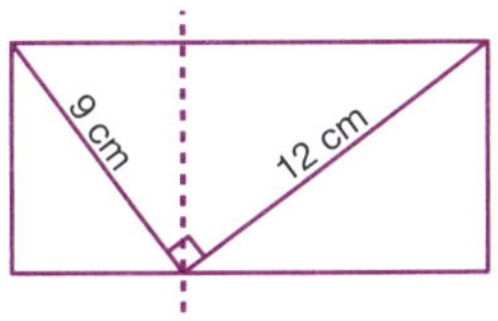

As $\frac{1}{2} \times 9 \times 12 = 54$, the area of the triangle is 54 cm². The triangle is exactly half the rectangle, so the area of the rectangle is 108 cm².

31. **8 cm**

As 10 × 3 = 30, the total length of wire is 30 cm. As 30 – 14 = 16 and half of 16 is 8, the length of the other two sides is 8 cm.

32. **55 cm**

As 2.2 × 100 = 220, the perimeter is 220 cm. As 220 ÷ 4 = 55, the length of each side is 55 cm.

33. **16 cm²**

As 4 × 4 = 16, the square has a side length of 4 cm. The dimensions of the rectangle are 8 cm by 2 cm. As 8 × 2 = 16, the area of the rectangle is 16 cm².

34. **12 L**

As 12 × 3 = 36 and 36 ÷ 6 = 6, it will take 6 L for each coat. As 6 × 2 = 12, Jannah will need 12 L of paint.

35. **48 cm²**

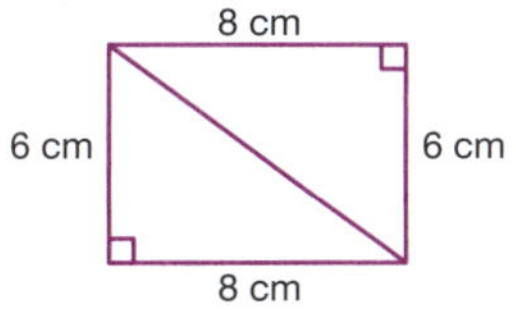

The triangles are joined along the longest side. The rectangle has sides 8 cm by 6 cm. As 8 × 6 = 48, the area is 48 cm².

Unit 6B PAGE 22

1. **2560 cm**

Converting m to cm will mean a bigger number. As there are 100 cm in 1 m, then 25.60 × 100 is 2560. This means 25.6 m = 2560 cm.

2. **6.1 km**

Converting mm to km will mean a smaller number. As there are 1000 mm in 1 m, and 1000 m in 1 km, then there are 1 000 000 mm in 1 km. As 6 100 000 ÷ 1 000 000 is 6.1, then 6 100 000 mm = 6.1 km.

3. **3.9 km**

Converting cm to km will mean a smaller number. As there are 100 cm in 1 m, and 1000 m in 1 km, then there are 100 000 cm in 1 km. As 390 000 ÷ 100 000 is 3.9, this means 390 000 cm = 3.9 km.

4. **24 300 m²**

There are 10 000 m² in 1 hectare (ha). As 2.43 × 10 000 is 24 300, then 2.43 ha = 24 300 m².

5. **3.5 m**

As 135 ÷ 100 = 1.35, then 135 cm = 1.35 m. Also, as 750 ÷ 1000 = 0.75, then 750 mm = 0.75 m.

$$\begin{array}{r} 1.35 \\ 1.40 \\ +\ 0.75 \\ \hline 3.50 \end{array}$$

The sum of the lengths is 3.5 m.

6. **20.1 km**

As there are 1000 m in 1 km, then 1500 m is 1.5 km.

$$\begin{array}{r} 1.5 \\ 12.0 \\ +\ \ 6.6 \\ \hline 20.1 \end{array}$$

The total distance was 20.1 km.

7. **136.5 cm**

As 1.82 m is 182 cm, then $\frac{3}{4}$ of 182 is 182 ÷ 4 × 3.

$$\begin{array}{r} 45.5 \\ 4\overline{)18^{2}2.^{2}0} \end{array}$$

This means 182 ÷ 4 × 3 is 45.5 × 3 which is 136.5. Dominic is 136.5 cm tall.

8. **7250 mm**

There are 1000 mm in 1 m. This means 7000 mm are in 7 m. Also, as $\frac{1}{4}$ of 100 is 25, then $\frac{1}{4}$ of 1000 is 250. As 7000 + 250 is 7250, then $7\frac{1}{4}$ m = 7250 mm.

9. **6516 m**

$$\begin{array}{r} 362 \\ \times \quad 18 \\ \hline 2896 \\ 3620 \\ \hline 6516 \end{array}$$

The length of the course is 6516 m.

10. **102.5 m**

As 5000 \$2 coins make up \$10 000, then use 20.5 × 1000 × 5 = 20 500 × 5.

$$\begin{array}{r} 20\,500 \\ \times \qquad 5 \\ \hline 102\,500 \end{array}$$

The length is 102 500 mm or 102.5 m.

11. **40.5 cm, 406 mm, 0.409 m, 403 cm**

Change each length to millimetres. 0.409 m is 409 mm, 403 cm is 4030 mm, 40.5 cm is 405 mm, 406 mm. The order of numbers is 405, 406, 409, 4030. The order of lengths is 40.5 cm, 406 mm, 0.409 m, 403 cm.

12. **63.19 m**

There are 1000 m in 1 km. Converting km to m means there will be a larger number. For 0.063 19 × 1000 move the decimal point 3 places to the right. This means 0.063 19 × 1000 = 63.19. There are 63.19 m.

13. **9.15 cm**

A regular octagon has 8 equal sides.

$$\begin{array}{r} 9.1\ 5 \\ 8\overline{)73.^{1}2^{4}0} \end{array}$$

Each side is 9.15 cm long.

14. 18 cm

The perimeter is twice the sum of the length and width: $2 \times (5\frac{3}{4} + 3\frac{1}{4})$. As 5 + 3 is 8 and $\frac{3}{4} + \frac{1}{4}$ is 1, then $5\frac{3}{4} + 3\frac{1}{4}$ is 8 + 1 = 9. As 2 × 9 = 18, the perimeter is 18 cm.

15. 6 cm

If the perimeter is 38 cm, then the sum of the length and width is 19 cm. As 13 + width is 19, the width is 6 cm.

16. 2.96 m

The square will have a side length of 74 cm. As 74 × 4 is 296, the perimeter is 296 cm, or 2.96 m.

17. 126 cm²

Equal lengths are shown on the shape, so as 12 ÷ 2 is 6, the top lengths are 6 cm each. As 12 – 9 is 3, the missing vertical length is 3 cm. The shape can be split into 2 rectangles. As 12 × 9 + 6 × 3 is 108 + 18, which is 126, the area is 126 cm².

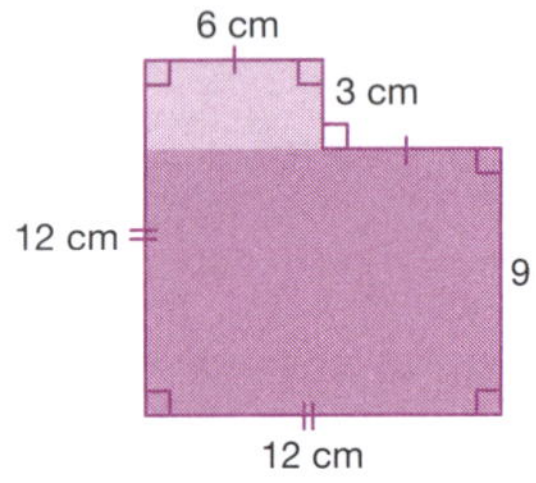

18. 44 cm

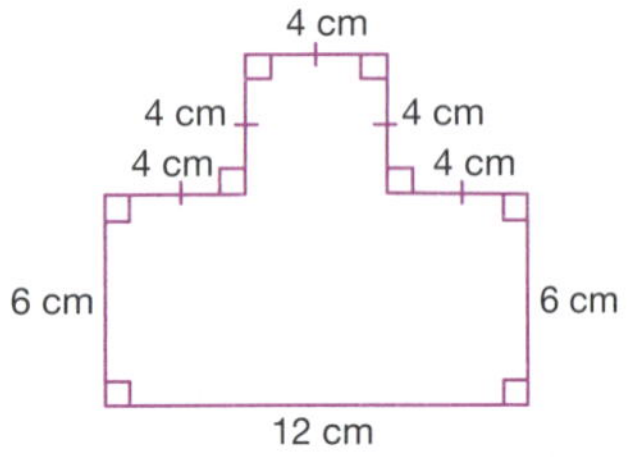

As 12 + 2 × 6 + 5 × 4 is 12 + 12 + 20 which is 44, the perimeter is 44 cm.

19. 5.7 m

As 85 cm is 0.85 m, then the perimeter is 2 × (2 + 0.85) which is 2 × 2.85 = 5.7. The perimeter is 5.7 m.

20. 80 cm

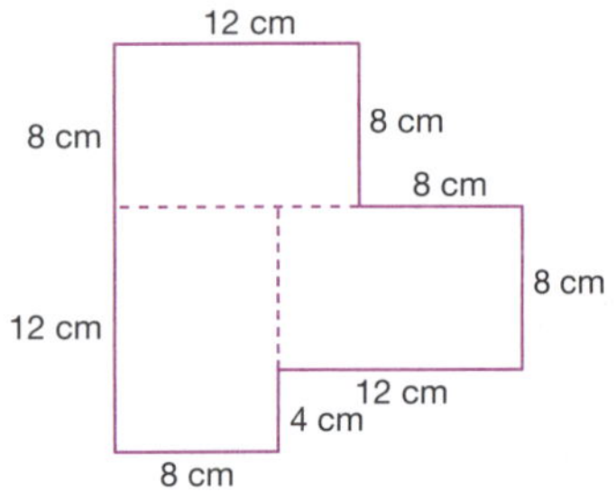

As 3 × 12 + 5 × 8 + 4 is 36 + 40 + 4 = 80, the perimeter is 80 cm.

21. 29 cm²

As 9 – (4 + 2) is 9 – 6 = 3, the squares have side lengths 2 cm, 3 cm and 4 cm. As $2^2 + 3^2 + 4^2$ is 4 + 9 + 16 = 29, the area is 29 cm².

22. 300 cm²

As the perimeter = 2 × (length + width), then 70 = 2 × (length + 15). This means the length + 15 = 35, which means the length is 20 cm. As 20 × 15 is 300, the area is 300 cm².

23. 144 cm²

As 72 ÷ 2 is 36, the sum of the length and width is 36. As 36 ÷ 3 is 12, the width is 12 cm and the length is 24 cm. To find the area, 24 × 12 = 2 × 12 × 12 = 288. The triangle is half the rectangle, so the area of the shaded triangle is 144 cm².

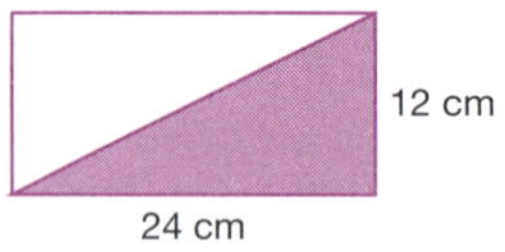

24. 24 cm²

As 8 + 10 + height = 24, then the height is 6 cm. The area of a triangle is $\frac{1}{2}$ × base × height. As $\frac{1}{2} \times 8 \times 6$ is 24, the area is 24 cm².

25. 432 cm²

The perimeter would be 96 cm which means the sum of the length and width is 48. As 48 ÷ 4 = 12 the width is 12 cm and the length 36 cm. As 36 × 12 is 432, the area is 432 cm².

26. 8 cm

As the perimeter is 26 cm, then the sum of the length and width is 13 cm. Look for two numbers that add to 13 and multiply to give 40. The numbers are 8 and 5, and so the length is 8 cm.

27. 144 cm²

As a regular octagon has 8 equal sides, and 8 × 6 is 48, the perimeter is 48 cm. As 48 ÷ 4 is 12, each side of the square is 12 cm long.
As 12 × 12 = 144, the area is 144 cm².

28. 3 cm

The shaded area is $\frac{3}{4}$ of the large square. If $\frac{3}{4}$ of a number is 27, then $\frac{1}{4}$ of the number is 9, and so the area of the small square is 9 cm², and hence the length of a side of the small square is 3 cm.

29. 288 cm²

As 16 + 8 = 24 and 12 + 8 = 20, the dimensions of the frame are 24 cm by 20 cm. The area of the cardboard is 24 × 20 – 16 × 12 = 480 – 192 = 288. The area is 288 cm².

30. 24 cm

As 14 × 8 = 112, the area of the rectangle was 112 cm². As 112 – 76 = 36, the area of the square is 36 cm². This means the side length of the square is 6 cm. As 6 × 4 = 24, the perimeter is 24 cm.

31. 20 cm

Opposite sides of a rectangle are equal. In the large rectangle 2 lengths = 3 widths. This means for the large rectangle, as well as each small rectangle, the length is one-and-a-half times the width. As 120 ÷ 5 = 24, the area of each small rectangle is 24 cm². Look for two numbers that multiply to give 24, where the larger is one-and-a-half times the smaller. The dimensions are 6 cm and 4 cm. As 2 × (6 + 4) = 20, the perimeter is 20 cm.

32. 124 cm

If a square on the top row has an area of 64 cm², the side length is 8 cm. As 6 × 8 = 48, the length of the rectangle is 48 cm. As there are 8 squares on the bottom row, and 48 ÷ 8 = 6, each square in the bottom row has a side length of 6 cm.
As 8 + 6 = 14, the dimensions of the rectangle are 48 cm by 14 cm.
As 2 × (48 + 14) = 124, the perimeter is 124 cm.

Unit 7A

PAGE 24

1. 3080 g

There are 1000 g in 1 kg. Converting kg to g will mean a larger number. As 3.080 × 1000 is 3080, there are 3080 g.

2. 7.84

There are 1000 g in 1 kg. Converting g to kg will mean a smaller number. As 7840 ÷ 1000 is 7.84, there are 7.84 kg.

3. $\frac{2}{5}$

There are 1000 mL in 1 L. 400 out of 1000 is $\frac{400}{1000}$, which is $\frac{400 \div 100}{1000 \div 100}$, or $\frac{4}{10}$, which is $\frac{2}{5}$. This means 400 mL is $\frac{2}{5}$ L.

4. 1500 cm³

As 1000 cm³ = 1 L, then multiplying by 1.5 gives 1500 cm³ = 1.5 L.

5. 350 g

$$\begin{array}{r} 0.35 \\ 3\overline{)1.05} \end{array}$$

The average mass is 0.35 kg, which is 350 g.

6. 7.2 kg

You need to multiply 1.44 × 5.

$$\begin{array}{r} 144 \\ \times \quad 5 \\ \hline 720 \end{array}$$

As 1.44 × 5 has 2 decimal places, then 1.44 × 5 is 7.20, or 7.2. The mass is 7.2 kg.

7. 4.2 kg

As 4.8 + 3.6 is 8.4, and 8.4 ÷ 2 is 4,2, the average mass is 4.2 kg.

8. 3.59 kg

As 590 g is 0.59 kg, then there are 3.59 kg.

9. 3000 kg

As there are 1000 L in 1 kL, and 3 × 1000 is 3000, then the mass is 3000 kg.

10. 840 cm³

The volume is length × width × height. As 14 × 10 × 6 is 140 × 6 which is 840, the volume is 840 cm³.

11. 12.65 kL

There are 1000 L in 1 kL. Converting L to kL will mean a smaller number. As 12 650 ÷ 1000 is 12.65, there are 12.65 kL.

12. 8 L

The volume is side × side × side. As 20 × 20 × 20 is 8000, the volume is 8000 cm³. As 1 cm³ = 1 mL, the capacity is 8000 mL, or 8 L.

13. 1200 mL

The volume is 15 × 10 × 8 which is 150 × 8 = 1200. The volume is 1200 cm³, which is 1200 mL.

14. 108 mL

As 6 × 6 × 3 is 36 × 3 = 108, the volume of water is 108 cm³, or 108 mL. This means another 108 mL of water is needed to fill the cube.

15. 7.8 kg

There are 13 cubes. As 13 × 6 is 78, then 13 × 0.6 is 7.8 and the total mass is 7.8 kg.

16. 480 cm³

As 48 × 10 is 480, the volume is 480 cm³.

17. 1280 cm³

Multiply 16 × 8 × 10, which is 160 × 8.

$$\begin{array}{r} 160 \\ \times \quad 8 \\ \hline 1280 \end{array}$$

The volume is 1280 cm³.

18. 2880 cm³

As 12 × 12 × 20 is 144 × 20 = 2880, the volume is 2880 cm³.

19.

20. 1600

As twice 2 h 30 min is 5 h, the screening commences 5 h after 1100. This means the third screening starts at 1600.

21. 0853

As 51 – 28 is 23, it takes 23 min to travel from York to Concord. Add 23 min to 0830 to get 0853.

22. 35 min

Find the time between 3:30 and 4:05. From 3:30 to 4:00 is 30 min then to 4:05 is 5 min.

As 30 + 5 = 35, Maddison waits for 35 min.

23. 2 h 40 min

All time differences are the same. From 1110 to 1350 is 2 h 40 min.

Unit 7B PAGE 25

1. 67 kg

There are 1000 kg in 1 tonne. Converting tonne to kg will mean a larger number. As 0.067 × 1000 is 67, there are 67 kg.

2. 56 000

There are 1000 mg in 1 g, and 1000 g in 1 kg. This means there are 1 000 000 mg in 1 kg. Converting kg to mg will mean a larger number. In 0.056 000 × 1 000 000, the decimal point moves 6 places, so there are 56 000 mg.

3. $\frac{1}{30}$

There are 1000 g in 1 kg, and so 6000 g in 6 kg. 200 out of 6000 is $\frac{200}{6000}$, which is $\frac{200 \div 100}{6000 \div 100}$, or $\frac{2}{60} = \frac{1}{30}$.

This means 200 g is $\frac{1}{30}$ of 6 kg.

4. 0.96 L

There are 1000 cm³ in 1 L. Converting cm³ to L will mean a smaller number. As 960 ÷ 1000 is 0.96, there are 0.96 L.

5. 10.08 kg

$$\begin{array}{r} 420 \\ \times \quad 24 \\ \hline 1\,680 \\ 8\,400 \\ \hline 10\,080 \end{array}$$

The total mass is 10 080 g, which is 10.08 kg.

6. 12.75 kg

The number sentence is 1.5 + 1.25 × 9 which is 1.5 + 11.25 = 12.75. The total mass is 12.75 kg.

7. 41.25 kg

The average is (41.5 + 40 + 43.9 + 39.6) ÷ 4.

$$\begin{array}{r} 41.5 \\ 40.0 \\ 43.9 \\ +\quad 39.6 \\ \hline 165.0 \end{array}$$

This means (41.5 + 40 + 43.9 + 39.6) ÷ 4 = 165 ÷ 4

$$\begin{array}{r} 41.2\,5 \\ 4\overline{)165.{}^{1}0{}^{2}0} \end{array}$$

The average mass is 41.25 kg.

8. 10.005 L

As 5 mL is 0.005 L, then there are 10.005 L.

9. 4.82 kg

There is 4.5 L of water when it is half full. The water has a mass of 4.5 kg. As 320 g is 0.32 kg, and 4.5 + 0.32 is 4.82, the total mass is 4.82 kg.

10. 7.2 m³

30 cm is 0.3 m. The volume is length × width × height. First, 12 × 2 × 0.3 = 24 × 0.3. As 24 × 3 is 72, then 24 × 0.3 = 7.2. Henry needs 7.2 m³ of soil.

11. 0.003 kL, 3080 mL, 3.27 L, 3600 mL

Change all capacities to litres. 3080 mL is 3.08 L, 0.003 kL is 3 L, 3600 mL is 3.6 L, 3.27 L. These numbers from smallest to largest are 3, 3.08, 3.27, 3.6. This means, from least to greatest, the order is 0.003 kL, 3080 mL, 3.27 L, 3600 mL.

12. 20 mL

There are 2000 mL in 2 L. The number sentence is 2000 – 330 × 6, which is 2000 – 1980 = 20. There is 20 mL of soft drink remaining.

13. 2.42 L

If the perimeter of the square is 44 cm the side length is 11 cm. The volume is 11 × 11 × 20 which is 121 × 20 = 2420. As the volume is 2420 cm³, the capacity is 2.42 L.

14. 640 mL

12 × 10 × 8 is 120 × 8 which is 960. As two-thirds of the prism needs to be filled then 960 ÷ 3 × 2 is 320 × 2 = 640 and so another 640 mL of water is needed.

15. 625 g

There are 20 cubes in the solid. The mass of each cube is 12.5 ÷ 20, which is 1.25 ÷ 2.

$$\begin{array}{r} 0.625 \\ 2\overline{)1.25^{1}0} \end{array}$$

Each cube has a mass of 0.625 kg, or 625 g.

16. 6 cm

As length × width × height is volume, then 10 × 8 × height is 480. This means 80 × height is 480. As 480 ÷ 80 = 48 ÷ 8, which is 6, the height is 6 cm.

17. 640 cm²

The dimensions of the prism are 10 cm by 8 cm by 8 cm. As 8 × 8 is 64, and 64 × 10 is 640, the volume is 640 cm².

18. 3 min 20 s

200 mL every second means 1000 mL, or 1 L, every 5 s. As 40 × 5 is 200, it will take Nicola 200 s, which is 3 min 20 s.

19.

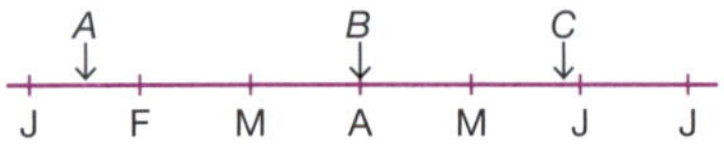

20. 1945

Three times 2 h 45 min is 3 × 2 = 6 h and 3 × 45 = 135 min. Now, 135 min is 2 h 15 min. Adding the times gives 8 h 15 min. The answer is 1130 plus 8 h 15 min which is 1945.

21. 1010

From 0751 to 0847 is 4 minutes short of 1 hour. From 1106 subtract 1 hour and then add 4 minutes is 1010.

Unit 8A PAGE 26

1. *P*(–2, 3), *Q*(2, –2)

To reach *P*, leave the origin and 2 to the left and 3 up gives (–2, 3). To reach *Q*, leave the origin and 2 to the right and 2 down gives (2, –2).

2. 5 units

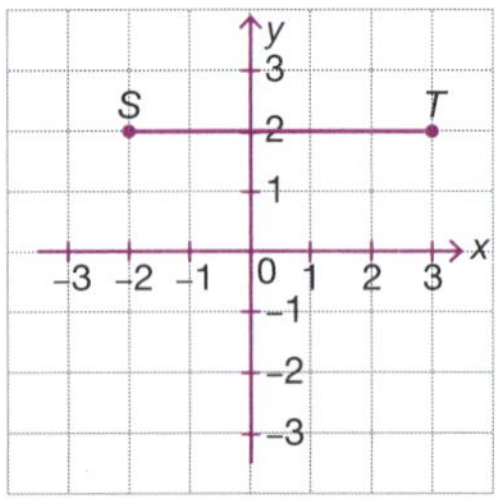

From –2 to 0 is 2 units and then to 3 is another 3 units. As 2 + 3 is 5 the length is 5 units.

3. square

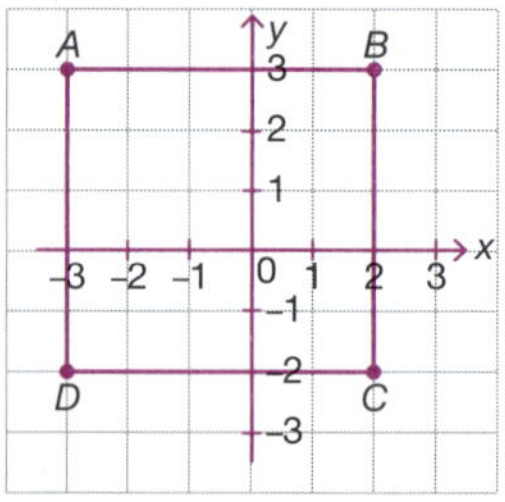

The shape is a square with side length 5 units.

4. *D*(–2, –1)

Point *D* will be under *A* and to the left of *C*. This means the coordinates of *D* are (–2, –1).

5. *Y*(3, –2)

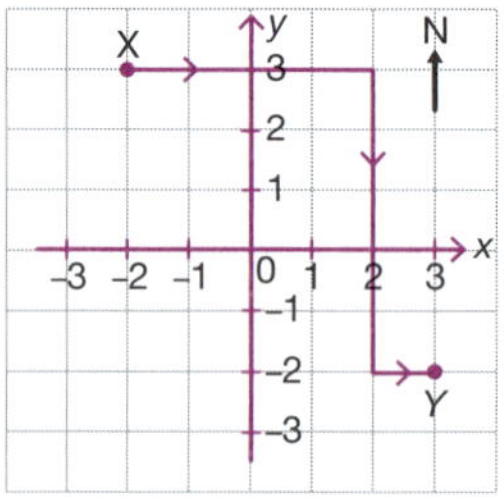

6. 2, 2

The shape has been translated 2 units down and 2 units right.

7.

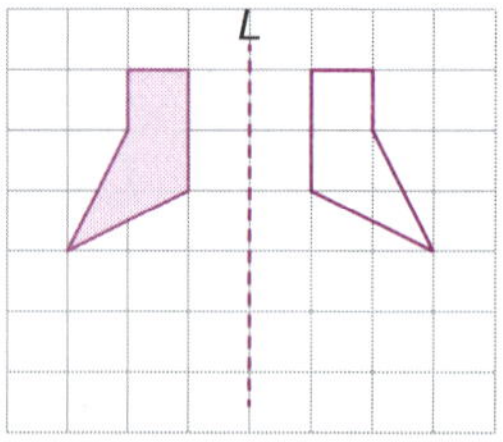

8.

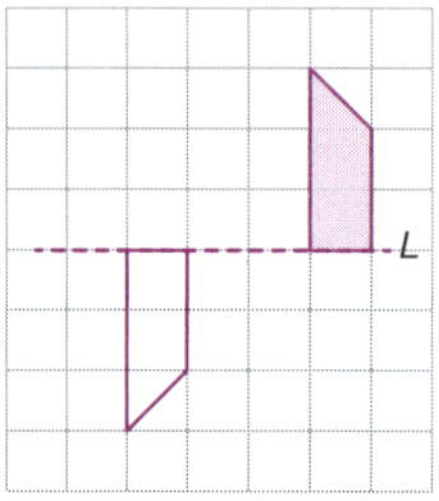

9.

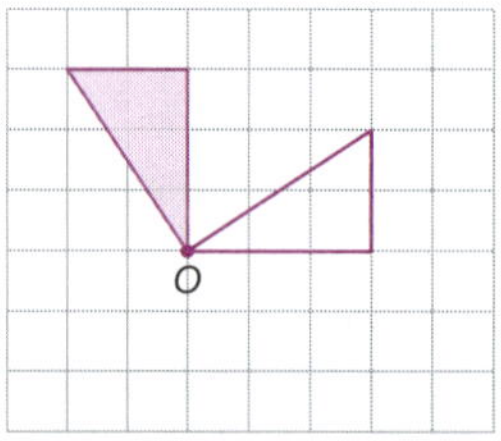

10.

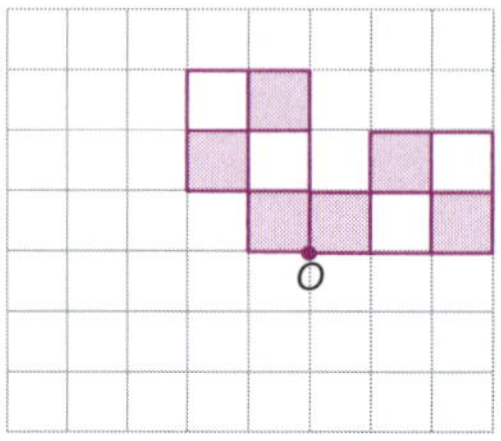

11. 117°

The two angles form a straight angle which means they add to 180°. As 180 – 63 is 117, the angle measures 117°.

12. 32°

The two angles form a right angle which means they add to 90°. As 90 – 58 is 32, the angle measures 32°.

13. 154°

The angle and 154° are vertically opposite angles which are equal. This means the angle measures 154°.

14. 105°

The two angles form an angle of revolution which means they add to 360°. As 360 – 255 is 105, the angle measures 105°.

15. 63°

The two angles form a straight angle which means they add to 180°. As 180 – 117 is 63, the angle measures 63°.

16. 73°

The two angles are vertically opposite and so are equal. The angle measures 73°.

17. 140°

The three angles form an angle of revolution which means they add to 360°. As 100 + 120 is 220, and 360 – 220 is 140, the missing angle is 140°.

18. 41°

The two angles form a right angle which means they add to 90°. As 90 – 49 is 41, the angle measures 41°.

19. 110°

The three angles form an angle of revolution which means they add to 360°. As 160 + 90 is 250, and 360 – 250 is 110, then the missing angle is 110°.

20. 65°

The three angles form an angle of revolution which means they add to 360°. As 145 + 150 is 295, and 360 – 295 is 65, then the missing angle is 65°.

21. 17°

The three angles form a straight angle which means they add to 180°. As 90 + 73 is 163, and 180 – 163 is 17, then the missing angle is 17°.

22. 92°

The three angles form a straight angle which means they add to 180°. As 48 + 40 is 88, and 180 – 88 is 92, the angle measures 92°.

Unit 8B PAGE 28

1.

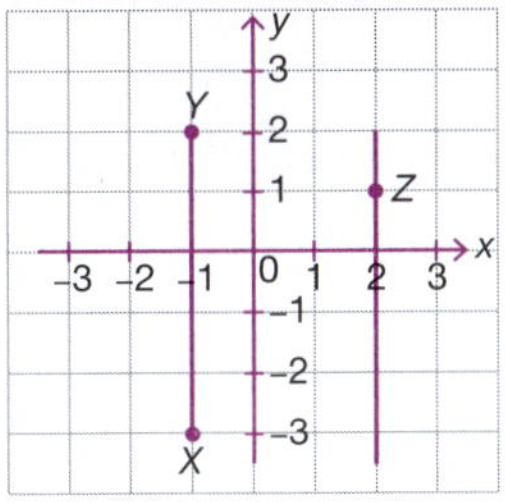

2. (0, 1)

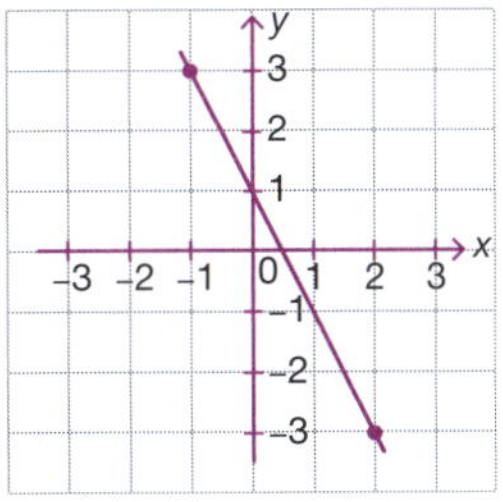

The line also passes through (0, 1).

3. *S*(–2, –2), 15 units²

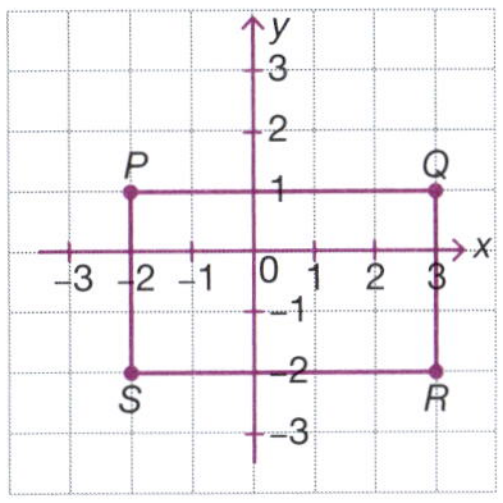

S has the coordinates (–2, –2), and the dimensions of the rectangle are 5 units by 3 units. As 5 × 3 is 15, the area is 15 units².

4. *P*(–2, 2)

As *SR* is 4 units then *P* will be 4 units to the left of *Q*.

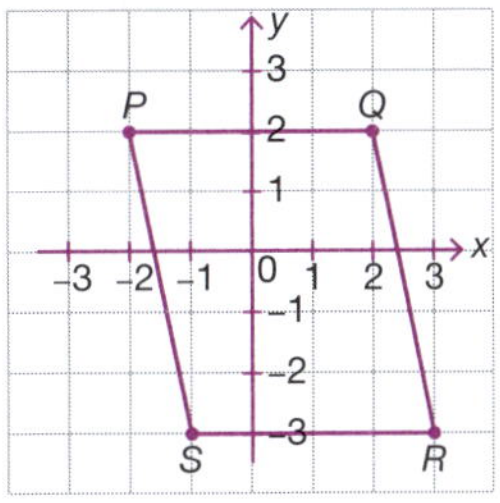

5. 8 units²

The base is 4 units and the height 4 units. As $\frac{1}{2} \times 4 \times 4$ is 8, the area is 8 units².

6. *C*(3, –2)

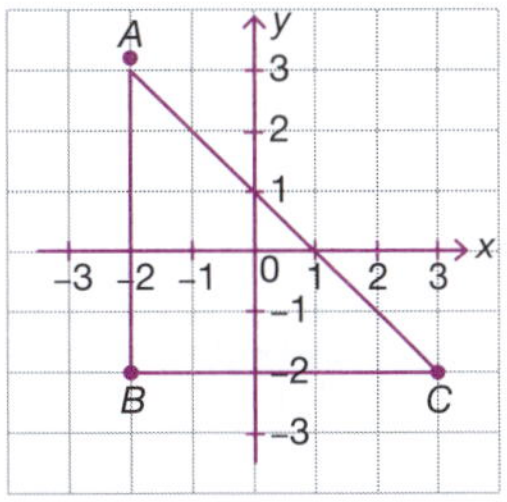

7.

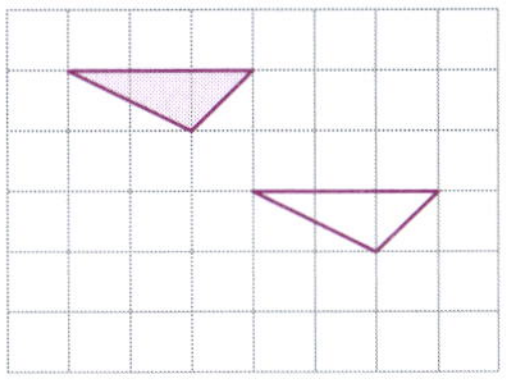

8.

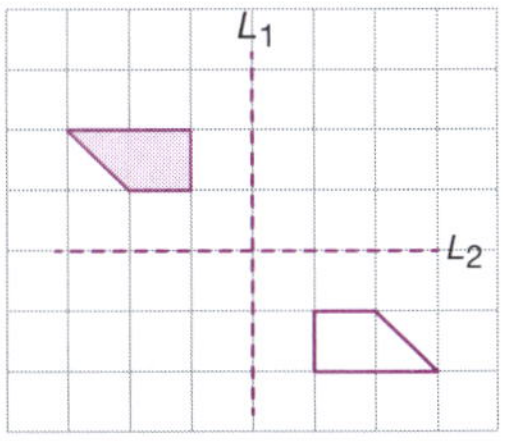

9. Translate 1 unit down, reflect (in either order)

The shape is translated 1 unit down and then reflected about the line. Alternatively, the reflection could be first and then the translation.

10.

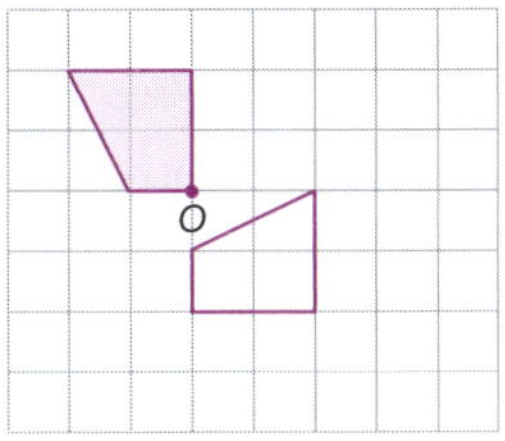

11.

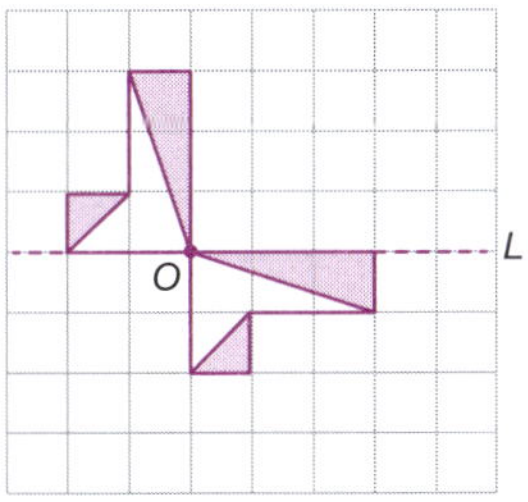

12. 38°

The three angles form a straight angle which means they add to 180°. As 180 – (90 + 52) is 180 – 142 which is 38, the angle measures 38°.

13. 20°

The three angles form a right angle which means they add to 90°. As 90 – (34 + 36) is 90 – 70 which is 20, the angle measures 20°.

14. 65

The 148° angle is vertically opposite the sum of 83° and x°. As 148 – 83 is 65, $x = 65$.

15. 262

The three angles form an angle of revolution which means they add to 360°. As 52 + 46 is 98, then $x + 98$ is 360. As 360 – 98 is 262, $x = 262$.

16. 86

The two angles are vertically opposite and so are equal. This means $x + 50 = 136$, and so $x = 136 - 50$ which is 86.

17. 30

The three equal angles add to form a right angle which means they add to 90°. As 90 ÷ 3 is 30, each angle measures 30°. This means $x = 30$.

18. 75

The three angles form an angle of revolution which means they add to 360°. As 155 + 90 is 245, and 360 – 245 is 115, then $x + 40$ is 115. As 115 – 40 is 75, then $x = 75$.

19. 63

The four angles form an angle of revolution which means they add to 360°. 144 + 90 is 234, and 360 – 234 is 126. Two times x is 126. This means $x = 63$.

20. 60

The two angles form a straight angle which means they add to 180°. As 180 ÷ 3 is 60, then $x = 60$.

21. 50

The two angles form a straight angle which means they add to 180°. As $x + x + 80$ is 180 and 180 – 80 is 100, then $x + x$ is 100. This means that $x = 50$.

Unit 9A PAGE 30

1. 15

The probability of a head is $\frac{1}{2}$. As $\frac{1}{2}$ of 30 is 15, then the expected number is 15 times.

2. $\frac{1}{5}$

As 4 + 1 is 5, and there is 1 white ball, then the probability is $\frac{1}{5}$.

3. $\frac{2}{3}$

20 out of 30 is written as $\frac{20}{30}$, which is $\frac{2}{3}$. The probability is $\frac{2}{3}$.

4. $\frac{1}{4}$

5 + 9 + 6 is 20, and there are 5 red cubes. The probability is $\frac{5}{20}$, which is $\frac{1}{4}$.

5. **0.4**

Express each as a decimal: 0.4 = 0.40, $\frac{1}{4}$ = 0.25, 35% = 0.35. Comparing 40, 25 and 35, the largest number is 40, so the most likely event has a probability of 0.4.

6. **60**

As there are six faces on the dice, the probability of a 5 is $\frac{1}{6}$ or, in theory, a 5 appears once every 6 rolls.

As 6 × 10 is 60, the best estimate is that a 5 appears 10 times in 60 rolls of the dice.

7. $\frac{3}{8}$

There are 8 sectors on the spinner and 3 out of the 8 sectors are odd numbers. The probability is written as $\frac{3}{8}$.

8. **0.05**

The probability is $\frac{1}{20}$ which is $\frac{5}{100}$, or 0.05.

9. **36**

As 6 × 6 = 36, the highest possible result is 36.

10. 

0.6 is $\frac{6}{10}$, which is the same as $\frac{3}{5}$.

This means 3 out of 5 balls are black.

11. **3**

The probability of a 2 is $\frac{3}{8}$. The expected number of times is 3 (out of 8).

12. **60%**

As 1 whole is 100% and 100 – 40 is 60, the probability of no rain is 60%.

13. **60%**

There are 6 black balls out of 10 balls. The probability is $\frac{6}{10} = \frac{60}{100}$, which is 60%.

14. $\frac{1}{200}$

As Cameron has 1 ticket out of 200, the probability is $\frac{1}{200}$.

15. $\frac{1}{3}$

The spinner is a hexagon and so has 6 sections. 5 takes up 2 sections out of 6. This means the probability is $\frac{2}{6}$, which is rewritten as $\frac{1}{3}$.

16. **4**

As 4 is divisible by both 2 and 4, the smallest number of cards is 4.

17. 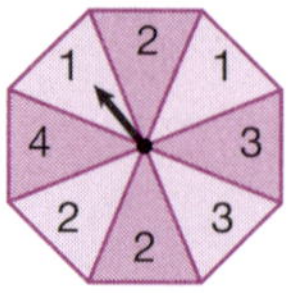

There needs to be as many 3s as 1s, so write in two 1s. Also there needs to be one 4.

18. **0.26**

As 1 – 0.74 is 0.26, the probability of the event not occurring is 0.26.

19. $\frac{1}{6}$

The probability is $\frac{1}{6}$, regardless of the first result.

20. $\frac{1}{4}$

There are 8 letters and 2 of them are As. The probability is $\frac{2}{8}$, which is $\frac{1}{4}$.

Unit 9B PAGE 31

1. **30**

The probability of a 2 or 3 is $\frac{2}{6}$, which is $\frac{1}{3}$. As 90 ÷ 3 is 30, then a 2 or 3 is expected 30 times.

2. **16**

As 4 + 1 is 5, and there are 4 black balls, the probability of a black ball is $\frac{4}{5}$. Find $\frac{4}{5}$ of 20: as 20 ÷ 5 × 4 is 4 × 4 = 16, the expected number of black balls is 16 times.

3. $\frac{1}{2}$

4 or more means 4, 5 or 6 so 3 of the 6 numbers on the dice. The chance is written as $\frac{3}{6} = \frac{1}{2}$.

4. $\frac{1}{2}$

Colour	Number
red	3
blue	7
green	4

As 3 + 7 + 4 is 14, and there are 7 blue cubes, the probability is $\frac{7}{14}$, which is $\frac{1}{2}$.

5. **26%**

Express each as a decimal: $\frac{2}{5} = \frac{4}{10}$ = 0.40, 26% = 0.26, 0.39 and $\frac{3}{10}$ = 0.30.

Comparing 40, 26, 39 and 30, the smallest number is 26, so the least likely event has a probability of 26%.

6. **30**

The prime numbers on a dice are 2, 3 and 5. The probability of a prime is $\frac{3}{6}$, which equals $\frac{1}{2}$. As 2 × 15 is 30, the best estimate is 30 rolls of the dice.

7. **12**

Out of the 8 sectors, 2 are numbered 4. The probability of a 4 is $\frac{2}{8}$, which is $\frac{1}{4}$. As 48 ÷ 4 is 12, the expected number of times is 12.

8. **0.45**

There are 9 numbers that are less than 10, so this is a probability of $\frac{9}{20} = \frac{45}{100}$, which is 0.45.

9. $\frac{1}{3}$

There are 2 odd numbers out of 6. The probability is $\frac{2}{6}$, which is $\frac{1}{3}$.

10. 

40% is $\frac{40}{100}$, which is $\frac{4}{10}$, or $\frac{2}{5}$.

This means 2 out of the 5 balls are black.

11. 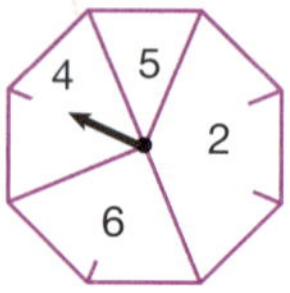

12. $\frac{2}{5}$

As $1 - (\frac{1}{5} + \frac{2}{5})$ is $1 - \frac{3}{5}$ which is $\frac{2}{5}$, the probability of a green ball is $\frac{2}{5}$.

13. 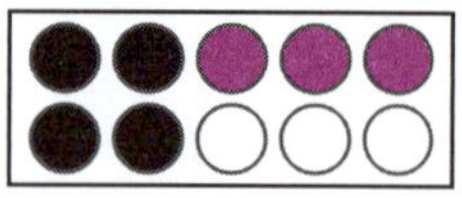

There are 10 balls in the box.

As 40% is $\frac{4}{10}$, there are 4 black balls.

As 30% is $\frac{3}{10}$, there are 3 pink balls.

As 10 – 4 – 3 is 3, there are 3 white balls.

14. **0.01**

As Erica has 10 tickets out of 1000, the probability is $\frac{10}{1000}$ which is $\frac{1}{100}$.

This can be written as 0.01.

15. 120

Even numbers are 2 and 6. As 2 takes up 1 section and 6 takes up 3 sections, the probability of spinning an even number is $\frac{4}{6}$, which is $\frac{2}{3}$. Now $\frac{2}{3}$ of 180 is 180 ÷ 3 × 2, which is 60 × 2 = 120. The expected number of times is 120.

16. 45

As there are 30 green balls, there must be 15 yellow balls. As 30 + 15 is 45, there are 45 balls in the bucket.

17. 5

As 12 is divisible by both 3 and 4, the smallest number of cards is 12.

As 12 ÷ 3 is 4 there are 4 red cards, and as 12 ÷ 4 is 3 there are 3 green cards. As 12 – 4 – 3 is 5, the smallest number of blue cards is 5.

18. 125

As heads appeared 150 times, then tails appeared 50 times out of 200. This represents a probability of $\frac{50}{200}$, which is $\frac{1}{4}$. As 500 ÷ 4 is 125, it is likely about 125 tails will be tossed.

Unit 10A PAGE 32

1. 10

As 4 + 3 + 2 + 1 is 10, then 10 students have curly hair.

2. $\frac{2}{5}$

There were 5 students who walked home and 2 of them were girls. This is written as $\frac{2}{5}$.

3. 16

As 7 + 9 is 16, there are 16 students who can play chess.

4. 41

As 18 + 23 is 41, there were 41 young people who preferred coffee.

5. 15

As 4 + 11 is 15, then 15 90-year-olds have a driver's licence.

6. 16

As 9 + 7 is 16, then 16 students read at least 4 books.

7. 38

As 12 + 10 + 7 + 9 is 38, then 38 students received a distinction or a credit.

8. 20

As 16 + 4 is 20, then 20 people have a landline phone.

9. 34

As 12 + 9 + 13 is 34, there are 34 sedans in the carpark.

10. 14

As 8 + 6 is 14, then 14 males liked summer or winter.

11.

	Yes	No	Total
Girls	10	2	12
Boys	6	8	14
Total	16	10	26

12.

	Beach	Pool	Movies	Total
Males	12	7	8	27
Females	16	10	12	38
Total	28	17	20	65

13.

	Year 7	Year 12	Total
Males	70	55	125
Females	85	65	150
Total	155	120	275

14.

	Brown	Blue	Other	Total
Boys	8	4	1	13
Girls	9	2	1	12
Total	17	6	2	25

15.

	Red	Green	Blue	Yellow	Total
Prisms	8	7	6	5	26
Cylinders	3	2	4	5	14
Total	11	9	10	10	40

16. 55

As 21 + 23 + 4 + 7 is 55, a total of 55 people selected Europe or Africa.

17. 3

As 3 + 5 = 8 and 3 + 2 is 5, then the difference is 8 – 5 which is 3. This means 3 more boys had a banana or an apple than had a mandarin or orange.

18. $\frac{7}{20}$

As 4 + 6 + 3 + 7 is 20, and 4 + 3 is 7, then $\frac{7}{20}$ of the crayons in Box B are red or green.

19. 16

As 6 + 10 is 16, then 16 students have a pet.

20. $\frac{2}{3}$

As 4 + 2 is 6 there are 6 left-handed students. As 4 of these 6 students are girls, then the fraction is $\frac{4}{6}$, or $\frac{2}{3}$.

21. $\frac{4}{15}$

As 8 + 7 + 11 + 4 is 30, the fraction is $\frac{8}{30}$, which is $\frac{4}{15}$.

22. As 30 ÷ 3 is 10, there are 10 cards of each shape.

	Square	Triangle	Rectangle
Red	4	5	5
Blue	2	2	4
Yellow	4	3	1

Unit 10B PAGE 34

1. 25%

As 3 + 1 is 4, there are 4 red-haired students. As 1 student has curly red hair, then 1 out of 4 is written as $\frac{1}{4}$, or 25%.

2. $\frac{1}{4}$

The number of boys is 3 + 2 + 3 = 8.

Two boys travelled by car, so the fraction is $\frac{2}{8}$, which is $\frac{1}{4}$.

3. $\frac{1}{4}$

As 7 + 8 + 9 + 4 is 28, and 7 girls play chess, then the fraction is $\frac{7}{28}$, which is $\frac{1}{4}$.

4. 2

As 23 + 2 + 1 is 26 and 18 + 4 + 2 is 24, then the difference is 26 – 24 which is 2. There were 2 more females than males surveyed.

5. $\frac{4}{15}$

As 4 + 11 is 15, there are 15 90-year-olds who have a licence. As 4 women have a licence, the fraction is $\frac{4}{15}$.

6. 75%

As 3 + 9 is 12 there are 12 girls. 9 girls read at least 4 books. $\frac{9}{12}$ is $\frac{3}{4}$, which is written as 75%.

7. 9

As 2 + 1 + 12 + 10 + 7 + 9 is 41, and 50 – 41 is 9, then 9 students did not receive an award.

8. $\frac{1}{5}$

The number of people with a landline is 16 + 4 = 20. 4 are less than 40. The fraction is $\frac{4}{20} = \frac{1}{5}$.

9. $\frac{1}{4}$

As 4 + 4 + 8 is 16, there are 16 SUVs. 4 are white so the fraction is $\frac{4}{16}$, which is $\frac{1}{4}$.

10. 7

As 6 + 9 is 15 and 5 + 3 is 8, then 15 – 8 is 7. This means 7 more workers liked spring than those who liked autumn.

11.

	Yes	No	Total
Girls	10	5	15
Boys	6	7	13
Total	16	12	28

12. 14

60 – (20 + 8 + 18) is 60 – 46 = 14. 14 students play an instrument but no sport.

13.

	Beach	Pool	Movies	Total
Males	6	5	7	18
Females	11	3	8	22
Total	17	8	15	40

14. 91

	Year 9	Year 11	Total
Males	85	61	146
Females	91	77	168
Total	176	138	314

There are 91 females in Year 9.

15. 10%

	Brown	Blue	Other	Total
Boys	39	7	4	50
Girls	37	10	3	50
Total	76	17	7	100

10 out of 100 were blue-eyed girls, which is $\frac{10}{100}$, or 10%.

16. $\frac{1}{4}$

As 4 × (3 + 2) is 20, and 3 + 2 is 5, then 5 out of 20 blocks are red or yellow prisms. As $\frac{5}{20} = \frac{1}{4}$, then $\frac{1}{4}$ of the blocks were red or yellow prisms.

17. $\frac{6}{25}$

The number of women was 12 + 23 + 8 + 7 = 50, and 12 women selected America, so the fraction is $\frac{12}{50}$, which is $\frac{6}{25}$.

18. 80%

The number of green crayons was 5 + 3 + 2 = 10. 5 + 3 = 8, which is the number in Boxes A + B so $\frac{8}{10}$, or 80% of green crayons are not in Box C.

19. $\frac{1}{7}$

The number of students is 6 + 10 + 4 + 8 = 28. The fraction is $\frac{4}{28}$, or $\frac{1}{7}$.

20. 30%

As 4 + 15 + 2 + 9 is 30, and there are 9 right-handed boys, then the fraction is $\frac{9}{30}$, or $\frac{3}{10} = \frac{30}{100}$, which is 30%.

21. 50%

As 8 + 7 + 11 + 4 is 30, and 8 + 7 is 15, then $\frac{15}{30}$, or $\frac{1}{2}$, of the students played sport. This means 50% of the students played sport.

22. As 45 ÷ 3 is 15, every row and every column needs to add to 15.

	Square	Triangle	Rectangle
Red	2	7	6
Blue	9	5	1
Yellow	4	3	8

Section 2

Unit 1A

PAGE 36

1. 28, 746, 3000

The last digit in an even number has to be even (0, 2, 4, 6 or 8). This means the even numbers are 28, 746 and 3000.

2.

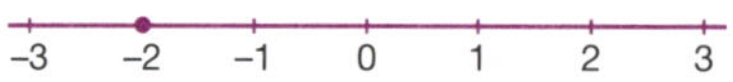

3. 3625

$$\begin{array}{r} 6000 \\ -\ 2375 \\ \hline 3625 \end{array}$$

The larger number is 3625.

4. $\frac{1}{4}, \frac{2}{8}$

1 column out of 4 columns is $\frac{1}{4}$.

2 squares out of 8 squares is $\frac{2}{8}$.

The fractions are $\frac{1}{4}$ and $\frac{2}{8}$.

5. $\frac{1}{2}$

As $\frac{3}{8}$ and $\frac{1}{8}$ have the same denominator, and as 3 + 1 is 4, then $\frac{3}{8} + \frac{1}{8} = \frac{4}{8}$. This can be rewritten as $\frac{4 \div 4}{8 \div 4} = \frac{1}{2}$.

6. 3.16

Rewrite 2.3 as 2.30.

$$\begin{array}{r} 2.30 \\ +\ 0.86 \\ \hline 3.16 \end{array}$$

7. 43%

A percentage is a fraction with a denominator of 100, so $\frac{43}{100}$ is 43%.

8. $99

129 – 30 is 129 – 29 – 1 which is 100 – 1 = 99. The new price is $99.

9. 5.85

Check the difference between the numbers:

$$\begin{array}{r} 5.15 \\ -\ 4.80 \\ \hline 0.35 \end{array}$$

The pattern is increasing by 0.35. As 5.50 + 0.35 is 5.85, the next number is 5.85.

10. 4

As 3 × 2 is 6, then 10 – 3 × 2 is 10 – 6, which is 4.

11. 3761 mm

Converting m to mm will mean a bigger number. As there are 1000 mm in 1 m, then 3.761 × 1000 is 3761. This means 3.761 m = 3761 mm.

12. 3670 g

There are 1000 grams in 1 kg. Converting kg to g will mean a larger number. As 3.670 × 1000 is 3670, there are 3670 g.

13.

14.

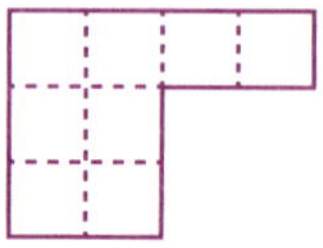

15. *A*(3, 1), *B*(–1, –2)

To reach *A*, leave the origin and 3 to the right and 1 up is (3, 1). To reach *B*, leave the origin, 1 to the left, and 2 down is (–1, –2).

16. 65°

An acute angle measures less than 90°. This means the acute angle is 65°.

17. 25

The probability of a head is $\frac{1}{2}$. As $\frac{1}{2}$ of 50 is 25, then the expected number is 25 times.

18. 24

As 13 + 11 is 24, there are 24 students who own a pet.

Unit 1B PAGE 37

1. 54, 2400

As 54 ÷ 6 is 9 and 2400 ÷ 6 is 400, the two numbers are 54 and 2400. 609 ÷ 6 is 101 with a remainder of 3 and 6661 ÷ 6 is 1110 with a remainder of 1.

2. –3

3. 6145

  3280
+ 2865
  6145

The unknown number is 6145.

4. $\frac{1}{4}$, $\frac{4}{16}$, $\frac{2}{8}$

There is a total of 16 sectors in the circular shape. 4 out of 16 are shaded which is $\frac{4}{16}$. Considering pairs of sectors, out of 8 pairs of sectors there are 2 shaded. This is $\frac{2}{8}$. There are 4 quarters in the circle and 1 of these is shaded. This is $\frac{1}{4}$. The fraction shaded can be written as $\frac{1}{4}$, $\frac{4}{16}$ or $\frac{2}{8}$.

5. $1\frac{3}{5}$

As $\frac{7}{10}$ and $\frac{9}{10}$ have the same denominator, and as 7 + 9 is 16, then $\frac{7}{10} + \frac{9}{10} = \frac{16}{10}$. This can be rewritten as $1\frac{6}{10}$ which is $1\frac{3}{5}$.

6. 10.061

Rewrite each decimal with 3 decimal places.

  4.981
  5.000
+ 0.080
 10.061

7. 67%

A percentage is a fraction with a denominator of 100, so $\frac{670}{1000} = \frac{670 \div 10}{1000 \div 10} = \frac{67}{100}$ is 67%.

8. $1.60

Multiply 4 cents by 40. As 4 × 40 is 160, the discount was $1.60.

9. 7.27

Check the difference between the numbers:

  6.71
– 6.43
  0.28

The pattern is increasing by 0.28.

  6.99
+ 0.28
  7.27

The next number is 7.27.

10. 10

16 ÷ 8 is 2 and 4 × 2 is 8. This means 16 ÷ 8 + 4 × 2 is 2 + 8, which is 10.

11. 6.498 km

Converting mm to km will mean a smaller number. As there are 1000 mm in 1 m, and 1000 m in 1 km, then there are 1 000 000 mm in 1 km. As 6 498 000 ÷ 1 000 000 is 6.498 this means 6 498 000 mm = 6.498 km.

12. 650 kg

There are 1000 kg in 1 tonne. Converting tonne to kg will mean a larger number. As 0.650 × 1000 is 650, there are 650 kg.

13.

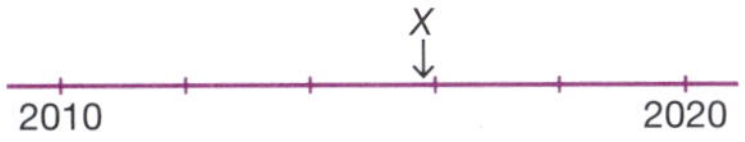

As 18 – 3 is 15, Noah was born in November 2015.

14.

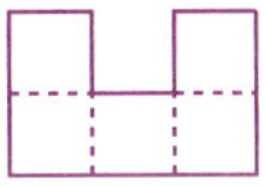

15. 5 units

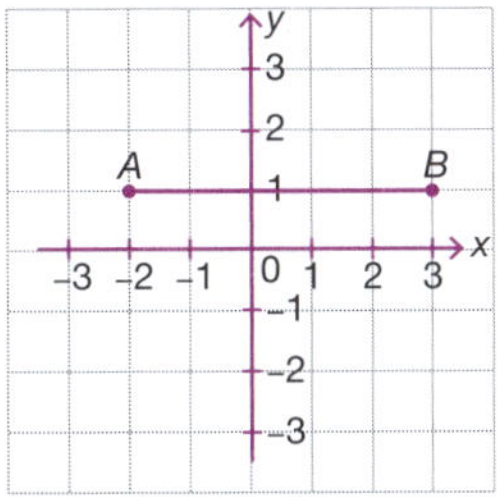

The length of *AB* is 5 units.

16. true

Yes, the angle must be obtuse. For example, if one angle is 89°, then the other angle is 91°.

17. 20

The probability of a 5 or 6 is $\frac{2}{6}$, which is $\frac{1}{3}$. As 60 ÷ 3 is 20, a 5 or 6 is expected 20 times.

18. 4

There are 13 + 3 = 16 girls and 11 + 1 = 12 boys. As 16 – 12 is 4, there are 4 more girls in the class than boys.

Unit 2A PAGE 38

1. yes

When two odd numbers are added, the result is always even. For example, 3 + 5 is 8.

2.

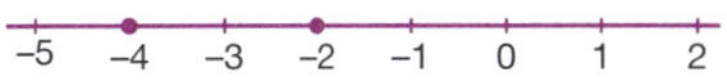

3. 250

  2800
+ 4200
  7000

He sells a total of 7000 chicks. As 7250 – 7000 is 250, Frank has 250 chicks remaining.

4. $\frac{4}{10}$, $\frac{2}{5}$

4 squares out of 10 squares is $\frac{4}{10}$.

2 columns out of 5 columns is $\frac{2}{5}$.

The fractions are $\frac{4}{10}$ and $\frac{2}{5}$.

5. $2\frac{4}{5}$

Add the fractions first: $\frac{1}{5} + \frac{3}{5}$ is $\frac{4}{5}$.

This means $\frac{1}{5} + 2 + \frac{3}{5}$ is $2\frac{4}{5}$.

6. 3.4

Rewrite with 1 decimal place.

  12.0
– 8.6
   3.4

7. 57%

To rewrite as a percentage, multiply by 100%: 0.57 × 100% is 57%.

8. $351

1250 – 899 is 1250 – 900 + 1. This is 350 + 1 which is 351. The amount of discount was $351.

9. 4.1

1.4 – 0.5 = 1.4 – 0.4 – 0.1 which is 0.9. The pattern is adding 0.9. The next number is 3.2 + 0.9 = 4.1.

10. 2

As 10 + 3 is 13, then 15 – 13 is 2.

11. 830 cm

Converting m to cm will mean a bigger number. As there are 100 cm in 1 m, then 8.3 × 100 = 8.30 × 100, which is 830. This means 8.3 m = 830 cm.

12. 6.74

There are 1000 grams in 1 kg. Converting g to kg will mean a smaller number. As 6740 ÷ 1000 is 6.74, there are 6.74 kg.

13.

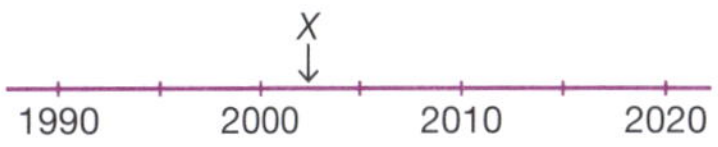

14.

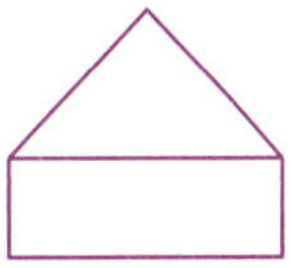

15.

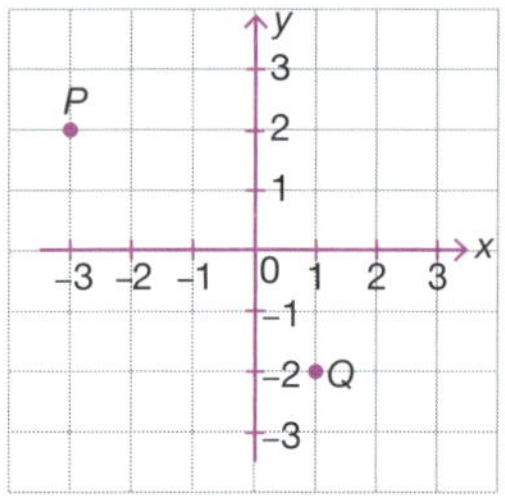

16. 145°

An obtuse angle measures more than 90°, but less than 180°. This means the obtuse angle is 145°.

17. $\frac{2}{5}$

As 3 + 2 is 5, there are 5 balls. As there are 2 blue balls, the probability is $\frac{2}{5}$.

18. 26

As 11 + 15 is 26, there are 26 adults who preferred coffee.

Unit 2B PAGE 39

1. ♥ + 2

The difference between consecutive odd numbers is 2. This means 2 more than an odd number is the next odd number.

2. –2

3. 600 km

$$\begin{array}{r} 2210 \\ -\ \ 800 \\ \hline 1410 \end{array}$$

After the first day Lara had 1410 km to drive.

$$\begin{array}{r} 1410 \\ -\ \ 810 \\ \hline 600 \end{array}$$

Lara drove 600 km on the second day.

4. $\frac{6}{12}, \frac{1}{2}, \frac{2}{4}$

6 squares out of 12 squares is $\frac{6}{12}$.

Half of the rectangle is shaded so $\frac{1}{2}$.

2 columns out of 4 columns is $\frac{2}{4}$.

The fractions are $\frac{6}{12}, \frac{1}{2}$ and $\frac{2}{4}$.

5. $5\frac{3}{5}$

Add the whole numbers first: 1 + 4 is 5. Now, add the fractions: $\frac{2}{5} + \frac{1}{5}$ is $\frac{3}{5}$.

This means $1\frac{2}{5} + 4\frac{1}{5}$ is $5\frac{3}{5}$.

6. 0.94

First, work out 3 – 1.2:

$$\begin{array}{r} 3.0 \\ -\ \ 1.2 \\ \hline 1.8 \end{array}$$

Now 1.8 – 0.86:

$$\begin{array}{r} 1.80 \\ -\ \ 0.86 \\ \hline 0.94 \end{array}$$

7. 306%

To rewrite as a percentage, multiply by 100%: 3.06 × 100% is 306%.

8. $2025

Add 1689 and 336.

$$\begin{array}{r} 1689 \\ +\ \ 336 \\ \hline 2025 \end{array}$$

The original price was $2025.

9. 2.33

$$\begin{array}{r} 4.19 \\ -\ \ 3.26 \\ \hline 0.93 \end{array}$$

The pattern is adding 0.93. The missing number is 1.4 + 0.93.

$$\begin{array}{r} 1.40 \\ +\ \ 0.93 \\ \hline 2.33 \end{array}$$

The missing number is 2.33.

10. 2.2

$$\begin{array}{r} 5.2 \\ -\ \ 3.8 \\ \hline 1.4 \end{array}$$

This means 3.6 – (5.2 – 3.8) is 3.6 – 1.4, which is 2.2.

11. 0.79 cm

Converting mm to cm will mean a smaller number. As there are 10 mm in 1 cm, you need to work out 7.9 ÷ 10. This means the decimal point will move 1 place to the left. As 7.9 ÷ 10 is 0.79, then 7.9 mm = 0.79 cm.

12. 5 430 000

There are 1000 mg in 1 g, and 1000 g in 1 kg. This means there are 1 000 000 mg in 1 kg. Converting kg to mg will mean a larger number. In 5.430 000 × 1 000 000, the decimal point moves 6 places, so there are 5 430 000 mg.

13.

As 2009 – 12 is 1997, they got married in December 1997.

14.

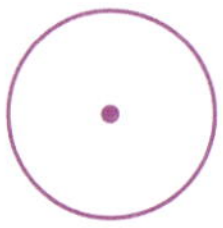

15. 3 units

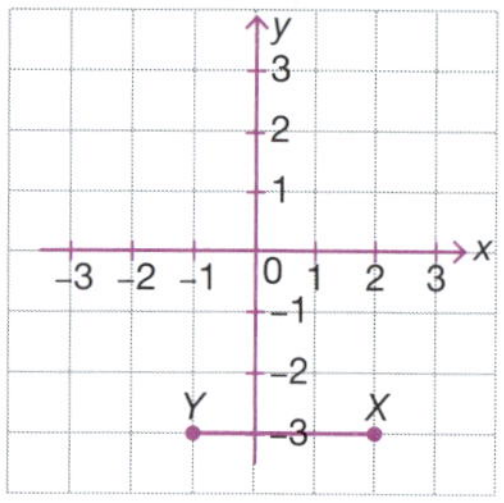

The length of XY is 3 units.

16. true

Yes, it is possible; for example 100°, 120° and 140°.

17. 30

3 + 2 is 5, so there are 5 balls. As there are 3 red balls, the probability is $\frac{3}{5}$.

You need to find $\frac{3}{5}$ of 50: as 50 ÷ 5 × 3 is 10 × 3 = 30, the expected number of red balls is 30.

18. 21

As 15 + 6 is 21, then 21 women preferred coffee or tea.

Unit 3A PAGE 40

1. 10

There are 10 odd numbers: 1, 3, 5, 7, 9, 11, 13, 15, 17 and 19.

2. –2 and –1

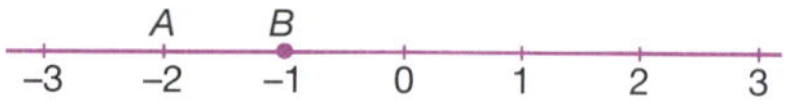

3. 14

As 28 + 16 is 44, and 58 – 44 is 14, there are 14 children on the bus.

4. $\frac{4}{10}$

For $\frac{4}{10}$ divide both top (numerator) and bottom (denominator) numbers by 2: $\frac{4}{10} = \frac{4 \div 2}{10 \div 2} = \frac{2}{5}$

5. $\frac{7}{10}$

$\frac{1}{10}, \frac{3}{10}$ and $\frac{3}{10}$ have the same denominator. As 1 + 3 + 3 is 7, then $\frac{1}{10} + \frac{3}{10} + \frac{3}{10} = \frac{7}{10}$.

6. 3.48

Look at the digit in the third decimal place: as it is 6, then increase the 7 to 8. The answer is 3.48.

7.

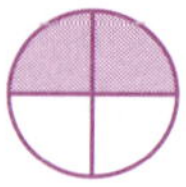

50% is $\frac{50}{100}$. $\frac{50}{100} = \frac{50 \div 50}{100 \div 50} = \frac{1}{2}$. Half of the circle is shaded.

8. **$2430**

You need to add 2250 and 180.

$$\begin{array}{r} 2250 \\ +\ \ 180 \\ \hline 2430 \end{array}$$

The original price was $2430.

9. **30**

The pattern is multiplying by 10. As 3×10 is 30, the next number is 30.

10. **32**

As $6 \div 3 = 2$, then $30 + 6 \div 3 = 30 + 2$, which is 32.

11. **2 ha**

There are 10 000 m^2 in 1 hectare (ha). As 20 000 ÷ 10 000 is 2, then 20 000 m^2 = 2 ha.

12. $\mathbf{\frac{3}{5}}$

There are 1000 mL in 1 L. 600 out of 1000 is $\frac{600}{1000}$, which is $\frac{600 \div 100}{1000 \div 100} = \frac{6}{10}$, which is $\frac{3}{5}$. This means 600 mL is $\frac{3}{5}$ L.

13.

14.

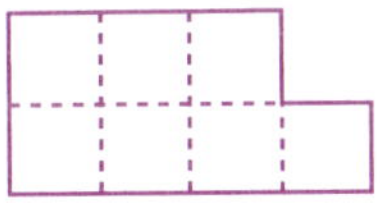

15.

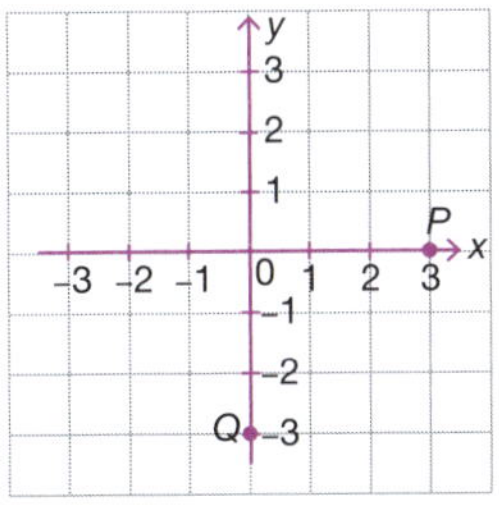

16. **322°, 183°**

A reflex angle measures more than 180°, but less than 360°. This means the reflex angles are 322° and 183°.

17. $\mathbf{\frac{3}{5}}$

15 out of 25 is written as $\frac{15}{25}$, which is $\frac{3}{5}$.

18. **60**

As 24 + 36 is 60, then 60 have a driver's licence.

Unit 3B PAGE 41

1. ☺ + 7

An even number plus an odd number is always odd. As 7 is odd, then ☺ + 7 is odd.

2. $\mathbf{-1\frac{1}{2}}$

3. **15 200**

$$\begin{array}{r} 276 \\ -\ \ 76 \\ \hline 200 \end{array}$$

The two numbers are 200 and 76.

As $76 \times 2 = 152$, then $76 \times 200 = 15\,200$.

The product is 15 200.

4. $\mathbf{\frac{4}{6}, \frac{20}{30}}$

$\frac{4}{6} = \frac{4 \div 2}{6 \div 2} = \frac{2}{3}$ and $\frac{20}{30} = \frac{20 \div 10}{300 \div 10} = \frac{2}{3}$.

5. $\mathbf{1\frac{3}{8}}$

As $\frac{3}{8}$, $\frac{7}{8}$ and $\frac{1}{8}$ have the same denominator, and as 3 + 7 + 1 is 11, then $\frac{3}{8} + \frac{7}{8} + \frac{1}{8} = \frac{11}{8}$, which is $1\frac{3}{8}$.

6. **9.00**

Look at the digit in the third decimal place: as it is 5, then increase the second 9 to 0 which then increases the first 9 to a zero, and then increases the 8 to a 9. The answer is 9.00.

7. 75% is $\frac{75}{100}$. As $\frac{75}{100} = \frac{75 \div 25}{100 \div 25} = \frac{3}{4}$, then 3 out of 4 columns are shaded.

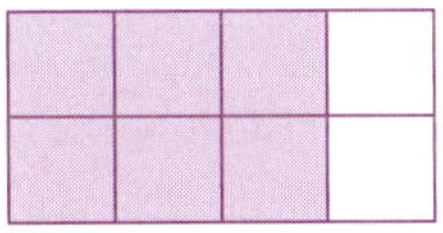

8. **$1600**

Last week's price was four-quarters of the price. If 1200 is three-quarters of the price, then by dividing by 3, one-quarter of the price was 400. As 400×4 is 1600, the price was $1600.

9. **1.75**

The pattern is dividing by 2.

$$2\overline{)3.5^{1}0}\ = 1.75$$

The next number is 1.75.

10. **4**

First, 400 ÷ 100 is 4, and then 4×2 is 8 and finally 8 ÷ 2 is 4. This means $400 \div 100 \times 2 \div 2 = 4$.

11. **37 500 m^2**

There are 10 000 m^2 in 1 hectare (ha). As $3.75 \times 10\,000$ is 37 500, then 3.75 ha = 37 500 m^2.

12. $\mathbf{\frac{1}{50}}$

There are 1000 g in 1 kg, and so 5000 g in 5 kg. 100 out of 5000 is $\frac{100}{5000}$, which is $\frac{100 \div 100}{5000 \div 100}$, or $\frac{1}{50}$. This means 100 g is $\frac{1}{50}$ of 5 kg.

13. As 2012 – 34 is 2012 – 12 – 22 = 1978, Brock's dad was born in 1978.

14.

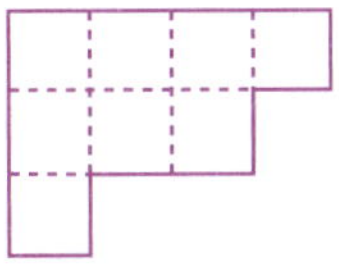

15. **origin**

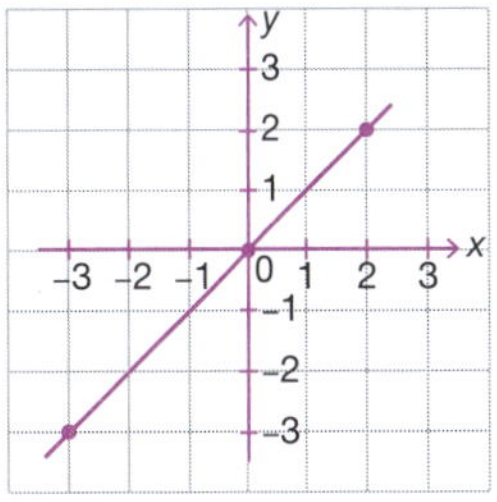

The line passes through (0, 0) which is the origin.

16. **false**

No, the other two angles do not have to be acute. For example, 200° is a reflex angle, 50° is acute and 110° is obtuse.

17. $\mathbf{\frac{5}{6}}$

At least 2 means 2, 3, 4, 5 or 6. The probability is 5 out of 6 which is written as $\frac{5}{6}$.

18. $\mathbf{\frac{3}{4}}$

As 36 + 12 is 48, there are 48 males. The fraction is 36 out of 48 = $\frac{36}{48} = \frac{36 \div 12}{48 \div 12} = \frac{3}{4}$.

Unit 4A PAGE 42

1. **2, 3, 5, 7, 11, 13**

A prime number has only 2 factors. This means the primes are 2, 3, 5, 7, 11 and 13.

2. **–2 °C**

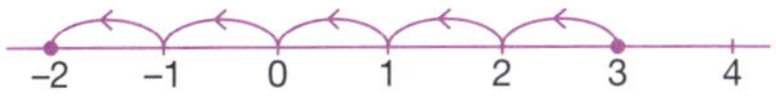

From 3, count backwards 5 which gives –2. The temperature is –2 °C.

3. **20**

As half of 40 is 20, Dan should give Adam 20 comic books.

4. **3**

For $\frac{6}{8}$ divide both top (numerator) and bottom (denominator) numbers by 2: $\frac{6}{8} = \frac{6 \div 2}{8 \div 2} = \frac{3}{4}$.

5. $\frac{5}{6}$

Use a related denominator: as 2 and 3 are factors of 6, rewrite the fractions as sixths. $\frac{1}{2} = \frac{1 \times 3}{2 \times 3} = \frac{3}{6}$ and $\frac{1}{3} = \frac{1 \times 2}{3 \times 2} = \frac{2}{6}$.

This means $\frac{1}{2} + \frac{1}{3} = \frac{3}{6} + \frac{2}{6} = \frac{5}{6}$.

6. **3.8**

First, 3.6 – 0.2 is 3.4. Now, adding 0.4 gives 3.8.

7.

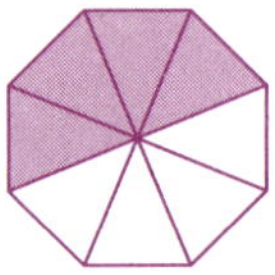

50% is $\frac{50}{100}$. As $\frac{50}{100} = \frac{50 \div 50}{100 \div 50} = \frac{1}{2}$, or $\frac{4}{8}$ then 4 out of 8 sections are shaded.

8. **\$72**

As 10% is one-tenth, you need to divide 80 by 10 which is 8.

As 80 – 8 = 72, the new price is \$72.

9. **2**

The pattern is adding $\frac{3}{5}$. The next number is $1\frac{2}{5} + \frac{3}{5}$. As $\frac{2}{5} + \frac{3}{5} = \frac{5}{5}$, or 1, then $1\frac{2}{5} + \frac{3}{5} = 2$.

10. **10**

As 24 ÷ 6 is 4, then 24 ÷ 6 + 6 is 4 + 6, which is 10.

11. **500**

There are 1000 mm in 1 m. As half of 1000 is 500, then $\frac{1}{2}$ metre = 500 mm.

12. **1.7 L**

There are 1000 mL in 1 L, and so 2000 mL in 2 L. As 2000 – 300 is 1700, there is 1700 mL, or 1.7 L remaining.

13.

14.

15. **1**

The y-value is always 2 more than the x-value. 2 more than –1 is 1. The missing number is 1.

16. **60°**

The two angles form a straight angle which means they add to 180°. As 180 – 120 is 60, the angle measures 60°.

17. **500**

The probability of a tail is $\frac{1}{2}$. As $\frac{1}{2}$ of 1000 is 500, then the expected number is 500 times.

18. **39**

As 12 + 9 + 4 + 14 is 39, there were 39 under 30-year-olds surveyed.

Unit 4B PAGE 43

1. **8**

A composite number has more than 2 factors. This means the numbers are 12, 14, 15, 16, 18, 20, 21 and 22, which is 8 numbers.

2. **4 °C**

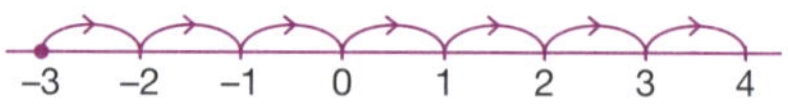

From –3, count forward 7 which gives 4. The temperature was 4 °C.

3. **15**

As 12 × 5 is 60, Edna was 60 when Ebony was 5. This means there is an age difference of 55 years. Edna is 55 years older than Ebony.

As 70 – 55 = 15, Ebony will be 15.

4. **4**

$\frac{12}{16} = \frac{12 \div 4}{16 \div 4} = \frac{3}{4}$. This means the missing number is 4.

5. $1\frac{5}{12}$

Use a related denominator: as 3 and 4 are factors of 12, rewrite the fractions as twelfths. $\frac{2}{3} = \frac{2 \times 4}{3 \times 4} = \frac{8}{12}$ and $\frac{3}{4} = \frac{3 \times 3}{4 \times 3} = \frac{9}{12}$.

This means $\frac{2}{3} + \frac{3}{4} = \frac{8}{12} + \frac{9}{12} = \frac{17}{12}$, which can be rewritten as $1\frac{5}{12}$.

6. **4.83**

$$\begin{array}{r} 3.00 \\ -\ 1.07 \\ \hline 1.93 \end{array}$$

Now, add 1.93 and 2.9:

$$\begin{array}{r} 1.93 \\ +\ 2.90 \\ \hline 4.83 \end{array}$$

7.

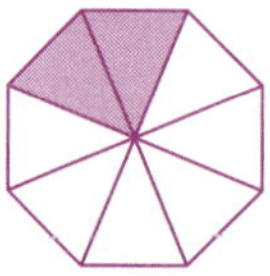

25% is $\frac{25}{100}$. As $\frac{25}{100} = \frac{25 \div 25}{100 \div 25} = \frac{1}{4}$ or $\frac{2}{8}$, then two out of the eight triangles are shaded.

8. **\$180**

As 10% is $\frac{1}{10}$, then 900 ÷ 10 is 90.

This means 20% is 90 × 2 = 180.

This is a saving of \$180.

9. $3\frac{3}{4}$

The first two numbers have whole numbers of 5, then the next two numbers have whole numbers of 4. The missing number will have a whole number of 3.

Also, the $\frac{3}{4}$ and $\frac{1}{4}$ are alternating. The next number will be $3\frac{3}{4}$. (The answer could also be found using a pattern of subtracting $\frac{2}{4}$.)

10. **1**

As 15 × 2 is 30 and 30 ÷ 6 is 5, then 15 × 2 ÷ 6 is 5. Also 2 × 2 is 4. This means 15 × 2 ÷ 6 – 2 × 2 = 5 – 4, which is 1.

11. **5750 mm**

There are 1000 mm in 1 m. This means 5000 mm are in 5 m. Also, as $\frac{3}{4}$ of 100 is 75, then $\frac{3}{4}$ of 1000 is 750.

As 5000 + 750 is 5750, then $5\frac{3}{4}$ m = 5750 mm.

12. **10 L**

$$\begin{array}{r} 16.3 \\ 4.8 \\ +\ 18.9 \\ \hline 40.0 \end{array}$$

Now, subtract 40 from 50, which is 10. There is 10 L of petrol in the tank.

13.

14.

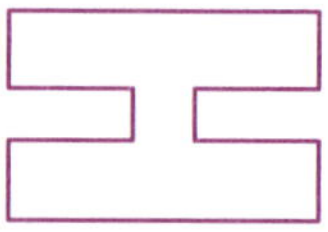

15. **20 units²**

The dimensions are 5 units by 4 units. As 5 × 4 is 20, the area is 20 units².

16. **44°**

The three angles form a straight angle which means they add to 180°. As 180 – (90 + 46) is 180 – 136 which is 44, the angle measures 44°.

17. **1050**

The probability of a 4 is 1 in 6, or $\frac{1}{6}$. As $\frac{1}{6}$ of 6300 is 6300 ÷ 6 = 1050, then the most likely number of times is 1050.

18. 3

As 14 + 12 is 26, and 9 + 14 is 23, then the difference is 26 – 23 = 3. This means 3 more people use the internet.

Unit 5A PAGE 44

1. 23, 29

The prime numbers are 23 and 29.

2. cooler

As –4 is less than 2, then the temperature is cooler.

3. 9

12 + 11 + 4 is 27. As 27 ÷ 3 is 9, the average is 9.

4. $\mathbf{\frac{1}{2}}$

3 out of 6 circles are shaded.

$\frac{3}{6} = \frac{3 \div 3}{6 \div 3} = \frac{1}{2}$.

5. $\mathbf{\frac{1}{3}}$

There are 3 thirds in one whole. $1 - \frac{2}{3}$ is $\frac{3}{3} - \frac{2}{3} = \frac{1}{3}$.

6. 10.95

$$\begin{array}{r} 365 \\ \times \quad 3 \\ \hline 1095 \end{array}$$

As there are 2 decimal places in the question, then the answer has 2 decimal places. This means 3.65 × 3 = 10.95.

7. 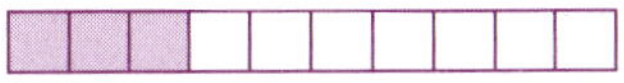

30% is $\frac{30}{100}$. As $\frac{30}{100} = \frac{30 \div 10}{100 \div 10} = \frac{3}{10}$, then 3 out of 10 sections are shaded.

8. 10%

As 20 – 18 is 2, the discount is $2. This means a discount of 2 out of 20, which is $\frac{2}{20}$, or $\frac{1}{10}$ which is 10%.

9. 8.2

$$\begin{array}{r} 5.8 \\ -\ 4.6 \\ \hline 1.2 \end{array}$$

The pattern rule is adding 1.2. 7 + 1.2 = 8.2. The missing number is 8.2.

10. 20

The number sentence is $\frac{1}{2} \times (12 + 28)$. As 12 + 28 is 40, then $\frac{1}{2}$ of 40 is 20.

11. 67 m

Converting cm to m will mean a smaller number. As there are 100 cm in 1 m, then 6700 ÷ 100 is 67. This means 6700 cm = 67 m.

12. 2000

As 1000 cm^3 = 1 L, then 2000 cm^3 = 2 L.

13. 19 years

One unit equals 2 years. As *P* is halfway between 1996 and 1998, the house was purchased in 1997. As *Q* is pointing to 2016, Joshua sold in 2016. From 1997 to 2016 is 3 + 16 = 19 years.

14. 18

A hexagonal prism has 18 edges, so Liana will need 18 straws.

15. 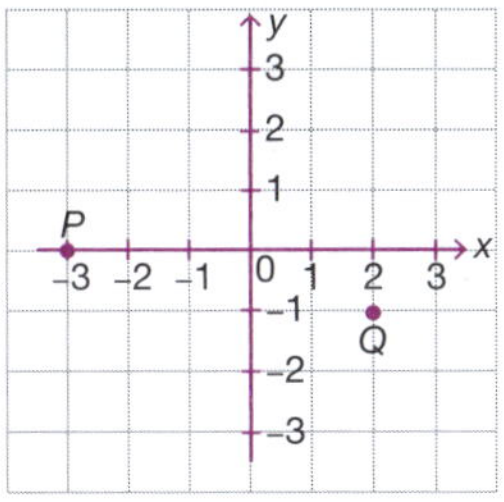

16. 54°

The two angles form a right angle which means they add to 90°. As 90 – 36 is 54, the angle measures 54°.

17. $\mathbf{\frac{1}{4}}$

As 8 + 7 + 5 is 20, there are 20 cubes. As there are 5 green cubes, the probability is $\frac{5}{20}$, which is $\frac{1}{4}$.

18. 16

As 3 + 9 + 4 is 16, there were 16 vehicles sold on the weekends.

Unit 5B PAGE 45

1. 4

The composite numbers are 4, 6, 8 and 9. This means there are 4 composite numbers.

2. <

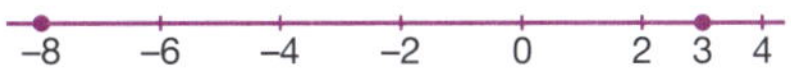

As –8 is to the left of 3 on the number line, then –8 is less than 3. This means –8 < 3.

3. 149 cm

If the average height is 158 cm then the total height will be 158 × 3 which is 474 cm. Aiden is 164 cm and Sam is 161 cm. As 164 + 161 = 325, and 474 – 325 = 149, Carter is 149 cm tall.

4. $\mathbf{\frac{3}{4}}$

6 out of 8 circles are shaded.

$\frac{6}{8} = \frac{6 \div 2}{8 \div 2} = \frac{3}{4}$.

5. $\mathbf{1\frac{2}{5}}$

Think of the question as $1 + 1 - \frac{3}{5}$. This is $1 + \frac{5}{5} - \frac{3}{5}$, which is $1 + \frac{2}{5}$, or $1\frac{2}{5}$.

6. 168.36

$$\begin{array}{r} 732 \\ \times \quad 23 \\ \hline 2\,196 \\ 14\,640 \\ \hline 16\,836 \end{array}$$

As there are 2 decimal places in the question, then the answer has 2 decimal places. This means 7.32 × 23 = 168.36.

7. 50% is $\frac{50}{100}$. As $\frac{50}{100} = \frac{50 \div 50}{100 \div 50} = \frac{1}{2}$, then half of the shape is shaded. This means $2\frac{1}{2}$ squares out of the 5 squares are shaded.

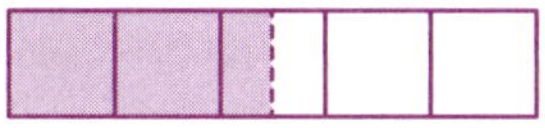

8. 25%

As 600 – 450 is 150, the discount is $150. This means a discount of 150 out of 600, which is $\frac{150}{600}$.

$\frac{150}{600} = \frac{15}{60} = \frac{1}{4}$ which is 25%.

9. 0.625

The pattern rule is dividing by 2.

$$2\overline{)1.25^{1}0} = 0.625$$

The missing number is 0.625.

10. 15

The number sentence is $\frac{3}{4} \times (48 - 28)$. As 48 – 28 is 20, you need to find $\frac{3}{4}$ of 20. As 20 ÷ 4 is 5, and 5 × 3 is 15, then $\frac{3}{4}$ of 20 is 15.

11. 0.042 m

Converting mm to m will mean a smaller number. As there are 1000 mm in 1 m, you need to find 42 ÷ 1000. Imagine 0042.0 ÷ 1000 is 0.042. This means 42 mm = 0.042 m.

12. 6.53 L

There are 1000 cm^3 in 1 L. Converting cm^3 to L will mean a smaller number. As 6530 ÷ 1000 is 6.53, there are 6.53 L.

13. C

One unit equals 2 years. As *A* is pointing to 1996, Abigail was born in 1996. Students are about 12 years old when they start high school. As 1996 + 12 is 2008, Abigail started high school in 2008. *C* is pointing to 2008.

14. 12

A hexagonal pyramid has 12 edges, so Michelle will need 12 straws.

15. 14 units

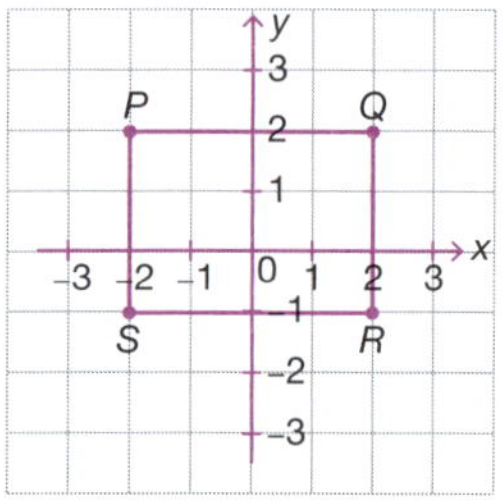

The dimensions are 4 units by 3 units. As 2 × (4 + 3) is 2 × 7 = 14, the perimeter is 14 units.

16. 25°

The three angles form a right angle which means they add to 90°.
As 90 – (29 + 36) is 90 – 65 which is 25, the angle measures 25°.

17. $\frac{1}{3}$

Colour	Number
Red	4
Blue	3
Green	2

As 4 + 3 + 2 is 9, and there are 3 blue cubes, then the probability is $\frac{3}{9}$, which is $\frac{1}{3}$.

18. 48

As 12 + 17 + 3 + 3 + 9 + 4 is 48, a total of 48 vehicles were sold.

Unit 6A PAGE 46

1. 55, 36

A composite number has more than 2 factors. The composite numbers in the list are 55 and 36.

2. profit, over

The words are profit (not loss) and over (not under).

3. 320

$$\begin{array}{r} 100 \\ 110 \\ +\ 110 \\ \hline 320 \end{array}$$

The total score was 434 points.

4.

Shade 1 column out of 4 columns.

5. $\frac{2}{5}$

As $\frac{7}{10}$ and $\frac{3}{10}$ have the same denominator, and as 7 – 3 is 4, then $\frac{7}{10} - \frac{3}{10} = \frac{4}{10}$. This can be rewritten as $\frac{2}{5}$.

6. $7.40

$$\begin{array}{r} 185 \\ \times\ \ 4 \\ \hline 740 \end{array}$$

As there are 2 decimal places in the question, then the answer has 2 decimal places. The answer is $7.40.

7. 35%

To rewrite as a percentage, multiply by 100%: 0.35 × 100% is 35%.

8. $87

A discount of 50% means that the new price is half of the original price. As 174 ÷ 2 is 87, the new price is $87.

9. 3.7, 3.3, 2.9, 2.5

3.7 – 0.4 is 3.3. 3.3 – 0.4 is 2.9.
2.9 – 0.4 is 2.5.

The pattern is 3.7, 3.3, 2.9, 2.5.

10. 22

The number sentence is 10 + 4 × 3. As 4 × 3 is 12, then 10 + 4 × 3 = 10 + 12, which equals 22.

11. 2160 mm

There are 1000 mm in 1 m, which means that 1.4 m is 1400 mm.

$$\begin{array}{r} 760 \\ +\ 1400 \\ \hline 2160 \end{array}$$

The total length is 2160 mm.

12. 16 cm³

The solid has 2 layers of 4 × 2 = 8 cubes. As 2 × 8 is 16, the volume is 16 cm^3.

13. 8:40 pm

As 40 + 20 is 60, each band starts on the hour. This means Postscript starts at 8 pm, and they finish playing at 8:40 pm.

14.

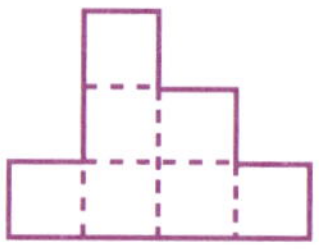

15. square

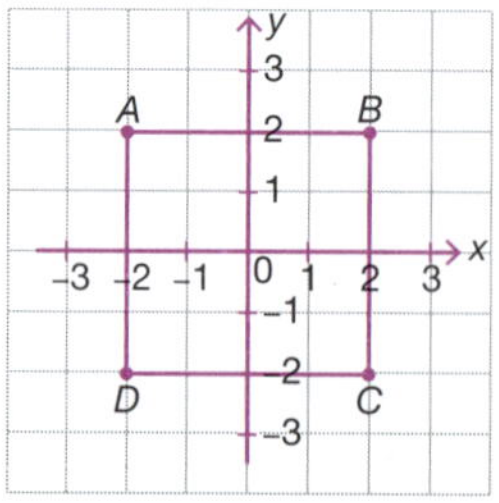

As all sides are equal, the shape is a square.

16. 124°

The angle * and 124° are vertically opposite which means they are equal and the angle is 124°.

17. 0.3

Express each as a decimal: $\frac{1}{4}$ = 0.25, 0.3 = 0.30 and 24% = 0.24.
Comparing 25, 30 and 24, the largest number is 30, so the most likely event has a probability of 0.3.

18. 34

As 16 + 18 is 34, then 34 students received a distinction.

Unit 6B PAGE 47

1. 121

The prime numbers are 2, 3, 5, 7, 11, 13 … The fifth prime number is 11.
11^2 = 11 × 11, which is 121.

2. losing $20

The opposite to winning is losing. This means the opposite to winning $20 is losing $20.

3. 8

Total is 16 + 20 = 36.

Noah will end up with one-third of the cars, and 36 ÷ 3 is 12. Noah has 20 cars, but ends up with 12, so he must give 20 – 12 = 8 cars.

4.

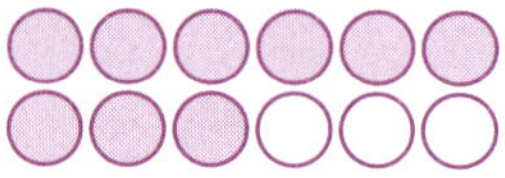

There are 12 circles and so a quarter is 3 circles. Shade 3 lots of 3 circles, which is 9 out of 12 circles.

5. $\frac{2}{3}$ **kg**

Subtract: $2 - 1\frac{1}{3}$. This is $2 - 1 - \frac{1}{3}$ which is $1 - \frac{1}{3}$. As $\frac{3}{3} - \frac{1}{3} = \frac{2}{3}$, Isaiah has $\frac{2}{3}$ kg remaining.

6. $26.75

$$\begin{array}{r} 775 \\ \times\ \ 3 \\ \hline 2325 \end{array}$$

As there are 2 decimal places in the question, then the answer has 2 decimal places. The magazines cost $23.25.

$$\begin{array}{r} 50.00 \\ -\ 23.25 \\ \hline 26.75 \end{array}$$

7. 160

Rewrite 1.6 as 1.60. To rewrite as a percentage, multiply by 100%: 1.60 × 100% is 160%.

8. 25%

199 is close to 200 and 149.25 is close to 150. As 200 – 150 is 50, the discount is 50 out of 200, which is $\frac{1}{4}$, or 25%.

9. **4.5, 5.15, 5.8, 6.45**
4.50 + 0.65 is 5.15. 5.15 + 0.65 is 5.8. 5.80 + 0.65 is 6.45.

10. **13**
The number sentence is (23 + 16) − (17 + 9). 23 + 16 is 39 and 17 + 9 is 26. This means (23 + 16) − (17 + 9) = 39 − 26, which is 13.

11. **2.43 m**
As 24 ÷ 100 = 0.24, then 24 cm = 0.24 m. Also, as 890 ÷ 1000 = 0.89, then 890 mm = 0.89 m.

$$\begin{array}{r} 0.24 \\ 1.30 \\ +\ 0.89 \\ \hline 2.43 \end{array}$$

The sum of the lengths is 2.43 m.

12. **18 cm³**
The bottom layer has 4 × 2 = 8 cubes, the second layer 3 × 2 = 6 cubes and the top layer 2 × 2 = 4 cubes. As 8 + 6 + 4 is 18, the volume is 18 cm³.

13. **2255**
As 40 + 15 is 55, each band starts 55 min after the last band started. So Cheerleader started at 2105, Emerson at 2200 and La Roma at 2255.

14.

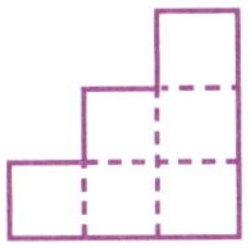

15. **15 units²**

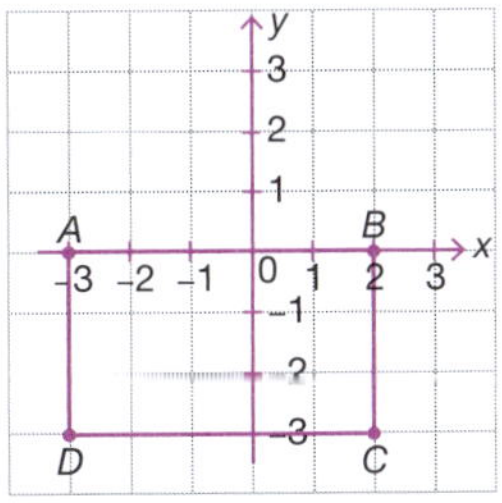

The dimensions are 5 units by 3 units. As 5 × 3 is 15, the area is 15 units².

16. **42°**
The 125° angle is vertically opposite the sum of 83° and *. As 125 − 83 is 42, the angle measures 42°.

17. $\mathbf{\frac{12}{40}}$
Express each as a decimal:
$\frac{2}{5} = \frac{4}{10} = 0.40$, 32% = 0.32, 0.35 and $\frac{12}{40} = \frac{3}{10} = 0.30$. Comparing 40, 32, 35 and 30, the smallest number is 30, so the least likely event has a probability of $\frac{12}{40}$.

18. $\mathbf{\frac{1}{2}}$
As 10 + 10 is 20, 20 students received a credit. 10 were males so the fraction is 10 out of 20 which is $\frac{10}{20}$, or $\frac{1}{2}$.

Unit 7A PAGE 48

1. **6**
The prime numbers are 2, 3, 5, 7, 11, 13. This means there are 6 players.

2. **loss, decrease, under**
The words are loss (not profit), decrease (not increase) and under (not over).

3. **30 km**

$$\begin{array}{r} 16 \\ 35 \\ 28 \\ +\ 41 \\ \hline 120 \end{array}$$

Now, the average is 120 ÷ 4 which is 30. Kalyn cycles an average of 30 km each day.

4. **88**
$\frac{1}{2}$ of 176 is 176 ÷ 2 which is 88.

5. $\mathbf{\frac{1}{2}}$
Use a related denominator: as 6 and 3 are factors of 6, rewrite $\frac{1}{3}$ as sixths.
$\frac{1}{3} = \frac{1 \times 2}{3 \times 2} = \frac{2}{6}$. This means $\frac{5}{6} - \frac{1}{3}$ is $\frac{5}{6} - \frac{2}{6} = \frac{3}{6}$, which can be rewritten as $\frac{1}{2}$.

6. **467.3**
Multiplying by 100 moves the decimal point 2 places to the right. This means 4.673 × 100 = 467.3.

7. **50%**
Two out of 4, or $\frac{2}{4}$ are shaded. $\frac{2}{4} = \frac{1}{2}$, which is 50% of the circles.

8. **$260**
If $130 is half the original price, you need to multiply 130 by 2.

$$\begin{array}{r} 130 \\ \times\ \ 2 \\ \hline 260 \end{array}$$

The original price was $260.

9. $\mathbf{\frac{3}{4}, 1, 1\frac{1}{4}, 1\frac{1}{2}}$
$\frac{3}{4} + \frac{1}{4} = 1$, $1 + \frac{1}{4} = 1\frac{1}{4}$,
$1\frac{1}{4} + \frac{1}{4} = 1\frac{2}{4} = 1\frac{1}{2}$
The numbers are $\frac{3}{4}$, 1, $1\frac{1}{4}$, $1\frac{1}{2}$.

10. **5**
First, 1.2 × 2 is 2.4. This means 2.6 + 1.2 × 2 = 2.6 + 2.4, which is 5.0, or 5.

11. **28.33 m**
There are 1000 mm in 1 m. As 1670 ÷ 1000 is 1.67, you need to work out 30 − 1.67.

$$\begin{array}{r} 30.00 \\ -\ \ 1.67 \\ \hline 28.33 \end{array}$$

There is still another 28.33 m remaining.

12. **395 g**

$$\begin{array}{r} 520 \\ -\ 125 \\ \hline 395 \end{array}$$

The mass is 395 g.

13. **1007**
As 53 − 17 is 36, it takes 36 min to travel from Benloch to Dunolly. To 0931, adding 36 min gives 1007.

14.

15. **5 units**
From −3 to 0 is 3 units, and then to 2 is 2 units. As 3 + 2 is 5, the length is 5 units.

16. **153°**
The two angles form a straight angle which means they add to 180°. As 180 − 27 is 153, the angle measures 153°.

17.

The probability is 3 out of 5, which is $\frac{3}{5}$.

18. **19**
As 8 + 11 is 19, then 19 students own a phone.

Unit 7B PAGE 49

1. **11**
There are 31 days in July. The prime numbers are 2, 3, 5, 7, 11, 13, 17, 19, 23, 29, 31. There are 11 numbers.

2. **being 15 m above sea level**
The opposite to below is above. The opposite to 15 m below sea level is 15 m above sea level.

3. **98**
The total for the 4 tests is 83 × 4 = 332. If her average in 5 tests is 86, then the total of the 5 tests would be 86 × 5 = 430. The difference in the totals is 430 − 332 which is 98. Zoey needs 98 in the next test.

4. 18

$\frac{3}{4}$ of 24 is 24 ÷ 4 × 3 which is 6 × 3 = 18.

5. $3\frac{3}{4}$ buckets

For $1\frac{1}{4} + 2\frac{1}{2}$, add the whole numbers and then the fractions.

As $\frac{1}{2}$ is $\frac{2}{4}$, the question is $1\frac{1}{4} + 2\frac{2}{4}$, which is $3\frac{3}{4}$. They picked $3\frac{3}{4}$ buckets of oranges.

6. 1000

Comparing 3.287 and 3287 (which is 3287.0), the decimal point has moved 3 places to the right. As 3.287 × 1000 = 3287, the missing number is 1000.

7. 75%

Three-quarters of the shape is shaded. To rewrite as a percentage, multiply by 100%.

$\frac{3}{4}$ of 100 is 100 ÷ 4 × 3 which is 25 × 3 or 75. The percentage is 75%.

8. $27

As 10% is $\frac{1}{10}$, then 135 ÷ 10 is 13.5. As 20% is 13.5 × 2 = 27, the saving is $27.

9. $\frac{1}{2}, \frac{5}{6}, 1\frac{1}{6}, 1\frac{1}{2}$

Use $\frac{1}{2} = \frac{3}{6}$ and $\frac{1}{3} = \frac{2}{6}$. Now, $\frac{3}{6} + \frac{2}{6}$ is $\frac{5}{6}$.

$\frac{5}{6} + \frac{2}{6}$ is $\frac{7}{6} = 1\frac{1}{6}$. $1\frac{1}{6} + \frac{2}{6} = 1\frac{3}{6} = 1\frac{1}{2}$.

10. 4.9

3.5 ÷ 5 is 0.7 and 16.8 ÷ 4 is 4.2. This means 3.5 ÷ 5 + 16.8 ÷ 4 = 0.7 + 4.2, which is 4.9.

11. 26.6 km

As there are 1000 m in 1 km, then you need to work out 850 ÷ 1000, which is 0.85.

$$\begin{array}{r} 0.85 \\ 16.30 \\ +\ \ 9.45 \\ \hline 26.60 \end{array}$$

The total distance was 26.6 km.

12. 40 kg

The average is (37.2 + 42.7 + 41.3 + 38.8) ÷ 4.

$$\begin{array}{r} 37.2 \\ 42.7 \\ 41.3 \\ +\ 38.8 \\ \hline 160.0 \end{array}$$

This means (37.2 + 42.7 + 41.3 + 38.8) ÷ 4 = 160 ÷ 4, which is 40.

The average mass is 40 kg.

13. 1130

From 0853 to 1016 is 7 min + 1 h + 16 min which is 1 h 23 min. From 1253 subtract 1 h 23 min. The time is 1130.

14.

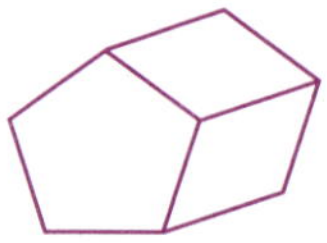

15. 10 units²

The base is 4 units and the height 5 units. As $\frac{1}{2}$ × 4 × 5 is 10, the area is 10 units².

16. 160°

The three angles form an angle of revolution which means they add to 360°. As 360 – (90 + 110) is 360 – 200, which is 160, the angle measures 160°.

17. As 2 + 2 + 1 is 5, the probability is 2 out of 5, which is $\frac{2}{5}$, or 0.4.

18. $\frac{1}{2}$

As 8 + 6 + 11 + 3 is 28, there are 28 students. 8 + 6 or 14 are boys. The fraction is $\frac{14}{28}$, or $\frac{1}{2}$.

Unit 8A PAGE 50

1. 1, 7

The two-digit number options are 30, 31, 37 and 38. Of these, the prime numbers are 31 and 37. The possible digits are 1 and 7.

2. –2, –1, 3, 4

When reading the numbers on the number line from left to right, the numbers are increasing. The order is –2, –1, 3, 4.

3. 1700

$$\begin{array}{r} 5600 \\ +\ \ 2700 \\ \hline 8300 \end{array}$$

The total in two estates is 8300.

$$\begin{array}{r} 10\ 000 \\ -\ \ \ 8\ 300 \\ \hline 1\ 700 \end{array}$$

There are 1700 people living in Bella Heights.

4. 10

$\frac{1}{4}$ of 40 is 40 ÷ 4 which is 10.

5. $\frac{7}{20}$

Use a related denominator: as 4 and 5 are factors of 20, rewrite the fractions as twentieths.

$\frac{3}{4} = \frac{3 \times 5}{4 \times 5} = \frac{15}{20}$ and $\frac{2}{5} = \frac{2 \times 4}{5 \times 4} = \frac{8}{20}$.

This means $\frac{3}{4} - \frac{2}{5}$ is $\frac{15}{20} - \frac{8}{20} = \frac{7}{20}$.

6. 37.24

$$\begin{array}{r} 532 \\ \times\ \ \ \ 7 \\ \hline 3724 \end{array}$$

As there are 2 decimal places in the question, then the answer has 2 decimal places. This means 5.32 × 7 is 37.24.

7. $<$

To rewrite $\frac{1}{10}$ as a percentage, multiply by 100%: $\frac{1}{10}$ of 100 is 100 ÷ 10 which is 10. The percentage is 10%. You can see 5% $<$ 10%.

8. $2.50

As 10% is $\frac{1}{10}$, you need to divide 25 by 10, which is 25.0 ÷ 10 = 2.5. The discount is $2.50.

9. 5.4

The sequence is 4.2, 4.8, 5.4. The number is 5.4.

10. $\frac{1}{10}$

As $\frac{2}{10} + \frac{4}{10} = \frac{6}{10}$, then $\frac{7}{10} - (\frac{2}{10} + \frac{4}{10}) = \frac{7}{10} - \frac{6}{10}$, which is $\frac{1}{10}$.

11. 8 cm

As there are 100 cm in 1 m, then you need to work out 1.73 × 100, which is 173. As 173 – 165 is 8, the difference in height is 8 cm.

12. 7.2 L

As 200 mL is 0.2 L, then 7 L 200 mL = 7.2 L.

13. 1052

As 43 – 19 is 24, it takes 24 min to travel from Wigram to Sockburn. To 1028, add 24 min to get 1052. Another method: the times in the second column are 1 h 9 min later than the times in the first column. This means 0943 + 1 h 9 min = 1052.

14.

15. **triangle**

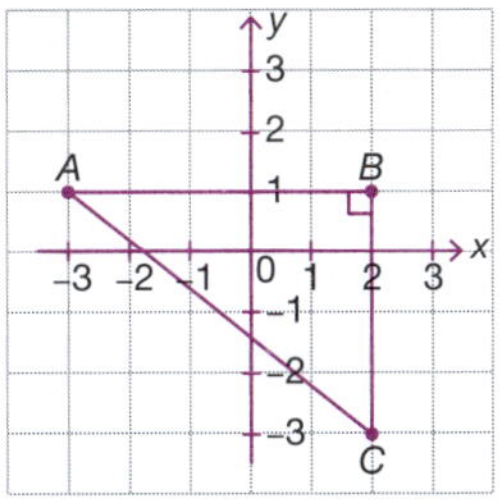

The shape is a triangle.

16. **35°**

The two angles form a straight angle which means they add to 180°. As 180 – 145 is 35, the angle measures 35°.

17. **60**

The probability of a 2 is $\frac{1}{6}$. As 6 × 10 is 60, the best estimate is 60 rolls of the dice.

18. **46**

As 26 + 5 + 15 is 46, there are 46 cars in the car park.

Unit 8B PAGE 51

1. **0, 1, 3**

The three-digit number options are 120, 121, 123 and 127. Of these, the composite numbers are 120, 121 and 123 (which is divisible by 3). The possible digits are 0, 1 and 3.

2. **–11, –5, –2, 2**

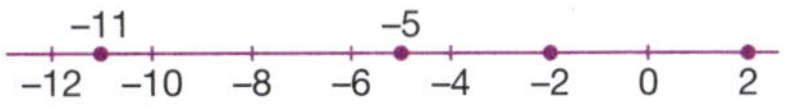

When reading the numbers on the number line from left to right, the numbers are in ascending order. The order is –11, –5, –2, 2.

3. **11**

If the average of 3 ages is 12, the total will be 3 × 12 = 36. As 36 – 9 – 16 is 11, Peyton is 11 years old.

4. **42**

$\frac{7}{10}$ of 60 is 60 ÷ 10 × 7 which is 6 × 7 = 42.

5. **$\frac{1}{2}$ m**

The question is $\frac{9}{10} - \frac{2}{5}$. Use a related denominator: as 10 and 5 are factors of 10, rewrite $\frac{2}{5}$ as tenths. As $\frac{2}{5} = \frac{4}{10}$, then $\frac{9}{10} - \frac{4}{10} = \frac{5}{10}$, which can be written as $\frac{1}{2}$.

6. **70.5**

2.35 × 30 is 2.35 × 10 × 3, which is 23.5 × 3.

$$\begin{array}{r} 235 \\ \times \quad 3 \\ \hline 705 \end{array}$$

This means 23.5 × 3 is 70.5.

7. **$\frac{8}{100}$, 9%, 0.37, 40%**

Change each into a percentage:

40%, $\frac{8}{100}$ = 8%, 0.37 = 37%, 9%.

From smallest to largest, the order is 8%, 9%, 37%, 40%. The ascending order is $\frac{8}{100}$, 9%, 0.37, 40%.

8. **$25.20**

As 10% is $\frac{1}{10}$, then 21 ÷ 10 = 2.1.

This means 20% is 2.1 × 2 = 4.2.

As 21 + 4.2 = 25.2, Ellie's new hourly rate is $25.20.

9. **4.1**

The sequence is 8.3, 7.6, 6.9, 6.2, 5.5, 4.8, 4.1 … The number is 4.1.

10. **$\frac{1}{2}$**

First, work out $\frac{1}{2} - \frac{1}{4}$, which is $\frac{2}{4} - \frac{1}{4} = \frac{1}{4}$. Now, $\frac{3}{4} - (\frac{1}{2} - \frac{1}{4}) = \frac{3}{4} - \frac{1}{4}$, which is $\frac{2}{4}$, or $\frac{1}{2}$.

11. **4.14 m**

As there are 1000 mm in 1 m, then you need to work out 640 ÷ 1000, which is 0.64.

$$\begin{array}{r} 3.50 \\ +\,0.64 \\ \hline 4.14 \end{array}$$

Josie's plank was 4.14 m long.

12. **20.03 kg**

As 30 g is 0.03 kg, then 20 kg 30g = 20.03 kg.

13. **1255**

From 0943 to 1107 is 17 min + 1 h + 7 min which is 1 h 24 min. From 1419 subtract 1 h 24 min. The answer is 1255.

14.

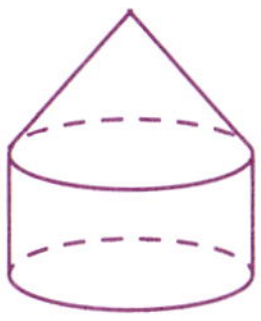

15.

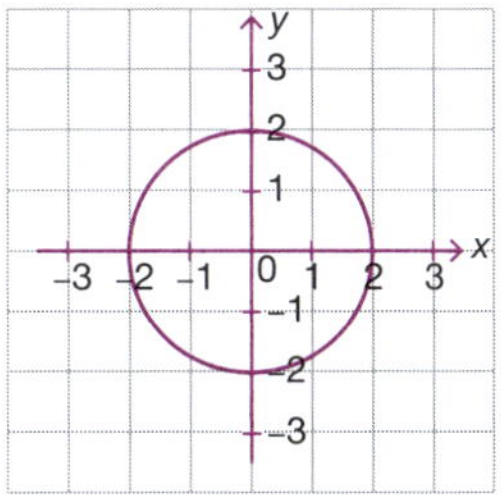

16. **100°**

The * angle is vertically opposite the sum of 48° and 52°. As 48 + 52 is 100, the angle measures 100°.

17. **120**

The prime numbers on a dice are 2, 3 and 5. The probability of a prime is $\frac{3}{6}$, which equals $\frac{1}{2}$. As 2 × 60 is 120, the best estimate is 120 rolls of the dice.

18. **$\frac{3}{5}$**

As 26 + 4 + 5 + 15 is 50, and 26 + 4 is 30, then the fraction is $\frac{30}{50}$, or $\frac{3}{5}$.

Unit 9A PAGE 52

1. **3760, 3765**

The digit on the end of a number divisible by 5 is either 0 or 5. The two numbers are 3760 and 3765.

2. **8, 0, –2, –5**

When reading the numbers on the number line from right to left, the numbers are decreasing. The order is 8, 0, –2, –5.

3. **31 383**

$$\begin{array}{r} 3\,487 \\ \times \quad 9 \\ \hline 31\,383 \end{array}$$

The answer is 31 383.

4. **8**

$\frac{1}{6}$ of 48 is 48 ÷ 6 which is 8.

5. **$\frac{3}{8}$**

As $\frac{5}{8}$, $\frac{3}{8}$ and $\frac{1}{8}$ have the same denominator, and as 5 – 3 + 1 is 3, then $\frac{5}{8} - \frac{3}{8} + \frac{1}{8} = \frac{3}{8}$.

6. **0.75**

$$5\overline{)3.7^{2}5}\quad 0.75$$

7. **0.85**

Consider 85 as 85.0. To rewrite as a decimal, divide by 100, which means the decimal point moves 2 places to the left. 85.0 ÷ 100 is 0.85. This means 85% = 0.85.

8. **$324**

As 10% is $\frac{1}{10}$, divide 360 by 10 to get 36. The price has dropped $36. As 360 – 36 is 360 – 30 – 6 which is 330 – 6 = 324, Nathan pays $324 for the guitar.

9. **11.4, 11.61, 11.82, 12.03**

11.40 + 0.21 is 11.61. 11.61 + 0.21 is 11.82. 11.82 + 0.21 is 12.03. The numbers are 11.4, 11.61, 11.82, 12.03.

10. **$1\frac{3}{4}$**

As $\frac{5}{8} + \frac{3}{8} = \frac{8}{8}$, or 1.

This means $\frac{3}{4} + (\frac{5}{8} + \frac{3}{8}) = \frac{3}{4} + 1 = 1\frac{3}{4}$.

11. **8.7 m**

$2\overline{)17.4}$ = 8.7

Michael still has 8.7 m to build.

12. **160 L**

Find two-thirds by dividing by 3, and then multiplying this answer by 2. As 240 ÷ 3 is 80, and 80 × 2 is 160, there is 160 L in the container.

13. **1 h 3 min**

1348 to 1448 is 1 h. Then to 1451 is 3 min. This is a total of 1 h 3 min.

14. **5**

A triangular prism has 5 faces.

15. ***Y* (−2, −2)**

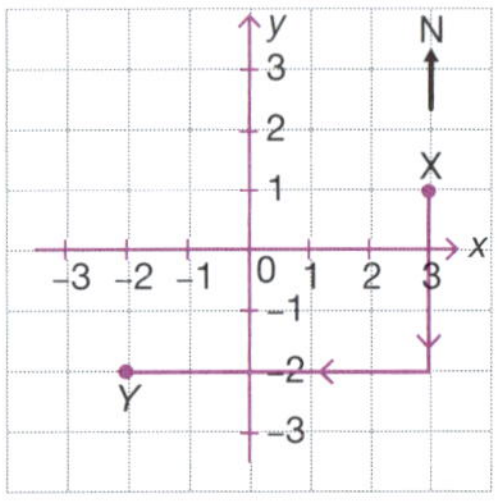

16. **154°**

The two angles form a straight angle which means they add to 180°. As 180 − 26 is 154, the angle measures 154°.

17. **0.4**

As he either rides or catches the bus then 1 − 0.6 = 0.4 gives the probability of catching the bus.

18. **5**

As 4 + 1 is 5, then 5 boys liked summer or spring.

Unit 9B PAGE 53

1. **5412, 5442, 5472**

The digits in a number divisible by 3 add to a number that is divisible by 3. As 5 + 4 + 2 is 11, then the missing digit could be a 1, 4 or 7. The three numbers are 5412, 5442 or 5472.

2. **6, 3, −1, −7, −12**

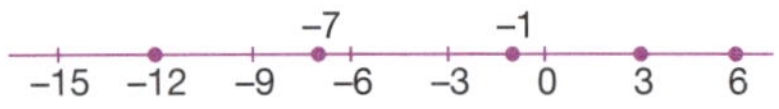

When reading the numbers on the number line from right to left, the numbers are in descending order. The order is 6, 3, −1, −7, −12.

3. **26 964**

```
     963
×     28
   7 704
  19 260
  26 964
```

The answer is 26 964.

4. **8**

If $\frac{2}{3}$ of the balls are red then $\frac{1}{3}$ are not red. $\frac{1}{3}$ of 24 is 24 ÷ 3 = 8. There are 8 balls that are not red.

5. **$\frac{5}{12}$**

The question is $1 - \frac{1}{4} - \frac{1}{3}$. Use a related denominator: as 4 and 3 are factors of 12, rewrite the fractions as twelfths.

As $1 = \frac{12}{12}$, $\frac{1}{4} = \frac{3}{12}$ and $\frac{1}{3} = \frac{4}{12}$, then $1 - \frac{1}{4} - \frac{1}{3} = \frac{12}{12} - \frac{3}{12} - \frac{4}{12}$, which is $\frac{5}{12}$.

Daniel received $\frac{5}{12}$ of the marbles.

6. **14.03**

$6\overline{)84.18}$ = 14.03

7. **0.052**

To rewrite as a decimal, divide by 100, which means the decimal point moves 2 places to the left. Think of 5.2 as 005.2, which means 005.2 ÷ 100 is 0.052. This means 5.2% = 0.052.

8. **$24 600**

As 25% is $\frac{1}{4}$, divide 32 800 by 4.

$4\overline{)32800}$ = 8200

As 32 800 − 8200 is 24 600, the new price is $24 600.

9. **120, 30, 7.5, 1.875**

120 ÷ 4 is 30. 30 ÷ 4 is 7.5.

$4\overline{)7.500}$ = 1.875

The numbers are 120, 30, 7.5, 1.875.

10. **3**

As $\frac{3}{10} + \frac{7}{10} = \frac{10}{10}$, or 1, then

$3\frac{3}{10} + \frac{7}{10} = 3 + 1$, which is 4.

This means $\frac{3}{4} \times (3\frac{3}{10} + \frac{7}{10}) = \frac{3}{4} \times 4$, which is 3.

11. **3.4 km**

Multiply 85 by 4000. As 85 × 4 is 340, then 85 × 4000 is 340 000. This means she has walked 340 000 cm, or 3400 m, or 3.4 km.

12. **48 L**

As the tank is one-quarter full, then another three-quarters is needed to fill the tank so three-quarters = 36. As 36 ÷ 3 is 12, then one-quarter of a tank is 12 L, and so four-quarters is 4 × 12 = 48. The total capacity is 48 L.

13. **1746**

From 1451 to 1500 is 9 min, to 1533 is 33 min. This is a total of 42 min. To 1704 add 42 min, which is 1746.

14. **9**

The square-based pyramid has 5 faces and the cube has 6 faces. But a face on each solid is not painted. As 4 + 5 is 9, there are 9 painted faces.

15. **(−1, 0)**

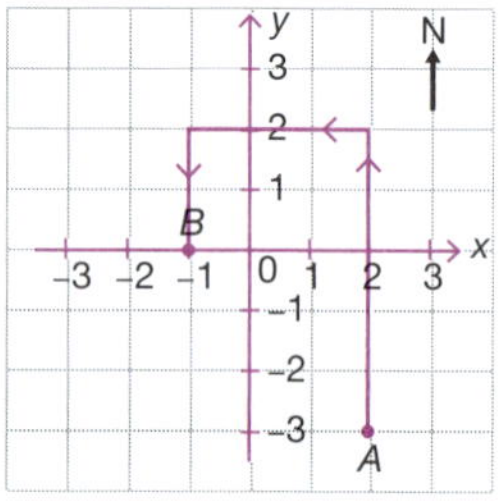

16. **85°**

The three angles form a straight angle which means they add to 180°. As 180 − (45 + 50) is 180 − 95 which is 85, the angle measures 85°.

17. **10**

As the probability is $\frac{2}{7}$, or 2 out of 7, Layla cycles 2 days each week. As 5 × 2 is 10, Layla will cycle 10 times.

18. **5**

As 4 + 9 is 13 and 5 + 3 is 8, then 13 − 8 is 5. This means 5 more students liked winter than the number who liked autumn.

Unit 10A PAGE 54

1. **13, 17**

A prime number has only two factors. From the list the numbers are 13 and 17.

2. **−6 °C**

The temperatures in order from the coldest are −6 °C, then −3 °C, −0.5 °C and 7 °C.

3. **403**

$9\overline{)3627}$ = 403

4. **6**

$\frac{1}{10}$ of 60 is 60 ÷ 10 which is 6.

5. $\frac{7}{12}$

Use a related denominator: as 4 and 3 are factors of 12, rewrite the fractions as twelfths. $\frac{1}{4} = \frac{1 \times 3}{4 \times 3} = \frac{3}{12}$ and $\frac{1}{3} = \frac{1 \times 4}{3 \times 4} = \frac{4}{12}$. This means $\frac{1}{4} + \frac{1}{3}$ is $\frac{3}{12} + \frac{4}{12} = \frac{7}{12}$, which is $\frac{7}{12}$.

6. **1.03**

$$\begin{array}{r} 1.03 \\ 4\overline{)4.1^{1}2} \end{array}$$

7. **9**

10% is $\frac{10}{100}$ which is $\frac{1}{10}$. To find $\frac{1}{10}$ of 90 divide 90 ÷ 10 = 9.

8. **$630**

As 10% is $\frac{1}{10}$, divide 700 by 10 to get 70. The price has dropped $70. As 700 – 70 = 630, Nora pays $630.

9. **8.05**

As 7.35 – 7.00 is 0.35, the pattern is adding 0.35.

$$\begin{array}{r} 7.70 \\ +\ 0.35 \\ \hline 8.05 \end{array}$$

The missing number is 8.05.

10. **4 × (6 + 2) = 32**

6 + 2 is 8 and 4 × 8 is 32. The correct number sentence is 4 × (6 + 2) = 32.

11. **1.15 km**

There are 1000 m in 1 km.
As 1250 ÷ 1000 is 1.25 km, subtract 1.25 from 2.4.

$$\begin{array}{r} 2.40 \\ -\ 1.25 \\ \hline 1.15 \end{array}$$

Sarah needs to swim 1.15 km.

12. **1 kL**

There are 1000 kg in 1 tonne. As the water has a mass of 1000 kg, there must be 1000 litres, or 1 kL.

13. **53 min**

From 1348 to 1400 is 12 min, and to 1441 is 41 min. As 12 + 41 is 53, the time is 53 min.

14. **no**

No; this does not make a cube without a lid. The shape could be a pentagonal prism without a base and a lid.

15. ***Y*(0, –1)**

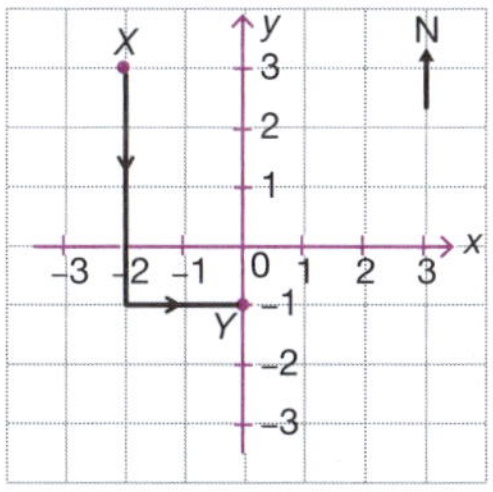

16. **26°**

The two angles form a right angle which means they add to 90°. As 90 – 64 is 26, the angle measures 26°.

17. $\frac{5}{8}$

There are 8 sectors on the spinner and 5 out of the 8 sectors are even numbers. This is written as $\frac{5}{8}$.

18. **5**

46 boys travelled by bus and 41 girls travelled by car. As 46 – 41 is 5, there were 5 more boys than girls.

Unit 10B PAGE 55

1. **41, 43, 47, 53, 59**

A prime number has only two factors. The prime numbers are 41, 43, 47, 53 and 59.

2. **–4.5 °C, –2.5 °C, –1.5 °C, 2.5 °C**

Coldest to warmest is in ascending order, or from smallest to largest. The order is –4.5 °C, –2.5 °C, –1.5 °C and 2.5 °C.

3. **248**

Average is the total of the 5 numbers divided by 5.

$$\begin{array}{r} 360 \\ 280 \\ 260 \\ 180 \\ +\ 160 \\ \hline 1240 \end{array}$$

$$\begin{array}{r} 248 \\ 5\overline{)12^{2}4^{4}0} \end{array}$$

The average is 248.

4. **18**

$\frac{2}{3}$ of 27 is 27 ÷ 3 × 2 which is 9 × 2 = 18. This means 18 students are in the choir.

5. **$12\frac{1}{4}$ h**

The question is $6\frac{3}{4} + 5\frac{1}{2}$. Use a related denominator: as 4 and 2 are factors of 4, rewrite $\frac{1}{2}$ as quarters. $\frac{1}{2} = \frac{2}{4}$.

Now $6\frac{3}{4} + 5\frac{1}{2}$ is $11 + \frac{3}{4} + \frac{2}{4}$ which is $11 + \frac{5}{4}$. This is $11 + 1\frac{1}{4}$, which is $12\frac{1}{4}$.

Mila worked $12\frac{1}{4}$ hours.

6. **22.99**

$$\begin{array}{r} 22.99 \\ 8\overline{)18^{2}3^{7}.9^{7}2} \end{array}$$

7. **42**

70% is $\frac{70}{100}$ which is $\frac{7}{10}$.

Find $\frac{7}{10}$ of 60 which is 60 ÷ 10 × 7 = 6 × 7 = 42.

8. **25% of $280**

640 ÷ 10 is 64. 280 ÷ 4 is 70. 138 ÷ 2 is 69. The greatest discount is 25% of $280.

9. **0.4**

Look at the first two numbers. As 1.6 × 4 is 6.4, the pattern is dividing by 4. As 1.6 ÷ 4 (or 0.1 × 4) is 0.4, the missing number is 0.4.

10. **20 – 4 × (3 + 2) = 0**

As 3 + 2 is 5 and 4 × 5 is 20, then 20 – 20 is 0. The correct number sentence is 20 – 4 × (3 + 2) = 0.

11. **3.165 m**

Andrew needs 100 coins. As 31.65 × 100 is 3165, the coins would cover 3165 mm, which is 3.165 m.

12. **2.6 kg**

$$\begin{array}{r} 2.25 \\ 4\overline{)9.^{1}0^{2}0} \end{array}$$

There are 2.25 L of water when it is one-quarter full. This water has a mass of 2.25 kg. As 350 g is 0.35 kg, and 2.25 + 0.35 is 2.6, the total mass is 2.6 kg.

13. **1454**

1639 is 1 h 6 min after 1533. So add 1 h 6 min on to 1348, which is 1454.

14.

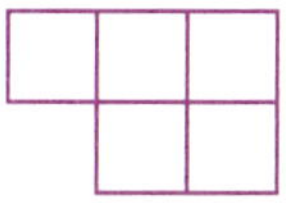

15. ***R*(–2, 1)**

As *Q* is 4 units to the right of *P*, the coordinates of *Q* are (2, –3). From *Q*, look north-west to *R* which is north of *P*. This means the coordinates of *R* are (–2, 1).

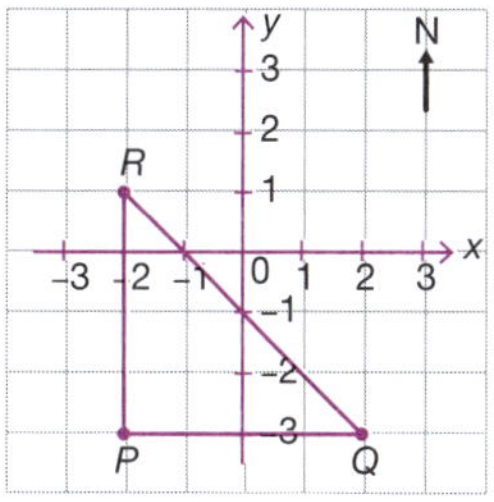

16. 32

The three angles form a straight angle which means they add to 180°. This means that $x + 58$ is 90.
As 90 – 58 is 32, the angle measures 32°, and so $x = 32$.

17. 10

Out of the 8 sectors, 2 are numbered 3. The probability of a 3 is $\frac{2}{8}$, which is $\frac{1}{4}$.
As 40 ÷ 4 is 10, the expected number of times is 10.

18. 6

As 46 + 38 is 84 and 37 + 41 is 78, then 84 – 78 is 6. This means 6 more students travelled by bus than the number who travelled by car.

Unit 11A — PAGE 56

1. 16, 25, 36, 49

$4^2 = 16$, $5^2 = 25$, $6^2 = 36$ and $7^2 = 49$. The square numbers are 16, 25, 36 and 49.

2. negative 10

The opposite of positive 10 (+10) is negative 10 (–10).

3. 7

The missing number is the answer to 140 ÷ 20. This has the same answer as 14 ÷ 2 which is 7.

4. 2

$\frac{1}{4}$ of 8 is 8 ÷ 4 which is 2. This means 2 red marbles are in the bag.

5. 4

Add the whole numbers and the fractions separately. 1 + 2 is 3 and $\frac{1}{2} + \frac{1}{2}$ is 1. As 3 + 1 is 4, then $1\frac{1}{2} + 2\frac{1}{2} = 4$.

6. 1.567

Dividing by 10 moves the decimal point 1 place to the left. This means 15.67 ÷ 10 = 1.567.

7. 73%

100 – 27 = 80 – 7 = 73. This means 73 out of 100 cars had departed the carpark, which is $\frac{73}{100}$, or 73%.

8. 40%

As 10 – 6 is 4, the price has reduced by \$4 out of \$10. As $\frac{4}{10}$ is $\frac{40}{100}$, the discount is 40%.

9. $1\frac{3}{4}$

Look at the numerators. The sequence is 3, 5, ☐, 9, 11 … The missing fraction is $\frac{7}{4}$, which is $1\frac{3}{4}$.

10. 8

16 ÷ 4 × 2 is 4 × 2 which is 8.

11. 56.4 cm

A regular hexagon has 6 equal sides.

$$\begin{array}{r} 94 \\ \times \quad 6 \\ \hline 564 \end{array}$$

As 94 × 6 is 564, then 9.4 × 6 is 56.4. The perimeter is 56.4 cm.

12. 20 L

As 1 cm³ = 1 mL, or 1000 cm³ = 1 L, then 20 000 cm³ = 20 L.

13. 1547

18 + 29 is 47. This means the train arrives at 1547.

14. square pyramid

The net forms a square pyramid.

15. 4, 5

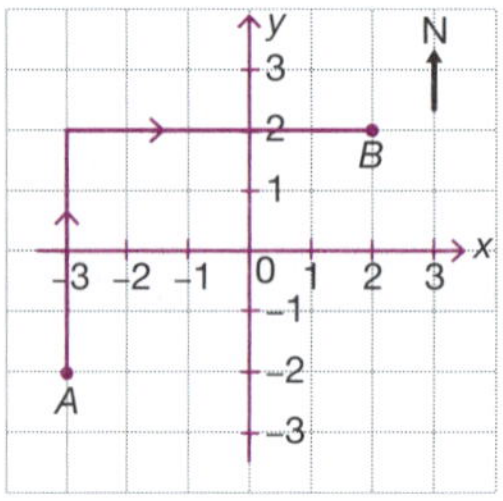

B is 4 units north of A and 5 units east of A.

16. 143°

The angles * and 143° are vertically opposite so are equal. This means the angle is 143°.

17. 0.02

The probability is $\frac{1}{50}$, or $\frac{2}{100}$, which is 0.02.

18.

	Yes	No	Total
Boys	9	4	13
Girls	12	3	15
Total	21	7	28

Unit 11B — PAGE 57

1. 15, 21, 28, 36

Triangular numbers have differences that are increasing by 1. The differences in the four numbers are 2, then 3, then 4. This means 10 + 5 is 15, 15 + 6 is 21, 21 + 7 is 28 and 28 + 8 is 36. The missing numbers are 15, 21, 28 and 36.

2. positive 8.4 (+8.4, or 8.4)

The opposite of negative is positive. This means the opposite is positive 8.4, or +8.4, or 8.4.

3. 394

The missing number is the answer to 15 760 ÷ 40. This has the same answer as 1576 ÷ 4.

$$\begin{array}{r} 394 \\ 4\overline{)1576} \end{array}$$

The missing number is 394.

4. 80

$\frac{2}{5}$ of 200 is 200 ÷ 5 × 2 which is 40 × 2 = 80. Andrew has read 80 pages.

5. $3\frac{1}{5}$ m

$10 - 6\frac{4}{5}$ is $10 - 6 - \frac{4}{5}$. This is $4 - \frac{4}{5}$, which is $3\frac{1}{5}$. Ross dug $3\frac{1}{5}$ m on Sunday.

6. 100

Comparing 124 (which is 124.0) and 1.24, the decimal point has moved two places to the left. As 124 ÷ 100 = 1.24, the missing number is 100.

7. 84%

$\frac{168}{200} = \frac{168 \div 2}{200 \div 2} = \frac{84}{100}$, which is 84%.

8. 25%

As 80 – 60 is 20, the price has reduced by \$20 000 out of \$80 000. As $\frac{20}{80}$ is $\frac{1}{4}$, the discount is 25%.

9. $5\frac{1}{3}$

As $7 - 6\frac{1}{6} = \frac{5}{6}$, the pattern is subtracting by $\frac{5}{6}$. As $6\frac{1}{6} = \frac{37}{6}$, then $\frac{37}{6} - \frac{5}{6}$ is $\frac{32}{6}$, which is $5\frac{2}{6}$, or $5\frac{1}{3}$.

The missing number is $5\frac{1}{3}$.

10. 24

First, work out 12 × 2 ÷ 6.
As 12 × 2 is 24, and 24 ÷ 6 is 4, then 12 × 2 ÷ 6 = 4.
This means 28 – 12 × 2 ÷ 6 = 28 – 4 which is 24.

11. 7.7 cm

A regular octagon has 8 equal sides.

$$\begin{array}{r} 7.7 \\ 8\overline{)61.6} \end{array}$$

Each side is 7.7 cm long.

12. 0.025 kg, 115 000 mg, 125 g, 0.2 kg

Change all masses to grams. 125 g, 0.2 kg is 200 g, 115 000 mg is 115 g, 0.025 kg is 25 g. These numbers from smallest to largest are 25, 115, 125, 200. This means from lightest to heaviest, the order is 0.025 kg, 115 000 mg, 125 g, 0.2 kg.

13. 1847

Use 37 = 24 + 13. From 1924 subtracting 24 min gives 1900, and then subtracting 13 min results in 1847.

14. 8

The square pyramid has 8 edges.

15. 4 north, 5 west

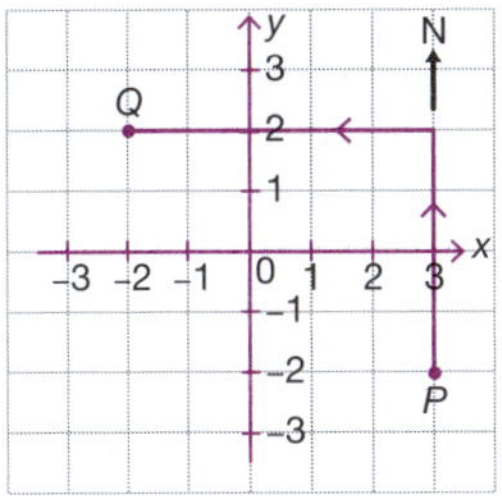

Q is 4 units north of *P* and 5 units west of *P*.

16. 73

The three angles form a straight angle which means they add to 180°. As 42 + 65 is 107, then x + 107 is 180. As 180 – 107 is 73, the angle measures 73°, and so x = 73.

17. 0.52

There are 13 odd numbers out of 25. The probability of an odd number is $\frac{13}{25}$, or $\frac{52}{100}$, which is 0.52.

18.

	Yes	No	Total
Boys	12	3	15
Girls	10	5	15
Total	22	8	30

Unit 12A PAGE 58

1. 13

As 2^2 is 2 × 2 = 4 and 3^2 = 3 × 3 is 9, then 4 + 9 = 13.

2. –5

The opposite of positive is negative. This means the opposite is –5.

3. 12

☐ × 20 = 240. The missing number is the answer to 240 ÷ 20 which is the same answer as 24 ÷ 2. This means the missing number is 12.

4. $\frac{1}{6}$

Two out of 12 bananas are ripe. $\frac{2}{12} = \frac{2 \div 2}{12 \div 2} = \frac{1}{6}$. This means $\frac{1}{6}$ of the bananas are ripe.

5. $19\frac{1}{2}$ **km**

$4\frac{1}{4} + 15\frac{1}{4}$ is $19\frac{2}{4}$ which is $19\frac{1}{2}$. Leah's total distance was $19\frac{1}{2}$ km.

6. 5.4

$5\overline{)27.0}$ = 5.4

7. 0.4

$\frac{2}{5}$ is 2 ÷ 5, which is $5\overline{)2.0}$ = 0.4. Another method is $\frac{1}{5}$ is 0.2, then $\frac{2}{5}$ is 2 × 0.2 which is 0.4.

8. $176.50

  199.90
– 23.40
  176.50

The new price is $176.50.

9. $92.50

Adding $87.50 and $2.50 is $90. Adding another $2.50 is $92.50. The cost will be $92.50.

10. (15 – 5) × 2 = 20

15 – 5 is 10 and 10 × 2 is 20. The correct number sentence is (15 – 5) × 2 = 20.

11. 14 cm

The perimeter is 4 × $3\frac{1}{2}$. First, 4 × 3 is 12, and 4 lots of $\frac{1}{2}$ is 2. As 12 + 2 is 14, the perimeter is 14 cm.

12. 960 cm^3

The volume is length × width × height. As 12 × 10 × 8 is 120 × 8 which is 960, the volume is 960 cm^3.

13. 1803

Use 24 = 21 + 3. From 1739 to 1800 is 21 min. Add another 3 min to get 1803.

14.

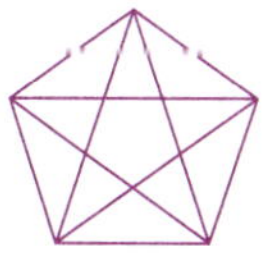

There are 5 diagonals.

15. (–3, –2)

The only point west is (–3, –2).

16. 130°

The two angles form an angle of revolution which means they add to 360°. As 360 – 230 is 130, the angle is 130°.

17. $\frac{1}{3}$

The square numbers are 1 and 4. As there are 2 square numbers out of 6 the probability is $\frac{2}{6}$, or $\frac{1}{3}$.

18.

	Work	No work	Total
Sport	14	12	26
No sport	10	6	16
Total	24	18	42

Unit 12B PAGE 59

1. 1 and 36

Square numbers are 1, 4, 9, 16, 25, 36, 49, 64, 81 … Triangular numbers are 1, 3, 6, 10, 15, 21, 28, 36, 45, 55, 66, 78, 91 … The two numbers in common are 1 and 36.

2. 11 (or +11)

The opposite of negative is positive. This means the opposite is positive 11, or +11, or 11.

3. 480

☐ ÷ 16 = 30. The missing number is the answer to 30 × 16. As 16 × 3 = 48, then 16 × 30 = 480. The number is 480.

4. $\frac{5}{8}$

As 16 – 6 is 10, there are 10 out of 16 seats empty. $\frac{10}{16} = \frac{10 \div 2}{16 \div 2} = \frac{5}{8}$. This means $\frac{5}{8}$ of the seats are empty.

5. $\frac{1}{3}$

You need to find the difference between $\frac{5}{6}$ and $\frac{1}{2}$. Rewrite $\frac{1}{2}$ as sixths: $\frac{5}{6} - \frac{3}{6}$ is $\frac{2}{6}$, or $\frac{1}{3}$ of the box.

6. 70

$5\overline{)348.645}$ = 69.729

348.645 ÷ 5 is 69.729, or 70 to the nearest whole.

7. 0.625

$\frac{5}{8}$ is 5 ÷ 8, which is $8\overline{)5.000}$ = 0.625. Another method is $\frac{1}{8}$ is 0.125, then $\frac{5}{8}$ is 5 × 0.125 which is 0.625.

8. $116.82

First, $64.90 × 2 is $129.80. As 10% is dividing by 10, 129.80 ÷ 10 is 12.98.

  129.80
– 12.98
  116.82

The total amount is $116.82.

9. 27.1 km

19.3 + 3 lots of 2.6.

```
   19.3
    2.6
    2.6
+   2.6
   27.1
```

Monica will run 27.1 km.

10. 16 ÷ (2 + 6) × 3 + 1 = 7

2 + 6 is 8 and 16 ÷ 8 is 2.
Now, 2 × 3 is 6, plus 1 is 7.
The correct number sentence is 16 ÷ (2 + 6) × 3 + 1 = 7.

11. 8 cm

The perimeter is twice the sum of the length and width: $2 \times (2\frac{1}{2} + 1\frac{1}{2})$. As 2 + 1 is 3 and $\frac{1}{2} + \frac{1}{2}$ is 1, then $2\frac{1}{2} + 1\frac{1}{2}$ is 4. $2 \times (2\frac{1}{2} + 1\frac{1}{2}) = 2 \times 4$ which is 8. The perimeter is 8 cm.

12. 2700 cm³

The volume is length × width × height. As 25 × 12 × 9 is 25 × 4 × 3 × 9 = 100 × 27, which is 2700, the volume is 2700 cm³.

13. 2142

From 2305, subtracting 1 h gives 2205. Subtracting 5 min gives 2200, and then another 18 min is 2142.

14. 9

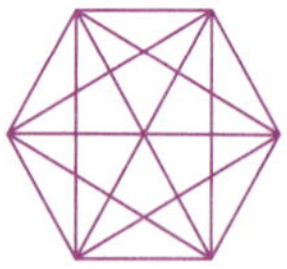

There are 9 diagonals.

15. (2, 3)

The only point is (2, 3).

16. 116

The three angles form an angle of revolution which means they add to 360°. As 84 + 160 is 244, then x + 244 is 360. As 360 − 244 is 116, the angle measures 116°, and so x = 116.

17. 70

The probability of rolling a 2 is $\frac{1}{6}$. As $\frac{1}{6}$ of 420 is 420 ÷ 6 = 70, the expected number is 70.

18.

	Work	No work	Total
Sport	11	6	17
No sport	12	9	21
Total	23	15	38

Unit 13A PAGE 60

1. 40

7^2 is 49 and 3^2 is 9. $7^2 - 3^2$ is 49 − 9, which is 40.

2. −5, 5

5 units to the left of 0 is −5 and 5 units to the right of 0 is 5 (or +5).

3. 1315

```
   2485
 − 1170
   1315
```

This means 1315 males applied.

4. $\frac{1}{2}$

26 out of 52 cards is $\frac{26}{52}$.

As $\frac{26}{52} = \frac{26 \div 26}{52 \div 26} = \frac{1}{2}$, then $\frac{1}{2}$ of the cards are red.

5. $\frac{3}{10}$

The question is $\frac{7}{10} - \frac{2}{5}$. Rewrite $\frac{2}{5}$ as tenths: $\frac{2}{5} = \frac{2 \times 2}{5 \times 2} = \frac{4}{10}$. This means $\frac{7}{10} - \frac{2}{5} = \frac{7}{10} - \frac{4}{10}$ which is $\frac{3}{10}$.

6. 1.74 m

You need to find 0.87 × 2.

```
   87
×   2
  174
```

As there are 2 decimal places in the question, then the answer has 2 decimal places. Logan was 1.74 metres tall.

7. $\frac{1}{4}$

Change each to a percentage: $\frac{1}{4}$ is 25%, 0.18 is 18% and 20%. This means $\frac{1}{4}$ is the largest.

8. $120

As 10% is $\frac{1}{10}$, then 150 ÷ 10 is 15. This means 20% is 30. As 150 − 30 is 120, the desk will cost $120.

9. 13

Counting the matchsticks, the pattern is 4, 7, 10 which is adding 3. As 10 + 3 is 13, there will be 13 matchsticks in the fourth shape.

10. $360

The number sentence to be used is (14 + 16) × 12. As 14 + 16 is 30, and 30 × 12 is 360, Jack will be paid $360.

11. 1.8 cm

The length of each side is found using 7.2 ÷ 4.

```
  1.8
4)7.³2
```

The length of each side is 1.8 cm.

12. 3.97 kg

870 g is 0.87 kg and 950 g is 0.95 kg.

```
   0.87
   1.10
   0.95
 + 1.05
   3.97
```

The total mass is 3.97 kg.

13. 1 h 14 min

From 11:48 to 12:00 is 12 min. Then 1 h to 1:00 and then 2 min to 1:02. This is a total of 1 h 14 min.

14. 

The square and rectangle

15. *D* (−2, −3)

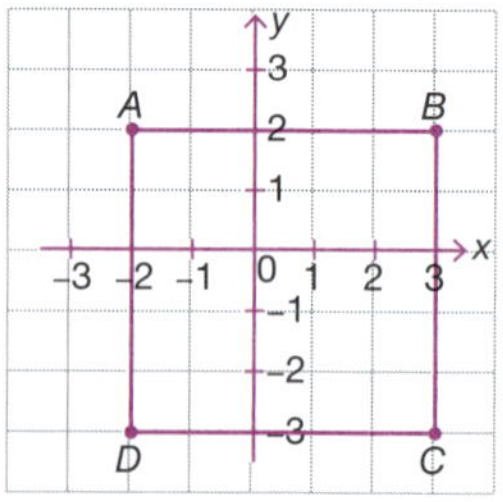

16. 39°

The two angles are vertically opposite and so are equal. This means the angle measures 39°.

17. 18

As 6 + 6 + 6 is 18, the highest total is 18.

18.

	AFL	League	Netball	Other
Males	16	11	4	10
Females	11	6	12	18
Total	27	17	16	28

Unit 13B PAGE 61

1. 16 and 28

Here are some square numbers: 1, 4, 9, 16, 25, 36 … Here are some triangular numbers: 1, 3, 6, 10, 15, 21, 28, 36, 45 … As 16 + 28 is 44, the numbers are 16 and 28.

2. −4, 8

6 units to the left of 2 is −4 and 6 units to the right of 2 is 8 (or +8).

3. 2 732 087

```
   3 389 981
 −   657 894
   2 732 087
```

This means 2 732 087 people were not born overseas.

4. $\frac{1}{4}$

As 12 – 6 – 3 is 3, there are 3 green balls out of a total of 12.

As $\frac{3}{12} = \frac{3 \div 3}{12 \div 3} = \frac{1}{4}$, then $\frac{1}{4}$ of the balls are green.

5. $\frac{7}{20}$

The question is $1 - \frac{1}{4} - \frac{2}{5}$. Use a related denominator: as 4 and 5 are factors of 20, rewrite the fractions as twentieths.

As $1 = \frac{20}{20}$, $\frac{1}{4} = \frac{5}{20}$ and $\frac{2}{5} = \frac{8}{20}$, then $1 - \frac{1}{4} - \frac{2}{5} = \frac{20}{20} - \frac{5}{20} - \frac{8}{20}$, which is $\frac{7}{20}$.

This means $\frac{7}{20}$ of the rectangle is unshaded.

6. **$6.40**

$$\begin{array}{r} 2.49 \\ +\ 3.89 \\ \hline 6.38 \end{array}$$

The cost is $6.38 which is $6.40 to the nearest 10 cents.

7. **0.5, $\frac{4}{8}$**

Change each to a percentage: $\frac{1}{5}$ is 20%, 0.5 is 50%, 0.05 is 5% and $\frac{4}{8} = \frac{1}{2} = 50\%$.

This means 0.5 and $\frac{4}{8}$ both equal 50%.

8. **$285**

50% means the second pair is half price. As 190 ÷ 2 is 95, the second set costs $95. As 190 + 95 is 190 + 100 – 5 which is 290 – 5 = 285, Jack will pay $285.

9. **19**

Counting the matchsticks, the pattern is 4, 7, 10 which is adding 3. Continuing the pattern: 13, 16, 19. There will be 19 matchsticks in the sixth shape.

10. **$406**

The number sentence to be used is (5 + 8 + 9 + 7) × 14. As 5 + 8 + 9 + 7 is 29, need to find 29 × 14.

$$\begin{array}{r} 29 \\ \times\ 14 \\ \hline 116 \\ 290 \\ \hline 406 \end{array}$$

Ella earns $406.

11. **5 cm**

If the perimeter is 42 cm, the sum of length and width is 21 cm. As 16 + width is 21, the width is 5 cm.

12. **14.2 kg**

As 14.5 – 1.2 is 13.3, the mass of the second bag is 13.3 kg. As 14.5 + 13.3 is 27.8, the mass of the third bag is found using 42 – 27.8.

$$\begin{array}{r} 42.0 \\ -\ 27.8 \\ \hline 14.2 \end{array}$$

The mass of the third bag is 14.2 kg.

13. **2:29 pm**

Use 27 + 29 = 56. From 1:33, add 56 min. This means 1:33 plus 27 min is 2:00, and another 29 min is 2:29. The train arrives at 2:29 pm.

14. **regular octagon**

The diagonals of a rhombus and a kite are different lengths, and a triangle has 0 diagonals.

15. **S(–5, –4)**

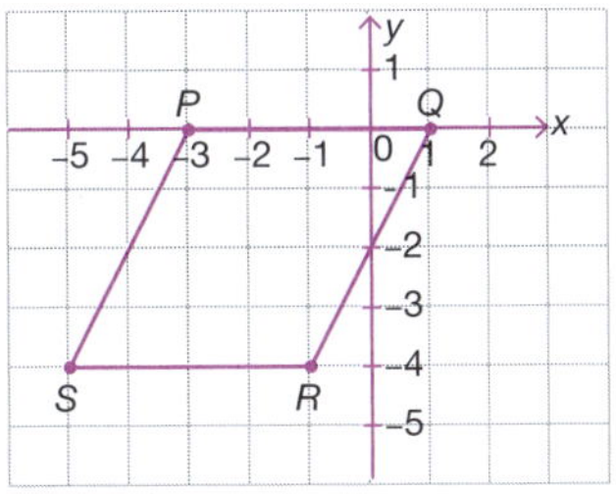

16. **51**

The three angles form an angle of revolution which means they add to 360°. As x + 164 + 145 is 360, then x is 360 – (164 + 145) = 360 – 309 which is 51. This means the angle measures 51°, and so x = 51.

17. **5**

Rolling a 1 and a 6 is a difference of 6 – 1 = 5.

18.

	AFL	League	Netball	Other
Males	21	14	6	5
Females	12	16	15	11
Total	33	30	21	16

Unit 14A PAGE 62

1. **25**

$3^2 + 4^2 = 9 + 16$ which is 25.

2. **0, 8**

4 units to the left of 4 is 0 and 4 units to the right of 4 is 8 (or +8).

3. **108**

$$11\overline{)1188} = 108$$

4. **12**

$\frac{1}{6}$ of 72 is 72 ÷ 6 which is 12. There are 12 sold vehicles.

5. **2**

$1\frac{2}{3} + \frac{1}{3} = 1 + \frac{2}{3} + \frac{1}{3}$. This is 2.

6. **54**

Multiplying by 1000 moves the decimal point 3 places to the right. This means 0.054 × 1000 = 54.

7. **70%**

As $\frac{1}{10}$ is 10% so $\frac{7}{10}$ is 7 × 10% = 70%.

8. **$150**

As 25% is $\frac{1}{4}$, you need to divide 600 by 4.

$$4\overline{)6^{2}00} = 150$$

The discount is $150.

9. **15**

Counting the dots, the pattern is 1, 3, 6 which are the triangular numbers. The difference is 2, then 3, then 4 and so on. The first five triangular numbers are 1, 3, 6, 10, 15. There will be 15 dots in the fifth shape.

10. **34**

The number sentence is 10 + 3 × 8. As 3 × 8 is 24, then 10 + 3 × 8 = 10 + 24 which is 34.

11. **12 cm**

The length of each side is found using 48 ÷ 4, which is 12.

The length of each side is 12 cm.

12. **3.75 kL**

There are 1000 L in 1 kL. Converting L to kL will mean a smaller number. As 3750 ÷ 1000 is 3.75, there are 3.75 kL.

13. **1 h 18 min**

From 12:53 to 1:00 is 7 min. To 2:00 is 1 h and then to 2:11 is 11 min. This is a total of 1 h 18 min.

14.

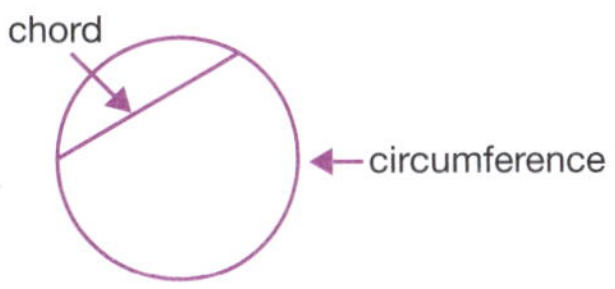

15. **4 units**

A diagonal is from (–2, 0) to (2, 0). As 2 + 2 is 4, the diagonal is 4 units.

16. **87°**

The two angles form a straight angle which means they add to 180°. As 180 – 93 is 87, the angle measures 87°.

17.

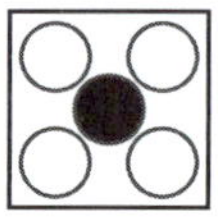

0.2 is $\frac{2}{10}$, which is the same as $\frac{1}{5}$. This means 1 out of 5 balls is black.

18.

	Beach	Pool	Movies	Total
Males	13	10	11	34
Females	17	15	8	40
Total	30	25	19	74

Unit 14B PAGE 63

1. 990

Look at the differences between consecutive triangular numbers. As 861 – 820 is 41, then the difference is 903 – 861 = 42, then a difference of 43. As 946 + 44 is 990, the next number is 990.

2. –10, –2

4 units to the left of –6 is –10 and 4 units to the right of –6 is –2.

3. 1096

$$\begin{array}{r} 1096 \\ 12\overline{)13152} \end{array}$$

The farmer has used 1096 cartons.

4. $\frac{3}{7}$

The prime numbers are 2, 3, 5, 7, 11, 13. This means 6 out of 14 numbers are prime. As $\frac{6}{14} = \frac{6 \div 2}{14 \div 2} = \frac{3}{7}$, then $\frac{3}{7}$ of the numbers are prime.

5. $\frac{1}{2}$

First, $1\frac{1}{4}$ is $\frac{5}{4}$.

This means $1\frac{1}{4} - \frac{3}{4} = \frac{5}{4} - \frac{3}{4} = \frac{2}{4}$, which can be rewritten as $\frac{1}{2}$.

6. 387.1

Rewrite the question as 3.871 × 25 × 4, which is 3.871 × 100. As multiplying by 100 moves the decimal point 2 places to the right, then 3.871 × 100 = 387.1.

7. 65%

By multiplying numerator and denominator by 5, $\frac{13}{20} = \frac{13 \times 5}{20 \times 5} = \frac{65}{100}$.

This is written as 65%.

8. $84

5% is half of 10%. As 10% is $\frac{1}{10}$, first divide 1680 by 10 which is 168. Now divide 168 by 2 which is 84.
The saving is $84.

9. 9th

Counting the dots, the pattern is 1, 3, 6 which are triangular numbers. The difference is 2, then 3, then 4 and so on. The triangular numbers are 1, 3, 6, 10, 15, 21, 28, 36, 45 … As 45 is the ninth triangular number, the ninth shape will be made from 45 dots.

10. 30

The number sentence is 5 × (1.5 + 4.5).

$$\begin{array}{r} 1.5 \\ +\ 4.5 \\ \hline 6.0 \end{array}$$

5 × (1.5 + 4.5) is 5 × 6 = 30.

11. 5.38 m

The perimeter is twice the sum of the length and width. Change 94 cm to 0.94 m.
The perimeter is 2 × (1.75 + 0.94).

$$\begin{array}{r} 1.75 \\ +\ 0.94 \\ \hline 2.69 \end{array}$$

This means 2 × (1.75 + 0.94) = 2 × 2.69 which is 5.38. The perimeter is 5.38 m.

12. 4 L, 4050 mL, 4.15 L, 0.005 kL

Change all capacities to litres. 4050 mL is 4.05 L, 4.15 L, 0.005 kL is 5 L, 4L. These numbers from smallest to largest are 4, 4.05, 4.15, 5. This means, from least to greatest, the order is 4 L, 4050 mL, 4.15 L, 0.005 kL.

13. 2:28 pm

As 36 – 19 = 17, the train was 17 min late. As 11 + 17 is 28, the train arrived at 2:28 pm.

14.

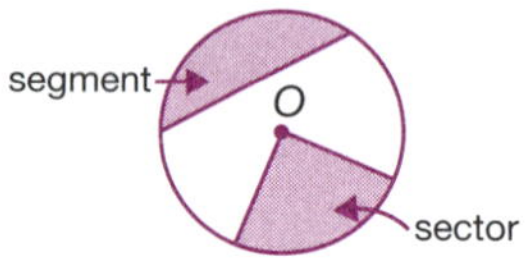

15.

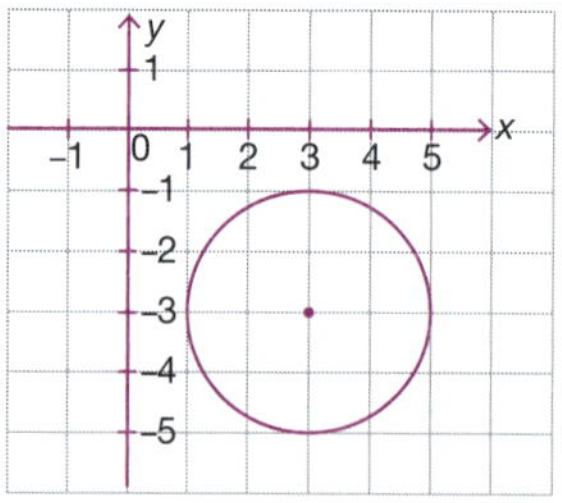

16. 79

Vertically opposite angles are 148° and the sum of x and 69. This means x + 69 is 148 which means x is 148 – 69 = 79. The angle measures 79°, and so x = 79.

17.

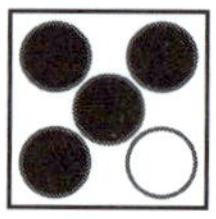

80% is $\frac{80}{100}$, which is $\frac{4}{5}$. This means 4 out of 5 balls are black.

18.

	Beach	Pool	Movies	Total
Males	10	11	7	28
Females	9	5	8	22
Total	19	16	15	50

Unit 15A PAGE 64

1. 36

$10^2 - 8^2$ = 100 – 64 is 36.

2. 4

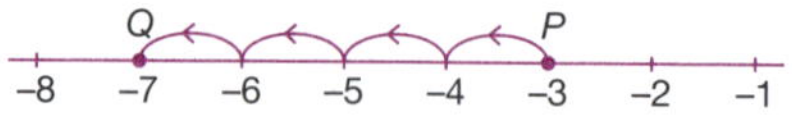

There are 4 jumps from P to Q. This means the difference between –3 and –7 is 4.

3. 3600

$$\begin{array}{r} 65\,000 \\ -\ 61\,400 \\ \hline 3\,600 \end{array}$$

3600 starters did not finish.

4. $\frac{1}{4}$

Ava used 3 out of 12 eggs.
As $\frac{3}{12} = \frac{3 \div 3}{12 \div 3} = \frac{1}{4}$, then Ava used $\frac{1}{4}$ of the eggs.

5. 2

$\frac{4}{5} + \frac{3}{5} = \frac{7}{5}$, which can be rewritten as $1\frac{2}{5}$. The missing number is 2.

6. $2387

You need to find 238 735 ÷ 100. As dividing by 100 moves the decimal point 2 places to the left, then 238 735 ÷ 100 = 2387.35. To the nearest whole, this is 2387, which means each person receives $2387.

7. 80

50% is $\frac{1}{2}$, and $\frac{1}{2}$ of 160 = 160 ÷ 2 = 80.
This means 50% of 160 is 80.

8. $1.45

As 10% is $\frac{1}{10}$, divide $14.50 by 10 which is $1.45. The discount is $1.45.

9. 26

Counting the matchsticks, the pattern is 6, 11, 16 which is adding 5. As 16 + 5 + 5 is 26, there will be 26 matchsticks in the fifth shape.

10. 35

There are five 9s to be subtracted. The question can be rewritten as $80 - 5 \times 9$ which is $80 - 45 = 35$.

11. 3.65 km

There are 1000 mm in 1 m and 1000 m in 1 km. This means there are 1 000 000 mm in 1 km. As there will be a smaller number of km than mm, use 3 650 000 ÷ 1 000 000, which is 3.65. There are 3.65 km.

12. 3 L

The volume is $15 \times 10 \times 20$ which is $150 \times 20 = 3000$. The volume is 3000 cm^3, which is 3 L.

13. 1502

The difference between 1423 and 1117 is 3 h 6 min. As 1156 + 3 h 6 min is 1502, the bus arrives at 1502.

14. 5 cm

The diameter is twice the radius. $2\frac{1}{2} + 2\frac{1}{2}$ is 5. The diameter is 5 cm.

15. 3, 2

The triangle has been translated 3 units down and 2 units right.

16. 74°

The two angles are vertically opposite and so are equal. The angle measures 74°.

17. $\frac{1}{8}$

As $3 + 9 + 8 + 4$ is 24, there are 24 students. If 3 students scored 7, the probability is $\frac{3}{24}$, which is $\frac{1}{8}$.

18.

	Year 7	Year 8	Total
Males	78	80	158
Females	79	85	164
Total	157	165	322

Unit 15B PAGE 65

1. 500

$10^2 + 20^2 = 100 + 400$ which is 500.

2. 5 degrees

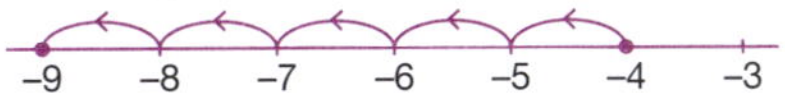

There are 5 jumps from –4 and –9. This means the difference between –4 °C and –9 °C is 5 degrees.

3. 4 993 797 000

$$\begin{array}{r} 5\,000\,000\,000 \\ -\quad 6\,203\,000 \\ \hline 4\,993\,797\,000 \end{array}$$

4. 12 km

$\frac{1}{4}$ of 16 is 16 ÷ 4 which is 4 km. As 16 – 4 is 12, Jacob still has 12 km to complete.

5. 7

Use a related denominator: as 8 and 12 are factors of 24, rewrite the fractions as twenty-fourths. $\frac{3}{8} = \frac{9}{24}$ and $\frac{11}{12} = \frac{22}{24}$.

This means, $\frac{3}{8} + \frac{11}{12} = \frac{9}{24} + \frac{22}{24} = \frac{31}{24}$, which can be rewritten as $1\frac{7}{24}$.

The missing number is 7.

6. 330 g

Vihaan has 50 \$2 coins. Find 6.6×50. This means $6.6 \times 10 \times 5$ is $66 \times 5 = 330$. The mass is 330 g.

7. 72

As 20% is $\frac{1}{5}$, you need to work out 360 ÷ 5.

As $5\overline{)360}$ gives 72, then 20% of 360 is 72.

8. \$28

First find 10% which is 140 ÷ 10 = 14. As 10% is 14 then 20% is 28. This means a saving of \$28.

9. 51

Counting the matchsticks, the pattern is 6, 11, 16 which is adding 5. The tenth shape will be made using 6 + 9 lots of 5 matchsticks. As $6 + 9 \times 5$ is $6 + 45$ which is 51, there will be 51 matchsticks in the tenth shape.

10. 81

There are five 13s to be added. The question can be rewritten as $16 + 13 \times 5$ which is $16 + 65 = 81$.

11. 4.52 m

There are 1000 m in 1 km. Converting km to m means there will be a larger number. For $0.004\,52 \times 1000$ move the decimal point 3 places to the right. This means $0.004\,52 \times 1000 = 4.52$. There are 4.52 m.

12. 400 mL

There are 2000 mL in 2 L. The number sentence is $2000 - 320 \times 5$, which is $2000 - 1600 = 400$. There is 400 mL of soft drink remaining.

13. 1230

First find the difference in the departure times of 1254 and 1407. From 1254 to 1300 is 6 min, to 1400 is 1 h and to 1407 is 7 min. This means there is a time difference of 1 h 13 min. Now add this to 1117 to get 1230.

14. 7.535 cm

As the diameter is twice the radius, you need to divide 15.07 by 2.

$2\overline{)15.070}$ gives 7.535

The radius is 7.535 cm.

15.

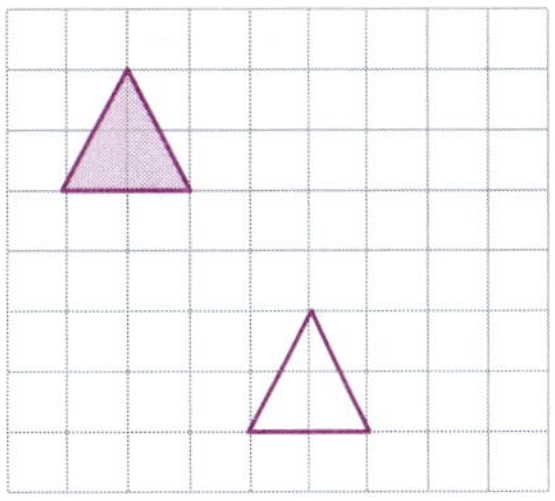

16. 32

The two angles are vertically opposite and so are equal.

This means $x + 40 = 72$, and so $x = 72 - 40$ which is 32.

17. $\frac{1}{2}$

As $3 + 9 + 8 + 4$ is 24, there are 24 students. As $8 + 4 = 12$ students scored at least 9, the probability is $\frac{12}{24}$, which is $\frac{1}{2}$.

18. 75

	Year 9	Year 10	Total
Males	85	75	160
Females	80	70	150
Total	165	145	310

There are 75 males in Year 10.

NAPLAN-style Test 1 PAGES 66–69

1. 45

As 1.5×6 is 9, Michelle has a total of 9 L of milk. As each glass contains 200 mL, then 5 glasses contain 1000 mL, or 1 L. As 5×9 is 45, Michelle can fill 45 glasses.

2. \$600

As 110×20 is 2200, the total of ticket sales is \$2200. As 2200 – 1600 is 600, the profit will be \$600.

3. D

A rise of 7 and a fall of 9 means overall a fall of 2. This means it is 2° colder than –3.5 °C which is –5.5 °C.

4. C

As 2 + 3 is 5, and 4×5 is 20, the question is 8 + 20 – ☐ = 10. This means 28 – ☐ = 10, and so the missing number is 18.

5. C

For 77 ÷ 100, the decimal point moves two places to the left. This means 77.0 ÷ 100 is 0.77.

6. 22

First, as 12 + 10 + 8 + 9 is 39, the number of green glasses was 50 – 39 = 11. As $\frac{11}{50}$ were green the percentage is 22%.

7. 40

As 16 ÷ 4 is 4, and 4 × 3 is 12, then $\frac{3}{4}$ of \$16 is \$12. As 16 + 2 × 12 is 40, the cost will be \$40.

8. 19

The total of the five sums will be 5 × 7 is 35. As 35 – 16 = 19, the sum of the five bottom faces is 19.

9. 30

As 10% represents 3 students, then by multiplying by 10, 100% represents 30 students. There are 30 students in the class.

10. 10

If in 10 years their total ages is 45, their total ages today is 45 – 20 = 25. This means the two ages are 15 and 10. Justin is 10 years old.

11. C

Express each fraction as a denominator of 36. $\frac{7}{12} = \frac{21}{36}$, $\frac{5}{6} = \frac{30}{36}$, $\frac{4}{9} = \frac{16}{36}$, $\frac{0}{1} = 0$. As $\frac{1}{2} = \frac{18}{36}$, and 16 is closest to 18, then $\frac{4}{9}$ is the closest.

12. 8

Packet As: As 30 ÷ 5 is 6, and 6 × 12 is 72, Elise will spend \$72. Packet Bs: As 30 ÷ 3 is 10, and 10 × 8 is 80, Elise will spend \$80. As 80 – 72 = 8, Elise will save \$8.

13. 210

20 minutes is $\frac{1}{3}$ hour. The distance is speed × time. As 90 × 2 = 180, and 90 × $\frac{1}{3}$ is 30, then 180 + 30 = 210. This means Bill has travelled 210 km.

14. 36 000

As 30 × 60 is 1800, the pool is filling at the rate of 1800 L per hour. As 1800 × 5 is 9000, the pool contains 9000 L when it is one-quarter full. As 9000 × 4 = 36 000, the pool holds 36 000 L when it is full.

15. 432

There are two rectangles with dimensions 12 cm by 8 cm, two rectangles with dimensions 12 cm by 6 cm and two rectangles with dimensions 8 cm by 6 cm. As 2 × 12 × 8 + 2 × 12 × 6 + 2 × 8 × 6 is 192 + 144 + 96 = 432, the area is 432 cm^2.

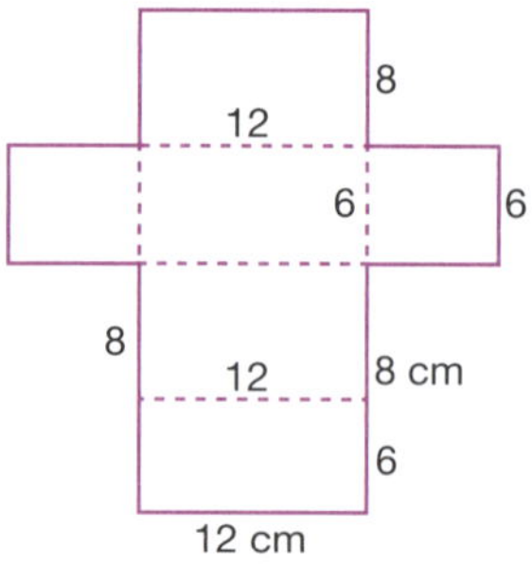

16. 78

1 + 4 × 2 + 4 × 3 + 3 × 4 + 5 × 5 + 6 × 2 + 8 = 1 + 8 + 12 + 12 + 25 + 12 + 8 which equals 78. The students bring a total of 78 cans.

17. D

Rotate 90° in a clockwise direction, translate 4 units right, then translate 1 unit down.

18. D

As 4 + 6 + 8 + 10 + 12 is 40, there are 40 balls in the box. As 0.25 is $\frac{1}{4}$, you need to find $\frac{1}{4}$ of 40. As 40 ÷ 4 is 10, and as there are 10 orange balls, the colour is orange.

19. 52

As vertically opposite angles are equal then x + 90 = 142. As 142 – 90 is 52, then x = 52.

20. 54

First, find the area of the three white triangles, and subtract from the area of the square. The shaded area is 12 × 12 – ($\frac{1}{2}$ × 6 × 6 + $\frac{1}{2}$ × 6 × 12 + $\frac{1}{2}$ × 6 × 12). This is 144 – (18 + 36 + 36) which is 144 – 90 = 54. The area is 54 cm^2.

Unit 16A PAGE 70

1. 1, 4, 25, 100

The factors of 100 are 1, 2, 4, 5, 10, 20, 25, 50, 100. From this list the square numbers are 1, 4, 25 and 100.

2. 6

There are 6 jumps from A to B. This means the difference between 1 and –5 is 6.

3. 740

74 × 5 × 2 is 74 × 10 which is 740.

4. 4

Compare the denominators: 15 has been divided by 3 to get 5. $\frac{12}{15} = \frac{12 \div 3}{15 \div 3} = \frac{4}{5}$. The missing number is 4.

5. $\frac{1}{8}$

The question is $\frac{5}{24} - \frac{1}{12}$. Rewrite $\frac{1}{12}$ as $\frac{2}{24}$. Now, $\frac{5}{24} - \frac{1}{12} = \frac{5}{24} - \frac{2}{24} = \frac{3}{24}$ which can be rewritten as $\frac{1}{8}$. There is still $\frac{1}{8}$ of the cake remaining.

6. 82.5 kg

You need to find 0.825 × 100. As multiplying by 100 moves the decimal point 2 places to the right, then 0.825 × 100 = 82.5. The total mass is 82.5 kg.

7. 75 km

As 10% is $\frac{1}{10}$, you need to work out 750 ÷ 10 which is 75. Brett has flown 75 km.

8. \$1290

50% is half price. This means the normal price is twice the price paid. As 645 × 2 is 1290, the normal price is \$1290.

9. –4

The pattern rule is subtracting 7. As 3 – 7 is –4, the missing number is –4.

10. 11

As 17 + 15 is 32, then 43 – (17 + 15) is 43 – 32 which is 11.

11. 94 cm^2

The shape can be split into two rectangles. To find the missing length add 9 and 2 which is 11. As 11 × 8 + 3 × 2 is 88 + 6, which is 94, the area is 94 cm^2.

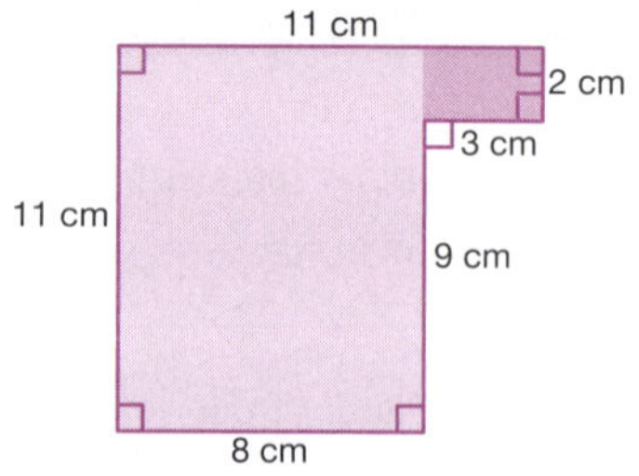

12. 42 g

As 420 ÷ 10 is 42, each serving is 42 g.

13. 1338

From 1036 to 1147 is 1 h 11 min. Adding this time to 1227 is 1338.

14. quadrant

As 90 × 4 is 360, the sector is called a quadrant.

15. 2, 2

The shape has been translated 2 units left and 2 units down.

16. 62°

The two angles form a straight angle which means they add to 180°. As 180 – 118 is 62, the angle measures 62°.

17. 6

The probability of a 1 is $\frac{2}{8}$, which is $\frac{1}{4}$. As $\frac{1}{4}$ of 24 is 24 ÷ 4 = 6, the expected number is 6 times.

18.

	Brown	Blue	Other	Total
Males	38	6	6	50
Females	32	4	14	50
Total	70	10	20	100

Unit 16B PAGE 71

1. 55

As, $1^2 = 1$, $2^2 = 4$, $3^2 = 9$, $4^2 = 16$ and $5^2 = 25$, the numbers are 1, 4, 9, 16, 25. Now 1 + 9 + 4 + 16 + 25 is 55, the sum is 55.

2. 11 degrees

From 8 °C to 0 °C is 8 degrees and from 0 °C to –3 °C is 3 degrees. As 8 + 3 is 11, the difference is 11 degrees.

3. 86 400

The number of tissues is 36 × 100 × 24.

$$\begin{array}{r} 36 \\ \times\ \ 24 \\ \hline 144 \\ 720 \\ \hline 864 \end{array}$$

As 864 × 100 is 86400, the number of tissues is 86 400.

4. 11

$2\frac{6}{8} = \frac{22}{8}$. The question is $\frac{22}{8} = \frac{\square}{4}$.
Compare the denominators: 8 has been divided by 2 to get 4.
$\frac{22}{8} = \frac{22 \div 2}{8 \div 2} = \frac{11}{4}$. The missing number is 11.

5. Nora

$\frac{3}{4} + \frac{1}{5} = \frac{15}{20} + \frac{4}{20} = \frac{19}{20}$. Over 2 days, Josh drove $\frac{19}{20}$ of a day and so Nora drove for $1\frac{1}{20}$ days. This means Nora drove the greater distance.

6. 0.17

As 10^2 is 100, the question is 17 ÷ 100, or 17.0 ÷ 100. As dividing by 100 moves the decimal point 2 places to the left, then 17.0 ÷ 100 = 0.17.

7. 36

As 100 – 40 is 60, you need to find 60% of 60. As 10% is $\frac{1}{10}$ then 60% is $\frac{6}{10}$. As 60 ÷ 10 × 6 is 6 × 6 = 36, then 36 students have not flown overseas.

8. $91

First find 10% which is 130 ÷ 10 = 13. As 10% is 13 then 30% is 13 × 3 = 39. As 130 – 39 is 91, the new price is $91.

9. –11

The pattern rule is subtracting 3. The tenth number will be 16 – 9 lots of 3. As 16 – 9 × 3 which is 16 – 27. From 16, subtracting 16 gives 0, and there is another 11 to subtract. This means 16 – 27 is –11.

10. 13

As 72 ÷ 6 is 12, then 16 – 12 is 4. This means 17 – (16 – 72 ÷ 6) = 17 – 4 which is 13.

11. 171 cm²

Equal lengths are shown on the shape, so as 18 ÷ 2 is 9, the lengths are 9 cm each. The shape can be split into two rectangles. As 7 × 9 + 12 × 9 is 63 + 108, which is 171, the area is 171 cm².

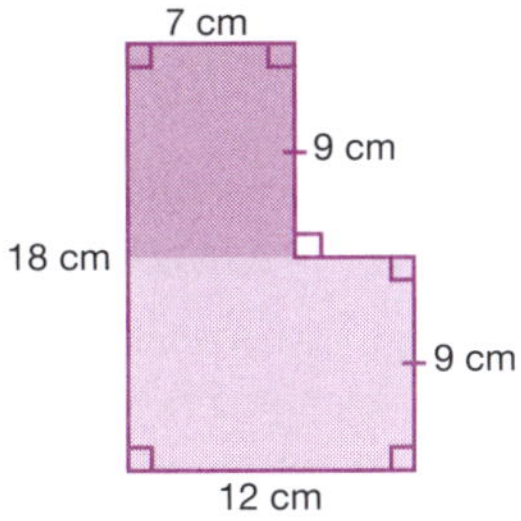

12. 3.6 L

As 240 ÷ 4 = 60, the machine pours 60 mL every second. As 60 × 60 is 3600, the machine pours 3600 mL, or 3.6 L, every minute.

13. 1314

You need to find the difference in the arrival times between 1225 and 1503. From 1225 to 1300 is 35 min, to 1500 is 2 h, and to 1503 is 3 min. This is a total of 2 h 38 min. Now add this on to 1036. Adding 2 h is 1236, adding 24 min is 1300 and then another 14 min is 1314.

14. 30°

As 360 ÷ 12 is 30, each of the sectors will have an angle of 30°.

15.

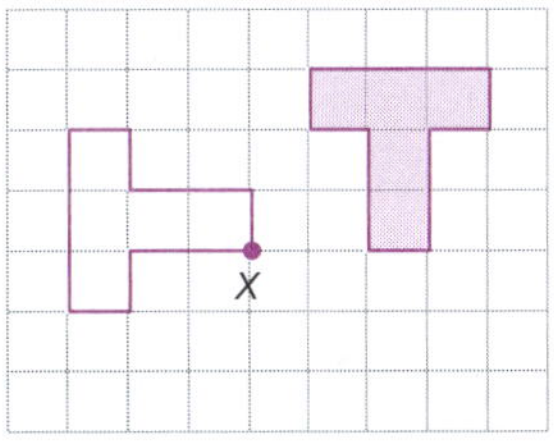

16. 86

The two angles form a straight angle which means they add to 180°. As 180 – 64 is 116, then x + 30 = 116. As 116 – 30 is 86, then x = 86.

17.

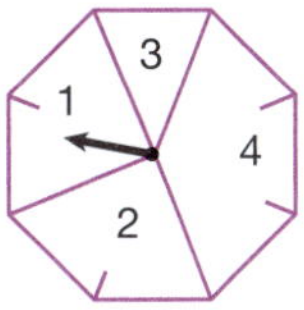

18. 42%

	Brown	Blue	Other	Total
Males	42	4	2	48
Females	43	6	3	52
Total	85	10	5	100

42 out of 100 were brown-eyed males, which is $\frac{42}{100}$, or 42%.

Unit 17A PAGE 72

1. 3, 12

The factors are 1, 2, 3, 4, 6, 8, 12, 16, 24 and 48. From the list, the numbers are 3 and 12.

2. –3

Use 5 = 2 + 3. Starting at 2, take away 2 gives 0 and then take away another 3 gives –3.

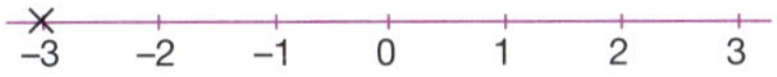

3. 75 km/h

$$\begin{array}{r} 75 \\ 9\overline{)67^{4}5} \end{array}$$

Luke's average speed is 75 km/h.

4. 3

Compare the denominators: 24 has been divided by 6 to get 4.
$\frac{18}{24} = \frac{18 \div 6}{24 \div 6} = \frac{3}{4}$. The missing number is 3.

5. $\frac{2}{7}$

First, $\frac{2}{7} + \frac{3}{7} = \frac{5}{7}$.

Now $1 - \frac{5}{7}$ is $\frac{7}{7} - \frac{5}{7}$ which is $\frac{2}{7}$.

6. 39.7

$$\begin{array}{r} 4.760 \\ 34.900 \\ +\ \ 0.023 \\ \hline 39.683 \end{array}$$

The nearest tenth means rounding to one decimal place. For 39.683, there is an 8 in the second decimal place. This means the 6 rounds up to 7, and the sum is 39.7.

7. 25%

Three out of 12 is written as $\frac{3}{12}$. As $\frac{3}{12} = \frac{3 \div 3}{12 \div 3} = \frac{1}{4}$, you need to change $\frac{1}{4}$ to a percentage. As $\frac{1}{4} \times 100\%$ is 25%, Geoff has used 25% of the eggs.

8. $1050

As 25% is $\frac{1}{4}$, divide 4200 by 4.

$$4\overline{)42^{2}00}\quad = 1050$$

The discount is $1050.

9. 36

The number of dots forms the pattern 1, 4, 9. These are the square numbers. As 6^2 is 36, there will be 36 dots in the sixth shape.

10. 7

$\frac{12 + 16}{4}$ can be rewritten as $(12 + 16) \div 4$. As 12 + 16 is 28, then $\frac{12 + 16}{4} = 28 \div 4$ is 7.

11. 1746 m

The perimeter is found using $2 \times (482 + 391)$.

$$\begin{array}{r} 482 \\ +\ 391 \\ \hline 873 \end{array}$$

This means $2 \times (482 + 391) = 2 \times 873$ which is 1746. The perimeter is 1746 m.

12. 5.1 kg

As 170×30 is 5100, the total mass is 5100 g, or 5.1 kg.

13. 1601

Heath should catch the second bus which leaves at 1601, as it arrives in Camira at 1714 which is 5:14 pm.

14. 20 cm

The chord *AB* does not pass through the centre and so is less than the diameter (24 cm). This means 20 cm is the best estimate.

15.

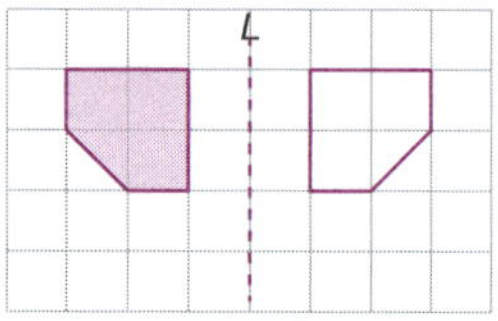

16. 50°

The three angles form a straight angle which means they add to 180°. As one of the angles is 90°, then the other two angles add to 90°. As 90 – 40 is 50, the angle measures 50°.

17. 20%

As 1 whole is 100% and 100 – 80 is 20, then the probability of no rain is 20%.

18.

	Red	Green	Blue	Yellow	Total
Prisms	8	7	7	8	30
Cylinders	6	3	7	4	20
Total	14	10	14	12	50

Unit 17B PAGE 73

1. 45

The multiples common to 3 and 5 are 15, 30, 45 … As 45 is between 40 and 50, there are 45 lollies in the bag.

2. –6

Use 10 = 4 + 6. Starting at 4, take away 4 gives 0 and then take away another 6 gives –6.

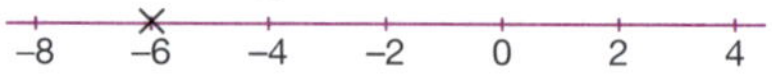

3. 860 km/h

From 8 am to 5 pm is 9 hours.

$$9\overline{)77^{5}40}\quad = 860$$

The average speed was 860 km/h.

4. 5, 4

Compare the denominators: 80 has been divided by 4 to get 20. $\frac{20}{80} = \frac{20 \div 4}{80 \div 4} = \frac{5}{20}$. Also, for $\frac{5}{20} = \frac{1}{\square}$, compare the numerators. 5 has been divided by 5 to get 1. $\frac{5}{20} = \frac{5 \div 5}{20 \div 5} = \frac{1}{4}$.

The missing numbers are 5 and 4.

5. $\frac{7}{30}$

The fraction remaining was $1 - \frac{1}{10} - \frac{2}{3}$. As $1 - \frac{3}{30} - \frac{20}{30}$ which is $1 - \frac{23}{30} = \frac{7}{30}$, there was $\frac{7}{30}$ of a bucket of water remaining.

6. 55.2

$$\begin{array}{r} 87.050 \\ -\ \ 31.861 \\ \hline 55.189 \end{array}$$

For 55.189, the digit in the second decimal place is an 8 so 55.189 is 55.2, to the nearest tenth.

7. 6

As 100 – 70 is 30, then 30% of the students have not brought lunch from home. As 10% is $\frac{1}{10}$ then 30% is $\frac{3}{10}$. As $20 \div 10 \times 3$ is $2 \times 3 = 6$, then 6 students have not brought lunch from home.

8. $80

As 10% is $20 \div 10 = 2$, then 20% is 4. The price of each T-shirt is 20 – 4 = 16. As 16×5 is 80, Steve will pay $80.

9. 900

The number of dots forms the pattern 1, 4, 9. These are the square numbers. In the 30th shape there will be 30^2 dots. As 3×3 is 9, then 30×30 is 900. There will be 900 dots in the 30th shape.

10. 3

$\frac{60 - 12 \times 3}{4 + 4}$ can be rewritten as $(60 - 12 \times 3) \div (4 + 4)$.

First, $60 - 12 \times 3$ is 60 – 36 which is 24. Also, 4 + 4 is 8. This means $\frac{60 - 12 \times 3}{4 + 4} = \frac{24}{8} = 24 \div 8 = 3$.

11. 250 m

As 10 000 m^2 is 1 ha, then 20 000 m^2 equals 2 ha. As length × 80 = 20 000, then length = 20 000 ÷ 80, which is 2000 ÷ 8 = 250. The length is 250 m.

12. 73.8 kg

You need to find $410 \times 15 \times 12$. As 15×12 is 180, then multiply 410 by 180.

$$\begin{array}{r} 41 \\ \times\ \ 18 \\ \hline 328 \\ 410 \\ \hline 738 \end{array}$$

As 41×18 is 738, then 410×180 is 73 800. The mass is 73 800 g, which is 73.8 kg.

13. 1811

4:45 pm is 1645. She has to wait for the next bus which leaves at 1748 and arrives in Coorinda at 1811.

14. 8 cm^2

As 360 ÷ 3 is 120, the sector makes up one-third of the circle. As 24 ÷ 3 is 8, the area of the sector is 8 cm^2.

15.

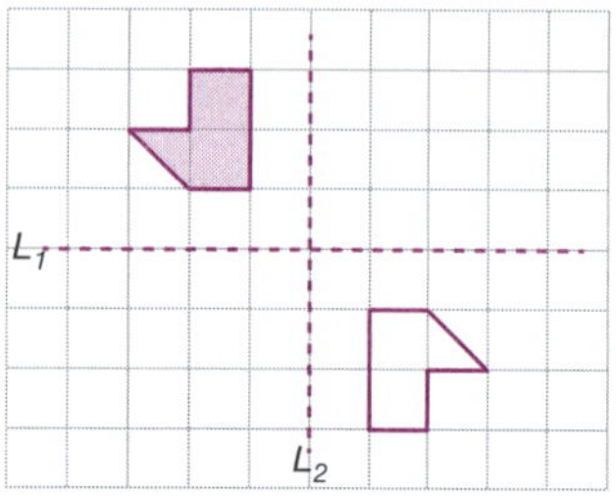

16. **65**

The three angles form a straight angle which means they add to 180°. As one of the angles is 50°, then the other two angles add to 130°. As the angles are equal then they both measure 65°. This means x is 65.

17. $\frac{1}{6}$

As $1 - (\frac{1}{2} + \frac{1}{3})$ is $1 - (\frac{3}{6} + \frac{2}{6})$ which is $\frac{6}{6} - \frac{5}{6} = \frac{1}{6}$, the probability of a green ball is $\frac{1}{6}$.

18. $\frac{9}{25}$

As 9 + 6 + 8 + 9 + 5 + 4 + 5 + 4 is 50, and 5 + 4 + 5 + 4 is 18, then the fraction that are cylinders is $\frac{18}{50} = \frac{9}{25}$.

Unit 18A PAGE 74

1. **8**

The factors of 16 are 1, 2, 4, 8, 16 and the factors of 40 are 1, 2, 4, 5, 8, 10, 20, 40. The largest factor common to both is 8.

2. **1**

Use 4 = 3 + 1. Starting at –3, add 3 gives 0 and then add another 1 gives 1.

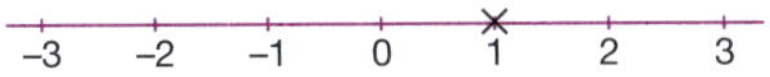

3. **5356**

$$\begin{array}{r} 5\,3\,5\,6 \\ 5\overline{)2\,6\,{}^{1}7\,{}^{2}8\,{}^{3}0} \end{array}$$

4. $\frac{5}{6}$

Divide 2 into both numerator and denominator: $\frac{10}{12} = \frac{10 \div 2}{12 \div 2} = \frac{5}{6}$

5. $\frac{3}{4}$ **L**

Add $\frac{1}{4} + \frac{1}{2}$. Use a related denominator: as 4 and 2 are factors of 4, rewrite $\frac{1}{2}$ as quarters.

As $\frac{1}{2} = \frac{1 \times 2}{2 \times 2} = \frac{2}{4}$ then $\frac{1}{4} + \frac{1}{2} = \frac{1}{4} + \frac{2}{4}$ which is $\frac{3}{4}$. There is now $\frac{3}{4}$ litre of juice in the jug.

6. **5.25**

The average is found by adding the numbers and dividing the total by 4. As 6 + 8 + 3 + 4 is 21, you need to find 21 ÷ 4.

$$\begin{array}{r} 5.2\,5 \\ 4\overline{)21.{}^{1}0\,{}^{2}0} \end{array}$$

The average is 5.25.

7. **500**

As 10% is $\frac{1}{10}$ you need to work out 5000 ÷ 10, which is 500. There are 500 Tigers' supporters at the game.

8. **\$2.50**

10% of \$5.00 is 50 cents. As 50 × 5 is 250, the senior will save \$2.50.

9. **19**

Counting the matchsticks, the pattern is 4, 7, 10 which is adding 3. The sixth shape will be made using 10 + 3 + 3 + 3 which is 19. There will be 19 matchsticks in the sixth shape.

10. **17**

As 6^2 is 36 and 3 × 8 is 24,
$6^2 - 3 \times 8 + 5 = 36 - 24 + 5$ which is 17.

11. **32 cm²**

The area of a triangle is $\frac{1}{2}$ × base × height. As $\frac{1}{2} \times 8 \times 8$ is 32, the area is 32 cm².

12. **0.75 kg**

$$\begin{array}{r} 125 \\ \times \quad 6 \\ \hline 750 \end{array}$$

The total amount of butter is 750 g, which is 0.75 kg.

13. **1426**

4 pm is 1600. The second bus arrives in Chesterton at 1533. This bus leaves Hammond at 1426.

14. **triangular prism**

The net forms a triangular prism.

15.

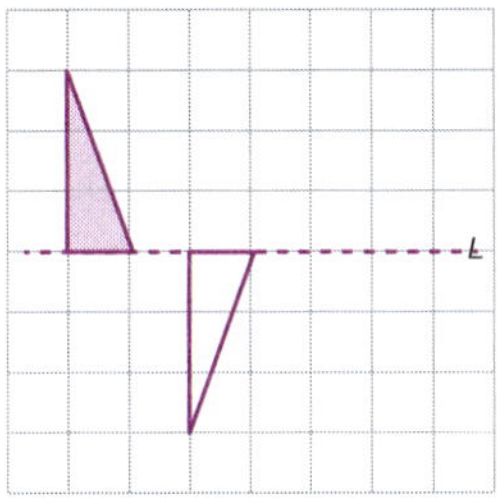

16. **70°**

The three angles form a straight angle which means they add to 180°. As one of the angles is 90°, then the other two angles add to 90°. As 90 – 20 is 70, the angle measures 70°.

17. **40%**

There are 4 white balls out of 10 balls. The probability is $\frac{4}{10} = \frac{40}{100}$, which is 40%.

18. **26**

As 8 + 6 + 5 + 7 is 26, a total of 26 people.

Unit 18B PAGE 75

1. **425, 681**

As 425 has 5 as a factor it has more than 2 factors. Also, for 681, adding the digits 6 + 8 + 1 gives 15. This is a multiple of 3, which means 681 has a factor of 3 and so 681 has more than 2 factors. The two composite numbers are 425 and 681.

2. **–4**

Using the number line, starting at –10 and adding 6 gets to –4.

3. **399**

$$\begin{array}{r} 26 \\ \times \quad 15 \\ \hline 130 \\ 260 \\ \hline 390 \end{array}$$

As 390 + 9 is 399 there are 399 students at the assembly.

4. $\frac{1}{3}$

$\frac{45}{135} = \frac{45 \div 5}{135 \div 5} = \frac{9}{27} = \frac{9 \div 9}{27 \div 9} = \frac{1}{3}$

5. $\frac{5}{12}$

The question is $1 - \frac{1}{4} - \frac{1}{3}$. Use a related denominator: as 4 and 3 are factors of 12, rewrite the fractions as twelfths.

As $1 = \frac{12}{12}$, $\frac{1}{4} = \frac{3}{12}$ and $\frac{1}{3} = \frac{4}{12}$, then $1 - \frac{1}{4} - \frac{1}{3} = \frac{12}{12} - \frac{3}{12} - \frac{4}{12}$, which is $\frac{5}{12}$.

6. **22.74 °C**

$$\begin{array}{r} 21.7 \\ 23.9 \\ 18.4 \\ 22.5 \\ +\ 27.2 \\ \hline 113.7 \end{array}$$

As there are 5 days, you need to divide 113.7 by 5:

$$\begin{array}{r} 22.7\,4 \\ 5\overline{)11\,{}^{1}3.{}^{3}7\,{}^{2}0} \end{array}$$

The average temperature was 22.74 °C.

7. **60**

First 100 – 75 is 25. Aria has to read another 25%, which is $\frac{1}{4}$ of the book. As 240 ÷ 4 is 60, Aria has 60 pages remaining.

8. **\$36**

The total cost is 30 × 6 = 180.
As 10% is 180 ÷ 10 = 18, then 20% is 18 × 2 = 36. The saving is \$36.

9. **37**

Counting the matchsticks, the pattern is 4, 7, 10 which is adding 3. The 12th shape will be made using 4 + 11 lots of 3. As 4 + 11 × 3 is 4 + 33 = 37, there will be 37 matchsticks in the 12th shape.

10. **100**

4 + 3 × 2 is 4 + 6 which is 10. This means $(4 + 3 \times 2)^2 = 10^2 = 100$.

11. **30 cm^2**

The longest side (13 cm) is opposite the largest angle (90°). This means the base and height are 5 cm and 12 cm (or 12 cm and 5 cm). As the area of a triangle is $\frac{1}{2}$ × base × height, then $\frac{1}{2} \times 12 \times 5$ is 30. The area is 30 cm^2.

12. **6 000 000**

As there are 1000 g in 1 kg, and 1000 kg in 1 t, then there are 1 000 000 g in 1 t. Multiplying by 6, there are 6 000 000 g.

13. **1613**

2:25 pm is 1425. He needs to wait to catch the third bus which leaves at 1501, arriving in Shorewood at 1613.

14. **rectangular pyramid**

The net forms a rectangular pyramid.

15. **translate 4 units right, reflect**

Translate 4 units right, reflect in line *L*.

16. **45**

The three angles form a straight angle which means they add to 180°. As one of the angles is 90°, then the other two angles add to 90°. As the angles are equal, they both measure 45°. This means *x* is 45.

17.

As 50% is $\frac{5}{10}$, there are 5 black balls.
As 30% is $\frac{3}{10}$, there are 3 black balls.
As 10 – 5 – 3 is 2, there are 2 shaded balls.

18. $\mathbf{\frac{1}{5}}$

As 10 + 17 + 8 + 5 is 40, and 8 women selected Asia, the fraction is $\frac{8}{40}$, which is $\frac{1}{5}$.

Unit 19A PAGE 76

1. **37**

The next prime after 32 is 37, as the factors of 37 are 1 and 37.

2. **up 2 floors (+2)**

Going down 3 floors is –3 and then going up is +5. From –3 counting on 5 gives 2. This means a combined effect of going up 2 floors.

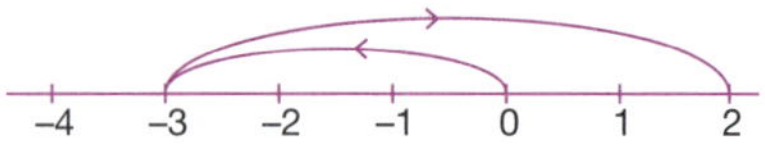

3. **10 800**

There are 60 seconds in a minute and 60 minutes in an hour. The number of seconds is 60 × 60 × 3. As 6 × 6 × 3 is 36 × 3 which is 108, so 60 × 60 × 3 is 10800. There are 10 800 s in 3 hours.

4. **8**

Multiply both numerator and denominator by 4: $\frac{2}{3} = \frac{2 \times 4}{3 \times 4} = \frac{8}{12}$.
The missing number is 8.

5. $\mathbf{3\frac{3}{4}}$ **h**

Add $2\frac{1}{2}$ and $1\frac{1}{4}$. For the fractions, rewrite both fractions with a related denominator.
As $\frac{1}{2} = \frac{1 \times 2}{2 \times 2} = \frac{2}{4}$, the question is $2\frac{2}{4} + 1\frac{1}{4}$, which is $3\frac{3}{4}$. Pavel trained for $3\frac{3}{4}$ h.

6. **$51.45**

```
  438.15
– 386.70
   51.45
```

Amanda earned $51.45 more this week.

7. **3000 L**

25% is the same as $\frac{1}{4}$ so find $\frac{1}{4}$ of 12 000, which is 12 000 ÷ 4. As 12 ÷ 4 is 3, then 12 000 ÷ 4 is 3000. There is 3000 L of water in the tank.

8. **$294**

As 10% is 1470 ÷ 10 = 147, then 20% is 147 × 2, which is 294. The saving will be $294.

9. **21**

Counting the dots, the pattern is 1, 5, 9 which is adding 4. As 9 + 4 + 4 + 4 is 21, there will be 21 dots in the sixth shape.

10. **2747**

The number sentence is 10 000 – (6753 + 500).

```
  6753
+  500
  7253
```

This means 10 000 – (6753 + 500) = 10 000 – 7253.

```
  10 000
–  7 253
   2 747
```

Andrew needs another 2747 points.

11. **28 cm**

As area = length × width, then 45 = length × 5. This means the length is 45 ÷ 5 which is 9. The perimeter is 2 × (9 + 5) = 2 × 14, which is 28. The perimeter is 28 cm.

12. **168 kg**

Find 2400 × 70. As 24 × 7 is 168, then 2400 × 70 = 168 000. The mass is 168 000 g, which is 168 kg.

13. **1407**

3:40 pm is 1540. Jane can catch the second bus arriving at 1542. This bus leaves Fletcher at 1407.

14. **triangular pyramid**

The net forms a triangular pyramid (tetrahedron).

15.

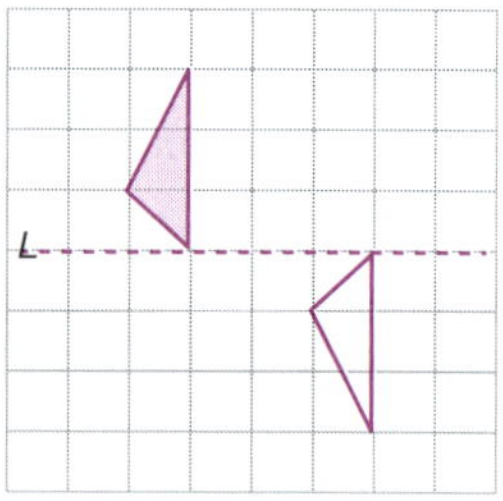

16. **160°**

The three angles form an angle of revolution which means they add to 360°. As 90 + 110 is 200, and 360 – 200 is 160, the angle measures 160°.

17. $\mathbf{\frac{1}{100}}$

As Sam has 1 ticket out of 100, the probability is $\frac{1}{100}$.

18. **8**

18 + 16 = 34 selected Biology.
12 + 14 = 26 selected Physics. As 34 – 26 is 8, then 8 more people selected Biology than selected Physics.

Unit 19B PAGE 77

1. **6**

The lowest multiple common to both 6 and 4 is 12. This means a square can be made with side length of 12 cm. As 12 ÷ 6 is 2 and 12 ÷ 4 is 3, there are 2 rows of 3 cards which is 6 cards.

2. **down 7° (–7)**

Going down 10 degrees is –10 and then going up is +3. From –10 counting on 3 gives –7. This means a combined effect of a fall of 7 degrees, which can be written as –7.

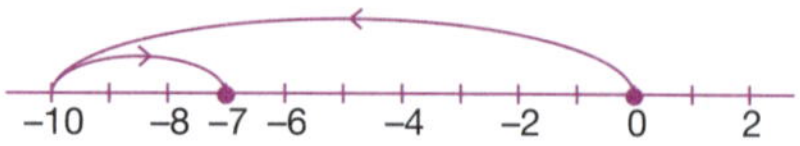

3. **2928 h**

June and September have 30 days each, and July and August have 31. The number of days is 15 + 31 + 31 + 30 + 15 which is 122.

Each day has 24 hours so multiply 122×24.

$$\begin{array}{r} 122 \\ \times \quad 24 \\ \hline 488 \\ 2440 \\ \hline 2928 \\ \hline \end{array}$$

Ella had lived for 2928 h.

4. $\mathbf{\frac{11}{20}}$

Use a related denominator of 20.

$\frac{1}{2} = \frac{10}{20}$ and $\frac{3}{5} = \frac{12}{20}$. The middle of 10 and 12 is 11. The middle of $\frac{1}{2}$ and $\frac{1}{3}$ is $\frac{11}{20}$.

5. $\mathbf{15\frac{1}{4}}$ **m**

$21\frac{1}{2} + 27\frac{1}{4}$ is $21\frac{2}{4} + 27\frac{1}{4} = 48\frac{3}{4}$. Now, work out $64 - 48\frac{3}{4}$. This is $64 - 48 - \frac{3}{4}$ $= 16 - \frac{3}{4}$ which is $15\frac{1}{4}$. Layla threw the javelin $15\frac{1}{4}$ m.

6. **0.0045**

For $4.5 \div 1000$, imagine $0004.5 \div 1000$. The decimal point moves 3 places to the left. This means $4.5 \div 1000$ is 0.0045.

7. **144 km**

20% is the same as $\frac{1}{5}$ so find $\frac{1}{5}$ of 120.

As $5\overline{)120}$ = 24, then Noah is increasing the distance by 24 km. As $120 + 24$ is 144, Noah plans to ride 144 km.

8. **$153**

As 10% is $180 \div 10 = 18$, then 5% is $18 \div 2$, which is 9. Now, $18 + 9$ is 27, so the discount is $27. As $180 - 27$ is 153, the price is $153.

9. **10th**

Counting the dots, the pattern is 1, 5, 9 which is adding 4. The pattern continues: 13, 17, 21, 25, 29, 33, 37. This means there will be 37 dots in the tenth shape.

10. **9.5 kg**

The number sentence is $(5 \times 8 + 3 \times 12) \div (5 + 3)$. This is $(40 + 36) \div 8$, which is $76 \div 8 = 9.5$. The average mass is 9.5 kg.

11. **112 cm²**

As the perimeter = 2 × (length + width), then 44 = 2 × (length + 8). This means the length + 8 = 22, which means the length is 14 cm. As $14 \times 8 = 112$, the area is 112 cm^2.

12. **7 200 000 kL**

There are 1000 kilolitres in 1 megalitre, and 1000 megalitres in 1 gigalitre. This means there are 1 000 000 kilolitres in 1 gigalitre.

As $7.2 \times 1\,000\,000$ is 7 200 000, there are 7 200 000 kL.

13. **1828**

2:23 pm is 1423. The second bus does not stop in Nulkaba. He needs to wait for the third bus which arrives in Nulkaba at 1828.

14. **triangular pyramid**

The net forms a triangular pyramid (tetrahedron).

15. **translate 3 units right, reflect**

Translate 3 units right, reflect in line *L*.

16. **60**

The three angles form a straight angle which means they add to 180°. All angles are equal and as $180 \div 3$ is 60, each angle measures 60°. This means $x = 60$.

17. **0.05**

As Sam has 5 tickets out of 100, the probability is $\frac{5}{100}$, or 5 hundredths, which is written as 0.05.

18. **22%**

As $12 + 10 + 18 + 10 + 14 + 12 + 16 + 8$ is 100, and $10 + 12$ is 22, then 22 out of 100 selected Chemistry.

As $\frac{22}{100} = 22\%$, then 22% of the students selected Chemistry.

Unit 20A PAGE 78

1. **29**

The prime numbers are 2, 3, 5, 7, 11, 13, 17, 19, 23, 29 … This means the tenth prime number is 29.

2. **south 4 km (–4)**

Going north for 3 km is +3 and then going south for 7 km is –7. From 3 counting backwards by 7 gives –4. This means a combined effect of travelling south for 4 km, which can be written as –4.

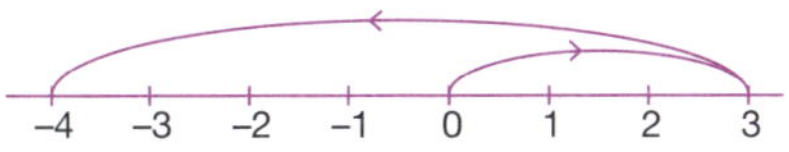

3. **58 112**

The missing number is the answer to 7264×8.

$$\begin{array}{r} 7\,264 \\ \times \quad 8 \\ \hline 58\,112 \\ \hline \end{array}$$

The missing number is 58 112.

4. $\mathbf{\frac{1}{5}}$

There are 60 min in an hour.

12 out of 60 is

$\frac{12}{60} = \frac{12 \div 12}{60 \div 12} = \frac{1}{5}$.

5. $\mathbf{\frac{5}{8}}$

The missing number is $1 - \frac{3}{8}$, which is $\frac{8}{8} - \frac{3}{8} = \frac{5}{8}$.

6. **$73.40**

Divide 220.20 by 3:

$$3\overline{)22^{1}0.^{1}20} = 73.40$$

Each person paid $73.40.

7. **80%**

16 marks out of 20 is recorded as $\frac{16}{20}$. Change this to an equivalent fraction with a denominator of 100:

$\frac{16}{20} = \frac{16 \times 5}{20 \times 5} = \frac{80}{100}$, which is 80%. Grayson scored 80% for his quiz.

8. **10%**

Writing as a fraction $\frac{200}{2000} = \frac{1}{10}$, which is 10%. The percentage discount is 10%.

9. **28**

Counting the matchsticks, the pattern is 4, 10, 16 which is adding 6. The fifth shape will be made using $16 + 6 + 6$ which is 28. There will be 28 matchsticks in the fifth shape.

10. $\mathbf{\frac{1}{6}}$

First, $\frac{1}{2} + \frac{1}{3}$ is $\frac{3}{6} + \frac{2}{6} = \frac{5}{6}$. This means $1 - (\frac{1}{2} + \frac{1}{3}) = 1 - \frac{5}{6}$, which is $\frac{1}{6}$.

11. **48 cm**

If the perimeter is 24 cm, the side length of each of the squares is 6 cm. The dimensions of the new shapes are 18 cm by 6 cm.

As $2 \times (18 + 6) = 2 \times 24 = 48$, the perimeter of the new shape is 48 cm.

12. **104 kg**

To find one-fifth, divide by 5

As $520 \div 5$ is 104, the maximum weight is 104 kg.

13. **9:53 am**

1:20 pm is 1320. The second bus arrives in Bethany at 1328 which is too late. Jamal needs to catch the first bus, which leaves Weston at 0953, which is 9:53 am.

14. **0**

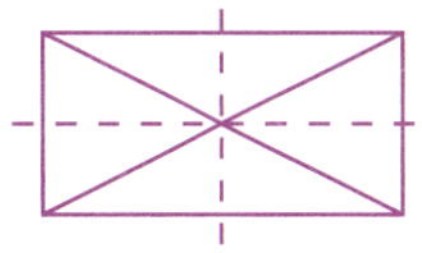

The dotted lines of symmetry are different to the diagonals.

15.

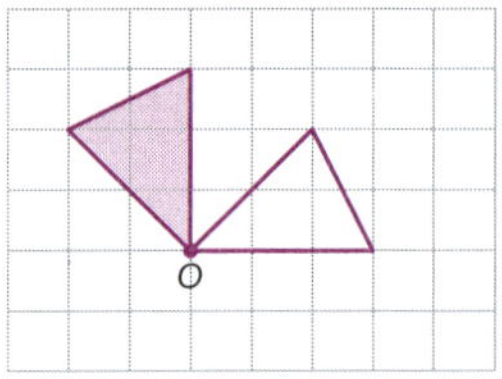

16. 50°

The three angles form an angle of revolution which means they add to 360°. As 160 + 150 is 310, and 360 – 310 is 50, the angle measures 50°.

17. $\mathbf{\frac{3}{8}}$

There are 3 balls that are not black (they are white). As there are 8 balls the probability is $\frac{3}{8}$.

18. 4

As 9 + 6 = 15 had bananas and 6 + 5 = 11 had mandarins, the difference is 15 – 11 = 4. This means 4 more students had a banana than students who had a mandarin.

Unit 20B — PAGE 79

1. 72

The lowest multiple common to 4, 3 and 2 is 12. This means the cube can be made with side length of 12 cm. As 12 ÷ 4 is 3, 12 ÷ 3 is 4 and 12 ÷ 2 is 6, there are 3 × 4 × 6 = 72 prisms.

2. losing \$25 (–25)

This could be thought of as winning \$10 and then losing \$35. Winning \$10 is +10 and then losing \$35 is –35. As 35 = 10 + 25, then the combined effect is losing \$25, which can be written as –25.

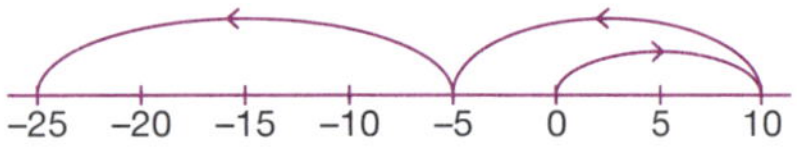

3. 194 208

The missing number is the answer to 5712 × 34.

$$\begin{array}{r} 5\,712 \\ \times \quad 34 \\ \hline 22\,848 \\ 171\,360 \\ \hline 194\,208 \end{array}$$

The missing number is 194 208.

4. $\mathbf{\frac{5}{8}}$

There are 24 h in a day. 15 out of 24 is $\frac{15}{24} = \frac{15 \div 3}{24 \div 3} = \frac{5}{8}$.

5. $\mathbf{\frac{1}{2}}$

The missing number is $1\frac{1}{6} - \frac{2}{3}$. First, $1\frac{1}{6} = \frac{7}{6}$ and $\frac{2}{3} = \frac{4}{6}$. This means $1\frac{1}{6} - \frac{2}{3}$ is $\frac{7}{6} - \frac{4}{6} = \frac{3}{6}$, which can be rewritten as $\frac{1}{2}$.

6. 2.79 kg

$$\begin{array}{r} 0.93 \\ 2\overline{)1.86} \end{array}$$

The second package had a mass of 0.93 kg.

$$\begin{array}{r} 1.86 \\ +\ 0.93 \\ \hline 2.79 \end{array}$$

The total mass was 2.79 kg.

7. 35%

$$\begin{array}{r} 36\,500 \\ +\ 28\,500 \\ \hline 65\,000 \end{array} \qquad \begin{array}{r} 100\,000 \\ -\ 65\,000 \\ \hline 35\,000 \end{array}$$

Mila received 35 thousand dollars out of 100 thousand dollars. As $\frac{35}{100}$ is 35%, Mila received 35% of the total amount.

8. 40%

Dividing by 10 is finding 10%. Multiplying this answer by 4 is finding 40%.

9. ninth

Counting the matchsticks, the pattern is 4, 10, 16 which is adding 6. Continuing the pattern: 22, 28, 34, 40, 46, 52. There will be 52 matchsticks in the ninth shape.

10. $\mathbf{\frac{3}{4}}$

First, $1\frac{1}{2} + \frac{1}{4}$ is $1\frac{2}{4} + \frac{1}{4} = 1\frac{3}{4}$. This means $2\frac{1}{2} - (1\frac{1}{2} + \frac{1}{4}) = 2\frac{1}{2} - 1\frac{3}{4}$. Now, rewriting these as improper fractions, and then using a related denominator, $2\frac{1}{2} - 1\frac{3}{4} = \frac{5}{2} - \frac{7}{4} = \frac{10}{4} - \frac{7}{4} = \frac{3}{4}$.

11. 80 cm

If the area of each small square is 100 cm^2, then the side length of the small square is 10 cm. This means each side of the large square is 20 cm. As 4 × 20 is 80, the perimeter of the large square is 80 cm.

12. 5304 kg

Multiply 22.1 × 240.

$$\begin{array}{r} 221 \\ \times \quad 240 \\ \hline 8\,840 \\ 44\,200 \\ \hline 53\,040 \end{array}$$

As 221 × 240 is 53 040, then 22.1 × 240 = 5304.0, which is 5304. The total mass is 5304 kg.

13. 6:26 pm

There is only one bus she can catch which leaves Lawson at 1557 and arrives in Davis City at 18:26, which is 6:26 pm.

14. 4

There are 4 diagonals that are also axes of symmetry.

15.

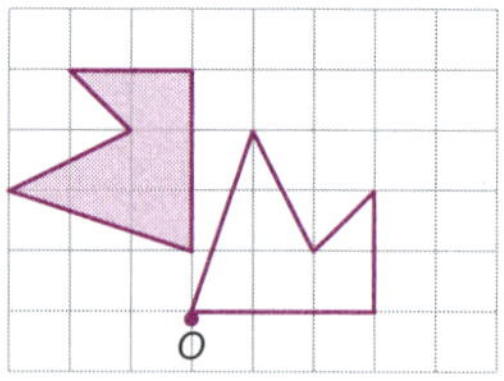

16. 90

The four angles form an angle of revolution which means they add to 360°. As all angles are equal and 360 ÷ 4 is 90 then each angle is 90°. This means $x = 90$.

17. 75%

There are 6 black balls out of 8 balls. This is a probability of $\frac{6}{8} = \frac{3}{4}$, which can be written as 75%.

18. 30%

As 9 + 8 + 6 + 4 + 6 + 7 + 5 + 5 is 50, and 8 + 7 is 15, then 15 out of 50 packed an apple. As $\frac{15}{50} = \frac{30}{100}$, which is 30%, then 30% of the students packed an apple.

Unit 21A — PAGE 80

1. 8

The composite numbers between 7 and 19 are 8, 9, 10, 12, 14, 15, 16, 18. This means there are 8 composite numbers.

2. 5, 9

From 4, move to the right 5 units gets to 9. This means 4 + 5 = 9.

3. 41

The average is the sum of the three ages divided by 3.

$$\begin{array}{r} 67 \\ 44 \\ +\ 12 \\ \hline 123 \end{array}$$

As 123 ÷ 3 is 41, the average age is 41 years old.

4. $\frac{1}{2}, \frac{5}{8}, \frac{3}{4}$

$\frac{5}{8}, \frac{1}{2} = \frac{1 \times 4}{2 \times 4} = \frac{4}{8}$ and $\frac{3}{4} = \frac{3 \times 2}{4 \times 2} = \frac{6}{8}$.

As the order is 4, 5, 6 then the order of fractions is $\frac{1}{2}, \frac{5}{8}, \frac{3}{4}$.

5. **1**

The missing number is $\frac{3}{10} + \frac{7}{10}$, which is $\frac{10}{10}$, or 1.

6. **10.5 °C**

The temperature will be 3.6 + 18.8 − 11.9.

$$\begin{array}{r} 18.8 \\ +\ 3.6 \\ \hline 22.4 \end{array}$$

Now subtract 22.4 − 11.9:

$$\begin{array}{r} 22.4 \\ -\ 11.9 \\ \hline 10.5 \end{array}$$

The temperature will be 10.5 °C.

7. **12**

25% is the same as $\frac{1}{4}$. This means 25% of 48 is $\frac{1}{4}$ of 48, which is 48 ÷ 4 = 12. Arthur gave 12 marbles to Theo.

8. **$300**

10% is 1500 ÷ 10 which is 150, and so 20% is 150 × 2 = 300. The discount is $300.

9. **32**

Counting the matchsticks, the pattern is 7, 12, 17 which is adding 5. The sixth shape will be made using 17 + 5 + 5 + 5 which is 32. There will be 32 matchsticks in the sixth shape.

10. **false**

As 10 − 4 is 6, then (10 − 4) × 3 + 3 is 6 × 3 + 3 = 18 + 3 which is 21. As this is not 36, the number sentence is false.

11. **1430 mm, 1.32 m, 123 cm, 1.023 m**

Change each length to millimetres. 1.32 m is 1320 mm, 123 cm is 1230 mm, 1430 mm, 1.023 m is 1023 mm. The order of numbers is 1430, 1320, 1230, 1023. The order of lengths is 1430 mm, 1.32 m, 123 cm, 1.023 m.

12. **2 kg**

You need to find (123 − 115) ÷ 4, which is 8 ÷ 4 = 2. George needs to lose 2 kg each week.

13. **34 min**

1804 is 6:04 pm. From 5:30 to 6:00 is 30 min, and another 4 min is a total of 34 min.

14. **80 cm²**

The length is 10 cm and the width is 8 cm. As 10 × 8 is 80, the area is 80 cm².

15.

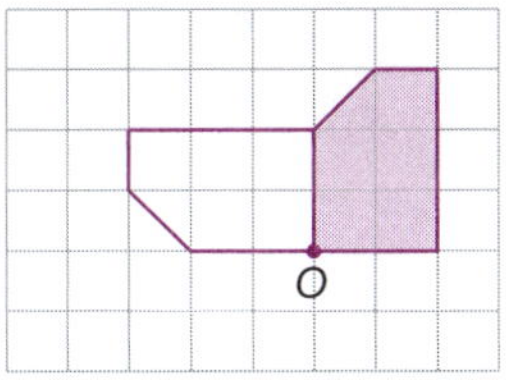

16. **130°**

The three angles form an angle of revolution which means they add to 360°. The two angles shown are 140° and 90°. As 140 + 90 is 230, and 360 − 230 is 130, the missing angle measures 130°.

17. $\frac{1}{4}$

The even numbers are 2 and 4. As 2 and 4 take up two-eighths of the spinner, the probability is $\frac{2}{8} = \frac{1}{4}$.

18. **21**

As 5 + 6 + 7 + 3 is 21, then 21 students have straight hair.

Unit 21B PAGE 81

1. **400**

Triangular numbers are 1, 3, 6, 10 … As 1 + 3 + 6 + 10 is 20, then $20^2 = 20 \times 20$ which is 400.

2. **−2, 4, 2**

From −2, moving to the right 4 units gets to 2. This means −2 + 4 = 2.

3. **715**

$$\begin{array}{r} 436 \\ 981 \\ +\ 728 \\ \hline 2145 \end{array}$$

As 2145 ÷ 3 is 715, an average of 715 bags were sold each day.

4. $\frac{11}{20}, \frac{3}{5}, \frac{7}{10}, \frac{3}{4}$

Rewrite each fraction with a denominator of 20: $\frac{3}{5} = \frac{12}{20}, \frac{11}{20}, \frac{3}{4} = \frac{15}{20}, \frac{7}{10} = \frac{14}{20}$. Comparing the numerators, the order is $\frac{11}{20}, \frac{3}{5}, \frac{7}{10}, \frac{3}{4}$.

5. $2\frac{1}{6}$

The missing number is $1\frac{1}{2} + \frac{2}{3}$. First, $1\frac{1}{2} = \frac{3}{2}$, and then change both fractions to sixths. $\frac{3}{2} + \frac{2}{3} = \frac{9}{6} + \frac{4}{6} = \frac{13}{6}$. This can be rewritten as $2\frac{1}{6}$.

6. **−2.4 °C**

You need to find −3.6 + 2.9 − 1.7: First, −3.6 + 2.9 is 2.9 − 3.6 which is −0.7. Now, −0.7 − 1.7 is −2.4. The temperature was −2.4 °C.

7. **$30**

40 + 35 is 75. As 100 − 75 is 25, Bonnie saved 25% of the money. Find 25% of $120. As 25% = $\frac{1}{4}$, and 120 ÷ 4 is 30, Bonnie saved $30.

8. **$162**

A 10% discount means a drop in price of $20 which means it will cost $180. A 10% discount on $180 means another drop of $18, which means Jordie pays $162.

9. **117**

Counting the matchsticks, the pattern is 7, 12, 17 which is adding 5. The next three numbers in the pattern are 22, 27, 32. As 7 + 12 + 17 + 22 + 27 + 32 = 117, there will be a total of 117 matchsticks in the first six shapes.

10. **12**

Find the values of the expressions inside the grouping symbols first: (40 − 4) ÷ 6 + 3 × (8 − 3 × 2) = 36 ÷ 6 + 3 × 2 = 6 + 6, which is 12.

11. **29 mm, 2.89 cm, 2.86 cm, 0.028 m**

Change each length to millimetres. 2.86 cm is 28.6 mm, 0.028 m is 28 mm, 29 mm, 2.89 cm is 28.9 mm. The order of numbers is 29, 28.9, 28.6, 28. The order of lengths is 29 mm, 2.89 cm, 2.86 cm, 0.028 m.

12. **2**

You need to find the pairs that sum to less than 180. 86 + 89 and 86 + 92 are the only pairings that have a sum less than 180. There are two different pairs.

13. **41 min**

As 1706 is 5:06 pm, then from 4:41 to 5:00 is 19 min, then to 5:06 is 6 min and then another 16 min is 41 min. Ellie waits 41 minutes.

14. **60 cm²**

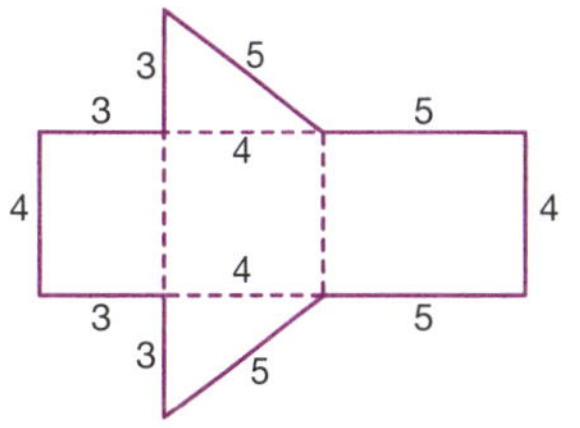

The answer is the sum of the areas of two rectangles, a square and two triangles. 4 × 3 + 5 × 4 + 4 × 4 + 2 × $\frac{1}{2}$ × 4 × 3 is 12 + 20 + 16 + 12 which is 60. The area is 60 cm².

15.

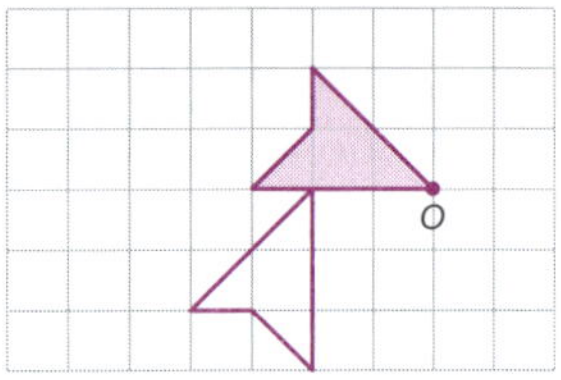

16. 55

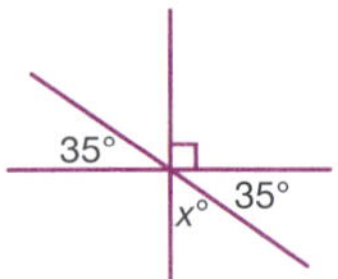

Using vertically opposite angles, $x°$, 35° and 90° form a straight angle. This means $x + 35 = 90$, which means x is 55.

17. 100

Numbers less than 4 1, 2 and 3. As these take up 5 out of the 8 sectors, the probability of a number less than 4 is $\frac{5}{8}$. $\frac{5}{8}$ of 160 is $160 \div 8 \times 5$ which is $20 \times 5 = 100$, so the expected number of times is 100.

18. $\mathbf{\frac{2}{3}}$

As 6 + 3 is 9, there are 9 blonde-haired students. As 6 students have straight blonde hair, then 6 out of 9 is written as $\frac{6}{9}$, which is $\frac{2}{3}$.

Unit 22A PAGE 82

1. 0

Square numbers are 1, 4, 9 … Square numbers larger than 1 have more than 2 factors. But 1 is not a prime number, so there are no numbers that are both square numbers and prime numbers.

2. 5, –1

From 4, moving to the left 5 units gets to –1. This means 4 – 5 = –1.

3. 216

$$\begin{array}{r} 18 \\ \times\ 12 \\ \hline 216 \end{array}$$

216 people can be seated at the venue.

4. $\mathbf{\frac{1}{2}, \frac{2}{3}, \frac{5}{6}}$

$\frac{1}{2} = \frac{1 \times 3}{2 \times 3} = \frac{3}{6}, \frac{5}{6}$ and $\frac{2}{3} = \frac{2 \times 2}{3 \times 2} = \frac{4}{6}$.

Now compare the numerators: the order is 3, 4, 5. The order of fractions is $\frac{1}{2}, \frac{2}{3}, \frac{5}{6}$.

5. $\mathbf{\frac{1}{2}}$

The missing number is $\frac{7}{10} - \frac{1}{5}$.

Rewriting $\frac{1}{5}$ as tenths,

$\frac{7}{10} - \frac{1}{5} = \frac{7}{10} - \frac{2}{10} = \frac{5}{10}$. This can be rewritten as $\frac{1}{2}$.

6. 17.4 km

$$\begin{array}{r} 4.8 \\ 7.3 \\ +\ 5.3 \\ \hline 17.4 \end{array}$$

Lewis drove a total distance of 17.4 km.

7. 2

There are 10 years in a decade.

As 20% is $\frac{2}{10}$, there are 2 years.

8. $36

As 20 × 2 is 40, and 10% of 40 is 40 ÷ 10 = 4, Meagan receives a discount of $4. As 40 – 4 = 36, the tickets will cost $36.

9. 41

Counting the matchsticks, the pattern is 6, 11, 16 which is adding 5. The eighth shape will be made using 16 + 5 + 5 + 5 + 5 + 5 which is 41. There will be 41 matchsticks in the eighth shape.

10. 3

As 24 – 12 is 12, then 4 × ☐ = 12. This means the missing number is 3.

11. 18 m²

The area is found using 5 × 3.6.

$$\begin{array}{r} 36 \\ \times\ 5 \\ \hline 180 \end{array}$$

There is 1 decimal place in the question, so 5 × 3.6 = 18.0, which can be written as 18. The area is 18 m².

12. 240 g

The volume is

$6 \times 4 \times 5$ is $6 \times 20 = 120\ \text{cm}^3$.

As 120 × 2 is 240, the mass is 240 g.

13. 50 min

0843 is 8:43 am. From 7:53 to 8:00 is 7 min then to 8:43 is another 43 min. As 7 + 43 is 50, she needs to wait 50 min.

14. 64 cm²

As 6 × 2 = 12, the square must have a side length less than 12 cm.

As 12 × 12 = 144, the area must be less than 144 cm². A possible area is 64 cm².

15. rotate 90° clockwise about *O*

The shape has been rotated 90° clockwise about *O*.

16. 60°

The three angles form a straight angle which means they add to 180°. The two angles shown are 70° and 50°. As 70 + 50 is 120, and 180 – 120 is 60, the missing angle measures 60°.

17. $\mathbf{\frac{1}{3}}$

As $\frac{2}{3} + \frac{1}{3} = 1$, and $\frac{2}{3}$ is twice $\frac{1}{3}$, then the probability of a head is $\frac{2}{3}$ and the probability of a tail is $\frac{1}{3}$.

18. 3

As 5 – 2 is 3, then 3 boys walked home.

Unit 22B PAGE 83

1. 7

Composite numbers are 4, 6, 8, 9 … and prime numbers are 2, 3, 5 … As 4 + 3 is 7, then 7 is the smallest number.

2. –2, 6, –8

From –2, moving to the left 6 units gets to –8. This means –2 – 6 = –8.

3. 2880

The number of oranges is 20 × 4 × 36. This is 36 × 80 which is 2880. There is a total of 2880 oranges.

4. $\mathbf{\frac{5}{6}, \frac{3}{4}, \frac{2}{3}, \frac{1}{2}}$

Rewrite each fraction with a denominator of 24:

$\frac{3}{4} = \frac{18}{24}, \frac{5}{6} = \frac{20}{24}, \frac{2}{3} = \frac{16}{24}, \frac{1}{2} = \frac{12}{24}$.

Comparing the numerators, the order is $\frac{5}{6}, \frac{3}{4}, \frac{2}{3}, \frac{1}{2}$.

5. $\mathbf{\frac{3}{4}}$

The missing number is $2\frac{1}{4} - 1\frac{1}{2}$. Change both mixed numerals to improper fractions: $2\frac{1}{4} = \frac{9}{4}$ and $1\frac{1}{2} = \frac{3}{2}$. Change $\frac{3}{2}$ to quarters: $\frac{9}{4} - \frac{3}{2} = \frac{9}{4} - \frac{6}{4} = \frac{3}{4}$.

6. 0.459

As 16.92 + 3.08 = 20, the question can be rewritten as 20 – ☐ = 19.541.

This means the missing number is 20 – 19.541.

$$\begin{array}{r} 20.000 \\ -\ 19.541 \\ \hline 0.459 \end{array}$$

The missing number is 0.459.

7. 6 km

As 100 – 60 is 40, Bodhi has 40% of 15 km still to walk. As 40% is $\frac{4}{10} = \frac{2}{5}$, you need to work out $\frac{2}{5}$ of 15, which is 15 ÷ 5 × 2. This is 3 × 2 = 6, which means Bodhi has 6 km to walk.

8. $84

As 100 – 80 = 20, the cost will be 20% of the original price. As 420 ÷ 10 = 42 which is 10%, then 20% is 84. The cost is $84.

9. 101

Counting the matchsticks, the pattern is 6, 11, 16 which is adding 5. The 20th shape will be made using 6 + 19 lots of 5 matchsticks. 6 + 19 × 5 is 6 + 95 which equals 101. The 20th shape is made from 101 matchsticks.

10. 16

First, 65 – 15 is 50, and 55 – 50 is 5. This means 100 ÷ (☐ + 4) equals 5. As 100 ÷ 5 is 20, then (☐ + 4) equals 20. This means the missing number is 16.

11. 50 cm

The pairs of numbers that multiply to give 24 are 1 and 24, 2 and 12, 3 and 8 or 4 and 6. The largest possible perimeter occurs in a rectangle with length 24 and width 1. As 2 × (24 + 1) is 2 × 25 = 50, the largest possible perimeter is 50 cm.

12. 32 cm²

The diagram is the net of a cube. If the capacity is 64 mL, then the volume is 64 cm³. As side × side × side = 64, each side is 4. There are two shaded squares, so as 2 × 4 × 4 = 32, the area is 32 cm².

13. 35 min

The bus arrives at 3 min before 0928 which is 0925, or 9:25 am. From 8:50 to 9:00 is 10 min, then to 9:25 is 25 min. As 10 + 25 is 35, Fatima waits for 35 min.

14. 340 cm²

As the square has an area of 100 cm², then the side length is 10 cm. Each of the triangles has a base length of 10 cm and a height of 12 cm. $4 \times \frac{1}{2} \times 10 \times 12 + 10 \times 10$ is 240 + 100 which is 340. The area is 340 cm².

15. rotate 90° anticlockwise about *O*, and translate down 1 unit

The shape has been rotated 90° anticlockwise about *O*, and translated 1 unit down.

16. 42

The three angles form a straight angle which means they add to 180°. As one of the angles is 90° the other two angles add to 90°. As $x + 48$ is 90, then $x = 90 - 48$ which is 42. The missing angle measures 42° and so $x = 42$.

17. 18

As $\frac{3}{4} + \frac{1}{4} = 1$, and $\frac{3}{4}$ is three times $\frac{1}{4}$, then the probability of a head is $\frac{3}{4}$. Now, $\frac{3}{4}$ of 24 is 24 ÷ 4 × 3 which is 6 × 3 = 18, so the expected number of heads is 18.

18. $\frac{1}{4}$

3 boys walked, 2 travelled by car and 3 caught the bus. As 3 + 2 + 3 is 8, there are 8 boys. 2 out of 8, or $\frac{2}{8} = \frac{1}{4}$ of the boys travelled by car.

Unit 23A PAGE 84

1. 1

The prime numbers are 2, 3, 5, 7, 11 … and the triangular numbers are 1, 3, 6, 10 … This means that 3 is the only number in common under 12.

2. –8, –7, –6

The numbers are –8, –7 and –6.

3. 2000, 300

Six hundred thousand is written as 600 000. This has 5 zeros so use 2000 × 300 which gives 600 000.

4. <

Rewrite each fraction with a denominator of 12: $\frac{2}{3} = \frac{2 \times 4}{3 \times 4} = \frac{8}{12}$ and $\frac{3}{4} = \frac{3 \times 3}{4 \times 3} = \frac{9}{12}$. As 8 < 9, then $\frac{2}{3} < \frac{3}{4}$.

5. $\frac{9}{10}$

First find $\frac{2}{5} + \frac{1}{2}$. Use a related denominator: as 5 and 2 are factors of 10, rewrite the fractions as tenths.

As $\frac{2}{5} = \frac{2 \times 2}{5 \times 2} = \frac{4}{10}$ and $\frac{1}{2} = \frac{1 \times 5}{2 \times 5} = \frac{5}{10}$.

As $\frac{2}{5} + \frac{1}{2}$ is $\frac{4}{10} + \frac{5}{10} = \frac{9}{10}$, Christopher has spent $\frac{9}{10}$ of his birthday money.

6. 92.5 km/h

The average speed is found by dividing the distance by the time. This means 370 ÷ 4:

$$\begin{array}{r} 92.5 \\ 4\overline{)37^{1}0.^{2}0} \end{array}$$

Gail's average speed was 92.5 km/h.

7. 720

90% is $\frac{90}{100}$, which is $\frac{9}{10}$. To find $\frac{9}{10}$ of 800, find 800 ÷ 10 × 9. This is 80 × 9 which is 720.

8. $1200

As 25% is $\frac{1}{4}$, and 1600 ÷ 4 = 400, the discount is $400. As 1600 – 400 is 1200, the cost will be $1200.

9. Shape 5

The number of matchsticks used forms a pattern: 5, 9, 13. The rule is adding 4. Continuing the pattern: 17, 21 … As 21 is the fifth number in the sequence, Shape 5 is formed using 21 matchsticks.

10. 6

The number sentence is $\frac{14 + 26}{2} - \frac{10 + 18}{2}$. This is rewritten as $\frac{40}{2} - \frac{28}{2} = \frac{12}{2}$, which is 6.

11. 11 cm

As 40 – 18 is 22, the two equal sides add to 22 cm. This means they are both 11 cm.

12. 512 cm³

You need to find 8 × 8 × 8 which is 64 × 8 = 512. The volume is 512 cm³.

13. 26 min

From 0703 to 0843 is 1 h 40 min. From 0739 to 0853 is 1 h 14 min. As 40 – 14 is 26, the second bus is 26 min quicker.

14. 8 cm³

The net is 6 squares so as 24 ÷ 6 is 4, the area of each square is 4 cm². This means a side length of 2 cm. As 2 × 2 × 2 is 8, the volume is 8 cm³.

15.

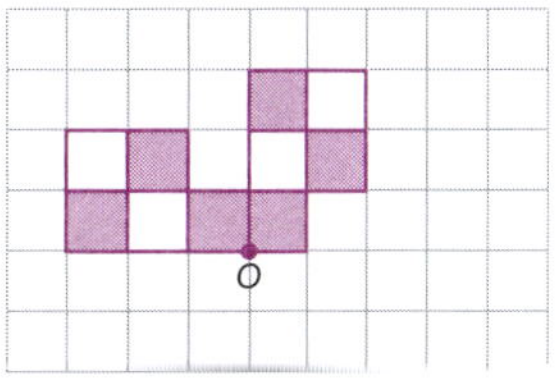

16. 80°

The three angles form a straight angle which means they add to 180°. As 40 + 60 is 100, and 180 – 100 is 80, the missing angle measures 80°.

17. There needs to be twice as many 3s as 5s, so write another 3 and 5.

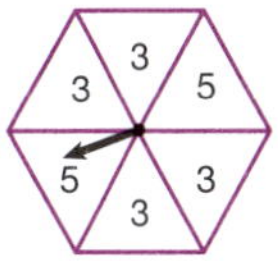

18. 22

As 12 + 10 is 22, then 22 Year 6 students voted for Arlo or Maeve.

Unit 23B PAGE 85

1. **15**

Looking for a number 3 more than a multiple of 4 and 3 more than a multiple of 6. The lowest multiple common to both 4 and 6 is 12. As 12 + 3 is 15, Colin picked 15 oranges.

2. **6**

The numbers are −4, −3, −2, −1, 0 and 1. This means there are 6 numbers between −5 and 2.

3. **272 000**

As 64 is 4 × 16 then 250 × 4 × 16 × 17 is 1000 × 16 × 17 or 16 000 × 17.

$$\begin{array}{r} 17 \\ \times\ \ 16 \\ \hline 102 \\ 170 \\ \hline 272 \end{array}$$

As 16 × 17 is 272, then 16 000 × 17 is 272 000.

4. **>**

Rewrite each fraction with a denominator of 12: $\frac{10}{3} = \frac{10 \times 4}{3 \times 4} = \frac{40}{12}$ and $\frac{13}{4} = \frac{13 \times 3}{4 \times 3} = \frac{39}{12}$. As 40 > 39, then $\frac{10}{3} > \frac{13}{4}$.

5. $\frac{3}{8}$

The question is $1 - \frac{3}{8} - \frac{1}{4}$. Use a related denominator: as 8 and 4 are factors of 8, rewrite $\frac{1}{4}$ as eighths. As $1 = \frac{8}{8}$ and $\frac{1}{4} = \frac{2}{8}$, $1 - \frac{3}{8} - \frac{1}{4} = \frac{8}{8} - \frac{3}{8} - \frac{2}{8} = \frac{3}{8}$.

This means $\frac{3}{8}$ of the pizza remains.

6. **600 km**

From 7 am to 2:30 pm is 7.5 hours. The distance travelled is speed × time, which is 80 × 7.5. As 7.5 × 80 is 7.5 × 10 × 8 is 75 × 8 = 600, Kendra travelled 600 km.

7. **176 cm**

As 10% = $\frac{1}{10}$, you need to find $\frac{1}{10}$ of 160, which is 160 ÷ 10 = 16. As 160 + 16 = 176, Rose is 176 cm tall.

8. **$13.41**

As $14.90 ÷ 10 is $1.49, the discount is $1.49.

$$\begin{array}{r} 14.90 \\ -\ \ 1.49 \\ \hline 13.41 \end{array}$$

The new price is $13.41.

9. **6**

The number of matchsticks used forms a pattern: 5, 9, 13. The rule is adding 4. Continuing the pattern: 17, 21, 25, 29 … As 5 + 9 + 13 + 17 + 21 + 25 is 90, Mollie can make 6 shapes in the pattern. (The next number in the sequence is 29 which means Mollie does not have enough matchsticks).

10. **2.4**

Find the total of all goals and divide by the total number of games.

The average is $\frac{8 \times 3 + 12 \times 2}{8 + 12}$ = (8 × 3 + 12 × 2) ÷ (8 + 12) = (24 + 24) ÷ 20, which is 48 ÷ 20, or 24 ÷ 10 = 2.4.

11. **64 cm²**

As the perimeter is 32 cm, the sum of the length and width is 16. The pairs that add to 16 are 1 and 15, 2 and 14, and so on. If the sides were 8 cm and 8 cm, the area would be 64 cm², which is the largest possible area. (Remember, a square is a rectangle.)

12. **8.5 cm**

Length × 8 × 10 is 680, which means 80 × length = 680. Find 680 ÷ 80, or 68 ÷ 8.

$$8\overline{)68.{}^{4}0}\quad = 8.5$$

The length is 8.5 cm.

13. **0902**

She needs to wait for the bus that arrives at 0832. This bus arrives in Lindisfarne at 0902.

14. **92 cm**

As the net has eight sides, and 120 ÷ 8 is 15, the side length of the isosceles triangles is 15 cm. When formed, the pyramid will have four edges of 15 cm and four edges on the square base of 8 cm. As 4 × 15 + 4 × 8 is 92, the sum of the edges is 92 cm.

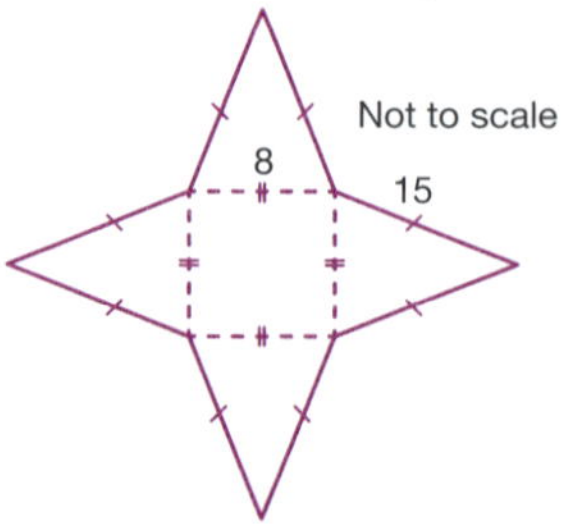

15.

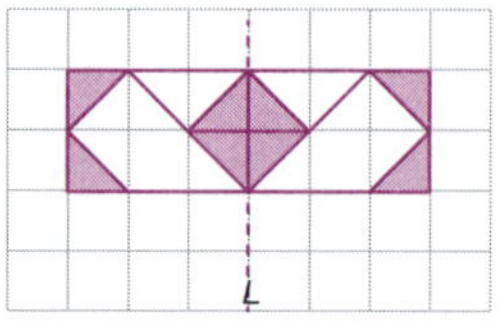

16. **35**

The angle 125° and the angle which is the sum of x and the right angle are vertically opposite angles. This means that $x + 90 = 125$. As 125 − 90 is 35, the angle is 35° and so $x = 35$.

17. There are 12 sections on the spinner.
As 12 ÷ 3 is 4, there are four 1s.
As 12 ÷ 4 is 3, there are three 2s.
As 12 ÷ 6 is 2, there are two 3s.
As 12 − (4 + 3 + 2) is 3, there are three 4s.

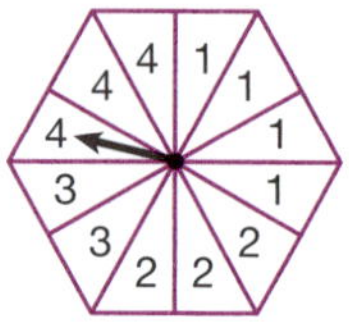

18. $\frac{5}{12}$

As 6 + 10 + 8 is 24, there are 24 Year 5 students. 10 out of 24 or $\frac{10}{24} = \frac{5}{12}$ of Year 5 voted for Oscar.

Unit 24A PAGE 86

1. **8**

Find composite even numbers less than 20. These numbers are 4, 6, 8, 10, 12, 14, 16 and 18. There are eight numbers.

2. **8 °C**

Think of a number line. From 6 to 0 is 6 and then from 0 to −2 is 2. As 6 + 2 is 8, the difference in temperatures is 8 °C.

3. **109**

$$\begin{array}{r} 84 \\ 162 \\ +\ \ 81 \\ \hline 327 \end{array}$$

The average is found using 327 ÷ 3.

$$3\overline{)32{}^{2}7}\quad = 109$$

The average daily attendance was 109.

4. The number line is marked in twelfths. $\frac{1}{4} = \frac{3}{12}$ and $\frac{5}{6} = \frac{10}{12}$.

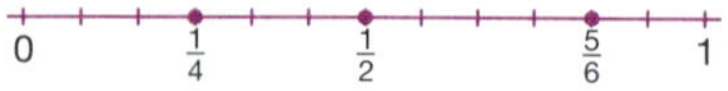

5. $\frac{7}{12}$

You need to add $\frac{1}{4}$ and $\frac{1}{3}$. Use a related denominator: as 4 and 3 are factors of 12, rewrite the fractions as twelfths. As $\frac{1}{4} = \frac{3}{12}$ and $\frac{1}{3} = \frac{4}{12}$, then $\frac{1}{4} + \frac{1}{3} = \frac{3}{12} + \frac{4}{12} = \frac{7}{12}$. This means $\frac{7}{12}$ of the students walked or travelled by car.

6. **$50.80**

1.27 × 40 is 1.27 × 10 × 4 which is 12.7 × 4.

```
  127
×   4
  508
```

As there is 1 decimal place in the question, then the answer has 1 decimal place. Joanne receives a pay rise of $50.8, which is $50.80.

7. **3500**

50% is $\frac{1}{2}$. If half of the tickets are sold, then half the tickets are still available. This means 3500 tickets are still available.

8. **$18**

As 16 – 12 = 4, then the discount as a fraction of the original price is $\frac{4}{16} = \frac{1}{4}$, which is 25%. Now as 24 ÷ 4 = 6, and 24 – 6 = 18, the price of a large pizza is $18.

9. **190**

46 + 1 is 47, then double is 94, so 94 is the fifth number. 94 + 1 is 95, then double is 190. 190 is the sixth number.

10. **10**

The number sentence is (80 – 30) ÷ 5, which is 50 ÷ 5 = 10. Paul gives his friends 10 golf balls each.

11. **1.144 m²**

Change 80 cm to 0.8 m. The area is found using 1.43 × 0.8.

```
  143
×   8
 1144
```

As there are 3 decimal places in the question, then 1.43 × 0.8 = 1.144. The area is 1.144 m².

12. **3.107 L**

340 mL is 0.34 L and 967 mL is 0.967 L.

```
  0.340
  0.967
+ 1.800
  3.107
```

The total is 3.107 L.

13. **23 min**

For the first bus, from 1121 to 1248 is 1 h 27 min. For the second bus, from 1408 to 1512 is 1 h 4 min. As 27 – 4 is 23, the second bus is 23 min quicker.

14. **15**

The solid is a pentagonal prism, which has 15 edges.

15.

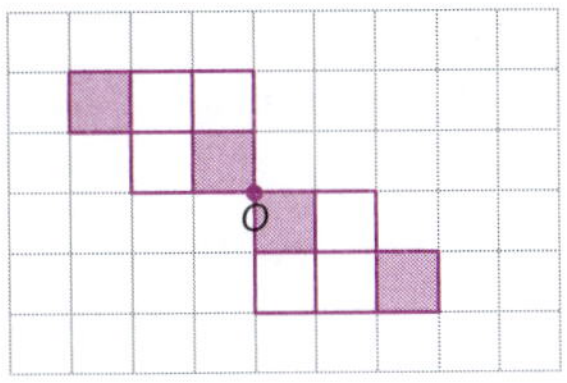

16. **120°**

The two angles form an angle of revolution which means they add to 360°. As 360 – 240 is 120, the angle measures 120°.

17. **0.72**

$\frac{36}{50}$ is $\frac{72}{100}$, which is 72 hundredths, or 0.72.

18. **62**

As 24 + 14 + 12 + 12 is 62, then 62 students visited on Tuesday or Friday.

Unit 24B PAGE 87

1. **48**

Looking for the lowest multiple of 8, 12 and 16. The number 48 is a multiple of all three numbers. The smallest number of chairs is 48.

2. **6 °C**

As the difference between 4 and 10 is 6, then the difference between –4 and –10 is also 6. The difference in temperatures is 6 °C.

3. **4145**

The second year had 2550 + 1761 = 4311, and the third year had 4311 + 1263 = 5574.

```
   2550
   4311
+  5574
 12 435
```

A total of 12 435 attended over the three years. As 12 435 ÷ 3 is 4145, then the average attendance was 4145.

4. The number line is marked in twelfths. $2\frac{1}{3} = 2\frac{4}{12}$ and $2\frac{3}{4} = 2\frac{9}{12}$.

5. $\frac{13}{30}$

The question is $1 - \frac{1}{6} - \frac{2}{5}$. Use a related denominator: as 6 and 5 are factors of 30, rewrite the fractions as thirtieths. $1 = \frac{30}{30}$, $\frac{1}{6} = \frac{5}{30}$ and $\frac{2}{5} = \frac{12}{30}$. This means $1 - \frac{1}{6} - \frac{2}{5}$ is $\frac{30}{30} - \frac{5}{30} - \frac{12}{30} = \frac{13}{30}$. This means $\frac{13}{30}$ of the circle is not coloured.

6. **$555**

As 12 × 2.5 is the same as 6 × 5 = 30, Sarah earns $30 per hour. Now, 18.5 × 30 is 18.5 × 10 × 3 is 185 × 3 which is 555. Sarah is paid $555.

7. **78**

As 30% is $\frac{3}{10}$, you need to find $\frac{3}{10}$ of 60, which is 60 ÷ 10 × 3 = 6 × 3 = 18. As 60 + 18 = 78, the number is 78.

8. **$45**

As 50% is half, then 60 ÷ 2 = 30, so the price is increased by $30. This means the price is $90. Discounting this by 50% means the price is half of $90, which is $45.

9. **69.8**

The fifth number is found by: 8.2 + 0.3 = 8.5 then double is 17. The sixth number is found by: 17 + 0.3 = 17.3 then double is 34.6. The seventh number is found by: 34.6 + 0.3 = 34.9 then double is 69.8.

10. **4**

The number sentence is (16 + 14 + 18 – 12) ÷ 9, which is 36 ÷ 9 = 4. Grace places four muffins in each of the bags.

11. **33.58 cm²**

Change 46 mm to 4.6 cm. The area is found using 7.3 × 4.6.

```
   73
×  46
  438
 2920
 3358
```

As there are 2 decimal places in the question, then 7.3 × 4.6 = 33.58. The area is 33.58 cm².

12. **265 mL**

The amount is (5.00 – 2.88) ÷ 8 which is 2.12 ÷ 8.

```
   0.265
8)2.1⁵2⁴0
```

There is 0.265 L or 265 mL in each glass.

13. **1854**

The first bus does not drop off in Kingstree, and the second bus does not pick up in Ridgeville. She has to catch the bus at Ridgeville at 1803, which arrives in Kingstree at 1854.

14.

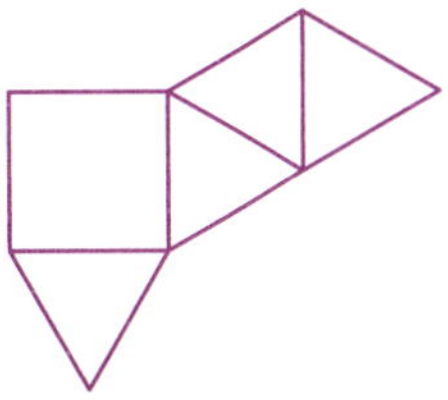

15.

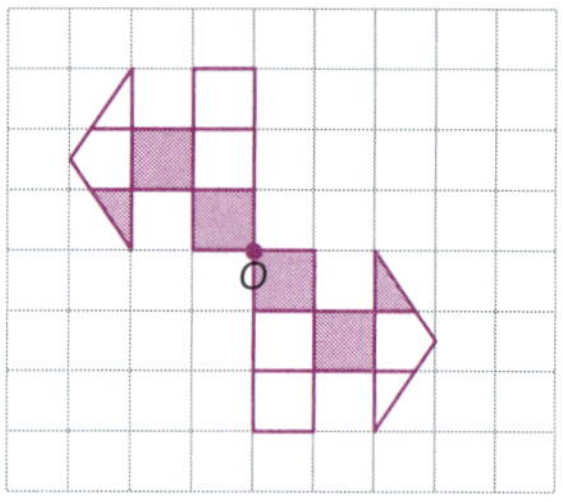

16. **227**

The three angles form an angle of revolution which means they add to 360°. This means $x + 46 + 87 = 360$. As $46 + 87$ is 133, and $360 - 133$ is 227, the angle measures 227°, and so $x = 227$.

17. **5**

60% is $\frac{60}{100}$, which is $\frac{6}{10}$, or $\frac{3}{5}$. This means 3 blue balls out of 5 balls. The smallest number of balls is 5.

18. **25%**

The total number of boys is $8 + 12 + 16 + 12 = 48$. As 12 boys visited on Friday and $\frac{12}{48} = \frac{1}{4}$, which is 25%, then 25% of the boys who went to the library were there on Friday.

Unit 25A PAGE 88

1. **2, 3, 11**

Look for two numbers that multiply to give 66. As 11×6 is 66, and 2×3 is 6, then $11 \times 2 \times 3$ is 66, and each of the numbers is prime. The numbers are 2, 3 and 11.

2. **2**

The pattern is adding 2. As $0 + 2$ is 2, the missing number is 2.

3. **9 h**

80 km/h means driving an average of 80 km every hour. The time is found by dividing 720 by 80.
As $720 \div 80 = 72 \div 8$, which is 9, it will take Aubrey 9 h.

4. The number line is marked in twelfths.
$\frac{1}{2} = \frac{6}{12}$ and $\frac{2}{3} = \frac{8}{12}$.

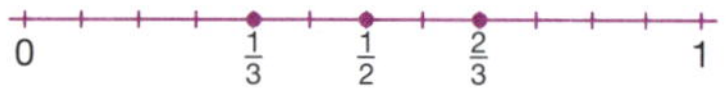

5. **310**

The whole book is five-fifths. As $62 \times 5 = 310$, the novel has 310 pages.

6. **$16.85**

$$4\overline{)67.40} = 16.85$$

Each paintbrush costs $16.85.

7. **7%**

Rewrite all as percentages: 7%, $0.6 = 0.60 = 60\%$, $\frac{8}{100} = 8\%$, $3 = 300\%$.
The smallest amount is 7%.

8. **$180**

As 10% is $\frac{1}{10}$, then $1740 \div 10$ is 174, which is less than 180. A discount of $180 is a better deal.

9. **30**

Counting the matchsticks, the pattern is 6, 10, 14 which is adding 4. The seventh shape will be made using $14 + 4 + 4 + 4 + 4 = 30$ matchsticks.

10. **16**

As $10 - 3 \times 2 = 10 - 6 = 4$, then $(10 - 3 \times 2)^2 = 4^2$, which is 16.

11. **4.68 cm**

The length of each side is found using $14.04 \div 3$.

$$3\overline{)14.04} = 4.68$$

The length of each side is 4.68 cm.

12. **4 L**

As half of 10 is 5, work out $40 \times 20 \times 5$. This is 40×100 which is 4000. As 4000 cm^3 is 4 L, 4 L is needed to fill the tank.

13. **8:14 pm**

The sunset time was 2014, which is 8:14 pm.

14. **cone**

A cone is formed.

15.

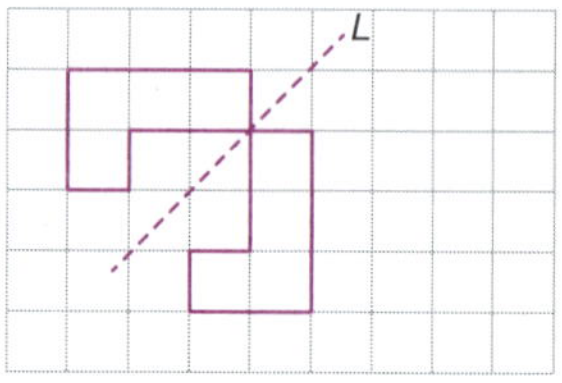

16. **15°**

The three angles form a straight angle. As one of the angles is 90°, then the other two angles also add to 90°. As $90 - 75$ is 15, the angle measures 15°.

17. **6**

As $\frac{1}{3}$ of 18 is $18 \div 3 = 6$, the Tigers won 6 games.

18. **11**

As $7 + 4$ is 11, then 11 students do not have siblings.

Unit 25B PAGE 89

1. **2**

To be even, the number must be a multiple of 2. That means that 2 must be one of the prime numbers.

2. **−4**

The pattern is subtracting 2. As $-2 - 2$ is -4, the missing number is -4.

3. **6:00 pm**

The time taken is found by dividing 600 by 75. Now, $600 \div 75$ is the same as $1200 \div 150$ which is the same as $2400 \div 300$. As $24 \div 3 = 8$, the trip takes 8 h. From 10 am adding 8 h gives 6:00 pm.

4. The number line is marked in tenths.
$3\frac{4}{5} = 3\frac{8}{10}$ and $4\frac{1}{10}$.

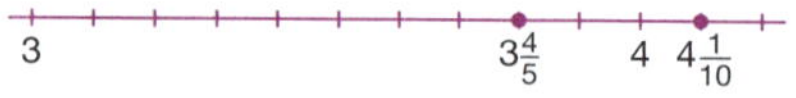

5. **250 km**

As $\frac{3}{8}$ of the trip is 150 km, then by dividing by 3, $\frac{1}{8}$ of the trip is 50 km.
Using $1 - \frac{3}{8} = \frac{5}{8}$, Layla still has $\frac{5}{8}$ of the trip to travel. Multiplying 50 by 5, she has 250 km to reach her destination.

6. **74.4, 74.4**

When 0.25 is multiplied by 4 the answer is 1. The first missing number is found by multiplying 18.6 by 4.

$$\begin{array}{r} 186 \\ \times \quad 4 \\ \hline 744 \end{array}$$

As there is 1 decimal place in the question, then the answer has 1 decimal place. This means $18.6 \times 4 = 74.4$.
The number sentence is $18.6 \div 0.25 = 74.4 \div 1 = 74.4$. The missing numbers are both 74.4.

7. **0.2**

$\frac{3}{5} = \frac{6}{10} = 0.6$. $0.2 + 0.6 = 0.8$.
As $25\% = \frac{1}{4}$, find $\frac{1}{4}$ of 0.8. As $8 \div 4$ is 2, then 25% of 0.8 is 0.2.

8. **$960**

$2000 - 1600$ is 400. The discount as a fraction of the original price is $\frac{400}{2000}$, which is $\frac{1}{5}$, or 20%.
As 10% of 1200 is 120, then 20% is 240. A discount of $240 on a price of $1200 makes the final price of the laptop $960.

9. **Shape 12**

Counting the matchsticks, the pattern is 6, 10, 14 which is adding 4. The sequence continues: 18, 22, 26, 30, 34, 38, 42, 46, 50. Shape 12 is made using 50 matchsticks.

10. 10

This is $\frac{1}{2}$ of 24 plus $\frac{1}{4}$ of 24 minus $\frac{1}{3}$ of 24. 12 + 6 − 8 = 10.

11. 48 cm²

As the perimeter is 28, then the sum of the length and width is 14. Two numbers that add to 14 and have a difference of 2 are 8 and 6. This means the dimensions are 8 cm and 6 cm. As 8 × 6 is 48, the area is 48 cm².

12. 9.6 L

The perimeter of the square is 80 cm which means the side length is 20 cm. The volume is 20 × 20 × 24 which is 400 × 24 = 9600. As the volume is 9600 cm³, the capacity is 9.6 L.

13. 14 h 19 min

0556 is 5:56 am and 2015 is 8:15 pm. From 5:56 to 6:00 is 4 min, then to midday is 6 h, then to 8 pm is 8 h and then to 8:15 is 15 min. This is a total of 14 h 19 min.

14.

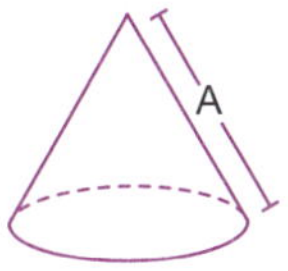

15.

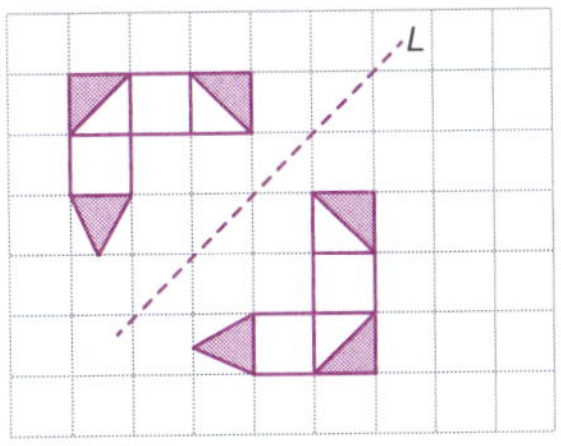

16. 245

The three angles form an angle of revolution which means they add to 360°. This means x + 39 + 76 = 360. As 39 + 76 is 115, and 360 − 115 is 245, the angle measures 245°, and so x = 245.

17. 12

The probability of winning is 0.4, and not winning is 0.6. 0.4 is $\frac{4}{10}$, or $\frac{8}{20}$. The team won 8 out of 20 games. As 20 − 8 is 12, the Tigers did not win 12 games.

18. 60%

As 4 + 6 is 10, there are 10 students who do not have a pet. As 6 out of 10 is $\frac{6}{10} = \frac{60}{100}$, which is 60%, then 60% of the students who do not have a pet have at least one sibling.

Unit 26A — PAGE 90

1. 2 and 3

As 2 and 3 are prime, and they are consecutive, they must be the numbers. Every other even number (except 0) is composite.

2. 7

The pattern is adding 3. As 4 + 3 is 7, the missing number is 7.

3. 135

67 500 ÷ 500 is the same as 675 ÷ 5.

$$\begin{array}{r} 1\,3\,5 \\ 5\overline{)6\,{}^{1}7\,{}^{2}5} \end{array}$$

This means 67 500 ÷ 500 is 135.

4. The number line is marked in eighths. $1\frac{1}{4} = 1\frac{2}{8}$.

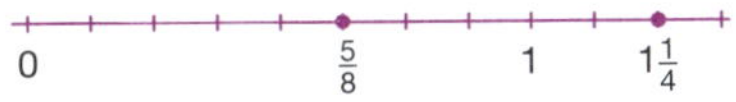

5. $\frac{3}{4}$ cup

$2 - 1\frac{1}{4}$ is $2 - 1 - \frac{1}{4}$, which is $1 - \frac{1}{4}$. As $1 = \frac{4}{4}$, then $\frac{4}{4} - \frac{1}{4}$ is $\frac{3}{4}$. Camilla borrowed $\frac{3}{4}$ of a cup.

6. 24.11 s

Add 23.71 and 0.4:

$$\begin{array}{r} 23.71 \\ +\ \ 0.40 \\ \hline 24.11 \end{array}$$

Emilee ran the race in a time of 24.11 s.

7. 20

100 − 90 is 10. This means 10% of 200 blocks not sold. As 10% = $\frac{1}{10}$, find 200 ÷ 10 which is 20. This means 20 blocks are not sold.

8. $360

As 25% is $\frac{1}{4}$, then 480 ÷ 4 is 120. If the price drops from $480 by $120 the new price is $360.

9. 20

The numbers in the first row are multiplied by 4 to give the corresponding numbers in the second row. As 5 × 4 is 20, the missing number is 20.

10. 25

The number sentence is $\frac{1}{2} \times (18 + 32)$. As 18 + 32 is 50, then $\frac{1}{2} \times (18 + 32) = \frac{1}{2} \times 50$, which is 25.

11. 8.04 cm

As a regular pentagon has five equal sides, you need to find 40.2 ÷ 5.

$$\begin{array}{r} 8.04 \\ 5\overline{)40.20} \end{array}$$

Each side is 8.04 cm.

12. 9.6 kg

As 3 × 4 is 12, there are 12 cubes in the solid. As 0.8 × 12 is 9.6, the mass of the solid is 9.6 kg.

13. 45 min

You need to find the elapsed time from 3:40 to 4:25. From 3:40 to 4:00 is 20 min then to 4:25 is 25 min. As 20 + 25 = 45, Hannah waits for 45 min.

14. 24 cm²

As 2 × 2 × 2 is 8, the side length of the cube is 2 cm. As 2 × 2 is 4, each square has an area of 4 cm². As there are 6 squares in the net, and as 6 × 4 is 24, the area of the net is 24 cm².

15.

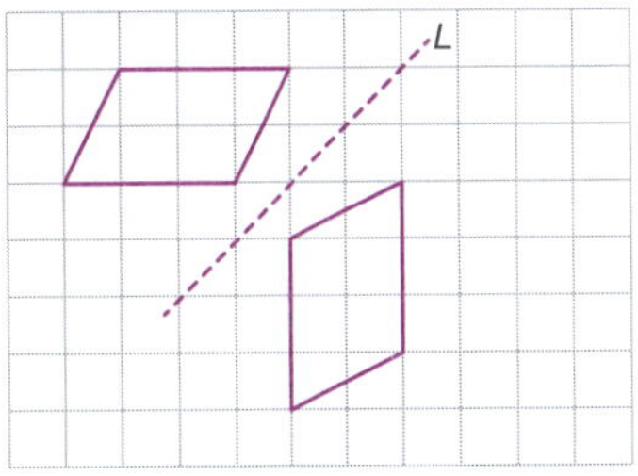

16. 70°

The three angles form an angle of revolution which means they add to 360°. As 260 + 30 is 290, and 360 − 290 is 70, the angle measures 70°.

17. 0.46

The two possible outcomes are the event occurring and not occurring. As 1 − 0.54 is 0.46, the probability of the event not occurring is 0.46.

18. $\frac{2}{5}$

As 3 + 2 is 5 there were 5 left-handed students. As 2 of these 5 students were boys, then the fraction is $\frac{2}{5}$.

Unit 26B — PAGE 91

1. 120th person

Look for a number, smaller than 200, that is a multiple of 5, 8 and 12. The only number is 120. This means the person 120th in line received all four items.

2. −1

The pattern is adding 5. As −6 + 5 is −1, the missing number is −1.

3. 2880 L

The number of litres is 12 × 6 × 4 × 10. As 12 × 6 is 72 and 72 × 10 is 720, the calculation needed is 720 × 4.

$$\begin{array}{r} 720 \\ \times\ \ \ 4 \\ \hline 2880 \end{array}$$

There are 2880 L of paint.

4. The number line is marked in sixths.

$-\frac{2}{3} = -\frac{4}{6}$ and $-1\frac{1}{2} = -1\frac{3}{6}$.

5. $\frac{1}{6}$

The question is $1 - \frac{1}{4} - \frac{1}{4} - \frac{1}{3}$. Use a related denominator: as 4 and 3 are factors of 12, rewrite the fractions as twelfths. $1 = \frac{12}{12}$, $\frac{1}{4} = \frac{3}{12}$ and $\frac{1}{3} = \frac{4}{12}$.

This means $1 - \frac{1}{4} - \frac{1}{4} - \frac{1}{3}$ is $\frac{12}{12} - \frac{3}{12} - \frac{3}{12} - \frac{4}{12} = \frac{2}{12}$, which can be rewritten as $\frac{1}{6}$. This means $\frac{1}{6}$ of the chocolates remain.

6. **18.66**

As 1673 × 2 is 3346, then 16.73 × 2 = 33.46, which is the total of the numbers. The difference between 33.46 and 14.8 will give the larger number.

$$\begin{array}{r} 33.46 \\ -\ 14.80 \\ \hline 18.66 \\ \hline \end{array}$$

The larger decimal is 18.66.

7. **24**

You need to work out 8% of 300. As 1% is 300 ÷ 100 = 3, then 8% is 8 × 3 = 24. This means 24 people were employed.

8. **$432**

$$\begin{array}{r} 384 \\ +\ \ 96 \\ \hline 480 \\ \hline \end{array}$$

The original price was $480.

As 10% is $\frac{1}{10}$, then 480 ÷ 10 is 48, and 480 − 48 = 432, so the price would have been $432.

9. **21**

The numbers in the second row are divided by 7 to give the corresponding numbers in the first row. As 147 ÷ 7 is 21, the missing number is 21.

10. **3**

As 16 ÷ 4 is 4, then $\frac{1}{4} \times (8 + 16 \div 4) = \frac{1}{4} \times (8 + 4)$, which is $\frac{1}{4} \times 12 = 3$.

11. **1.13 m**

Change each to metres: 320 mm = 0.32 m, 40 cm = 0.4 m, 1.2 and 2.6.

$$\begin{array}{r} 0.32 \\ 0.4 \\ 1.2 \\ +\ \ 2.6 \\ \hline 4.52 \\ \hline \end{array}$$

Now find 4.52 ÷ 4.

$$4\overline{)4.5^{1}2}\quad 1.13$$

The average length is 1.13 m.

12. **50 kg**

As 4 × 2 × 3 is 24, there are 24 cubes in the solid. Also, as 1.2 × 1000 = 1200, the mass of the solid is 1200 kg. Find 1200 ÷ 24, which is the same as 100 ÷ 2 = 50. Each of the cubes has a mass of 50 kg.

13. **1 h 10 min.**

25 min before 1:20 is 12:55. From 12:55 to 1:55 is 1 hour, and then another 10 min gives 2:05. Simon waited 1 h 10 min.

14. **94 cm²**

The net has 6 rectangles: 2 rectangles measuring 5 cm by 4 cm, 2 rectangles measuring 4 cm by 3 cm and 2 rectangles measuring 5 cm by 3 cm. As 2 × 5 × 4 + 2 × 4 × 3 + 2 × 5 × 3 is 40 + 24 + 30 is 94, the area of the net is 94 cm².

15.

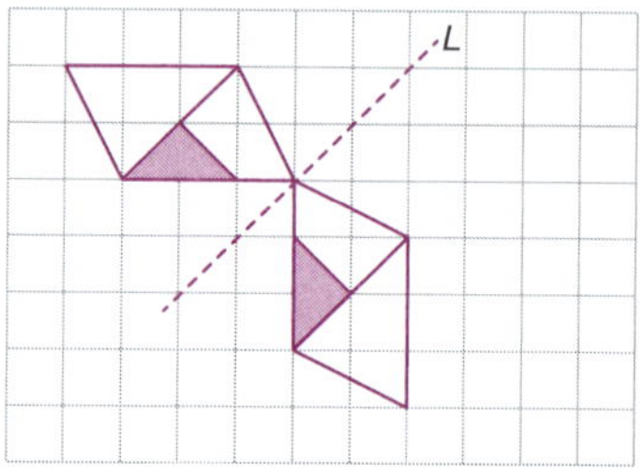

16. **40**

The three angles form a straight angle. As 180 − 100 is 80, then the two angles add to 80. As 80 ÷ 2 is 40, then they are both 40°, so $x = 40$.

17. $\frac{1}{4}$

The even numbers greater than 10 are 12, 14, 16, 18 and 20. This means the probability is 5 out of 20, which is $\frac{5}{20}$, or $\frac{1}{4}$.

18. **44%**

As 3 + 11 + 2 + 9 is 25, and there are 11 right-handed girls, then the fraction is $\frac{11}{25}$, or $\frac{44}{100}$, which is 44%.

Unit 27A — PAGE 92

1. **10**

The prime numbers are 2, 3, 5, 7, 11, 13, 17, 19, 23, 29. This means 10 students stood up.

2. **−3**

The pattern is subtracting 2. As −1 − 2 is −3, the missing number is −3.

3. **252**

The missing number is found using 12 × 21.

$$\begin{array}{r} 21 \\ \times\ \ 12 \\ \hline 252 \\ \hline \end{array}$$

The missing number is 252.

4. $\frac{1}{4}$, $\frac{9}{30}$

As 4 is greater than 3, then $\frac{1}{4}$ is less than $\frac{1}{3}$. Also, as $\frac{1}{3} = \frac{10}{30}$, then $\frac{9}{30}$ is less than $\frac{1}{3}$. The two fractions are $\frac{1}{4}$ and $\frac{9}{30}$.

5. **232**

The whole amount is four quarters. As 58 × 4 = 232, there are 232 students enrolled.

6. **4.79 km**

$$\begin{array}{r} 11.65 \\ -\ \ 6.86 \\ \hline 4.79 \\ \hline \end{array}$$

Jarrod ran 4.79 km on the second day.

7. **0.4,** $\frac{2}{5}$

40% = 0.40 = 0.4.

Also, 40% = $\frac{40}{100} = \frac{40 \div 20}{100 \div 20} = \frac{2}{5}$.

8. **$20**

As 20% is $\frac{1}{5}$, then 25 ÷ 5 = 5 and so the discount is $5. As 25 − 5 is 20, the new price is $20.

9. **5.7**

As 4.1 − 2.4 is 1.7, the rule is that 1.7 is added to numbers in the first row to give the corresponding numbers in the second row. 4 + 1.7 is 5.7. Another method could be used: as the numbers in both rows are increasing by 0.4, then the missing number is 5.3 + 0.4 which is 5.7.

10. **0.4**

0.56 + 0.24 is 0.80 = 0.8. Now, as 8 ÷ 2 is 4, then 0.8 ÷ 2 is 0.4.

11. **6 cm**

The area of a triangle is $\frac{1}{2}$ × base × height. As $\frac{1}{2}$ × 16 × height is 48, then 8 × height is 48. This means the height is 6 cm.

12. **1 L**

As 20 × 5 × 10.5 is 100 × 10.5 = 1050, the volume is 1050 cm³. This is 1.05 L which is close to 1 L.

13. **1 h 25 min**

All time differences are the same. From 9:30 to 10:55 is 1 h 25 min.

14. 27 cm³

As there are 14 equal sides, and $42 \div 14 = 21 \div 7 = 3$, each side is 3 cm. As $3 \times 3 \times 3$ is 27, the volume is 27 cm³.

15. (1, –1)

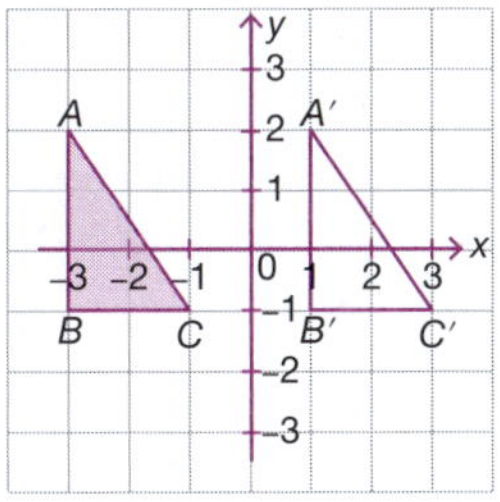

The coordinates of the image of *B*, shown as *B′*, are (1, –1).

16. 220°

The two angles form an angle of revolution which means they add to 360°. As 360 – 140 is 220, the angle measures 220°.

17. 0.2

As $1 - (0.3 + 0.5)$ is $1 - 0.8 = 0.2$, the probability is 0.2.

18. As 29 – 14 is 15, there are 15 boys in the class. Half of 14 is 7 so 7 girls are less than 150 cm, and 7 are at least 150 cm. As 15 – 6 is 9, there are 9 boys at least 150 cm tall.

	Boys	Girls
Less than 150 cm	6	7
At least 150 cm	9	7

Unit 27B PAGE 93

1. 230

There are 150 even numbers. Then as $300 \div 10$ is 30, there are 30 numbers with a last digit of 5. There are lots more multiples of 3, 7 and so on as well. Of the numbers, 230 would be the best estimate. (There are actually 237 composite numbers.)

2. –28

The pattern is subtracting 6.

As –22 – 6 is –28, the missing number is –28.

3. 81 648

$$\begin{array}{r} 126 \\ \times \quad 18 \\ \hline 1008 \\ 1260 \\ \hline 2268 \end{array}$$

The missing number is found using 2268×36.

$$\begin{array}{r} 2\,268 \\ \times \quad 36 \\ \hline 13\,608 \\ 68\,040 \\ \hline 81\,648 \end{array}$$

The missing number is 81 648.

4. $\mathbf{\frac{3}{8}}$

Rewrite both fractions as eighths.

$\frac{1}{4} = \frac{2}{8}$ and $\frac{1}{2} = \frac{4}{8}$. As the middle of 2 and 4 is 3, the middle of $\frac{2}{8}$ and $\frac{4}{8}$ is $\frac{3}{8}$.

5. 2500 L

As $1 - \frac{2}{5}$ is $\frac{3}{5}$, then $\frac{3}{5}$ of the tank is 1500 L. Dividing by 3 gives $\frac{1}{5}$ of the tank equalling 500 L. The whole tank is $\frac{5}{5}$, so multiplying by 5 gives 2500 L.

6. $67.96

169.9×40 is $169.9 \times 10 \times 4$ which is 1699×4:

$$\begin{array}{r} 1699 \\ \times \quad 4 \\ \hline 6796 \end{array}$$

As there are 2 decimal places in the question, then the answer has 2 decimal places. The cost is 6796 cents or $67.96.

7. $\mathbf{0.025, \frac{1}{40}}$

As 2% is 0.02, then $2\frac{1}{2}\%$ is 0.025. Also, $2\frac{1}{2}\% = \frac{2\frac{1}{2}}{100} = \frac{2\frac{1}{2} \times 2}{100 \times 2} = \frac{5}{200} = \frac{5 \div 5}{200 \div 5} = \frac{1}{40}$.

8. $40.50

As 25% is $\frac{1}{4}$, and $60 \div 4$ is 15, the price was first reduced by $15.

As 60 – 15 = 45, the price was $45. Now, as 10% is $\frac{1}{10}$, and $45 \div 10$ is 4.5, the second discount was $4.50. As $45 – $4.50 is $40.50, the beach towel was bought for $40.50.

9. 2.7

The numbers in the second row are half the corresponding numbers in the first row. As $5.4 \div 2$ is 2.7, the missing number is 2.7.

10. 22

The sum of 12 and 15 is 27. To work out $\frac{2}{3}$ of 27, use $27 \div 3$ to find a third, then multiply by 2 to find two thirds. As $27 \div 3 \times 2$ is 18, you need to add 4 and 18, which is 22.

11. 324 cm²

As a regular hexagon has 6 equal sides, and 12×6 is 72, the perimeter is 72 cm. As $72 \div 4$ is 18, each side of the square is 18 cm long. The area of the square is 18×18 which is $9 \times 2 \times 9 \times 2 = 81 \times 4$ which is 324. The area is 324 cm².

12. 28.8 kL

You need to find $80 \times 6 \times 60$, which is $480 \times 60 = 28\,800$. This means 28 800 L, or 28.8 kL, is released every hour.

13. 2:40 pm

You need to find the time 1 h 25 min before 4:05. From 4:05, subtracting 1 h gives 3:05, then subtracting 25 min gives 2:40. The plane left Sydney at 2:40 pm.

14. 84 cm²

There are three rectangles and two triangles in the net of the prism. For the rectangles, $5 \times 6 + 3 \times 6 + 4 \times 6 = 72$. For the triangles, $2 \times \frac{1}{2} \times 3 \times 4 = 12$. As 72 + 12 = 84, the area of the net is 84 cm².

15. (1, –2)

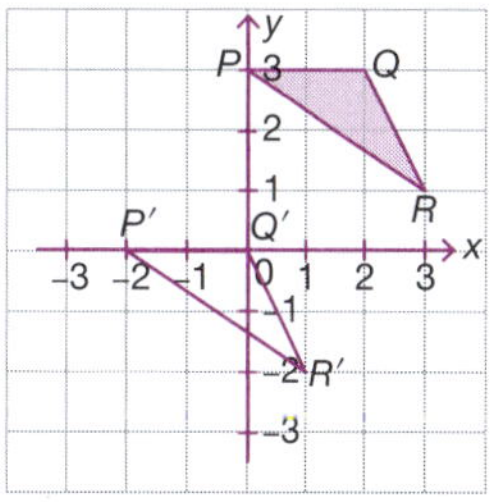

The coordinates of the image of *R*, shown as *R′*, are (1, –2).

16. 56

The three angles form an angle of revolution which means they add to 360°. As 360 – 248 is 112, and $112 \div 2$ is 56, the two angles are both 56°. This means $x = 56$.

17. 15

As 0.7 – 0.3 is 0.4 the probability of selecting a red marble is 0.4. As 0.4 represents 20 then 0.1 represents 5 and 0.3 represents 15. There must be 15 blue marbles.

18. As $28 \div 4$ is 7, there are 7 girls who are less than 150 cm tall. There are 15 boys and 13 girls, and three-fifths of 15 is $15 \div 5 \times 3$ which is 9. Also, $28 - (6 + 9 + 7)$ is 6.

	Boys	Girls
Less than 150 cm	6	7
At least 150 cm	9	6

Unit 28A PAGE 94

1. **8, 9, 10**

   Composite numbers are 4, 6, 8, 9, 10 … This means that 8, 9, 10 are the first three consecutive numbers that are composite.

2. **8 °C**

   You need to start at −4 and add 12. −4 + 4 gives 0 and then 0 + 8 is 8. The new temperature is 8 °C.

3. **160 cm**

$$\begin{array}{r} 165 \\ 148 \\ 171 \\ +\ 156 \\ \hline 640 \end{array}$$

   The total height is 640 cm.

$$4\overline{)6^{2}40}\quad 160$$

   The average height of the plants is 160 cm.

4. $\frac{5}{6}$

   Rewrite the fractions as twelfths.

   $\frac{2}{3} = \frac{2 \times 4}{3 \times 4} = \frac{8}{12}$; $\frac{5}{6} = \frac{5 \times 2}{6 \times 2} = \frac{10}{12}$;

   $\frac{3}{4} = \frac{3 \times 3}{4 \times 3} = \frac{9}{12}$. For 8, 10 and 9, the largest number is 10. This means the largest fraction is $\frac{5}{6}$.

5. $\frac{7}{8}$

   The question is $\frac{5}{8} + \frac{1}{4}$. Use a related denominator: as 8 and 4 are factors of 8, rewrite $\frac{1}{4}$ as eighths. Using $\frac{1}{4} = \frac{2}{8}$, then $\frac{5}{8} + \frac{1}{4}$ is $\frac{5}{8} + \frac{2}{8} = \frac{7}{8}$. This means $\frac{7}{8}$ of the stamps were Australian or European.

6. **$46.25**

$$3\overline{)13^{1}8.7^{1}5}\quad 46.25$$

   Each person paid $46.25.

7. **14**

   Finding 10% is finding $\frac{1}{10}$, which is dividing by 10. This means 140 ÷ 10 is 14.

8. **$60**

   If 10% is $40, then by dividing by 2, 5% is $20. As 10% + 5% is 15%, and $40 + $20 is $60, the discount would have been $60.

9. **divided by 2**

   Each number in the bottom row is half the corresponding number in the top row. The rule is 'Bottom number = Top number divided by 2'.

10. **6**

    The number sentence is (12 + 18) − 8 × 3. As 12 + 18 is 30, and 8 × 3 is 24, then (12 + 18) − 8 × 3 = 30 − 24, which is 6.

11. **20 cm**

    If the area of the enlarged square is 100 cm², then each side must be 10 cm. If the original dimensions have been doubled, they were originally 5 cm. As 4 × 5 is 20, the square had a perimeter of 20 cm.

12. **5 cm**

    As 10 × 10 × 10 is 1000, the volume of the cube is 1000 cm³. For the prism, 20 × 10 × height = 1000. As 20 × 10 is 200, then 200 × height is 1000. This means the height is 5 cm.

13. **1855**

    From 1531 to 1658 is 1 h 27 min. From 1728 adding 1 h gives 1828, then 27 min is 1855.

14. **312 cm²**

    The net is made from 4 rectangles and 2 squares.

    As 4 × 10 × 6 + 2 × 6 × 6 is 240 + 72 which is 312, the area is 312 cm².

15. 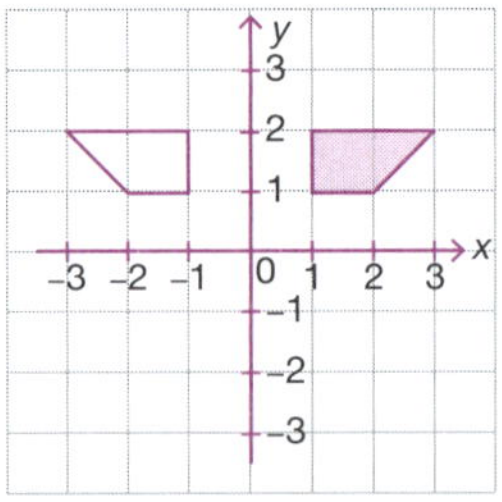

16. **100°**

    The three angles form an angle of revolution which means they add to 360°. As 150 + 110 is 260 and 360 − 260 is 100, the missing angle is 100°.

17. $\frac{4}{25}$

    As 8 + 16 + 6 + 20 is 50, and 8 girls have been to Melbourne, the probability is $\frac{8}{50}$, which is $\frac{4}{25}$.

18. As 40 ÷ 2 is 20 there are 20 boys and 20 girls. As 20 ÷ 2 is 10 there are 10 boys who can swim 200 m and as 20 ÷ 4 is 5, there are 5 girls who can swim 200 m.

	Can swim 200 m	Cannot swim 200 m
Girls	5	15
Boys	10	10

Unit 28B PAGE 95

1. **6**

   These numbers are 19, 29, 59, 79, 89 and 97. This means there are six numbers.

2. **−5.5 °C**

   As −2 − 3 is −5, then −2.5 − 3 is −5.5.

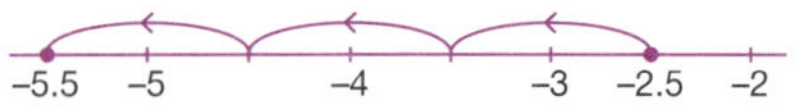

3. **22**

   Total number of goals in six games is 24 × 6 = 144. As 144 + 16 + 16 is 176, the total number of goals in eight games is 176. The average in eight games is 176 ÷ 8 which is 22 goals.

4. **Lincoln's**

   Allison has $\frac{5}{12}$ remaining and Lincoln has $\frac{3}{8}$ remaining. As $\frac{5}{12} = \frac{10}{24}$ and $\frac{3}{8} = \frac{9}{24}$, and 10 > 9 then $\frac{5}{12} > \frac{3}{8}$. There is more of Allison's cake remaining, so more of Lincoln's cake was eaten.

5. **48**

   You need to find the difference between the two fractions. $\frac{3}{4} = \frac{9}{12}$ and $\frac{1}{3} = \frac{4}{12}$. $\frac{3}{4} - \frac{1}{3}$ is $\frac{9}{12} - \frac{4}{12} = \frac{5}{12}$.

   As $\frac{5}{12}$ of the number is 40, then dividing by 5, $\frac{1}{12}$ of the number is 8. As $\frac{1}{2} = \frac{6}{12}$ then multiplying by 6, half the number is 48.

6. **$18.95**

   Divide 1137 by 10, then divide the result by 6. As 1137 ÷ 10 is 113.7, the cost will be 113.7 ÷ 6.

$$6\overline{)11^{5}3.^{5}7^{3}0}\quad 18.95$$

   The cost is $18.95 for each calculator.

7. **160**

   As 100 − 60 is 40, then 40% or $\frac{2}{5}$ of the people are females. As $\frac{2}{5}$ of 500 is 200 there are 200 females. As 100 − 20 is 80, then 80% of the females are not under 18 years old. As $\frac{80}{100} = \frac{160}{200}$, then 160 out of the 200 females were not under 18 years old.

8. **$900**

   As 100 − 10 is 90, then 90% of the original price is $810. Dividing by 9 10% is $90, and then multiplying by 10 gives 100% which is $900. The original price was $900.

9. squared

Each number in the bottom row is the square of the corresponding number in the top row. The rule is 'Bottom number = Top number squared.'

10. 15.1

As 2.1×8 is 16.8 and $6.8 \div 4$ is 1.7, then $2.1 \times 8 - 6.8 \div 4 = 16.8 - 1.7$, which is 15.1.

11. 420 cm²

If the area of the enlarged square is 400 cm², then, as 20×20 is 400, each side must be 20 cm. The dimensions of the rectangular tile are 28 cm and 15 cm.

```
   28
   15
  140
× 280
  420
```

The area of the rectangular tile is 420 cm².

12. 2.5 cm

1 litre of water is contained in 1000 cm³. The volume of water in the cube is $20 \times 20 \times \text{depth} = 1000$. As 20×20 is 400, then $400 \times \text{depth} = 1000$. This means the depth is $1000 \div 400$, which is $10 \div 4 = 2.5$. The depth is 2.5 cm.

13. 1759 and 2004

From 1829 to 1927 is 58 min. From 1701, adding 58 min gives 1759. This means *A* is 1759. From 1759 to 1836 is 37 min. From 1927, adding 37 min gives 2004. This means *B* is 2004.

14. 360 mL

The dimensions of the rectangular prism are 10 cm by 6 cm by 6 cm. As $10 \times 6 \times 6$ is 360, the volume is 360 cm³, which is a capacity of 360 mL.

15.

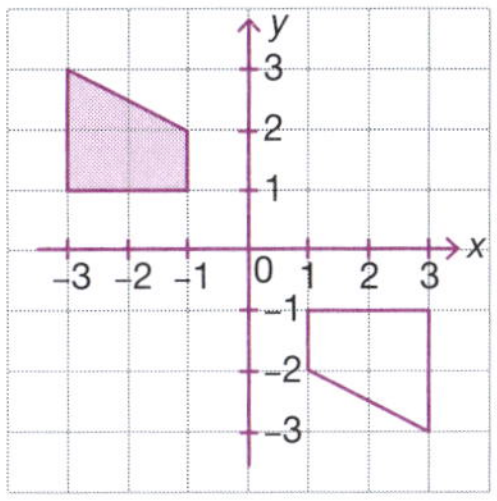

16. 26

There are four angles making up a straight angle that add to 180°. As one of the angles is 90°, the other three add to 90°. As 90 − 38 is 52, and $52 \div 2$ is 26, then two angles are each 26°. This means $x = 26$.

17. $\frac{10}{13}$

As 6 + 20 is 26, and 20 boys have not been to Melbourne, then the probability is $\frac{20}{26}$, which is $\frac{10}{13}$.

18. 40% is $\frac{40}{100}$, which is $\frac{2}{5}$. Now $\frac{2}{5}$ of 50 is $50 \div 5 \times 2$ which is 20. There are 20 boys and 30 girls. As $30 \div 3$ is 10, there are 10 girls who can swim 200 m. Also, as $20 \div 2$ is 10, there are 10 boys who cannot swim 200 m.

	Can swim 200 m	Cannot swim 200 m
Girls	10	20
Boys	10	10

Unit 29A — PAGE 96

1. 3, 5, 11

165 is divisible by 5: $165 \div 5$ is 33. Also, $33 = 11 \times 3$. As $5 \times 11 \times 3 = 165$, the prime factors are 3, 5 and 11.

2. −2

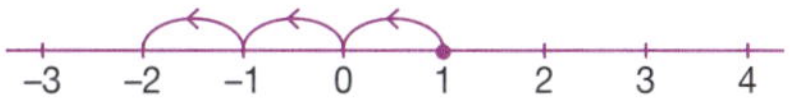

Starting at 1, moving to the left 3 units gets to −2.

3. 375

```
   25
×  15
  125
  250
  375
```

Mrs Dann handed out 375 pieces.

4. $2\frac{3}{4}$

$\frac{21}{8}$ is rewritten as $2\frac{5}{8}$. Compare $2\frac{3}{4}$ and $2\frac{5}{8}$. Look at $\frac{3}{4}$ and $\frac{5}{8}$. As $\frac{3}{4} = \frac{6}{8}$, then $2\frac{3}{4} > 2\frac{5}{8}$. The larger mixed numeral is $2\frac{3}{4}$.

5. 20 years

Owen's grandfather is $10 \times 6 = 60$ years old. Owen's father is $10 \times 4 = 40$ years old. As 60 − 40 is 20, the age difference is 20 years.

6. 14.56

```
   14.56
5)7²2.²8³0
```

7. 4

As $40\% = \frac{40}{100} = \frac{4}{10}$, we won 4 out of 10 games.

8. $330

As 25% is $\frac{1}{4}$, and $440 \div 4$ is 110, the price is discounted by $110. As 440 − 110 is 330, the discounted price will be $330.

9.

Top number	2	3	4	5
Bottom number	7	10	13	16

10. 5

As 12×2 is 24, and 36 − 24 is 12, then $60 \div (36 - 12 \times 2) = 60 \div 12$, which is 5.

11. 144 cm²

As $48 \div 4$ is 12, each side is 12 cm. As 12×12 is 144, the area of the square is 144 cm².

12. 40

By multiplying by 1000, 2.4 kg is 2400 g. Find $2400 \div 60$, which is $240 \div 6 = 40$. Eloise washed 40 loads.

13. 1741

Find the time from 1420 to 1550. From 1420 to 1520 is 1 h, and to 1550 is 30 min. This is a total of 1 h 30 min. Adding this time on to 1611 is 1741.

14. 60 cm

There are 14 equal lengths making up the perimeter.
As $70 \div 14 = 35 \div 7 = 5$, the length of each edge is 5 cm. As a cube has 12 edges and 12×5 is 60, the total length of edges is 60 cm.

15.

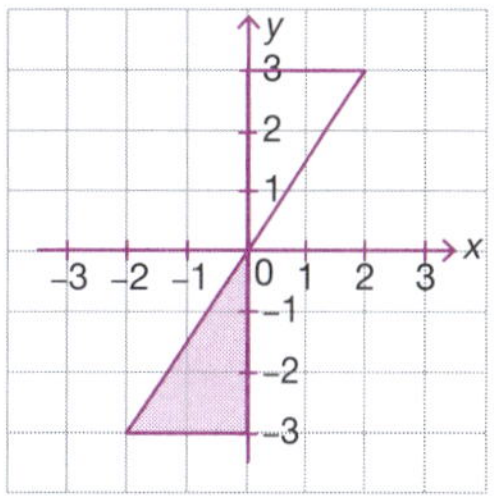

16. 50°

The three angles form a straight angle which means they add to 180°. As 100 + 30 is 130, and 180 − 130 is 50, the angle measures 50°.

17. $\frac{3}{8}$

The primes are 2, 3, 5, 7, 11, 13, 17, 19 and 23. The probability is $\frac{9}{24}$, which is $\frac{3}{8}$.

18. 126

As 48 + 78 is 126, there was a total of 126 customers.

Unit 29B — PAGE 97

1. 1024

The differences are 841 − 784 = 57, 900 − 841 = 59, 900 − 961 = 61.
This means the next number is 961 + 63 = 1024. The next number is 1024.

2. Tommy

The order is –10, –8, –3, +4. Tommy's score of –3 means he came third.

3. 1800 km

$$\begin{array}{r} 18 \\ 8\overline{)14{}^{6}4} \end{array}$$

Brooklyn has travelled 18 lots of 100 km. This means she has travelled 1800 km.

4. $-\frac{15}{4}, -3\frac{1}{2}, \frac{10}{3}, 3\frac{5}{6}$

Numbers to the left on a number line are smaller than those on the right.

Express as mixed numerals: $3\frac{5}{6}$, $-3\frac{1}{2}$, $\frac{10}{3} = 3\frac{1}{3}$, $-\frac{15}{4} = -3\frac{3}{4}$. From smallest to largest is $-3\frac{3}{4}, -3\frac{1}{2}, 3\frac{1}{3}, 3\frac{5}{6}$. The order is $-\frac{15}{4}, -3\frac{1}{2}, \frac{10}{3}, 3\frac{5}{6}$.

5. $\frac{1}{6}$

As $1 - \frac{1}{3}$ is $\frac{2}{3}$, then $\frac{2}{3}$ of the money is shared between the 4 children.

As $\frac{2}{3} = \frac{4}{6}$, each child received $\frac{1}{6}$ of the money.

6. $87.50

The difference between the two amounts is to be multiplied by 7.

$$\begin{array}{r} 50.00 \\ -\ 37.50 \\ \hline 12.50 \end{array}$$

Now $12.50 × 7:

$$\begin{array}{r} 1250 \\ \times\quad 7 \\ \hline 8750 \end{array}$$

As there are 2 decimal places in the question, then the answer has 2 decimal places. There will be $87.50 left.

7. 5%

$\frac{3}{4} + \frac{1}{5} = \frac{15}{20} + \frac{4}{20} = \frac{19}{20}$.

Now, $\frac{19}{20} = \frac{19 \times 5}{20 \times 5} = \frac{95}{100}$, which is 95%.

If 95% of the balls are red or blue, then 5% of the balls are green.

8. 40%

As 25% is $\frac{1}{4}$, and 200 ÷ 4 is 50, the price was $150. As 20% is $\frac{1}{5}$, and 150 ÷ 5 is 30, the total of the two discounts is $80. As a fraction, this discount is $\frac{80}{200} = \frac{40}{100}$, or 40% of the original price.

9.

Top number	6	8	10	12
Bottom number	3	7	11	15

10. 34

6 + 3 is 9 and 12 – 10 is 2. This means (6 + 3) × 4 – 4 ÷ (12 – 10) = 9 × 4 – 4 ÷ 2, which is 36 – 2 = 34.

11. 40 cm

As the length × 4 = 64, and 64 ÷ 4 is 16, the length of the rectangle is 16 cm. As 2 × (16 + 4) = 2 × 20 which is 40, the perimeter is 40 cm.

12. $\frac{3}{4}$

As 20 × 20 × 20 is 8000, the volume of the cube is 8000 cm³, which is a capacity of 8 L. As 6 L has been poured into the cube, it is $\frac{6}{8}$, or $\frac{3}{4}$ full.

13. 1839

Compare 1709 and 2016. The time difference is 3 h 7 min. Now add this time on to 1532. The third bus leaves at 1839.

14. 216 L

As there are 12 edges on a cube and 720 ÷ 12 = 360 ÷ 6 = 60, the side length is 60 cm. As 60 × 60 × 60 is 216 000, the volume is 216 000 cm³. This means a capacity of 216 000 mL, or 216 L.

15.

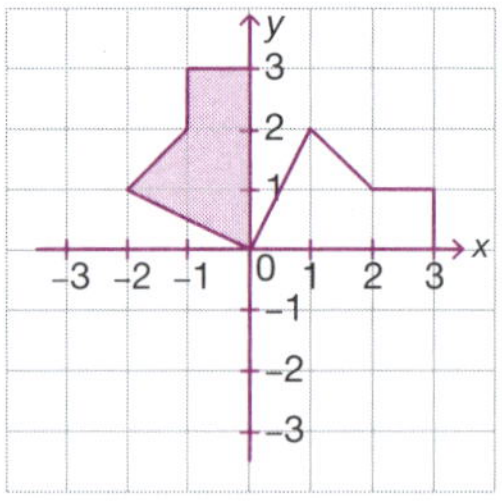

16. 74

The two angles are vertically opposite and so are equal. As x + 52 = 126, and 126 – 52 is 74, then x = 74.

17. 5

As $1 - \frac{1}{4}$, the probability of not choosing a red marble is $\frac{3}{4}$. If $\frac{3}{4}$ of the marbles are not red, then $\frac{1}{4}$ of the marbles is 15 ÷ 3 = 5. There were 5 red marbles in the bag.

18. 22%

As 35 + 48 + 88 + 53 + 78 + 98 = 400, there was a total of 400 customers throughout the day. The fraction is 88 out of 400, or $\frac{88}{400} = \frac{22}{100}$, or 22%.

Unit 30A — PAGE 98

1. 8

The square numbers less than 100 are 1, 4, 9, 16, 25, 36, 49, 64 and 81.

Of these numbers, all are composite except 1. There are eight numbers.

2. 19 °C

From –15 to 0 is 15 units and from 0 to 4 is 4 units. As 15 + 4 is 19, the difference is 19 °C.

3. 7.2 m

The length is 24 × 30 cm.

$$\begin{array}{r} 24 \\ \times\quad 30 \\ \hline 720 \end{array}$$

Fiona needs 720 cm, or 7.2 m.

4. $\frac{7}{8}$

Express both fractions as eighths: $\frac{3}{4} = \frac{6}{8}$ and $1 = \frac{8}{8}$. As the middle of 6 and 8 is 7, the fraction is $\frac{7}{8}$.

5. $1\frac{1}{12}$

Use a related denominator: as 2, 3 and 4 are factors of 12, rewrite the fractions as twelfths.

Using $\frac{1}{2} = \frac{6}{12}$, $\frac{1}{3} = \frac{4}{12}$ and $\frac{1}{4} = \frac{3}{12}$, then $\frac{1}{2} + \frac{1}{3} + \frac{1}{4}$ is $\frac{6}{12} + \frac{4}{12} + \frac{3}{12}$, which is $\frac{13}{12}$, or $1\frac{1}{12}$.

6. $149.85

$$\begin{array}{r} 69.95 \\ 69.95 \\ +\quad 9.95 \\ \hline 149.85 \end{array}$$

The total cost was $149.85.

7. 240

40% can be written as $\frac{40}{100}$. To find $\frac{40}{100}$ of 600, use 600 ÷ 100 × 40. This is 6 × 40 which is 240.

8. $72

As 50% is half price, and 36 ÷ 2 is 18, the cost of a child's ticket is $18. As 36 + 18 + 18 is 36 + 36 = 72, the total cost is $72.

9.

Top number	4	8	12	16
Bottom number	1	2	3	4

10. 0.5

1.2 + 1.8 is 3. This means 3.5 – (1.2 + 1.8) = 3.5 – 3 which is 0.5.

11. 4 cm

As 12 × 4 is 48, both rectangles have an area of 48 cm². As length × 6 is 48, the length of the second rectangle is 8 cm. The dimensions are 12 cm by 4 cm and 8 cm by 6 cm. The perimeters are 32 cm and 28 cm, which means there is a difference of 4 cm.

12. **0.96 kL**

As 120 × 100 × 80 is 12 000 × 80 = 960 000, the volume is 960 000 cm^3. This is a capacity of 960 L, which is 0.96 kL.

13. **1624**

Lola can catch the 1624 train, get off at Dartford and wait for the next train. She will arrive at 1748.

14.

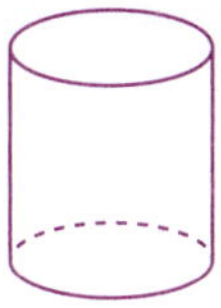

15.

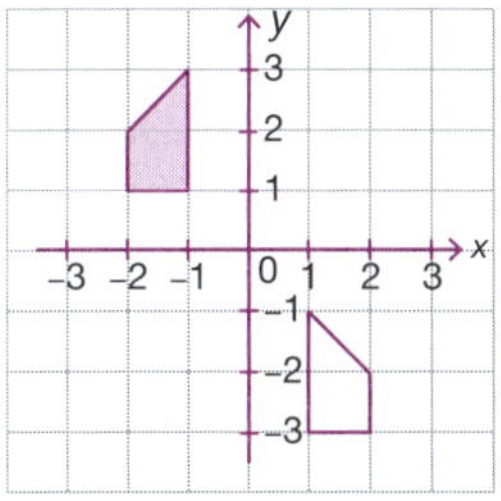

16. **70°**

The angles 150° and the sum of the angle * and 80° are vertically opposite angles and so are equal. As 150 – 80 is 70, the missing angle is 70°.

17. **24**

As 8 × 3 is 24, there are 24 balls in the bucket.

18.

	Beach	No beach
Movie	6	8
No movie	9	4

Unit 30B PAGE 99

1. **211**

201 and 207 are divisible by 3, 203 is divisible by 7 and 209 is divisible by 11. This means the first prime larger than 200 is 211.

2. **–$85**

You need to subtract 120 from 35 which is 35 – 120. Instead, work out 120 – 35 which is 85 and then place a negative sign in front. This means 35 – 120 is –85. The balance is –$85.

3. **92 m**

As 16 × 4 = 64, Aaron has used 64 m. As 64 + 28 is 92, there was originally 92 m of cable on the roll.

4. $\mathbf{2\frac{1}{12}}$

Express both mixed numerals as improper fractions with the same denominators: $1\frac{2}{3} = \frac{5}{3} = \frac{20}{12}$ and $2\frac{1}{2} = \frac{5}{2} = \frac{30}{12}$. As the middle of 20 and 30 is 25, the mixed numeral is $\frac{25}{12}$, which is $2\frac{1}{12}$.

5. **32 L**

The difference between $\frac{3}{4}$ and $\frac{1}{3}$ represents 20 L.

$\frac{3}{4} - \frac{1}{3}$ is $\frac{9}{12} - \frac{4}{12} = \frac{5}{12}$. As $\frac{5}{12}$ of a tank is 20 L then, by dividing, $\frac{1}{12}$ is 4 L.

As $1 - \frac{1}{3}$, another $\frac{2}{3}$, or $\frac{8}{12}$ of a tank is needed. As 4 × 8 is 32, it will take 32 L to fill the tank.

6. **1.41 m**

As the average of five heights is 1.47, then the total height is 1.47 × 5:

$$\begin{array}{r} 147 \\ \times \quad 5 \\ \hline 735 \end{array}$$

This means 1.47 × 5 is 7.35.

The total height of the three boys is 1.51 × 3:

$$\begin{array}{r} 151 \\ \times \quad 3 \\ \hline 453 \end{array}$$

This means 1.51 × 3 is 4.53.

The total height of the two girls is 7.35 – 4.53:

$$\begin{array}{r} 7.35 \\ -\ 4.53 \\ \hline 2.82 \end{array}$$

The average height of the girls is 2.82 ÷ 2 = 1.41, which means a height of 1.41 m.

7. **280 km**

30% of the distance is 120 km. Dividing by 3 means 10% of the distance is 40 km. As George still has 70% of the distance to drive, multiplying by 7 means 70% of the distance is 280 km. George still needs to drive 280 km.

8. **$1024**

As 20% is $\frac{1}{5}$, then 2500 ÷ 5 is 500. As 2500 – 500 = 2000, the price on Tuesday is $2000. As 2000 ÷ 5 is 400, and 2000 – 400 = 1600, the price on Wednesday is $1600. As 1600 ÷ 5 is 320, and 1600 – 320 = 1280, the price on Thursday is $1280. As 1280 ÷ 5 is 256, and 1280 – 256 = 1024, the price on Friday is $1024.

9.

Top number	5	8	11	14
Bottom number	25	64	121	196

10. **55**

First 48 – 24 is 24 and 24 ÷ 8 is 3, then adding 2 gives 5. Also, 4 × 2 is 8 so 3 + 8 is 11.

This means [(48 – 24) ÷ 8 + 2] × (3 + 4 × 2) = 5 × 11 which is 55.

11. **320 cm²**

If the perimeter is 36 cm, then the sum of the length and width is 18 cm. As 10 + width = 18, the width is 8. The dimensions of the original rectangle are 10 cm by 8 cm. This means the new rectangle has dimensions 20 cm by 16 cm. As 20 × 16 is 320, the area of the new rectangle is 320 cm^2.

12. **18 cm**

A capacity of 5.4 L is a volume of 5400 cm^3.

This means 20 × 15 × height = 5400, or 300 × height = 5400.

As 5400 ÷ 300 is the same as 54 ÷ 3 which is 18, the height is 18 cm.

13. **1748**

3:10 pm is 1510. If he catches the 1516 train to Dartford, and then waits for the 1725 train he will arrive in Maidstone at 1748.

14. **30 cm**

As the perimeter is 18, then the sum of length and width is 9. This means the dimensions of the rectangle are 6 cm by 3 cm. The circumference of the circle is the same as the length of the rectangle. As 6 + 6 + 3 + 3 + 6 + 6 is 30, the perimeter of the net is 30 cm.

15.

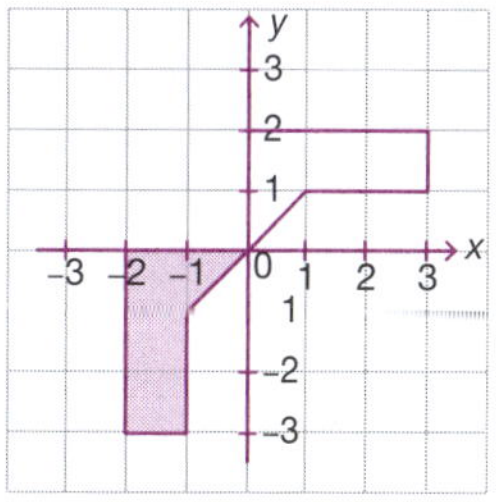

16. **63**

The four angles form an angle of revolution which means they add to 360°. As 144 + 90 is 234 and 360 – 234 is 126, the two missing angles add to 126°. As these two angles are equal, and 126 ÷ 2 is 63, then x = 63.

17. **12**

1 – (0.7 + 0.1) is 1 – 0.8 which is 0.2. The probability of a green card is 0.2. The probability of a blue card is half the probability of a green card, and as 24 ÷ 2 is 12, there must be 12 blue cards in the pile.

18.

	Beach	No beach
Movie	12	7
No movie	6	3

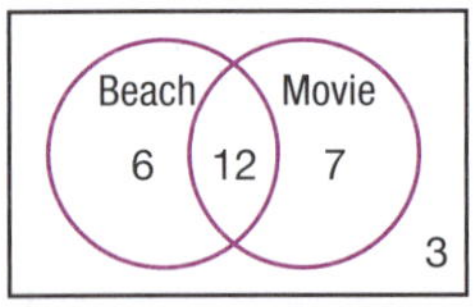

NAPLAN-style Test 2 PAGES 100–103

1. B and E

As 75% is $\frac{3}{4}$, you need to find the fractions that are equal to $\frac{3}{4}$.

As $\frac{30}{40} = \frac{30 \div 10}{40 \div 10} = \frac{3}{4}$ and $\frac{15}{20} = \frac{15 \div 5}{20 \div 5} = \frac{3}{4}$, Lyenna's maths test result could be $\frac{30}{40}$ or $\frac{15}{20}$.

2. 66°

Between north and east is a right angle. As 360 – (90 + 48 + 156) = 360 – 294, which is 66, the shaded angle is 66°.

3. 1.1 m

Remy: 1.25 m, Harriet: 0.95 m and Maddie: 1.1 m. (1.25 + 0.95 + 1.1) ÷ 3 is 3.3 ÷ 3 = 1.1. The average height was 1.1 m.

4. C

As 6 ÷ 2 × 3 is 9 and 8 – 4 is 4, the question is 20 – (4 + 9) + 8 ÷ 4 which is 20 – 13 + 2 = 9.

5. $4.80

As 191.9 – 179.9 is the same as 191 – 179 = 12, and 12 × 40 is 480, Gabrielle pays an extra 480 cents, or $4.80.

6. C

As 16 + 14 is 30, a total of 30 men had registered by Tuesday. As 30 ÷ 2 is 15, and 15 – 4 is 11, then 11 women registered on Tuesday.

7. 16

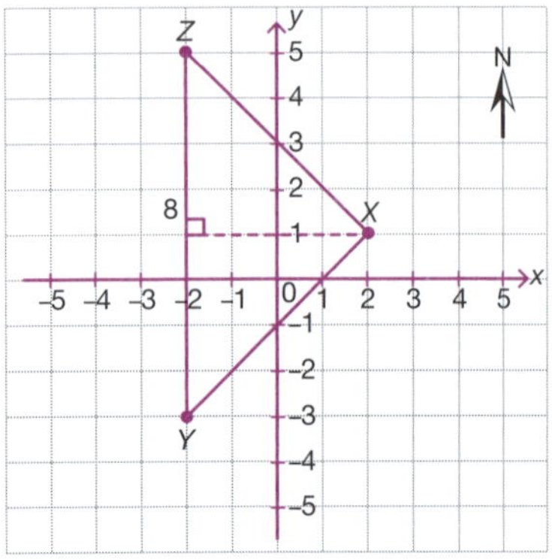

Z will have coordinates (–2. 5). The triangle has base 8 units and height 4 units.

Area $= \frac{1}{2} \times 8 \times 4$

$= 16$

The area is 16 units².

8. C

As 20 × 10 × 5 is 1000, the volume of the prism is 1000 cm³, which is a capacity of 1000 mL. As 2 L is 2000 mL, there must still be 1000 mL in the container.

9. A

As the perimeter is 36 cm, then the sum of the length and width is 18 cm. As 10 + width is 18 cm, the width is 8 cm. As 10 × 8 is 80, the area is 80 cm².

10. C

There are 4 red balls and 1 blue ball remaining in the bag. As 4 out of the 5 balls are red, the probability is $\frac{4}{5}$, which is $\frac{8}{10}$, or 0.8.

11. 2.36

The number line is marked in 0.02s. *X* is 2.36.

12. 17

The number of matchsticks used forms a pattern is 3, 5, 7 which is adding 2. Continuing the pattern is 9, 11, 13, 15, 17. This means the eighth shape is made using 17 matchsticks.

13. $80.10

As 10% is $\frac{1}{10}$, then the discount is 89 ÷ 10, which is 8.9. As 89.0 – 8.9 is 80.1, the price is $80.10.

14. 14

As 60 – 28 is 32, the sum of Chloe and Clare's ages is 32. Half of 32 is 16, and now adding and subtracting 2 gives 18 and 14. Clare is 18 and Chloe is 14.

15. 11

As 15 – 8 = 7, there are 7 Year 6 girls. As 11 – 7 = 4, there are 4 Year 5 girls. As 7 + 4 = 11, then 11 girls catch the bus.

16. 7

6 and 8 are both factors of 24. This means the lights flash together every 24 s. As 3 min is 180 s, the multiples of 24 less than 180 are 24, 48, 72, 96, 120, 144 and 168. The lights flash together seven times.

17. 72 cm

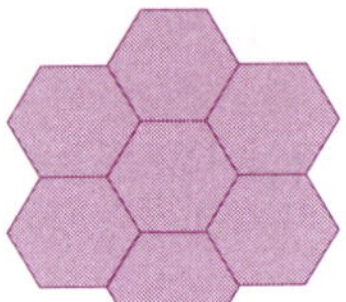

As 24 ÷ 6 is 4, each side of the hexagonal tile is 4 cm. The larger shape's border is formed using 3 sides of 6 hexagons. As 3 × 6 × 4 is 72, the perimeter is 72 cm.

18. 25

As 12 – (4 + 3) is 12 – 7 = 5, then the probability of selecting a blue ball is $\frac{5}{12}$. As $\frac{5}{12}$ of 60 is 60 ÷ 12 × 5 = 5 × 5 = 25, Violet expects 25 blue balls.

19. $5\frac{1}{4}$

As 12 – 4 = 8, there are 8 more numbers to reach the twelfth number. As the pattern is increasing by $\frac{1}{4}$, and 8 lots of $\frac{1}{4}$ is 2, then add 2 on to $3\frac{1}{4}$, which is $5\frac{1}{4}$.

20. B

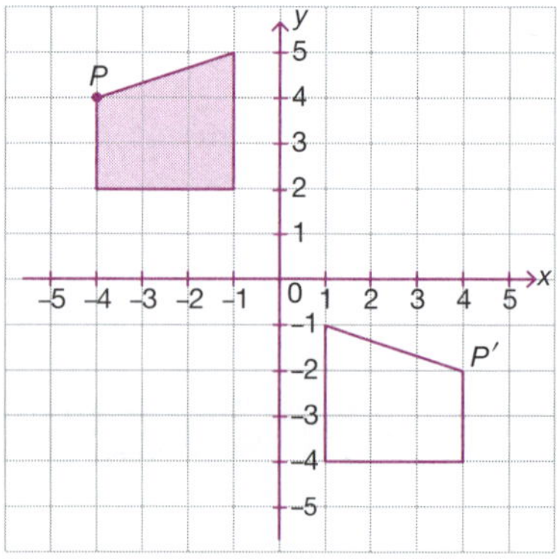

The coordinates of *P′* are (4, –2).

NOTES

NOTES